"This book is an excellent introduction to apologetics. It is devoted exclusively to the intellectual background and foundation introducing students to the study of apologetics. It gives an orientation to terms and concepts, identifies key thinkers, and addresses fundamental questions equipping the reader with essential background for further study of reasons for faith and answers to objections."

Norman L. Geisler
Distinguished Professor of Apologetics
Veritas Evangelical Seminary, Murrieta, CA (www.VeritasSeminary.com)

"I am very happy to see the publication of this very useful and understandable book by my friend, Lynn Gardner. Brother Gardner is more knowledgeable about apologetics than anyone else I am aware of in our Brotherhood. His discerning familiarity with the literature in this field, as evidenced by this book, is impressive. His handling of the introductory and background issues that lay the groundwork for doing apologetics is thorough, sound, and much needed. This book will probably be a required reading the next time I teach my seminary course on Basic Apologetics."

Jack Cottrell
Professor of Theology
Cincinnati Christian University, Cincinnati, Ohio

"When I first spoke to Lynn about this project, he indicated that he wanted to write a book that filled a gap in apologetic literature—one which was a true introduction to the nature and value and history of apologetics. Admittedly, this is something which, to some extent, you might find addressed in apologetic texts, but rarely—if ever—in a single volume. In this respect and a host of others, *Commending and Defending Christian Faith* is wildly successful. Lynn fuses his deep and wide knowledge of apologetics with rich pastoral spirit forged in the fires of decades of training and teaching. The result is an utterly contemporary and timeless introduction to the field that is both scholarly and devotional. Embrace the wisdom contained herein and you will love the Lord your God more fully with mind and heart, and be well equipped to continue to grow in that love."

David Peters
Associate Professor of Philosophy and Apologetics
Florida Christian College, Kissimmee, Florida

"Ours is a challenging age in which to defend the Christian faith. Now more than ever Christians need to know how to mount a reasonable and effective apologetic in the face of rampant secularism and religious pluralism. Lynn Gardner's *Commending and Defending Christian Faith* is a welcome resource. While most volumes on apologetics focus on the arguments and evidences that Christians enjoy thinking about and using, Gardner takes the reader back to the preliminary concepts that form a foundation for all of our various defenses of the faith. This is the logical starting point for a good study of Christian apologetics. The reader will benefit greatly from a cogent description of the prevailing anti-Christian worldview and appropriate apologetic methodology. And very much appreciated by this reader is Gardner's strong defense of the concept and reality of objective truth from God. The content and style of this book, as well as the clarity and passion of the author make this a worthy reading for anyone interested in the defense of our faith."

Johnny Pressley
Dean of the Graduate Seminary and Chairman of the Department of Theology
Cincinnati Christian Seminary, Cincinnati, Ohio

"Though it is true that postmodernism reigns in literature and social work and communications classes, much of the typical university curriculum is still based on rational inquiry and drawing conclusions from evidence. In recent years I have seen a resurgence of university students coming to me with basic questions about the validity of Christianity. Though some Christians have tossed aside classical apologetics as irrelevant to our day and age, church leaders and spiritual mentors of all types need to be prepared to help seekers and challenged believers sort through the issues that are raised by personal doubts and detractors of the faith. Lynn Gardner's book *Commending and Defending Christian Faith* is a well-written and insightful introduction as to why apologetics matter and how to put them to practical use. Dr. Gardner makes complex issues easy to understand for the layman, and gives practical examples of apologetics in action. *Commending and Defending Christian Faith* should be mandatory reading for preachers, youth ministers, campus ministers, youth workers of all sorts, and anyone else who seeks to direct others' spiritual journeys."

David Embree
Director, Christian Campus House and
Instructor, Department of Religious Studies, Missouri State University
Springfield, Missouri

"One of the greatest needs in the twenty-first century is for courageous defenders of the Christian faith. Dr. Lynn Gardner has dedicat-
ed his life's work to that end. This well-documented study is a
tremendous resource on the history, value, and approaches to
Christian apologetics. The amount of research in these pages is staggering—as attested to in the number of notes. The biographical profiles of influential apologetics past and present are a bonus feature.
Lynn Gardner is a scholarly believer in Christ whose style exempli-
fies the exhortation of Peter to always be ready to give a reason for
your beliefs—but to do so with 'gentleness and respect' (1 Peter
3:15). The author not only writes of his convictions, but has lived
them out in his own life, and with his children and grandchildren.
This book is of great value to college students in introductory apologetics courses, to pastors, and to any Christ-follower who is serious
about loving God with all their heart, soul, mind, and strength."

Jeff Bigelow
Senior Pastor, Rolling Hills Christian Church, Eldorado Hills, California
and former apologetics professor.

"Dr. Gardner's apologetics primer is the product of a lifetime. His
practical, basic presentation of reasoned faith reveal the desire of his
heart to defend God's truth to honest seekers. Brother Gardner
speaks from a deep well of having read practically everything written on the subject. We owe a debt to him for this gift and we must
heed his call to remain faithful to God's Word."

John Hunter
Associate Director of Seth Wilson Library,
Ozark Christian College, Joplin, Missouri,
and former editor.

"H. Lynn Gardner's *Commending and Defending Christian Faith* provides a splendid introduction to apologetics. The book covers topics
which are essential background for anyone who will be involved in
tackling more specific objections to the Christian faith. It lays a foundation of understanding which is vitally important for the person
seeking to defend Christian truth. While designed for the nonspecialist, it displays a wide-ranging familiarity with apologetic literature
and offers readers extensive resources on the subject. At the same
time, it offers a straightforward approach which combines biblical
conviction with practical application. Rooted in Scripture and

marked by clear thinking and a passion for the subject at hand, it will be useful both in the college classroom and the local church."

Jeff Robertson
Coordinator, Consortium for Online Education
and former apologetics professor.

"Once again, Lynn Gardner presents a compelling case for the gospel of Christ. He *commends and defends the faith* in a clear, relevant, concise, logical, and humble way. I would recommend this book to any serious Christ-follower who has a passion for removing the intellectual and cultural barriers that keep people from making a decision for Christ."

Doug Aldridge
Professor of Apologetics and Hermeneutics
Ozark Christian College, Joplin, Missouri

"Dr. Lynn Gardner has done it again. Another superb product crafted from history, philosophy, personal grit, and Scripture. The entire composition rings with the importance of truth, honesty, hope, morality, reason, and faith. Voices of the past and leading voices of today support the material he presents. The character profiles that grace the beginning of each chapter wonderfully complement the tone of the material to follow. The review questions will benefit the studious student. The work is readable and organized in a systematic fashion—covering basic materials introducing the field of apologetics. Dr. Gardner shows the importance of apologetics as a duty of every Christian worker. The last chapter alone is an invaluable tool for the reader. Moreover, by book's end, the concept of commending and defending Christian faith is much less a stranger and more so a close friend."

Michael Hand
Minister of the Christian Church, Chetopa, Kansas
and a graduate student

Commending & Defending
Christian Faith

Commending & Defending
Christian Faith

An
Introduction
to
Christian
Apologetics

H. Lynn Gardner

Foreword by Gary R. Habermas

COLLEGE PRESS
JOPLIN, MO • 1.800.289.3300
www.collegepress.com

In memory of my brother

Gregory Mark Gardner

(November 12, 1953–December 30, 2003)

Because of being severely handicapped
with cerebral palsy from birth,
he never walked on his own
and communicated only with great difficulty.
Still he had a productive life
and a strong influence on many.

He did not question God for his condition.
In his own way he gave a strong and
winsome testimony as he commended
his Christian faith to others.

Acknowledgements

I am grateful for Seth Wilson and my other teachers at Ozark Bible College, now Ozark Christian College, for the foundation they gave me in regard to how to think about commending and defending Christian faith. While never an apologetics major, yet all my studies have contributed to my work in apologetics.

The privilege of teaching apologetics to college students for forty years has sharpened my thinking and enriched my understanding. The opportunity to teach apologetics in local churches and in conferences has challenged me to speak in terms people can understand.

I want to express my appreciation to Gary R. Habermas for writing the Foreword. David Embree, Jeff Robertson, and John Hunter read each section of the book as it was written and made excellent suggestions. I am also indebted to David Peters, Michael Hand, and Herb Waterhouse who read the entire manuscript and made helpful comments. Dr. James North provided good observations on the two history chapters. Doug Aldridge used a prepublication form of the book as a text in his spring 2010 Apologetics course at Ozark Christian College. Many others were helpful in specific ways. I am grateful to the College Press team for believing in this project and seeing it to completion.

I want to thank my wife, Barbara. She is a good thinker and has helped me clarify many of my thoughts. She has heard me talk about this book for a long time. In fact I think I heard her say something like, "Perhaps we can get reacquainted after you are done with this book." She has been very patient.

Most of all, my prayer is that God's truth will be exalted and God will be glorified through this book.

Foreword

When I began publishing in the field of apologetics more than 30 years ago, it was often difficult to find publishers who were willing to issue contracts for such works. Granted, given that I was a new author, this may simply have been due to my lack of experience. But something else seemed to be a factor at that time, as well. Editors would occasionally explain that there was not much of a market for apologetic writings. Apparently, this was simply not one of the areas in which many readers were very interested. Generally, it seemed that "arguing" about what appeared to some to be rather sectarian positions was unpalatable to some, while the notion of religious tolerance was beginning to have its own profound influence.

But today, the situation is far different. Editors increasingly report that apologetics is one of the "hottest" publishing areas. What happened? It is definitely true that, as in almost all areas of life, things change. As the saying goes, "What goes around comes around." But something far less capricious seems also to be afoot. During these 30 years, the Western world has witnessed the influx of major cultural and academic trends such as the New Age Movement, the third quest for the historical Jesus, the New Atheism, and postmodernism. Many other far-reaching trends may be detected, as well.

All of a sudden, it seems, Christians now want answers. Many want to be more proactive. What can we say to our young people? How do we answer this or that perspective? How do I address my child's doubts? Perhaps most importantly, when surveys often indicate the good chance that our Christian students will often suffer a faith-crisis while attending college classes, with many reporting that they have actually walked away from their faith, parents are understandably tired of sitting on the sidelines and doing nothing. Enter the burgeoning field of best-selling apologetic authors and works.

More of our brightest minds have been drawn to the various fields of apologetic endeavor. One of the results of this genre explosion is that the published works include much specialized literature, as well. Increasingly, even narrow niches are being filled. Such is the demand today. While being a popular work, this latest volume by H. Lynn Gardner helps to fill such a slot. As he explains in the Introduction, during his four decades of teaching apologetics, Gardner searched in vain for a volume that provided "the intellectual background and foundation" to the field of apologetics. In other words, *Commending and Defending Christian Faith: An Introduction to Christian Apologetics* is not a book of Christian evidences. Lynn Gardner has already written one of those.[1]

Rather, it might be said that this volume provides some of the necessary spadework that needs to be provided *before* one should pursue the apologetic evidences themselves. For example, how do we understand and deal with the subjects of religious doubt and unbelief? Or, what can be said about how we think, know, and believe? After all, we must do these things *before* we use our minds to work through the evidences. Or how ought apologetics actually be practiced? How was it done in New Testament times by Jesus, Peter, and Paul? How do these methods look down through the centuries? And how can we best play the role of apologist in present times? These are the sorts of issues that Gardner pursues in this volume.

It should be noted, further, that this book was specially crafted for convenient use as a college textbook. Each chapter includes an outline, a couple of relevant quotations, along with

---

[1] Lynn Gardner, *Christianity Stands True: A Common Sense Look at the Evidence* (Joplin, MO: College Press, 1994). For another study of a subject often treated in apologetics courses, see Gardner's *Where Is God When We Suffer? What the Bible Says about Suffering* (Joplin, MO: College Press, 2007).

a profile of an individual whose life typifies some of the struggles and issues depicted in that particular discussion. Throughout the chapters, convenient charts summarize and categorize crucial distinctions. Likewise, each chapter concludes with review questions along with an annotated list of suggested resources. Further, the volume ends with a glossary of key terms. In short, this text is designed from start to finish as a tool to be adapted for classroom use. In fact, these helps are so self-explanatory that they are tailor-made even for those professors who do not specialize in the area of apologetics. The result is a volume that can be required along with a second text of Christian evidences to create a well-rounded approach to this subject. This is one way to more intentionally take the lead in affecting the next generation.

Gary R. Habermas
Distinguished Research Professor and Chair
Department of Philosophy and Theology
Liberty University
May, 2010

Table of Contents

Introduction

While in college I purchased a 520-page bargain book for fifty cents entitled *J. Gresham Machen: A Biographical Memoir.*[1] Machen, an early twentieth-century NT scholar, defended historic Christianity against theological liberalism. That book inspired me to want to teach students to be defenders of the faith.

In my forty years of teaching apologetics I searched in vain for a book devoted exclusively to the intellectual background and foundation introducing students to the study of apologetics. Usually introductory apologetics works begin briefly with introductory matters, but give most attention to the actual defense of Christianity. I do not present arguments for the existence of God and for the truth of Christianity, but rather I deal exclusively with issues preliminary to that study.

Christians often feel inadequate and unprepared to make a defense of their faith. As people read apologetics books they often encounter unfamiliar terms, concepts, and names. *Commending and Defending Christian Faith* introduces the reader to the what, why, and how of apologetics. This apologetics primer gives an orientation to terms and concepts, identifies key thinkers, and addresses fundamental questions equipping the reader with essential background for further study of reasons for faith and answers to objections.

It is a *"how to think about Christian apologetics"* book. It explores the basic issues believers should consider as they prepare to develop their own specific approach to an apologetic witness.

Christian discipleship training must include preparation for giving a defense of our faith. Persuasive rational, historical,

---

[1] Neb Stonehouse, *J. Gresham Machen: A Biographical Memoir* (Grand Rapids: Eerdmans, 1954).

and personal reasons have convinced me that Christianity is true. My passion in preaching and teaching has been to commend and defend the truth of God in the Spirit of Christ. The study of apologetics has forever enriched my life, and I have seen it strengthen the faith of many others.

Many do not see the importance of or need for apologetics. We hear these comments:

- ✧ "Apologetics won't work with postmoderns."
- ✧ "Objective truth doesn't exist."
- ✧ "Reason is a myth of the Enlightenment."
- ✧ "Twenty-first-century people want a spiritual experience that works for them in their preferred lifestyle."
- ✧ "Reason and truth are irrelevant. Experience validates spirituality."
- ✧ "If you try to prove things are true, you aren't living by faith."

Is apologetics still valid and viable today? How can we communicate our Christian faith to those who reject it? Can we have reasons for faith? Is Christianity true for all persons in all places? Or is any religion true for the person who sincerely believes it?

The word *apologetics* brings various images to peoples' minds. Many view it as saying you are sorry. War imagery comes to some who see apologetics as akin to taking scalps or at least prisoners. Others see apologetics as a philosophical exercise satisfying the intellectual interests of ivory tower scholars but with little relevance to the real world. Those who define religion in terms of mysticism or subjectivism consider apologetics as an unholy exaltation of human pride. Pluralists and relativists view a rational case for the unique claims of Christianity rooted in history as a futile, even bigoted, enterprise totally out of touch in an age tolerant of all faiths.

Apologetics is the rational defense of Christianity. It gives positive reasons for belief in God, Christ, and the Bible while removing obstacles to faith by answering false objections. We can make a rational case for Christian faith because Christianity is grounded in objective evidence. In 1 Peter 3:15 Peter uses the word *apologia* when exhorting us to give a reason for our Christian hope. In the Greek language this word described a reply or answer to an accusation brought against one in a court. Today we need to answer the false accusations and attacks brought against Christianity.

Apologetic questions hold front-page importance because of the strong expressions of unbelief facing all Christians in our culture. Aggressive world religions, the resurgence of militant atheism, blatant sensuality, postmodern relativism, pagan spirituality and mysticism, and self-centered humanism zealously challenge what we believe as Christians.

While an academic discipline, apologetics is also a spiritual and practical study. Apologetics is essential to the church's ministry of evangelism and discipleship. When the church ignores the biblical and historical foundations of Christianity, it creates a rootless religious experience of relationships and activities rather than true Christianity. If each person must find his or her own truth and we have no historical gospel truth to declare, we have no clear message and no incentive to evangelism.

> *Commending and Defending Christian Faith* presents information that one needs to know before beginning a serious study of the case for the existence of God, the deity of Jesus, and the inspiration and authority of the Bible. It is not a step-by-step manual detailing a defense, but rather a book on how to think about apologetics. It is truly an introduction to apologetics—an apologetics primer, a first book for one embarking on a study of apologetics.

Many Christians fear answering critics and defending their faith. Many feel inadequate and unprepared or lack the commitment and conviction to do so. Others defend their faith in an inappropriate manner—betraying rather than portraying Christ! Reading and thinking through *Commending and Defending Christian Faith* will help the reader gain confidence in witnessing for Christ whether in personal conversation, in responding to a skeptic or a seeker, in teaching a class, in preaching a sermon, or in answering children's questions. It will also prepare the reader for further apologetics studies and for better development of their own apologetic approach.

The writing style will appeal to undergraduates and thinking Christians. The material is organized and communicated in today's language for today's Christians. Even in our so-called postmodern world, believers can love God with their minds and hearts and give a strong witness for Christian faith. It can be an introductory textbook in apologetics courses used in combination with other books that give a defense of Christianity. Every Christian needs to prepare to defend his or her faith. This book can be that equipping tool.

Each chapter begins with the chapter outline, key quotations, and a profile giving a snapshot of a person or event relevant to the chapter. A list of review questions and a brief annotated list of important resources on the chapter's topic follow the text of the chapter.

Part One, "Challenges to Christian Faith," explores the landscape of doubt and unbelief. It defines terms and concepts and identifies key thinkers. Defenders of the faith need to know why some doubt or deny Christianity. Chapter 1 explains the nature of doubt and identifies kinds of doubt. Chapter 2 describes doubters in the Bible and gives suggestions for dealing with doubt. Chapter 3 defines several varieties of unbelief under the headings of secular, religious, and practical. Chapter 4 provides a brief snapshot of key thinkers in the development of unbelief in modern times. Chapter 5 states reasons for unbelief and the consequences of rejecting God.

The Second Part, "Foundations for Apologetics," discusses thinking, knowing, knowing truth, and believing. Chapter 6 investigates the misuse, the validity, and proper use of the mind. Chapter 7 discusses how we can gain genuine knowledge. Chapter 8 contends that truth is objective and knowable. In analyzing the nature of faith, chapter 9 relates reason, facts, and feelings to faith.

Part Three, "The Practice of Apologetics," discusses the need for apologetics and the biblical, historical, and methodological foundation and framework for the practice of apologetics. Chapter 10 answers the question, "Why should the Christian faith be defended?" Chapters 11 through 14 survey the defense of the faith in the NT and through church history. Chapter 15 helps the reader to recognize and evaluate different methods or approaches used in apologetics. Practical uses of apologetics are explored in Chapter 16. The concluding chapter (17) gives guidelines enabling one to commend and defend the faith in a manner pleasing to Christ. A glossary of terms used in apologetics is provided.

Commending and Defending Christian Faith will provide the following benefits for the reader. He or she will:

✧ Become familiar with apologetics vocabulary, concepts, and key thinkers who attack Christian faith and apologists who defend Christian faith.

✧ Understand the basic issues, questions, and challenges facing those who defend Christian faith.

✧ Be motivated to be defenders of the faith by learning about defending the faith from examples, practical opportunities, and guidelines.

A study of the defense of the faith is vital to preparing Christian leaders. An apologist is a combination of evangelist and thinker, preacher and teacher, and above all a living example of love, joy, and peace, found in Christ. A life of holiness, commitment, and prayerful dependence powerfully demonstrates the reality of the living personal God. As a shepherd, he or she seeks to rescue the lost by leading them to faith, returning the straying back to solid confidence, and feeding the hungry on the truth of God. Apologetics is for every Christian, not just elite academic specialists or veteran Christians.

Those who win people to Christian faith, and strengthen and mature believers in the faith, need to be well grounded in the faith themselves. They need to know not only what they believe but why they believe. Apologists need clear and rigorous thinking, historical perspective, burning zeal, deep trust in God, and a character manifesting grace and love.

Peter instructs Christians, *"But in your hearts regard Christ the Lord as holy, always being prepared to make a defense to anyone who asks you for a reason for the hope that is in you; yet do it with gentleness and respect"* (1 *Pet 3:15*). We must be prepared. We must be ready to give a defense of our hope. Communicating one's faith involves knowledge and skill, combined with a gentle, humble, Christ-like spirit.

We can *defend* the faith in a manner and spirit that does not *commend* and make attractive the message. We can *commend* the faith in a manner and spirit that does not *defend* the truth of the message. Both love and truth are essential. Paul instructs us to speak the truth in love (*Eph 4:15*). We must never manifest a haughty, self-righteous arrogance.

We commend the faith when our lives demonstrate a genuine gratitude and joy for receiving the grace of God. We must treat others with love and respect, ever realizing that "there but by the grace of God go I." Our goal is not to prove others wrong and ourselves right. We seek to save souls, not merely to win arguments. We want people to know God and come into a believing relationship with him. May God grant us grace, love, and power to commend and defend Christian faith in the Spirit of Christ.

Challenges to
Christian Faith

"O you of little faith, why did you doubt?"
Matthew 14:31

"Have mercy on those who doubt."
Jude 22

1

Understanding Doubt

Understanding Doubt	"Doubt is not the opposite of faith, nor is it the same as unbelief. Doubt is a state of mind in suspension *between* faith and unbelief so that it is neither of them wholly and it is each only partly."[1]
Profile: Billy Graham— A Crisis with Doubt	
I. The Uncertainty of Doubting	
A. New Testament words for doubt	Os Guinness
B. Value and dangers of doubt	"Unbelief is sin; but doubt, which is merely a special form of intellectual temptation, must like all temptation be distinguished from actual sin."[2]
II. Kinds of Doubt	
A. Factual doubts	
B. Philosophical doubts	
C. Emotional doubt	
D. Volitional doubt	Charles Hummel

[1] Os Guinness, *God in the Dark* (Wheaton: Crossway, 1996) 26. Emphasis in the original.
[2] Charles Hummel, *Doubters Welcome* (Downers Grove, IL: InterVarsity, 1968) 14.

Profile: Billy Graham—A Crisis with Doubt

Billy Graham wrestled with doubt the summer of 1949 before his Los Angeles crusade. He said, "The particular intellectual problem I was wrestling with, for the first time since my conversion as a teenager, was the inspiration and authority of the Scriptures. Seeming contradictions and problems with interpretation defied intellectual solutions, or so I thought. Could the Bible be trusted completely?"[3]

Several factors contributed to his crisis. Disturbing conversations with his increasingly skeptical friend, Charles Templeton, Graham's reading of neoorthodox theologians, a disappointing meeting in Altoona, Pennsylvania, the death of an uncle, and some health difficulties, all preceded the most intense point of his doubt.

He read scholars on both sides of the issue. He studied the Bible's claims and credentials. Christ's total trust in Scripture gave him assurance. On a moonlit August evening in the San Bernardino mountains Graham reached resolution, "Oh, God; I cannot prove certain things, I cannot answer some of the questions Chuck is raising and some the other people are raising, but I accept this Book by faith as the Word of God."[4]

His strong confidence in the reality of God and the deity of Jesus provided the basis for trusting Christ and Scripture in the areas he couldn't intellectually explain. Referring to this incident, he stated, "Not all my questions were answered, but a major bridge had been crossed. In my heart and mind, I knew a spiritual battle in my soul had been fought and won."[5]

---

[3] Billy Graham, *Just As I Am: The Autobiography of Billy Graham* (San Francisco: HarperSanFrancisco, 1987) 136.

[4] As quoted by John Pollock, *The Billy Graham Story* (Grand Rapids: Zondervan, 2003) 44.

[5] Graham, *Just As I Am*, 139.

A distraught father reported to Jesus that his disciples had failed to cast a demon out of his son. Jesus said, *"All things are possible for one who believes."* The father responded, *"I believe; help my unbelief!"* (**Mark 9:23-24**). The man was not saying he rejected God. He was confessing his struggle with doubt.

Do Christians sin when they doubt? How should a Christian deal with personal doubts and questions when they arise? How should church leaders respond to members who doubt? Can doubt lead to spiritual growth?

Confidence, certainty, and assurance lie at the heart of Christian faith. Christians believe in the reality of God, the deity of Christ, and the truth of the Bible. Convinced beyond a reasonable doubt that Christianity is true, believers submit in total trust and obedience to Christ as the Lord of their lives. Doubt disturbs this confidence.

Doubt is of little concern in insignificant matters, but of great concern in matters of consequence. I may question the meteorologist's prediction the temperature will rise to 80 degrees today. I may struggle with indecision and doubt regarding whether or not I should get a lung transplant in order to survive my terminal lung disease. The consequences of the second far outweigh the first. The more important the statement or person questioned, the greater urgency to address the doubt. Doubts about the existence of God and the lordship of Jesus assume huge significance. These decisions carry eternal consequences.

Ignoring cancer in your body or termites in the foundation of your house results in catastrophic consequences. Avoiding open discussion of the issue of doubt weakens the church. The rough reality of life exposes the shallow intellectual and spiritual foundation of many church members. Even well-grounded believers face situations that jar their confidence.

The church needs to be prepared to minister to persons dealing with honest questions and doubts. Young people going through a phase of questioning everything need to be given a secure setting where they can ask honest questions and be given resources to help them find satisfying answers. Many church members have never been taught the basis of Christian faith. Not having a solid foundation for their belief in Christianity, they are more vulnerable to doubt. Those with shallow faith still have real faith that needs nourishing. The deficiency rests not in Christianity but in the weak foundations of the person's faith.

We must not treat honest questions and genuine doubts about Christian faith lightly or harshly. We should not make people feel guilty because they want to know the truth. Honest doubt is not sinful. Treating doubters with criticism and contempt will only make the problem worse.

A healthy church helps those outside the church become believers in Christ and strengthens the faith of those in the church. Understanding doubt and its relationship to faith contributes to the ministry of evangelism and discipleship. It also prepares us to deal with questions that will come in our own lives.

Doubt is common to everyday life and to religious experience. Believers have doubts; unbelievers also have doubts. C.S. Lewis said that no matter what you believe, doubts will come. He acknowledges, "Now that I am a Christian I do have moods in which the whole thing looks very improbable; but when I was an atheist I had moods in which Christianity looked terribly probable."[6] Os Guinness says doubt "is not primarily a Christian problem, but a human problem. . . . The root of doubt is not in our faith but in our humanness."[7] After talking with doubters for more than twenty years, Gary R. Habermas believes "that virtually all Christians raise questions about God or their faith at some time."[8]

---

[6] C.S. Lewis, *Mere Christianity* (New York: Macmillan, 1952) 123.
[7] Os Guinness, *In Two Minds* (Downers Grove, IL: InterVarsity, 1976) 39.
[8] Gary R. Habermas, *The Thomas Factor: Using Your Doubts to Draw Closer to God* (Nashville: B & H, 1999) 10-11.

A vibrant and robust faith must be anchored in truth. We cannot commit ourselves unreservedly to something we believe to be false. Therefore we must deal honestly with our questions and doubts. Guinness comments, "A healthy understanding of doubt will act as a safeguard against today's widespread and unnecessary breakdown of faith. . . . What is most damaging is not that Christians doubt but that there seems to be so little honesty about doubt and so little understanding of how to resolve it. This must be changed."[9]

Myths about Doubt

1. Doubt is insignificant.
2. Doubt is rare.
3. Doubt is sin.
4. Doubt is unbelief.
5. Biblical leaders never doubted.
6. Christians don't have doubts.
7. Doubt can't lead to spiritual growth.
8. Doubt is a virtue.

The Uncertainty of Doubting

Doubt reveals a divided mind and uncertainty about a person or statement. Several Greek words are translated as doubt, each indicating a different aspect. The Greek word, *diakrino*, denotes an inner conflict of being torn between options. It means arguing with oneself, indecision, and lack of conviction. James says, *"But let him ask in faith, with no doubting, for the one who doubts is like a wave of the sea that is driven and tossed by the wind"* (Jas 1:6).

Peter Davids states:

James is not trying to encourage believers to stuff their doubts deep within and to drum up an emotional *feeling* of certainty,

---

[9] Guinness, *God in the Dark*, 15-16.

but to commit themselves. Faith for James is a single-minded commitment to God that trusts in God because God is God. Thus faith remains resting in God despite doubt and holds on through testing. Faith is the "but if not" of Daniel's friends (Dan. 3:18); the 'though he slay me yet will I trust him' of Job (Job 13:15). It is a confident trust in God or a resting in God despite the outward circumstances.[10]

The doubter lives with an inner battle between trust and distrust of God. While in a worship service, he or she may trust in God. "Outside, the same person faces the winds of adversity and, instead of trusting *despite feelings*, gives in and believes that only his or her own resources and cleverness can help. Like wind-tossed water, an unstable Christian sways back and forth."[11]

Douglas Moo contrasts faith and doubt. Faith indicates a confident, unwavering trust in God. Doubting means disputing with oneself and wavering with an inner conflict in loyalties.[12] Like the shifting sea

> . . . the divided person has no fixed beliefs and direction. Having no "anchor of the soul" (Heb. 6:19), he is a prey to every shifting wind of doctrine and contrary storm of opposition and persecution, and his loyalty to God is constantly threatened. He does not possess that unwavering confidence in God, uninfluenced by adversity and diverse opinions, that receives from the Lord what is asked.[13]

Jude calls Christians to *"Have mercy on those who doubt"* (*Jude 22*). When persons are wavering on Christian truth, mature Christian brothers or sisters need to come beside them and with love help them work through their questions. Treat them as you would want to be treated.

---

[10] Peter H. Davids, *James* (Peabody, MA: Hendrickson, 1989) 30.
[11] Ibid.
[12] Douglas J. Moo, *James* (Grand Rapids: Eerdmans, 1985) 64.
[13] Ibid., 64-65.

James 4:8 says doubt (*dipsychos*) is having a divided mind pulling an individual in two ways. Doubters are double-minded, double-hearted, which if unresolved leads to a double life. Their indecision pulls them in two directions, oscillating between competing positions.

Another Greek word, *distazo*, conveys the idea of hesitating because you have reservations about something. One's commitment is qualified instead of being unreserved. This is the word Jesus used when He spoke to Peter after he sank into the water, *"O you of little faith, why did you doubt?"* (*Matt 14:31*). He had a qualified faith, a weak faith, not an absent faith. His belief was "effective enough to motivate him but not effective enough to sustain him."[14] After Jesus' resurrection Matthew uses the same word to report, *"And when they saw him they worshipped him, but some doubted"* (*Matt 28:17*). Apparently they hesitated to believe.

In my preaching and teaching ministry I have encountered many sincere Christians troubled with doubts and many equally sincere believers not plagued with doubts. Struggling with intellectual difficulties makes one neither inferior nor superior to those who rest satisfied in their faith that Christianity is true. Edward Carnell noted that Christians have different types of minds, those "who are troubled with rational objections to the faith and demand answers, and those, on the other [hand], who are not."[15]

Those who think seriously about Christian truth can commonly expect to experience honest questions. William Lane Craig says, "The church tends to shuffle this problem under the rug. . . . Perhaps because Christians aren't supposed to have any doubts, we smile and pretend that this problem

---

[14] Michael J. Wilkins, *The NIV Application Commentary: Matthew* (Grand Rapids: Zondervan, 2004) 517.
[15] Edward Carnell, *An Introduction to Christian Apologetics*, 4th rev. ed. (Grand Rapids: Baker, 1948) 8.

doesn't exist. But it does, and nobody is exempt."[16] Craig continues, "A Christian who is thinking for himself will confront doubts; and doubt, if not properly dealt with, can be tremendously destructive of one's spiritual life. . . . A sort of secret battle rages within, destroying your spiritual life from the inside out, leaving you an empty shell."[17]

Those who struggle with doubts and difficulties must search for answers. Doubt can be healthy if it promotes an earnest search for truth. Doug Aldridge writes, "We should not run away from our doubts or deny our doubts but address them, because our faith is strengthened as we work through our doubts."[18]

We must hear or read a statement making an assertion before we can doubt it. After understanding the affirmation, we make a decision whether or not to accept it as true. Good thinking involves asking questions. Questions and doubts can refine a theory or our beliefs by exposing weaknesses or blind spots in our thinking. Raising exploratory questions can have positive value in helping us move from a naïve perception to a confident belief. Questioning can lead us to improved understanding, or it can lead us astray.

Investigative questions exercise a positive function assisting us in distinguishing truth from error. R.C. Sproul states, "To gain assurance of crucial truths often requires that we doubt premises we've accepted uncritically. Doubt forces us back to first principles. . . . Truth demands that we doubt what does not conform to truth."[19] He continues, "Doubt nags the soul. Still,

---

[16] William Lane Craig, *Hard Questions, Real Answers* (Wheaton, IL: Crossway, 2003) 31.

[17] Ibid., 33.

[18] Doug Aldridge, "Doubt and Rationality of Christian Belief," in *A Humble Defense: Evidence for the Christian Faith*, eds. Mark Scott and Mark Moore (Joplin, MO: College Press, 2004) 190.

[19] R.C. Sproul, ed. *Doubt and Assurance* (Grand Rapids: Baker, 1993) 10.

doubt can appear as a servant of truth. Indeed, it is the champion of truth when it wields its sword against what is properly dubious. It is a citadel against credulity. Authentic doubt has the power to sort out and clarify the difference between the certain and the uncertain, the genuine and the spurious."[20] The exercise of doubt in the search for truth assumes the validity of certain logical assumptions—the law of noncontradiction and the principle that an effect must have an antecedent cause.[21] Honest doubt can assist us in our search for truth.

Genuine doubt asks for information, desiring to know and understand. It can lead to a stronger faith and a better grasp of the truth. McGrath calls doubt a "spiritual growing pain."[22] Unbelief refuses to believe even in the face of good evidence. As we grow in personal maturity, we need to ask, "Am I convinced what I believe is really true?" A merely inherited or unexamined faith ill prepares us for the harsh realities of life. We need to evaluate our beliefs and make them our own. If Christianity is true, it can stand up to hard questioning. It is important that we are personally convinced of the truth of Christianity.

While honest doubt can lead to faith, dishonest doubt leads to unbelief. Charles Hummel draws the contrast, "Many times questions and doubts are a screen for self-will, an excuse not to believe so that we can carry on in our own way. Jesus Christ recognized this fact in dealing with men; he knew that doubt can be intellectual and spiritual thirst, while unbelief is refusal to drink even when the water is offered."[23] Unresolved doubts can lead to sin.

Unresolved and suppressed doubt will not go away. It can undermine the foundation of a Christian's faith. It has become

---

[20] Ibid., 16.
[21] Ibid., 16-17.
[22] Alister McGrath, *Doubting: Growing through the Uncertainties of Faith* (Downers Grove, IL: InterVarsity, 2006) 14.
[23] Hummel, *Doubters Welcome*, 14.

popular to question everything and commit to nothing. This doubting is serious because it leads to agnosticism and permanent suspension of judgment, and can result in settled unbelief and atheism.

Kinds of Doubt

We can categorize doubts by kinds or families.[24] Identifying the kind of doubt a person experiences is necessary in order to make an appropriate response. Four kinds of doubt will be explained—factual, philosophical, emotional, and volitional.

Factual doubts arise from ignorance and misinformation. They often result when we are presented with authoritative claims in matters outside our area of competence. Scholars make statements such as: "No intelligent scientist accepts the Genesis account of creation." "No biblical scholar believes that an apostle wrote a Gospel." "Educated people don't believe the Bible is inerrant." These statements can cause doubts for those uninformed of the facts in the case. Unfortunately, they assume scholarly authorities speak from knowledge. An honest investigation of the facts in the matter is the proper way to address doubts arising from ignorance and misinformation.

Persons who inherited a family faith or who for social reasons became involved in the church may later be plagued with doubt because they never settled the question of the truth of Christianity in their minds. Christianity claims to be true and welcomes investigation of its truth claims. Those experiencing factual doubt need to embark on a serious, thorough study of the rational and historical evidences for the truth of Christianity. "This type of doubt is silenced by facts, answered by truth, and reassured by understanding. . . . The best remedy for this type of doubt is to know the sure and sufficient reasons

---

[24] Stephen Board, *Doubt* (Downers Grove, IL: InterVarsity, 1972); Guinness, *God in the Dark*; Gary R. Habermas, *Dealing with Doubt* (Chicago: Moody Press, 1990).

God has given us, to know why we can know God is there, to know why we can trust his revelation as true, to know why we can be sure of his love and goodness, and to stand firm in our understanding of these truths."[25] The Christian faith provides information beyond what human reason can establish, but it is not against reason. Without good reasons for our faith, we become susceptible to doubt.

Philosophical doubts arise from wrong assumptions and wrong thinking. Our basic assumption about the nature of ultimate reality determines our view of God. Incorrect presuppositions result in a faulty view of God. When people hold distorted concepts of God, they cannot trust him. They blame God for what their false concepts say he is or does. "This type of doubt is not a matter of doubting the right presuppositions but believing the wrong ones. . . . The presuppositions are wrong, so the picture of God is wrong too. . . . If God really were like our picture of him, then the doubt would be valid. But it is our picture of God, not God, that is at fault, and the doubt is fueled solely by misunderstanding."[26] Such doubters fail to realize that God is not at all like they envision him. "Unable to see God as he is, they cannot trust him as they should, and doubt is the result."[27] This kind of doubter needs to know God as he really is and root out his or her misunderstandings of him.

A scientist declared he could never accept the resurrection of Christ because his naturalism was essentially opposed to the possibility of miracles. He closed his mind to the possibility of miracles, not because of the facts, but because of his assumption of naturalism. Merely presenting facts and evidences will not be enough to convince this type of doubter. We must challenge and refute the false philosophy and system confusion by demonstrating the mistaken reasoning.

[25] Guinness, *God in the Dark*, 89, 91.
[26] Ibid., 62, 65.
[27] Ibid., 58-59.

Doubts may result from the failure to distinguish between facts and the interpretations people place on the facts. I have a card with a fossil trilobite glued on it. A printed inscription states the fossil is 300 million years old. The fossil constitutes hard evidence of the creature that once lived on earth. However the statement that the trilobite is 300 million years old is an interpretation that makes many assumptions. The facts can yield other possible interpretations of the data.

We must allow facts to shape our thinking rather than reinterpreting the facts to fit our thinking. Doubts arising from this kind of confused thinking require that one clearly distinguish between the actual facts and the interpretation or explanation that others have given to these facts. All assumptions and interpretations must be open to correction if the facts warrant the change.

The philosophical doubter who has adopted false assumptions needs to be forced to see the logical conclusion of his or her position. Francis Schaeffer effectively used this technique in his cultural apologetic. He pushed unbelievers to see the unlivable consequences of their non-Christian assumptions.[28]

Emotional doubt arises from feelings. Doubts come when we are discouraged and lonely. Emotional doubt often emerges out of personal hurts, anxiety, depression, and other setbacks. "Emotional doubt is identified not so much by the sorts of questions that are asked but by the underlying reasons for those questions. . . . It frequently masquerades as factual doubt."[29] Emotional doubters judge issues by their feelings. "The key to identifying emotional uncertainty often involves

---

[28] Francis A. Schaeffer, *The God Who Is There*, 30th Anniversary Edition (Downers Grove, IL: InterVarsity, 1968, 1998).

[29] Gary R. Habermas, "Dealing with Emotional Doubt," in *Passionate Conviction: Contemporary Discourses on Christian Apologetics*, eds. Paul Copan and William Lane Craig (Nashville: B & H Academic, 2007) 245.

picking out any painful or distressed feelings *behind* the questions or issues."[30]

Habermas analyzes emotional doubt:

> What and how we think greatly influences both our feelings and our behavior. The result is that the most prominent influence on our emotional and volitional struggles is *not* the painful things that happen to us in life, but what we *say* or *think* to ourselves *concerning* these things in our lives. . . . What we tell ourselves *about* them is the most significant factor in our emotional lives. . . . This is why a study of Christian evidences may be helpful but will usually not solve the issues or take away the pain of emotional doubt. . . . to treat the emotional issues we must direct ourselves to what we tell ourselves.[31]

C.S. Lewis in *The Screwtape Letters* has the senior devil counsel his nephew to get Christians to concentrate their thoughts on their states of mind about God, not about God himself.[32] We can focus on our angry feelings against God for allowing our loved one to suffer but we fail to give attention to understand God's role in human suffering. Preoccupation with our feelings, our thoughts, our uncertainties, makes God seem unreal and far away.

C.S. Lewis describes the role emotions play in regard to doubt:

> I was assuming that if the human mind once accepts a thing as true it will automatically go on regarding it as true, until some real reason for reconsidering it turns up. In fact, I was assuming that the human mind is completely ruled by reason. But that is not so. For example, my reason is perfectly convinced by good evidence that anesthetics do not smother me and that properly trained surgeons do not start operating until I am unconscious. But that does not alter the fact that when they have me down on the table and clap their horrible mask over

---

[30] Ibid., 247.
[31] Ibid., 247-249.
[32] C.S. Lewis, *The Screwtape Letters* (Toronto: Bantam Books, 1982) Letter VI.

my face, a mere childish panic begins inside me. I start think-ing I am going to choke, and I am afraid they will start cutting up before I am properly under. In other words, I lose my faith in anesthetics. It is not reason that is taking away my faith; on the contrary, my faith is based on reason. It is my imagination and emotions. The battle is between faith and reason on one side and emotion and imagination on the other.[33]

Lewis describes a man who knows a pretty girl is a liar and can't be trusted. However, when with her he loses his faith in this knowledge and imagines she will be different this time. He plays the fool by telling her something he should never have revealed to her. His senses and emotions have destroyed his faith in what his reason knows to be true.[34]

Lewis then applies his point:

I am not asking anyone to accept Christianity if his best rea-soning tells him that the weight of the evidence is against it. That is not the point at which Faith comes in. But supposing a man's reason once decides that the weight of the evidence is for it. I can tell that man what is going to happen to him in the next few weeks. There will come a moment when there is bad news, or he is in trouble, or is living among a lot of other peo-ple who do not believe it, and all at once his emotions will rise up and carry out a sort of blitz on his belief. Or else there will come a moment when he wants a woman, or wants to tell a lie, or feels very pleased with himself, or sees a chance of making a little money in some way that is not perfectly fair: some moment, in fact at which it would be very convenient if Chris-tianity were not true. And once again his wishes and desires will carry out a blitz. I am not talking of moments at which any real new reasons against Christianity turn up. Those have to be faced and that is a different matter. I am talking about moments when a mere mood rises up against it.[35]

---

[33] Lewis, *Mere Christianity*, 122.

[34] Ibid.

[35] Ibid., 123. See *A Grief Observed* in which Lewis lays bare his struggle with doubt after his wife's death.

It is essential that we listen carefully to doubters so we can discover and understand the true cause of their doubt. After identifying the factors influencing their thinking, then we can address the real reason for their doubt.

Emotional doubt calls for clear thinking about the real issues. Fellowship with those who genuinely love the person provides an environment for the person to see beyond the emotional concerns to the fundamental questions of truth. Our subjective feelings and impressions often prove unreliable. Our faith needs to be grounded in the objective faithfulness of God shown throughout history.

Volitional doubt arises from the will. Doubts of the will come from the desire to be independent from God. Some unbelievers acknowledge no amount of evidence will persuade them to believe in God. Such doubt arises from a stubborn, rebellious will.

The person who wants to be totally self-sufficient and autonomous will doubt God. Os Guinness says, "If I am autonomous, God must go."[36] He comments on this doubt of rationalization.

> Contrary to what the doubter says, the problem is not in the belief but in the believer. It is not in the insufficiency of truth but in the ingratitude and self-sufficiency of the truster. In essence, this doubt holds nothing against truth except that it is inconvenient. It may express itself extremely vocally and raise a wide range of objections to the truth, but these are not genuine doubts. They are part of the propaganda exercise of doubt itself. The real bone of contention is that truth is unnecessary and unwelcome rather than untrustworthy.[37]

A college student admitted to Paul Little that he answered his intellectual questions and doubts. The student refused to accept Christ explaining, "Frankly, because it would mess up

[36] Guinness, *God in the Dark*, 43.
[37] Ibid., 50.

the way I'm living."[38] One may grant that Christianity is true but say, "It's not for me." This doubt arises from a subjective view of truth. This refusal to commit one's life to obey Christ has no good reason except personal preference. "Unless each of us wrestles with the truth for ourselves, we will end up with opinions rather than convictions."[39]

When the Jews questioned Jesus' teaching, He responded, *"My teaching is not mine, but his who sent me. If anyone's will is to do God's will, he will know whether the teaching is from God or whether I am speaking on my own authority"* (John 7:16-17). Jesus accused the Pharisees of willful refusal to believe what the Scriptures had said of him. He said they did not love God, preferring the glory of men rather than the glory of God. This was the basis of their doubt (John 5:39-47).

While the many forms of doubt are not unbelief, doubt can become unbelief. When one wills to doubt, then that doubt can develop into disbelief or unbelief. This kind of doubt is more a moral problem than merely an intellectual one. Paul pointed to a moral basis for those who believed what is false. He said they *"did not believe the truth but had pleasure in unrighteousness"* (2 Thess 2:12). He stated that those without special revelation should have known the *"eternal power and divine nature"* from the physical universe, but they refused to have God in their knowledge or give thanks to him. They exchanged the truth for a lie and worshiped the creature rather than the Creator. They chose to reject God because they chose a selfish lifestyle (Rom 1:19-31).

"Doubt arises naturally because truth that is unpracticed will soon be taken to be impracticable. And, since practicability is an absolute essential for a worldview, truth that is impractical will soon be discarded as untrue." Guinness con-

[38] Paul Little, *Know Why You Believe*, 3rd ed. (Downers Grove, IL: InterVarsity, 1988) 18.
[39] Guinness, *God in the Dark*, 103.

tinues, "It is not that the Christian faith is true because it works, but if it is not put to work, a severe doubt is cast over its truthfulness."[40]

Repentance is the only appropriate response for those who doubt because of a willful desire to disbelieve and disobey God. Christ requires that we surrender our right to run our lives as we please (*Gal 2:20; 1 Cor 6:19-20*). A doubter who refuses to surrender has moved into unbelief. Genuine love for this person will motivate us to remind him or her that abandoning Christ results in hopelessness and despair.

Reasonable and historical evidences for Christianity are helpful for those dealing with factual and philosophical doubt. However, in regard to emotional and volitional doubt, though they are of some help, evidences do not touch the underlying problem. Here a spiritual ministry is required.

Uncertainty lies at the heart of doubt. We must deal with our doubts so that we can have the assurance of a solid and unwavering faith.

Kinds of Doubts	Doubts Arising from:	The Doubter Needs
Factual Doubt	Ignorance or misinformation	Factual evidence
Philosophical Doubt	False assumptions and wrong thinking	Clear thinking
Emotional Doubt	Arising from feelings	Fellowship
Volitional Doubt	Arising from the will	Repentance

---

[40] Ibid., 117.

Review Questions

1. Explain Billy Graham's crisis with doubt. How did he resolve it?

2. Why is doubting Christianity a serious matter?

3. Why is it beneficial to understand the role of doubt in relation to faith?

4. List some myths about doubt.

5. State the essential idea of doubt.

6. List Greek words for doubt and the basic idea of each.

7. When are questions and doubts beneficial in the learning process?

8. When is doubt not beneficial?

9. List four kinds of doubt.

10. Explain and give an example of each kind of doubt.

11. What is the needed response to each of these kinds of doubt?

12. Provide an example of doubt you have experienced in your personal life.

Suggested Reading

Guinness, Os. *God in the Dark: The Assurance of Faith beyond a Shadow of Doubt.* Wheaton, IL: Crossway Books, 1996. Explains kinds of doubt and ways each may be resolved. An update of his work *In Two Minds* (InterVarsity Press, 1976).

Habermas, Gary R. *The Thomas Factor: Using Your Doubts to Draw Closer to God.* Nashville: Broadman & Holman, 1999. Explains factual, emotional, and volitional doubt.

Focuses on identifying emotional doubt giving suggestions for its treatment. Builds on his earlier work, *Dealing with Doubt* (Moody, 1990).

McGrath, Alister. *Doubting: Growing through the Uncertainties of Faith*. Downers Grove, IL: InterVarsity, 2006. Analyzes the complexities of doubt suggesting that doubt is an invitation to growth in faith. An updating of *The Sunnier Side of Doubt* (Zondervan, 1990).

"I desire to argue my case with God."
Job 13:2

*"Wage the good warfare,
holding faith and a good conscience.
By rejecting this, some have
made shipwreck of their faith."*
1 Timothy 1:18-19

2

Encountering Doubt

Encountering Doubt
Profile: Francis Schaeffer—
    Dealing with Doubt
  I. Biblical Doubters
    A. Job
    B. Psalmists
    C. Prophets
    D. John the Baptist
    E. Apostles
  II. Dealing with Doubt
    A. Examine your
       motives
    B. Realize questions
       are normal
	"Now that I am a Christian I do have moods in which the whole thing looks very improbable: but when I was an atheist I had moods in which Christianity looked terribly probable. This rebellion of your moods against your real self is going to come anyway. That is why Faith is such a necessary virtue: unless you teach your moods 'where they get off,' you can never be either a sound Christian or even a sound atheist."[1]
	                C. S. Lewis

[1] C.S. Lewis, *Mere Christianity* (New York: Macmillan, 1952) 123-124.

C. Honestly seek answers D. Don't expect exhaustive answers E. Turn your doubts into prayers F. Continue to study God's Word and fellowship with believers	"Get at the roots of the doubt by replacing the misbeliefs with truth. The lies need to be uprooted forcefully and removed one by one, while the firm application of truth promotes healing. The key is to *practice the truth.*" [2] <div align="right">Gary Habermas</div>

Profile: Francis Schaeffer—
Dealing with Doubt

As a young agnostic Francis Schaeffer started reading the Bible. He found answers to his philosophical questions and embraced the Christian faith. After seminary he served as a pastor in America. Francis and his wife, Edith, moved to Europe and ministered from their home, L'Abri, in Switzerland. Through his cultural apologetic expressed in his speaking and writing Schaeffer rescued the faith of many during the tumultuous sixties and seventies.

He describes a spiritual crisis in his life in 1951 that led him to reexamine his faith:

> During this time I felt a strong burden to stand for the historical Christian position, and for the purity of the visible Church. Gradually, however, a problem came to me—the problem of reality. This had two parts: first, it seemed to me that among many of those who held the orthodox position one saw little reality in the things that the Bible so clearly said should be the result of Christianity. Second, it gradually grew on me that my own reality was less than

[2] Habermas, "Dealing with Emotional Doubt" in *Passionate Conviction: Contemporary Discourses on Christian Apologetics*, eds. Paul Copan and William Lane Craig (Nashville: B & H Academic, 2007) 257.

it had been in the early days after I had become a Christian. I realized that in honesty I had to go back and rethink my whole position.

I told Edith that for the sake of honesty I had to go all the way back to my agnosticism and think through the whole matter. I'm sure that this was a difficult time for her and I'm sure she prayed much for me in those days. I walked in the mountains when it was clear and when it was rainy I walked backward and forward in the hayloft of the old chalet in which we lived. I walked, prayed, and thought through what the Scriptures taught as well as reviewing my own reasons for being a Christian.

As I rethought my reasons for being a Christian I saw again that there were totally sufficient reasons to know that the infinite-personal God does exist and that Christianity is true.[3]

Thirty years after this event Edith observed that we can't completely know another's struggles for honesty and sincerity. Neither can we copy or repeat another's experience. We can, however, learn from those who have survived spiritual struggles. Reflecting on her husband's experience, she wrote,

Sometimes it is important for someone to walk among thorns and sharp rocks in order to post warnings, or to mark the trail with freshly painted hiking signs, indicating the best path around some hornet's nest or a precipitous cliff. It isn't necessary for everyone to set forth in the wilderness to mark his or her own trail if others have walked that way before![4]

She continues, "He came out of that struggle to 'blaze a trail' for himself, but with markings for others to follow more easily." The "asbestos protection" of the honest answers he found to his honest questions prepared him to share the unshakable certainties with others.[5]

[3] Francis A. Schaeffer, *True Spirituality* (Wheaton, IL: Tyndale House, 1971) Preface.
[4] Edith Schaeffer, *The Tapestry: The Life and Times of Francis and Edith Schaeffer* (Waco, TX: Word, 1981) 355.
[5] Ibid.

Abraham trusted God even when he did not understand. He knew enough about God to know he could be trusted. Godly persons experience confusing situations and wrestle with doubt. We must not ignore honest questions and doubts. They should be addressed. We can learn how to encounter doubt from the experiences of individuals who have dealt with doubt.

Biblical Doubters

Job, a believer in patriarchal times, wrestled with questions, doubts, and despair when he lost his possessions, his ten children, and his health. Job expressed his perplexity about God, *"He destroys both the blameless and the wicked. When disaster brings sudden death, he mocks at the calamity of the innocent. The earth is given into the hand of the wicked; he covers the faces of its judges—if it is not he, who then is it?"* (Job 9:22-24). *"Why do you hide your face and count me as your enemy?"* (Job 13:24). *"Why do the wicked live, reach old age, and grow mighty in power?"* (Job 21:7).

Job complained bitterly to God (Job 7:11; 10:1; 23:2). *"I desire to argue my case with God"* (Job 13:2). He called on God to explain the justice in all this (Job 9:19,32; 14:3-4; 23:7; 31:35-37). He responded to God's silence, *"I call for help, but there is no justice"* (Job 19:7; see also Job 27:2). *"Let the Almighty answer me!"* (Job 31:35). Job blamed God for making him taste of bitterness and he defends his own integrity (Job 26:1–31:40; 27:2-6; 29–31).

In spite of horrific experiences Job did not deny or abandon God. He persevered, keeping his integrity and his faith. God did not reject him but in the end admonished, humbled, corrected, and blessed him. Rather than explain to Job why he suffered, God revealed His wisdom, power, and sovereignty more fully to Job (Job 38–42).[6] Knowing God is the key to over-

---

[6] Lynn Gardner, *Where Is God When We Suffer?* (Joplin, MO: College Press, 2007) 55-67.

coming doubt. John Mark Hicks says, "Genuine faith is a faith that ultimately trusts and hopes in God even though it struggles through doubt and despair."[7]

Other Bible persons questioned God. David cried out, *"How long, O God, is the foe to scoff? Is the enemy to revile your name forever?"* (*Ps 74:10*). The question "why?" appears frequently in the Psalms. *"Why, O LORD, do you stand afar off? Why do you hide yourself in times of trouble?"* (*Ps 10:1*). In the psalms of lament we find complaints but also cries for help. Victory over doubt and depression is found in expressing trust and praise to God.[8] Whom we turn to for help determines whether we find victory or defeat in doubt.

Habakkuk asked, *"O LORD, how long shall I cry for help, and you will not hear? Or cry to you 'Violence!' and you will not save? Why do you make me see iniquity, and why do you idly look at wrong?"* (*Hab 1:1-3*). He questioned God's use of such a wicked people as the Babylonians to punish the Israelites. God helped Habakkuk see that this was not the end of the story. The wicked will receive their just reward, but *"the righteous shall live by faith"* (*Hab 2:4*). In remembering the faithfulness of God in the past Habakkuk affirmed his unconditional trust in the power and majesty of the sovereign Lord over all the earth (*Hab 3:17-19*).

Tragedy filled Jeremiah's life—misunderstood by family, mistreated by priests, prophets, and kings, hated, and rejected by his people. He cursed the day he was born and asked *"Why did I come out from the womb to see toil and sorrow, and spend my days in shame?"* (*Jer 10:18*). He complained to God, *"Why does the way of the wicked prosper? Why do all who are treacherous thrive?"* (*Jer 12:1*). *"Why have you struck us down so that there is no healing for us?"* (*Jer 14:19*). *"Why is my pain increasing?"* (*Jer*

---

[7] John Mark Hicks, *Yet Will I Trust Him: Understanding God in a Suffering World* (Joplin, MO: College Press, 1999) 171.

[8] Gardner, *Where Is God When We Suffer?* 76-82.

15:18). He accused God of misleading him, *"O LORD, you have deceived me, and I was deceived; you are stronger than I, and you have prevailed. I have become a laughingstock all the day; everyone mocks me"* (*Jer 20:7*). Through it all he cared and grieved for his people. He prayed for understanding expressing confidence in God's power and steadfast love (*Jer 32:17-22*). Studying the prophets helps us realize that knowing and trusting the sovereign God of the universe is the key to dealing with our questions and doubts.

Jesus did not humiliate doubters. He did not demand a blind faith. To those troubled with honest questions and sincere doubts he gave good, solid reasons for faith in him. In his preaching, John the Baptist thundered the impending judgment the Messiah would bring. Jesus concentrated on healing and helping people and expressed his teaching about judgment in symbols.

While imprisoned at Machaerus, John the Baptist heard of *"the deeds of the Christ"* (*Matt 11:2*). Perhaps the months in prison may have demoralized him causing second thoughts. His patience grew thin. Jesus' ministry did not proceed as John had envisioned. John needed reassurance and clarification from Jesus. "John is concerned because his present experience does not match the message he gave about the Coming One's arrival, which promised blessing on those who repent and judgment on those who do not."[9]

Michael Wilkins says, "It is natural for John to experience perplexity as he languishes in prison, much as had earlier prophets such as Elijah (e.g., 1 Kings 19:1-18) when their human experience did not fully correspond with God's message through them."[10] His expectations of the Messiah did not harmonize with his situation in prison awaiting execution.

---

[9] Michael Wilkins, *The NIV Application Commentary: Matthew* (Grand Rapids: Zondervan, 2004) 413.
[10] Ibid., 413.

He sends his disciples to ask Jesus, *"Are you the one who is to come, or shall we look for another?"* And Jesus answers, *"Go and tell John what you hear and see: the blind receive their sight and the lame walk, lepers are cleansed and the deaf hear, and the dead are raised up"* (*Matt 11:3-5*). Jesus points to the evidence of His preaching and miracles that fulfilled prophecies made by *Isaiah* (*35:4-6; 29:18-19; 61:1*, cf. *Luke 4:17-21*). This objective evidence answered John's question thus strengthening his faith and reassuring his heart.

Keener does not believe the passage emphasizes John's weakness:

> But an argument that views John negatively misses the very thrust of the passage. Jesus could confront John's question no more graciously than he does in 11:4-6, quite in contrast with how he addresses his opponents and even wayward disciples (16:23; 23:13-33); far from invoking judgment as on one who had seen much and believed little (11:21-24), he had John's disciples recount to John what they had now seen for the first time (11:4-5) and pronounced a blessing on him if he would persevere (11:6). He calls John his promised forerunner (11:10), Elijah (11:14). He further chides a generation for not receiving that prophet (11:18-19; cf. 10:41), and makes John the greatest figure of history so far (11:11), even if John does not get to hear all the compliments (11:7).[11]

"Thus it seems most likely that Matthew recorded John's struggle with doubt not to condemn John, but to encourage subsequent disciples . . . whose faith would be tested by hardships: 'Blessed is the one who does not stumble on my account.' Yet even for such a prominent servant, Jesus provides a warning: no mortal is incapable of falling."[12]

Wilkins identifies one thing in this passage that "jolts" him:

[11] Craig S. Keener, *A Commentary on the Gospel of Matthew* (Grand Rapids: Eerdmans, 1999) 334.
[12] Ibid., 335.

John's question reassures us that if this great prophet has questions, it's all right for us to have questions as well. I need to be honest when I encounter situations that tax my faith or my understanding and be able to express when my experience baffles my expectations. There is where it is especially important to have colleagues and confidants who understand and can help us through situations that we may not have encountered before and which catch us unexpectedly off guard.[13]

The apostles doubted the report of the women about the angel's announcement of Christ's resurrection (*Luke 24:10-11*). It is true that Thomas doubted. As D.A. Carson clarifies, "The rubric 'doubting Thomas' is not entirely fair: had he been present when the risen Christ first manifested himself to the disciples, doubtless he too would have believed."[14]

When the apostles told Thomas that the risen Christ appeared to them, he responded that he would not believe until he had seen for himself. He insisted on very specific evidence. When Jesus met with Thomas he did not ignore, ridicule, or condemn him for his doubt. Jesus said, *"Put your finger here, and see my hands; and put out your hand, and place it in my side. Do not disbelieve, but believe"* (*John 20:27*).[15] Jesus presented evidence to dispel his doubt.

Dealing with Doubt

A college student who claimed to be an atheist relates, "Seven years ago when I was eleven, I questioned my Sunday School teacher about the reliability of the OT miracles. She said rather curtly that they were to be accepted not discussed. When I kept asking, she told me either to be quiet and believe

---

[13] Wilkins, *Matthew*, 430.

[14] D.A. Carson, *The Gospel according to John* (Grand Rapids: Eerdmans, 1991) 656.

[15] The NIV has "Stop doubting and believe."

them or leave. So I left."[16] A teenager asked questions about her Christian faith. Her pastor told her she was wrong to doubt and she should simply believe what she is taught. She abandoned Christ converting to Reformed Judaism.[17] Even if these leaders could not answer the questions, they should have cared enough to find someone who could.

Honest seekers really want to know the truth about Christianity. Is God real? Is Jesus God? Is the Bible true? Eternal consequences rest on how we answer these questions. These suggestions can help seekers of truth who are struggling with doubt.

1. *Examine your motives.* Is the question or doubt a smoke screen? Do you want to know the truth or do you just want to justify your sinful lifestyle? A minister's adultery made it easy for him to doubt the reality of hell.

2. *Realize questions are normal.* Bible characters and many Christians have doubted in their journey of faith. Timothy Keller says, "A faith without some doubts is like a human body without any antibodies in it." He states that people "too busy or indifferent to ask hard questions about why they believe as they do will find themselves defenseless against either the experience of tragedy or the probing questions of a smart skeptic."[18]

A seven-year-old son of a Christian professor announced to his father that he did not believe in God anymore. The wise father did not argue or rebuke him. He answered, "That's all right, son. God still believes in you." He soon was the father of an ex-atheist.[19] Respect the person's right to question. Do your

---

[16] Charles Hummel, *Doubters Welcome* (Downers Grove, IL: InterVarsity, 1968) 2.

[17] Winfried Corduan, *Reasonable Faith: Basic Christian Apologetics* (Nashville: B & H Publishers, 1993) 13.

[18] Timothy Keller, *Reason for God: Belief in an Age of Skepticism* (New York: Dutton, 2008) xvi-xvii.

[19] Hummel, *Doubters Welcome*, 18-19.

best to assist in finding help. Do not push them further into doubt. Preoccupation and anxiety can expand normal difficulties into impossible problems.

3. *Honestly seek answers.* Christianity welcomes investigation; it has nothing to hide. Francis Schaeffer never tired of saying, "Every honest question deserves an honest answer." Doubts about whether humans can survive indefinitely in a space station may not be important for you to research. But the eternal issues at stake in regard to the truth of Christianity demand your serious investigation.

Just because we do not know the answers to difficult questions does not mean no satisfying answers exist. Genuine humility requires that we do not equate what we do not know with what cannot be known.

What is the actual evidence for the doubt? Does the objection actually require more faith than the Christian faith? Keller writes, "In fairness you must doubt your doubts. My thesis is that if you come to recognize the beliefs on which your doubts about Christianity are based, and if you seek as much proof for those beliefs as you seek from Christians for theirs— you will discover that your doubts are not as solid as they first appeared."[20] Seekers after truth want to see both sides of the issue stated in its strongest form.

4. *Do not expect to have exhaustive answers.* Absolute certainty is not available for ultimate issues and worldviews. Truth is rational but it includes an element of mystery. We function every day on the basis of reasonable and practical certainty, not absolute proof. We do not know everything about our own selves, yet we believe we are real. We cannot understand everything about God, but can understand enough to have a solid basis for belief in him and his revelation of himself in Christ and in Scripture.

---

[20] Keller, *Reason for God*, xviii.

5. *Turn doubts into prayers.* Ask God to help resolve the questions and doubts. William Lane Craig advises, "When doubts come, then, don't try to hide them or pretend they don't exist. Take them to God in prayer and ask him to help you resolve them. Tell him honestly that, say, you doubt his existence or his being in Christ, or whatever doubt you may have. He cares for you and will help you. . . . When we have intellectual doubts that is the time as never before to deepen our spiritual lives and seek the fullness of God's Spirit."[21] Doubt at its core involves a spiritual battle for your soul (*Eph 6:12*).

6. *While seeking answers continue the study of God's Word and fellowship with believers.* After having doubts about the existence of God while in a Christian liberal arts college, philosophy major James Taylor recovered his confidence on a spring break mission trip to Mexico. "What I found during that trip was that the experience of Christian service, evangelism, worship, and fellowship revived my faith in God. This revival happened because through these experiences I had a strong sense of God's presence and activity."[22]

Taylor explains the importance of Christian fellowship while dealing with doubt:

> It is clear how this communal element can provide a powerful strengthening of one's faith in God, the Bible as the Word of God, and central Christian teachings that are based on the church's reading of Scripture throughout history. Human beings have a strong tendency to be influenced by their associates concerning what they believe and value. This is why doubters are best advised to continue fellowshiping and worshiping with a body of believers in spite of their doubt. . . . My own participation with a group of Christians on a mission trip played an important role in the rehabilitation of my faith.

---

[21] Craig, *Hard Questions, Real Answers* (Wheaton, IL: Crossway, 2003) 35.
[22] James E. Taylor, *Introducing Apologetics: Cultivating Christian Commitment* (Grand Rapids: Baker Academic, 2006) 10.

Doubters who instead spend the bulk of their time with unbelievers are likely to experience a further erosion of their faith as a result of the negative influence of these non-Christians.[23]

McGrath concurs, "Don't stop going to church or keeping company with other Christians if you feel you're going through a dry spell. Their support can keep you going."[24]

While studying in Europe in 1905–1906, J. Gresham Machen's contact with Wilhelm Hermann and other liberals created within him an overwhelming intellectual and spiritual struggle. Professor Hermann made theological liberalism attractive and heart-gripping by the force of his fervent religious spirit. Interpreting Christianity as primarily moral, he separated theology from history. Hermann denied the historical accuracy of the Gospels, yet he conveyed a subjective trust in Jesus.

Hermann's passion and joy in his subjective trust in Jesus captivated and inspired Machen. He describes his teacher, "He believes that Jesus is the one thing in all the world that inspires *absolute confidence*, and an *absolute*, joyful subjection; that through Jesus we come into communion with the living God and are made free from the world."[25] He writes in a letter, "I have been thrown all into confusion by what he says—so much deeper is his devotion to Christ than anything I have known in myself during the past few years."[26] Machen found this spirit a refreshing contrast to coldness and deadness in some orthodox churches.

This experience shook Machen's faith to the core. He had to answer this question: "Was faith a subjective experience or must faith be rooted in the historical facts of the Gospels?"

---

[23] Ibid., 279.

[24] Alister McGrath, *The Sunnier Side of Doubt* (Grand Rapids: Zondervan, 1990) 44.

[25] Letter from Machen quoted in Neb Stonehouse, *J. Gresham Machen: A Biographical Memoir* (Grand Rapids: Eerdmans, 1954) 107. Emphasis in the original.

[26] Ibid., 106.

Honestly seeking the truth, Machen came through this experience without losing his evangelical faith. Even though he still struggled with unsettled questions, Princeton Seminary asked him to teach Greek and German. The faculty sympathetically helped him deal with his doubt. He says of Francis L. Patton, "With infinite patience he brought me through my doubts and helped me in my difficulties."[27] Of his closest colleague, William Armstrong, Machen affirms, "The assistance that he has given me in the establishment of my Christian faith has been simply incalculable."[28] Through his time of doubting, his parents assured him of their confidence in him and their love for him. Machen acknowledged that the teaching and support they gave sustained him.

Not all doubters end up as casualties; in fact many of them become passionate apologists. Machen became an outstanding NT professor and strong apologist for the faith. He resolutely defended historic Christianity against the theological liberalism of his day.

D.W. Smith observes,

> The most effective apologist is likely to be someone who understands the real anguish and travail that often accompany religious doubt and so can approach the other person with a genuine pastoral concern and an ability to utilize the relevant biblical resources in relation to the struggles between faith and doubt.[29]

7. *If necessary, go back to square one and rethink the basis of your faith.* Os Guinness describes the *Square One Principle:*

---

[27] J. Gresham Machen, "Christianity in Conflict," in *J. Gresham Machen: Selected Shorter Writings* (Phillipsburg, NJ: P & R Publishing, 2004) 553.

[28] Quoted in Stonehouse, *J. Gresham Machen*, 209.

[29] D.W. Smith, "Agnosticism," in *New Dictionary of Christian Apologetics*, ed. by W.C. Campbell-Jack and Gavin McGrath (Downers Grove, IL: InterVarsity, 2006) 66.

Life can proceed with deceptive ease on the basis of a faith that was once vital but has become so taken for granted that it is no longer authentic. At that stage any pressure may be such a test for faith that the believer is faced with a choice; Give up or go back to square one. If we give up, then we abandon faith altogether. But if we go back to square one (and so back to our roots, back to our foundations, back to our beginning), we will find a faith that is solid and secure. The lesson of the Square One Principle is this: The person who has the courage to go back when necessary is the one who goes on in the end.[30]

The story of Francis Schaeffer at the beginning of this chapter stands as an example of one who was willing to rethink the foundation of his faith. When needed, it is better to honestly reexamine one's faith rather than skate through life on the thin ice of a shallow, superficial faith that lacks deep conviction.

Dealing with Doubt

1. Examine your motives.
2. Realize questions are normal.
3. Honestly seek answers.
4. Do not expect exhaustive answers.
5. Turn doubts into prayers.
6. Continue to study God's Word and to fellowship with believers.
7. If necessary, go back to "square one" and rethink the basis for your faith.

Doubt can be harmful or it can lead to growth. Toying with and feeding doubt in an intellectually dishonest and prideful way will be destructive to one's faith. Doubt in an honest search for truth can lead to deeper foundations and more vibrant spiritual growth.

---

[30] Os Guinness, *God in the Dark* (Wheaton: Crossway, 1996) 18.

William Lane Craig recounts his undergraduate days in the 1960s at Wheaton College. At that time of student unrest many considered it sophisticated to be doubters, even unbelievers. Craig remembers:

> An attitude was prevalent among the students that doubt was actually a virtue and that a Christian who did not doubt his faith was somehow intellectually deficient or naïve. But such an attitude is unbiblical and confused. It is unbiblical to think of doubt as a virtue. . . . Thinking about your faith is, indeed, a virtue; for it helps you to better understand and defend your faith. But thinking about your faith is not equivalent to doubting your faith.[31]

Craig says, "It troubled me deeply to see some of my classmates, whose intellectual abilities I admired, lose their faith and, to all appearances, reject Christ. This brought home to me in a powerful way how serious the problem of doubt can be."[32]

Observing this left a deep impression. Craig continues, "When I began teaching I resolved to do all I could to help my students stay in the faith while still exploring the intellectual issues about faith. In particular, I resolved never to present objections to Christianity without also presenting and defending various solutions to those objections. . . . We can challenge people to think more deeply and rigorously about their Christian faith without encouraging them to doubt their faith."[33]

I attended graduate school at Wheaton College in the 1960s. I, too, witnessed the attitude Craig describes in many students. It had the same effect on me. In my teaching career I have tried to build and strengthen faith. Spiritual leaders should be faith builders not play devil's advocate. It is never our job to encourage doubt. Doubts will surface on their own. Our job is to help people find honest answers to their honest questions and doubts when doubts arise.

---

[31] Craig, *Hard Questions, Real Answers*, 33.
[32] Ibid., 31.
[33] Ibid., 34.

Review Questions

1. What factors led to Francis Schaeffer's crisis with doubt?

2. How did he resolve this doubting?

3. Summarize Job's experience with questioning God.

4. What overall lesson can we learn from Job, the psalmists, Habakkuk, and Jeremiah about times of doubting and questioning God?

5. What answer did Jesus give to John's question?

6. Explain how Jesus dealt with honest questions and doubts of John the Baptist and Thomas (*Matt 11:2-6; Luke 7:18-23; John 20:24-29*).

7. Summarize what C.S. Lewis said in regard to the role emotions play in association with doubt.

8. Identify seven steps for dealing with doubt and doubters.

9. What helped Machen resolve his questions as he worked through a period of uncertainty?

10. Explain the *Square One Principle*.

11. What effect did seeing college students lose their faith have on William Lane Craig?

Suggested Reading

See pages 34-35.

"What if some were unfaithful?
Does their faithlessness nullify the faithfulness of God?
By no means!
Let God be true though every one were a liar."

Romans 3:3-4a

3
Varieties of Unbelief

Varieties of Unbelief	"The word *unbelief* is usually used
Profile: H.L. Willett—The Evolution of A Theological Liberal	of a willful refusal to believe or of a deliberate decision to disobey.
I. Secular Unbelief	So, while doubt is a state of sus-
A. Atheism	pension between faith and unbe-
B. Naturalism	lief, unbelief is a state of mind
C. Agnosticism	which is closed against God, an
D. Humanism	attitude of heart which disobeys
II. Religious Unbelief	God as much as it disbelieves the
A. Deism	truth."[1]
B. Polytheism	
C. Pantheism	
D. Panentheism	
E. Religious humanism	Os Guinness

[1] Guinness, *In Two Minds* (Dowers Grove, IL: InterVarsity, 1976) 28.

F. Non-Christian religions
G. Theological liberalism/modernism
H. Higher criticism
I. Cults/Alternative religions
III. Practical Unbelief
   A. Hypocrisy
   B. Unconscious disbelief
   C. Resentment
	"That Jones shall worship the god within him turns out ultimately to mean that Jones shall worship Jones. Let Jones worship the sun or moon, anything rather than the Inner Light; let Jones worship cats or crocodiles, if he can find any in his street, but not the god within."[2]
	
	G. K. Chesterton

Profile: H.L. Willett—The Evolution of a Theological Liberal

A case study of H.L. Willett (1864–1944) reveals one man's journey from being an orthodox believer to being a radical modernist. While a student at Bethany College in the 1880s he accepted the Bible as inerrant in its religious teachings and in its references to history and science. He graduated with his B.A. in 1886 and M.A. in 1887. Some change in his thinking began in 1887 as he limited inspiration to Bible doctrines and precepts.

After three years ministering in a local church, he entered Yale and began study for a doctorate in OT studies under William Rainey Harper, a noted liberal scholar. In 1893 he followed Harper to the University of Chicago. Willett received his Ph.D. in 1896 and began to teach at the University of Chicago. He helped found the Disciples Divinity House at the university and served as its first dean.

[2] G.K. Chesterton, *Orthodoxy: The Classic Account of a Remarkable Christian Experience* (Colorado Springs: WaterBrook Press, 1994, 2001) 109.

In 1899 he said an unknown prophet in the late inter-testament period wrote the book of Daniel. Jesus attributed the book to Daniel only to accommodate the views of his hearers. He affirmed the divided authorship of Isaiah and Zechariah. He suggested that the Gospel writers altered OT statements to better fit the life of Jesus. In 1902 Willett defined inspiration of the Bible as the record of a people's reflection and understanding of God, not the Word of God. In 1908 he wrote that the OT miracles were "fanciful narratives based on fact or legend and should not be taught to children as literal description of facts."[3] In 1909 he spoke of two documents in *I Samuel*, one with more primitive ideas.

In 1916 he described the Bible as an evolutionary development of religious ideas through the prophets, culminating in the ministry of Jesus. He accepted the documentary hypothesis of the Pentateuch, considering part of it written in the fifth century BC. He said *Joshua* and *Judges* were written then also. In 1917 he denied that the Bible is a book from God. He did not believe the biblical writers had any supernatural and inerrant knowledge of God's will. He said, "No error has ever resulted in greater discredit to the Scripture or injury to Christianity than that of attributing to the Bible such a miraculous origin and nature as to make it an infallible standard of morals and religion."[4] He measured inspiration by how one was inspired to a deeper spiritual experience. Willett moved from affirming full inerrancy to limited inerrancy, then after accepting radical higher criticism, to viewing the Bible as a merely human book.[5]

[3] H.L. Willett as quoted in the *Christian Standard* (August 15, 1902) 944-945.
[4] Herbert Lockwood Willett, *Our Bible: Its Origin, Character, and Value* (Chicago: The Christian Century Press, 1917) 16-17.
[5] James B. North, "The Significance of Biblical Inerrancy on the Bible Colleges of the Restoration Movement," *The Seminary Review* (1984), 109-

> Two immediate observations: First, one can begin as a believer in the Bible as God's Word and change to being one who denies the Bible is God's Word. Second, *"Let anyone who thinks that he stand take heed lest he fall"* (*1 Cor 10:12*).

Studying apologetics can be frustrating when you constantly encounter new and strange words that an author or speaker assumes you already know. Communication depends on a common understanding of terms. Word studies can be boring and dry as dust; but words really do reveal minds and connect us with people. Having working definitions of relevant terms is essential to a meaningful discussion of ideas. Understanding words in their accepted meaning makes possible effective and clear communication on the part of both the sender and receiver.

Words representing varieties of unbelief have importance because they represent persons who have held or now hold certain ideas. Learning a working definition of the generally accepted meaning of terms as you begin study of a discipline is important because it facilitates learning and saves time later. This chapter will introduce and briefly define various types of unbelief, such as, deism, agnosticism, and secular humanism. Some influential persons advocating these views will be identified. Chapter 4 will summarize the ideas of key thinkers whose ideas shaped modern unbelief. Knowing basic terms and concepts as well as being able to identify influential unbelievers prepares one for further study of apologetics.

One caution: don't label anyone thinking that you know all they believe just because you read a definition in a book. It is good to know the basic meaning of a term, but clarity of under-

---

123. For a comparison of Willet's views in 1899, 1917, and 1929 see William E. Tucker, *J. H. Garrison and Disciples of Christ* (St. Louis: Bethany Press, 1964) 91-92.

standing requires that you listen (or read) the individual's explanation of his or her beliefs. For example, a person may say he or she is an evolutionist. They may mean they believe that organisms change rather than affirming amoeba-to-man natural development. If we want others to respect and clearly understand what we believe, we must accord them the same privilege.

We all have a personal worldview whether or not we can state it. A worldview is a set of beliefs and assumptions by which we make sense of the world and life. What we think about reality, God, knowledge, truth, right and wrong, human beings, history, and values makes up our worldview. Preparing to defend the faith means understanding our own worldview and the worldview of those we attempt to lead to Christian faith. Determining one's basic worldview is important as we commend and defend Christian faith with a non-Christian.

Effective communication depends upon knowing general concepts. In the early stages of studying apologetics having brief working definitions will maximize your learning and make it more enjoyable. Detailed definition of terms can come later to avoid oversimplification.

As you increase your knowledge, you can refine your understanding of a concept. In listening to persons expressing unbelieving viewpoints, listen to what *they* say they believe. Avoid pigeonholing them into a dictionary definition. That is a good starting point, one which can be refined.

In this book unbelief represents the viewpoints of those who do not believe in the God of the Bible. This chapter will attempt to map the unbeliever's landscape by explaining terms and identifying thinkers under the classification of three areas of unbelief: secular, religious, and practical.

Secular Unbelief

Secular unbelief acknowledges no divine being or divine revelation. This includes atheism, naturalism, agnosticism, and humanism.

Views Concerning God's Existence

Theist—"I am convinced that God exists."

Doubter—"I have doubts about God's existence."

Agnostic (soft)—"I don't know whether or not God exists."

Agnostic (hard)—"I can't know whether or not God exists."
(Skeptic)

Atheist—"I know (or believe) that God does not exist."[6]

Atheism denies the existence of a divine being or beings. It is the denial of any kind of god existing either beyond the world or in the world. Prominent European atheists include Marx, Nietzsche, Freud, and Sartre.[7] Notable American atheists include John Dewey and Bertrand Russell.

Bertrand Russell (1872–1970) used his influence and writing to deny God and oppose Christianity. By age eighteen he considered himself a nontheist. He attacked Christianity and questioned the historical existence of Jesus. Russell saw Christians as "timid seekers after the childish comforts of a less adult age."[8]

British zoologist Richard Dawkins defends an atheistic worldview appealing to natural sciences, especially evolutionary biology. In *The Blind Watchmaker* (1986) he argues that science proves things with certainty while religion affirms falsehoods and oppresses people. He claims that science is free from faith. Alister McGrath, a former atheist, says of Dawkins's *The God Delusion*:

> Dawkins simply offers the atheist equivalent of slick hellfire preaching, substituting turbocharged rhetoric and highly selective manipulation of facts for careful, evidence-based think-

---

[6] Norman L. Geisler, *Baker Encyclopedia of Christian Apologetics* (Grand Rapids: Baker Books, 1999) 55.

[7] They will be discussed in Chapter 4.

[8] Bertrand Russell, *The Scientific Outlook* (London: Unwin, 1931) 30.

ing. Curiously, there is surprisingly little scientific analysis in *The God Delusion*. There's a lot of pseudoscientific speculation, linked with wider cultural criticisms of religion, mostly borrowed from older atheist writings.[9]

In addition to Dawkins, other atheists—Sam Harris and Christopher Hitchens—have recently written popular books. They argue that atheism is rational and mature and religion is irrational and childish. They are very dogmatic as well as emotional in their defense of atheism. With much media attention, they are getting their ideas before the public. Christians must not ignore this new atheist attack on Christianity. Christian apologists have produced effective responses to this challenge.[10]

Some of the arguments used by atheists for their denial of God include: the existence of evil and suffering, the apparent purposelessness of life, randomness of the universe, and the eternality of matter.[11]

Influential Atheists

Feuerbach: "There is no God."

Marx: Religion is the "opiate of the masses."

Nietzsche: "Where is God? We have killed him. God is dead."

Freud: God is "the fulfillment of the oldest, strongest, and most urgent wish of mankind."

Lenin: "Down with religion! Long live atheism!"

Sartre: Because no God exists all is permitted.

Dewey: A naturalistic faith based on nature, human potential, and democracy.

Russell: Rejected God, religion, and morality.

Dawkins: Evolution demands atheism.

Harris: Religion is irrational, childish, and oppressive.

---

[9] Alister McGrath and Joanna Collicutt McGrath, *The Dawkins Delusion? Atheistic Fundamentalism and the Denial of the Divine* (Downers Grove, IL: InterVarsity, 2007) 11.

[10] For a survey and response to the new atheism, see Gary R. Habermas, "The Plight of the New Atheism: A Critique," *Journal of the Evangelical*

Atheism denies the supernatural therefore it is naturalistic. *Naturalism* views the physical world as the only reality. Naturalists reject miracles since they deny any supernatural action in the natural world. *Scientific naturalism* views the physical world as the only reality and scientific knowledge as the only valid knowledge. Naturalists explain everything that exists in terms of matter in motion. *Positivism* holds that only the positive sciences using sense experience, verified by scientific demonstration, can establish genuine knowledge. *Logical positivism* holds that all statements not verified by sense experience are nonsense. Belief in God, the human spirit, and immortality, are rejected as unverifiable, emotional nonsense. Logical positivism dominated philosophy in the 1930s and 1940s but fell into disrepute because its verification statement itself was unverifiable.

Perhaps the most widespread form of secular unbelief is *agnosticism*. Agnosticism professes the inability to determine whether or not God exists, neither affirming belief in God nor denying the existence of God. Soft agnosticism holds that we don't know if God exists or not. The evidence is insufficient. God is unknown. Hard agnosticism or skepticism says that we can't know if God exists or not. No one can know. God is unknowable.

Agnostics claim no valid evidence exists to establish the reality of God. The question of God's existence remains open

Theological Society 51 (December 2008) 813-827. See also William Lane Craig and Chad Meister, eds., *God Is Great, God Is Good: Why Believing in God Is Reasonable and Responsible* (Downers Grove, IL: InterVarsity, 2009); Paul Copan and William Lane Craig, eds., *Contending with Christianity's Critics: Answering New Atheists & Other Objectors* (Nashville: B & H Publishing, 2009); Ravi Zacharias, *The End of Reason: A Response to the New Atheists* (Grand Rapids: Zondervan, 2008); R. Albert Mohler, Jr., *Atheism Remix: A Christian Confronts the New Atheists* (Wheaton, IL: Crossway Books, 2008); David Marshall, *The Truth behind the New Atheism: Responding to the Emerging Challenges to God and Christianity* (Eugene, OR: Harvest House, 2007); and Alister McGrath and Joanna Collicutt McGrath, *The Dawkins Delusion? Atheist Fundamentalism and the Denial of the Divine* (London: SPCK, 2007).

[11] Geisler, *Baker Encyclopedia of Christian Apologetics*, 56-57.

and unanswerable. Agnosticism has roots in the skepticism of Hume and of Kant (Enlightenment philosophers who will be introduced in the next chapter). They both questioned the mind's ability to know external reality; therefore no theoretical knowledge of God is possible. Thomas Huxley (1825–1895) coined the word *agnostic* in 1869. Huxley and Herbert Spencer (1820–1903), a social Darwinist, together with Charles Darwin (1809–1882), all considered themselves agnostics.

Agnostics profess to be open and objective, claiming they suspend judgment. In reality they decide the evidence is insufficient and therefore do not trust God. Rather than remaining noncommittal, the agnostic in effect decides against God. A total agnosticism that affirms that all reality is unknowable is self-defeating. It assumes some knowledge of reality in order to make that statement. Also one would have to be omniscient to know one cannot know reality.

Humanists emphasize human accomplishments, especially in literature, philosophy, and the arts. Some restrict humanism to secular worldviews, however some Christians have used the term to indicate care for and promotion of the well-being of human beings.

Secular humanism denies the existence of supernatural beings and is concerned for the physical and social well being of human beings. The two *Humanist Manifestos* of the twentieth century state the ideas of secular humanism. They deny God and reject miracles. Rejecting creation, they affirm evolution by natural processes alone. Ethics are relative and determined by humans. They advocate socialism, human self-sufficiency, and naturalistic religion. Humanism as a religion will be discussed later in this chapter.

Carl Sagan (1934–1996), an agnostic scientist, defended naturalistic evolution. He viewed the cosmos as a god. He loudly proclaimed, "The cosmos is all that is or ever was or ever will be."[12] He believed human beings were created in the image of the cosmos. Claiming to be scientific, Sagan's views were indeed religious making the cosmos as creator and object of moral duty and worship—even our source of salvation.

Religious Unbelief

Theism is belief in a personal God. Christianity is one specific expression of theism. Other forms include Judaism and Islam. *Revelation* refers to the communication from God to mankind. Various forms of religious unbelief will be identified.

Deism is the belief that God made the world, then locked it in natural law and has not intervened with the world or its events since. Deists reject supernatural revelation basing religion only on reason and nature. They believe in the existence of God, human moral obligations, as well as rewards and punishments in the afterlife. Deism flourished in the seventeenth and eighteenth centuries especially in France, England, and America. Thomas Paine and Thomas Jefferson were prominent deists in America. By the end of the nineteenth century deism ceased to be a major movement.

The deistic view of God lives on. Recently Antony Flew (b. 1923), a British philosopher, son of a Methodist minister, and at one time the world's most famous atheist, has affirmed belief in a deist type of God.[13] Sociologist Christian Smith has identified American civil religion as "moralistic therapeutic deism."

---

[12] Carl Sagan, *Cosmos* (New York: Random House, 1980) 4.

[13] Antony Flew with Roy Abraham Varghese, *There Is a God: How the World's Most Notorious Atheist Changed His Mind* (New York: Harper One, 2007) and "My Pilgrimage from Atheism to Theism: A Discussion between Antony Flew and Gary Habermas," in *God Is Great, God Is Good*, eds. Craig and Meister, 228-240.

Enlightenment Deism	Moralistic, Therapeutic Deism
1. God created the world.	1. God created the world.
2. He set it up to run by fixed natural laws.	2. God wants people to be good, nice, and fair to each other.
3. God does not intervene in the world.	3. The goal of life is to be happy and to feel good about one's self.
4. Human beings have a natural right to live a happy life.	4. God is uninvolved in one's life except when he is needed to resolve a problem.
5. Life after death with rewards and punishments.[14]	5. Good people go to heaven when they die.[15]

Polytheism believes in the existence of many gods. Various forms of paganism involve worship of many gods. The Mormon religion teaches that God was once a man and men can become gods. Mormon theology teaches that gods inhabit the universe who procreate "spirit children" who dwell in bodies on other planets. Some forms of Hinduism can also be regarded as polytheistic.

Spiritism is the belief that the world is inhabited by an infinite number of animistic and ancestral spirits, but the idea of a sovereign God is discounted.

Pantheism is the view that God and the world are identical. God is the world and the world is God. The rationalistic

[14] John Orr, *English Deism: Its Roots and Its Fruits* (Grand Rapids: Eerdmans, 1934).

[15] Christian Smith, "On 'Moralistic Therapeutic Deism' as U.S. Teenagers' Actual, Tacit, De Facto Religious Faith," **http://ptsem.edu/lectures/2005/Smith-Moralistic.pdf**. See Christian Smith and Melinda Lundquist Denton, *Soul Searching: The Religious and Spiritual Lives of American Teenagers* (New York: Oxford University Press, 2005).

philosophers Spinoza (1632–1677) and Georg Hegel (1770–1831) advocated a pantheistic worldview. Hegel believed reality is the unfolding of the Absolute Spirit through a dialectical process. Some hard-core environmentalists and certain neopagan groups recognize the divine presence in all things.

Panentheism is the view that God is the soul of the universe just as man's body has a soul. God evolves with the universe. God is in the world but not to be equated with the world. God is more than the world. The process philosophy of Alfred North Whitehead is the basis for this view. Process theology incorporates panentheism.

The recent *New Age Movement* has ridden a resurgence of interest in spirituality, incorporating a blend of eastern, occultic, and pantheistic teachings. It teaches reincarnation, and that we are all gods. Pagan perspectives and attitudes are taught in wicca (witchcraft), in goddess worship in radical feminism, and in nature-venerating religions. Contemporary paganism exhibits a pantheistic deification of nature. The practice of magic and occult rituals are often involved.

Eastern religions reject the God of the Bible and Christianity, holding to a pantheistic monism. *Hinduism*, the dominant religion of India, teaches reincarnation (a cycle of rebirth into another existence), karma (one's actions determine one's destiny in the next existence), and nirvana (final purification with absorption into the whole of reality when the wheel of reincarnation is escaped). *Buddhism*, developed from Hinduism, seeks to respond to suffering by achieving selflessness through an Eightfold Path thereby avoiding the reincarnation cycle and achieving nirvana.

Islam is monotheistic religion following the seventh-century teachings of Muhammad, a native of Saudi Arabia. Adherents of Islam, *Muslims*, submit to Allah (God). However Allah differs in significant respects from the God of the Bible. Muslims do not accept the resurrection or deity of Jesus. They accept Jesus as a prophet, but consider Muhammad the final and superior prophet. The Qur'an is their authoritative holy book. They accept only parts of the Bible. They believe Paul in his epistles corrupted the original teachings of Jesus. They also reject the writings of the apostle John as polluted by Greek philosophy.

Religious humanism considers human beings as the highest standard and value in the universe. Humanity is deified. Auguste Comte (1798–1857) in his "religion of humanity" advocated the deification of humanity in a nontheistic religious cult. He was the high priest and his mistress was high priestess of the Cult of Humanity. Robert Ingersoll, an unbelieving American lecturer, spoke of celebrating "the religion of Humanity." Unitarians, an American religious group, reject the deity of Jesus and advocate the divinity of mankind. In his *Religion without Revelation*, Julian Huxley (1887–1975) called his naturalistic worldview "the religion of evolutionary humanism." It is unbelief to dethrone God, but it is also unbelief to deify mankind.

Religious Views Concerning God

Theism—belief in a personal God

Deism—belief in a Creator who can be known only through reason and nature

Pantheism—belief that God and the world are the same

Polytheism—belief in many gods

Panentheism—belief that God is the soul of the universe and evolves with it

Humanism—human beings become their own god

Theological liberalism—rationalistic, naturalistic, humanistic reconstruction of Christianity

---

Theological liberalism modified Christianity in the light of modern culture and science. It is rationalistic in its view of knowledge, naturalistic in its view of reality, and humanistic in its values. Liberals rejected the Bible as an authoritative divine revelation and accepted naturalistic science and biblical criticism. They viewed the Bible as a record of mankind's evolving religious experiences.

F.D.E. Schleiermacher (1768–1844), a German theologian, taught that true religion was not orthodox doctrine nor piety but a feeling of absolute dependence upon the Infinite. Religion for him is not based on the Bible, which is only a record of various individuals' religious experiences. His stress on the immanence of God approached an experimental pantheism. He became the father of liberal Protestant theology by accommodating religion with modern culture.

Biblical higher criticism evaluates the authority and value of the biblical documents by naturalistic standards. Sometimes called the historical-critical method, it questions the Bible as any work of literature or history. Human thinking becomes the criterion for judging and interpreting the Bible. Critics attempt to explain authorship, manner and date of composition, authority and inspiration of biblical books by using rationalistic and naturalistic techniques applied to any literature. Higher criticism may be used in a neutral sense of study of the origin, authorship, composition, and date of a document. The leaders of the Higher Criticism movement approached the Bible as a natural human product. They ruled out divine revelation and supernatural guidance.

David Strauss (1808–1874), a German critic, saw Christianity as eternal ideas expressed through historical myth. A human Jesus lived in history. The early church transformed this human Jesus into a divine and supernatural Christ. The supernatural aspects of the Gospels are nonhistorical myths rather than actual, literal events.

F.C. Baur (1792–1860) applied the Hegelian dialectic to the interpretation of early Christianity. He saw Jewish Christianity as the thesis and Paul's Christianity as the antithesis. The alleged strife between Pauline and Petrine factions found a synthesis in the second century represented by Acts and the Pastoral Epistles (1 & 2 Timothy and Titus). His theory caused many to doubt the trustworthiness of the NT.

Julius Wellhausen (1844–1918) reinterpreted the OT according to rationalism and naturalism. The concept of God evolved from a tribal deity to an ethical and universal God. He viewed the first five books of the Bible (the Pentateuch) as having been edited together centuries later from the writings of four sources: Jehovist (J), Elohimist (E), Priestly (P), Deuteronomist (D); this concept is known as the Documentary Hypothesis. He considered the religion of Israel as a merely human religion.

Albrecht Ritschl (1822–1889) gave an ethical interpretation to Christianity. The purpose of the kingdom of God is to bind people of every race in a moral community of brotherly love. The church is to build brotherhood and not primarily to save souls. The father of the social gospel movement, Adolf Harnack (1851–1930), wanted to get back to simple, nonsupernatural Christianity. He wanted to get behind Paul's message of a divine Christ going back to the social message of a human Jesus. In his *What Is Christianity?* Harnack attempted to discard what he saw as historical husks from the Gospels and retain the kernel of love and brotherhood.

Many Christian denominations reinterpret Christianity so as to deny the orthodox view of God, Christ, and the Bible. *Theological liberalism* was a rationalistic, naturalistic, humanistic reinterpretation of Christianity. This theology gained a strong following in the late nineteenth and early twentieth century. Also called *modernism*, it wanted to be up-to-date and modern and constituted an innovation in the history of theology.

Liberals rejected God as Creator and Sovereign of the universe, believing rather in a divine Spirit involved in the world. The origin of the universe and the human race came by evolution not creation. They rejected hell and judgment in favor of the universal fatherhood of God and the brotherhood of man. The Bible is viewed as a natural record of man's evolutionary religious experience. It recorded man's search for God. They explained miracles as natural events. Jesus was a religious leader, but not God in the flesh nor our substitute Savior. He is a mere human being who left us a great example. Harry Emerson Fosdick (1878–1969) was "Mr. Liberalism" in America.

Neoorthodoxy, a mid-twentieth century theology, breaks with liberalism by emphasizing the transcendence of God and human sinfulness. God is viewed as Wholly Other. But, they do not accept full orthodoxy, representing a range from very liberal to conservative theologies. Neoorthodoxy generally accepts negative biblical criticism. Rationalism provided the epistemological foundation for liberalism. Neoorthodoxy built on an existential view of truth. Neoorthodox theologians do not view the Bible as propositionally true but believe it can become the Word of God when it speaks to the person's heart.

Rudolf Bultmann (1884–1976) as one of the founders of Form Criticism sees the Gospels as collections of sayings, miracle stories, and anecdotes about Jesus. Form critics seek to get behind the Gospel material to the actual Jesus who really lived. Bultmann concluded that we can know almost nothing for sure about Jesus of Nazareth. As one of the most influential NT scholars of the mid-twentieth century he maintained a skeptical attitude toward the NT.

Eta Linnemann was at one time a recognized German liberal NT scholar. She concluded that her historical-critical theology was based on naturalistic philosophies that exclude God's Word as a source of truth. "These philosophies simply presupposed that man could have no valid knowledge of the God of the Bible." She decided that her teaching was "the blind leading the blind" and repented of her misleading of her students. After being convinced that the Bible is God's inspired word, she left her teaching position in the German university. Eventually she served as a missionary teacher in Indonesia.[16]

Any view that humanizes God or deifies man expresses unbelief. Many unbelieving approaches in theology and biblical criticism, too diverse to mention here, have appeared in the last half of the twentieth century and the early twenty-first century.

When evaluating new theologies, we must look for any false philosophy behind the theology. Theological liberalism had its foundation in rationalistic naturalism. Neoorthodoxy was based in existentialism. Liberation theology advocated political and social revolution to deal with oppression of blacks, women, and the poor along the lines of Marxist ideology. Several in the Emergent Church Movement, influenced by postmodernism, base Christianity on spiritual experience rather than on any objectively verifiable truth. Any view that says objective truth is unknowable is a flawed and unsound worldview that cannot speak with certainty about anything.

In popular usage the term "cult" carries a disparaging connotation of a religious group with weird beliefs and often abusive behavior. In evangelical circles it has designated religious groups deviating significantly from orthodox Christianity. These groups, such as Mormonism and Jehovah's Witnesses, are offshoots from Christianity.

Mormonism teaches that the universe is inhabited by many gods who procreate spirit children who are given bodies and live on different planets. Mormons accept the authority of the Book of Mormon and certain other religious books as authorized scripture. They accept the Bible's inspiration when

---

[16] Eta Linnemann, *Historical Criticism of the Bible: Methodology or Ideology? Reflections of a Bultmannian Turned Evangelical* (Grand Rapids: Kregel, 1990) 18-19.

they consider it to be rightly translated. They give priority to their literature when a conflict with the Bible arises. Jesus is said to be a spirit brother with Lucifer.

The *Jehovah's Witnesses* reject the deity of Jesus, viewing him as the first creation of God, the archangel Michael. They spiritualize Jesus' resurrection and his second coming. Only 144,000 will share future heavenly glory; the rest of the saved will live on earth. Their version of the Bible, *The New World Translation of the Holy Scriptures*, is translated to fit their theology. To avoid affirming the deity of Jesus, their translation reads, "The Word was a god" (*John 1:1*).[17]

The term *new religious movements* refers to religious, spiritual, or ethical groups of recent origin not affiliated with any established church or religious body. These nonmainstream and alternate religious groups are of concern to Christian apologists because of their unbelieving views concerning God, Christ, and the Bible.

Practical Unbelief

Another kind of unbelief can be classed as *practical unbelief*. Some profess Christian faith but live as if God does not exist. They do not openly deny God. They just ignore him and are indifferent to him, organizing their lives independently without any reference to God. He is not a habitual concern for them. Their thoughts, decisions, and actions are not guided by a desire to please him and do his will. He is pushed aside by involvement with money, productivity, pleasure, and for the daily business of life.

God is tolerated with a smile. They give him token acknowledgement by periodic attendance at religious services.

---

[17] Ronald Enroth, *A Guide to New Religious Movements* (Downers Grove, IL: InterVarsity, 2005); Walter Martin and Ravi Zacharias, *The Kingdom of the Cults*, rev. and exp. (Minneapolis: Bethany House, 2005); and Apologetics Research Resource on Religious Movements, Cults, Sects, World Religions and Related Issues, **www.apologeticsindex.org**.

Even some evangelical church members accept any religious expression as valid—even if it is unbelieving or anti-Christian. Accepting relativism and tolerance, they approve of each person choosing to believe and live however they please. The culture of our day has reached the point where unbelief is less surprising than a strong, vibrant Christian faith lived day-by-day.

A *hypocrite* professes trust in God with his lips but denies it with his life. The Pharisees professed to honor God and to trust his word, but in practice they sought man's glory and refused to believe Jesus fulfilled God's prophecies (*John 6:44-46*). The hypocrite's professed belief in God makes no difference in his or her life. James said, *"Faith by itself, if it does not have works, is dead"* (*2:17*). Our obedient works do not save us but they do indicate whether or not we have genuine faith.

It is possible to believe on a conscious level yet be *unbelieving on the unconscious level.* Psychoanalyst Dr. Ignace Lepp assisted a client, Michael, with his personality problems. Michael defended everything about his Catholicism with fanaticism. Dr. Lepp observed, "In contrast with the rock-like faith he had evidenced, Michael's unconscious was full of uncertainty and doubt. It was to overcome these that in all conscious sincerity, he adhered to strict orthodoxy."[18]

Often the life-of-the-party type of personality is really trying to cover up deep inner emptiness and unhappiness. There exists a type of arrogant religious dogmatism and unrealistic idealism. For example, they refuse to admit that Christians may not receive their desired answers to prayers. Such overdone dogmatism may be a cover-up for deep inner insecurity and unprofessed unbelief.

One may profess faith in God, yet harbor bitterness and resentment against God because of a defect in one's appearance, a dysfunctional home life, personal suffering, other mis-

---

[18] Ignace Lepp, *Atheism in Our Time* (New York: Macmillan, 1963) 159.

fortune. Often those who are angry with God must see the love of God expressed through Christians before they can overcome their ill feelings toward God. A person with deep-seated psychological problems may need help from a professional Christian counselor. Mature Christian faith includes trust, love, and obedience to the Lord.

Unbelievers are persons made in the image of God and are deeply loved by God. We must not hate them as enemies. Jesus taught us to love our neighbor as ourselves. Respecting others means we should seek to understand them and act in their best interest. Unbelief is no trivial matter; it has eternal consequences. Unbelievers are persons for whom Christ died. We need a passion to study apologetics so we can be prepared to commend and defend the faith to those who do not yet know the Lord.

Review Questions

1. While in college Willett believed the inerrancy of the Bible. Summarize the view of the Bible he came to accept.

2. Why is it important to know the meaning of relevant terms in the study of apologetics?

3. This chapter classifies unbelief into what three categories?

4. Define atheism and naturalism.

5. Identify several influential atheists.

6. How does McGrath characterize the literature by the "new atheists"?

7. Distinguish between two forms of agnosticism.

8. Distinguish between what some Bible believers mean by humanism and secular humanism.

9. Briefly define theism, deism, pantheism, polytheism, and panentheism.

10. Who is called the father of theological liberalism?

11. How did the higher criticism movement view the Bible?

12. Define and state the key ideas of theological liberalism.

13. What view of knowledge was the basis for Liberalism?

14. What view of knowledge formed the basis for Neoorthodoxy?

15. How do groups such as Mormons and Jehovah's Witnesses differ from orthodox Christianity?

16. Give examples of practical unbelief.

Suggested Reading

Campbell-Jack, W.C., and Gavin McGrath. *New Dictionary of Christian Apologetics.* Downers Grove, IL: InterVarsity, 2006. Includes hundreds of articles that cover key topics, historic figures, and contemporary global issues relating to Christian apologetics.

Evans, C. Stephen. *Pocket Dictionary of Apologetics & Philosophy of Religion: 300 terms & thinkers clearly & concisely defined.* Downers Grove, IL: InterVarsity, 2002. A short work briefly defining some of the key terms needed to understand the philosophers and theologians in the area of apologetics.

Geisler, Norman L. *Baker Encyclopedia of Christian Apologetics.* Grand Rapids: Baker Books, 1999. A comprehensive reference work examining key issues, persons, and concepts related to Christian apologetics.

"They exchanged the truth about God for a lie and worshiped and served the creature rather than the Creator."

Romans 1:25

"If the foundations are destroyed, what can the righteous do?"

Psalm 11:3

4

Pioneers of Modern Unbelief

Pioneers of Modern Unbelief	"My grandfather preached
Profile: Charles Darwin—Evolutionist and Agnostic	the gospel of Christ;
Key Thinkers in the Development of Modern Unbelief	My father preached
I. The Seventeenth and Eighteenth Centuries	the gospel of Socialism;
A. Descartes	I preach the gospel of science."[1]
	Epitaph Sir Richard Gregory wrote for himself

[1] W.H.G. Armytage, *Sir Richard Gregory: His Life and Work* (New York: Macmillan, 1956). Quoted by Michael Green, *Avoiding Jesus: Answers for Skeptics, Cynics, and the Curious* (Grand Rapids: Baker Books, 2005) 38.

B. Spinoza C. Hume D. Kant II. The Nineteenth and Twentieth Centuries A. Darwin B. Marx C. Kierkegaard D. Nietzsche E. Freud F. Sartre	"The resolve to submit everything to the scrutiny of reason was the basic item on the agenda not only for Kant but for the Age of Enlightenment in general."[2] Colin Brown "To mention those four names [Marx, Darwin, Nietzsche, and Freud] together is to represent a massive cultural, intellectual, and epistemological shift. Each of these men contributed to human thought in a way that changed the conditions of belief, the intellectual foundations of all thought."[3] Albert Mohler

Profile: Charles Darwin— Evolutionist and Agnostic

Charles Darwin began as an orthodox Christian theist and creationist belonging to the Church of England. He stated in his *Autobiography*, "I remember my conviction that there is more in man than the mere breath of his body."[4] He recalled admitting "the extreme difficulty or rather impossibility of conceiving this immense and wonderful universe, including man . . . as the result of blind chance or

[2] Colin Brown, *Christianity & Western Thought: A History of Philosophers, Ideas & Movements from the Ancient World to the Age of Enlightenment* (Downers Grove, IL: InterVarsity, 1990) 1:286.

[3] R. Albert Mohler, Jr., *Atheism Remix: A Christian Confronts the New Atheists* (Wheaton, IL: Crossway Books, 2008) 21.

[4] Charles Darwin, *The Autobiography of Charles Darwin*, ed. by Nora Darwin Barlow (New York: W.W. Norton, 1993) 91.

necessity." He continued, "When reflecting I feel compelled to look to a First Cause having an intelligent mind in some degree analogous to that of man; and I deserve to be called a Theist."[5]

He said that by 1839 he viewed the OT as no more trustworthy than the Hindu holy books. He rejected miracles. "The more we know of the fixed laws of nature the more incredible do miracles become."[6] In his estimation, the Bible writers were ignorant and the Bible history was untrustworthy. "I gradually came to disbelieve in Christianity as a divine revelation." "Disbelief crept over me at a very slow rate, but was at last complete."[7]

By 1879 Darwin called himself an agnostic, denying ever being an atheist. Central to his developing unbelief was his desire to explain everything naturally. Fixed natural laws replaced God as his explanation of the world and human life.[8]

"Belief no longer functions as a unifying and defining element" of the American culture, according to James Turner.

It no longer provides a common heritage that underlies our diverse world views. . . . Unbelief has transformed the hopes, aspirations, purposes, and behavior of millions of unbelievers. . . . The option of godlessness has disintegrated our common intellectual life, both in formal disciplines like philosophy, science, and literature and in those informal habits of mind by which we, as a culture, experience and order our world.[9]

---

[5] Ibid., 30.

[6] Ibid., 85.

[7] Ibid., 86.

[8] Ibid., 84, 87.

[9] James Turner, *Without God, Without Creed: The Origins of Unbelief in America* (Baltimore: The Johns Hopkins University Press, 1985) 263.

God used to be the "central explanatory concept" but now our culture lacks a center.[10]

In seventeenth- and eighteenth-century Enlightenment Europe, many thinkers believed that human beings on their own could discover all truth and that the natural world was the only reality. They attempted to explain man and the world without God. The unbelief they initiated has continued into the twenty-first century.

Aleksandr Solzhenitsyn, a former unbeliever who came to faith in God in a Russian communist prison, speaks about the cause of the Russian communist revolution:

> I have spent well-nigh 50 years working on the history of the Russian Revolution; in the process I have collected hundreds of personal testimonies, read hundreds of books, and contributed eight volumes of my own. But if I were asked today to formulate as concisely as possible the main cause of the ruinous revolution that swallowed up some 60 million of our people, I could not put it more accurately than to repeat: 'Men have forgotten God.'[11]

He says if he were to identify the principal trait of the entire twentieth century it would be that "we have lost touch with our Creator."[12]

Unbelief may be either a deliberate refusal to believe in a personal God or a lack of belief or trust in any ultimate being. The unbeliever may deny that any kind of god or ultimate being exists at all or may trust in false gods. From a biblical and Christian viewpoint unbelief is a rejection or lack of belief in the living, personal God, who is revealed in Scripture and in Jesus Christ as divine Lord and Savior. It may manifest itself in denying or depersonalizing God or Christ, in rejecting the truth revealed in Scripture, or in deifying humanity or false gods.

---

[10] Ibid., 264.

[11] Aleksandr Solzhenitsyn, "Men Have Forgotten God," *National Review* (July 22, 1983) 872.

[12] Ibid.

What we believe about an ultimate being stands at the center of our worldview. It influences how we answer questions, such as: What is reality? What is a human being? and How should we live? It defines our deeply held beliefs shaping our fundamental orientation to life.

The NT uses two words for unbelief "both of which imply a certain obstinacy and resistance to truth (Rom. 11:20, 23; Eph. 2:2; 5:6; 1 Tim. 1:13; Heb. 3:12)."[13] One word (*apistia*) carries the idea of disbelief and mistrust; the other (*apeithes*) means disobedience and rebellion to God.[14] The disobedience springs from unbelief. Unbelief is a state of mind and disobedience is the behavior that issues from it.

This chapter does not attempt to answer or refute false ideas in the thinkers surveyed. The men listed have left a lasting legacy contributing to unbelief. Rather than give a comprehensive summary of each thinker's worldview, I have chosen to briefly identify their contributions to modern unbelief. They have established ways of thinking that have contributed to modern loss of confidence in the reality of God, the deity of Christ, and the trustworthiness and authority of the Bible.

The Seventeenth and Eighteenth Centuries

Rene Descartes (1596–1650) was a French mathematician considered to be the father of modern philosophy. As a rationalist he tried to establish all truth by reason alone. He believed that human beings are free and capable of establishing truth and being good without the aid of external sources. He trusted reason, but considered sensation acceptable only so far as reason validated it. Using the standards of clear and distinct ideas as tests of truth, Descartes saw God as a clear and distinct idea that he considered an innate idea.

---

[13] W. Stanford Reid, "Unbelief," in *Baker's Dictionary of Theology* (Grand Rapids: Baker Book House, 1960) 535.

[14] O. Becker, "Faith," in *The New International Dictionary of New Testament Theology*, ed. Colin Brown (Grand Rapids: Zondervan, 1975) 1:593.

While trying to counteract the growing skepticism of his day, his divorcing God from any historical revelation paved the way for increased skepticism about the knowledge of God. Descartes believed in God, however his God functioned as a philosophical abstraction to complete his worldview. He separated faith and religion from philosophy and science. His advocacy of human reason as the final authority supplanted the Bible as the final authority.

Blaise Pascal commented, "I cannot forgive Descartes. In all his philosophy he would have been quite willing to dispense with God. But he had to make Him give a fillip [flick of the finger against the thumb] to set the world in motion; beyond this he has no further need of God."[15] The French political revolutionaries liked Descartes because a limited God is an irrelevant God allowing freedom from any God or master. He made human autonomy of reason and will the basis for human welfare.

Baruch de Spinoza (1632–1677), a Dutch philosopher, continued the rationalistic method. His strict deductive rationalism reduced all truth to self-evident and mathematically knowable ideas. He held that only one ultimate substance exists (monism). One can call this substance either God or Nature. Equating God with nature (pantheism) rules out any supernatural personal Being or events. Spinoza rejected the God of theism and revealed religion. He considered miracles that people believed, miracles only because of the believer's ignorance and the promotion by religious leaders. As one of the earliest radical biblical higher critics, he rejected the traditional biblical authors and held that the writers of Scripture had only human powers. He alleged the Bible had contradictions and accommodations to false ideas of the culture of the day. He limited the Bible's authority to religious matters. Being a deter-

---

[15] Blaise Pascal, *Pensees* (Mineola, NY: Dover Publications, 2003 repr. of 1958 ed.) #77.

minist he denied human freedom. For him the goal of life was to understand nature and accept one's part in it. There is no life after death and no revealed religion.

Norman Geisler observes, "Indeed, virtually all of the central emphases in modern liberalism—from the statement that 'the Bible contains the Word of God' to the accommodation theory, rationalism, naturalism, the religion-only view, the moral criterion for canonicity, and even the allegorical interpretation of Scripture—are found in Spinoza."[16]

David Hume (1711–1776), a Scottish skeptic, sought to undermine the traditional arguments for the existence of God and the reasonableness of the truth-claims of Christianity. He particularly attacked belief in the reality of miracles. As an empiricist Hume believed that all knowledge comes two ways: through the senses or by reflection in the mind on ideas derived from sensations. He argued that knowledge can be found only in mathematics and in the experimental sciences. Religion is founded solely on faith, not reason.

He was skeptical of the existence of God and any knowledge not verified by human experience. He was skeptical of causality, the continuity and unity of the individual identity and self, and of God—because they cannot be discovered by the senses. Custom, not reason, is the basis of the concept of causality, according to Hume. He rejected the arguments for God's existence from cause and design as invalid because causality can't be proven, being an argument from analogy. Taste and feeling, not reason or facts, provides the basis of moral judgments.

According to Hume, uniform experience has established natural law which rules out all miracles as violations of natu-

---

[16] Norman L. Geisler, "Philosophical Presuppositions of Biblical Errancy," in *Inerrancy*, ed. by Norman L. Geisler (Grand Rapids: Zondervan, 1980) 319-320.

ral law. Appealing to universal experience he contended that it was more likely that witnesses are mistaken than that natural law was altered by a miracle. He argued that no testimony was sufficient to establish a miracle. His attack on miracles has done much to shape modern disbelief in miracles. Yet his argument is circular—defining miracles as impossible violations of natural law, then concluding that miracles have never happened. Hume's ideas have promoted skepticism about God, miracles, and revealed religion.

Immanuel Kant (1724–1804) stands, in many ways, as the most important philosopher of modern times. This German thinker attempted to combine British empiricism with Continental rationalism. He rejected empiricism's view that beliefs outside human experience could not be justified. He rejected the rationalist's unwillingness to admit empirical discoveries and their claim that knowledge of reality can be established by reason alone. He agreed with rationalists in accepting the validity of causality as coming from reason as an operation of the mind. With the empiricists he believed the raw material of information begins in and comes through the senses, but he added, the mind processes or filters it.

One does not actually perceive things as they actually are but only as the mind conditions them. So we can't really know what things actually are. Since the mind structures all knowledge, no way exists to get outside one's own being to actual reality before the concept is structured in the mind. We can only know appearances not the reality. Geisler summarizes Kant's view, "There is a great impassable gulf between the real world and our knowledge of it; we must remain agnostic about reality. We know only *that* it is there but can never know *what* it is."[17]

---

[17] Norman Geisler, *Christian Apologetics* (Grand Rapids: Baker Book House, 1976) 16.

W. Corduan summarizes,

> Kant declared that knowledge is not the mind's passive recep-
> tion of orderly truth from outside of itself, but the active work
> of the mind in formulating the very truths it is assimilating.
> . . . More specifically, as the mind receives the unprocessed
> sensory intuitions, it first imposes the forms of space and
> time on them and then makes sense of them by means of log-
> ical categories of judgment, which are grounded in the mind's
> own pure concepts of understanding. The result, according to
> Kant, is knowledge.[18]

Pure reason deals with material things (the phenomenal realm) but a subjective practical reason is necessary to deal with issues such as the existence of God, human freedom, and immortality of the soul (the noumenal realm). In Kant's view one can't know reality. We can only have a subjective knowledge of ultimate issues. His rejection of external authorities results in making one's own self the determiner of knowledge. He paved the way for a series of subjective and relativistic philosophies since, including existentialism and postmodernism.

Kant saw religion as nonsupernatural and subjectively revealed. Pure reason or science cannot demonstrate the existence of God. While he held that the objective reality of God cannot be proved, he acknowledged it can neither be refuted by speculative reason. We do not have objective knowledge of God. But rather God is a useful and necessary hypothesis or concept that enables us to organize our thoughts about the world and that provides the highest morality. The human being saves oneself by his or her own moral law. Kant believes that living by the moral imperative we can presuppose the existence of God, human freedom, and immortality. He denied the

---

[18] W. Corduan, "Kant, Immanuel," in *New Dictionary of Christian Apologetics*, ed. by W.C. Campbell-Jack and Gavin McGrath (Downers Grove, IL: InterVarsity, 2006) 384.

need for a divine revelation believing that man by his own reason could have found any truths contained in the Scriptures. Kant warned that religion should not be sought in objective historical events such as miracles, the incarnation, atonement through the cross, an authoritative Word of God, but in practical reason within the person.

Winfried Corduan states that Kant left behind a "legacy of subjectivity. It was he who first opened the door to the notion that to find knowledge we need to look inside the mind, not out to the world. There is no question that this open door made possible the subsequent arrival of phenomenology, existentialism, and postmodern relativistic philosophies."[19] Everett Ferguson says, "Kant was important for religious history for his sharp separation of faith and knowledge, his equation of religion with morality, and his skepticism of the philosophical proofs for the existence of God (although he argued for God's existence as a necessary postulate of the moral nature of man)."[20]

Wilbur M. Smith says Kant's philosophy, "the most influential philosophy of modern times, is diametrically, in every important sphere, *opposed to the great fundamental truths of the Christian faith by which alone man can ever be redeemed.*"[21]

The Nineteenth and Twentieth Centuries

The Industrial Revolution, the French Revolution, and the dethroning of traditional metaphysics by Kant's philosophy—all contributed to the forming of modern Europe.

Georg W.F. Hegel (1770–1831), a German rationalist, advocated a philosophy of Absolute Idealism. He believed reality

---

[19] Corduan, "Kant, Immanuel," 385.

[20] Everett Ferguson, *Church History, Reformation, and Modern* (Abilene: Biblical Research Press, 1967) 59.

[21] Wilbur M. Smith, *Therefore, Stand* (Natick, MA: W.W. Wilde, 1945) 15. Emphasis is in the original.

was the unfolding of the Absolute Mind or Spirit (God). History is the sphere of this progressive development of the Spirit. This unfolding Spirit proceeds in a dialectical process in which it generates a contradiction and later finds resolution in a higher unity.

According to Hegel, the God of the Bible is not the God of modern times. Winfried Corduan summarizes his view, "The distinction between God and man has been abolished, and both died at Calvary. Thus the ultimate Deity in Hegel's system is not to be identified with the God who disclosed Himself in the History of Israel and who became man in Jesus Christ. This new Deity is Absolute Spirit."[22] Corduan concludes, "Absolute Spirit is in fact the absolutized spirit of man."[23]

Hegel divorced knowledge and truth from historical facts grounding them within human subjectivity. Karl Marx's dialectical materialism and Søren Kierkegaard's existentialism both contain strong reactions to Hegel. Hegel advocated an evolution of truth before Darwin popularized the concept of biological evolution.

Charles Darwin (1809–1882). Nancy Pearcey points out:

> For some three hundred years after the scientific revolution, Christianity and science were thought to be completely compatible and mutually supporting. . . . Secularizing trends eventually began to threaten the harmony between science and religion, but its final collapse came abruptly in the late nineteenth century when Charles Darwin published his theory of evolution. Darwinism was implacably naturalistic, explaining life's origin and development by strictly natural causes. It was . . . the missing puzzle piece that completed a naturalistic picture of reality.[24]

[22] Winfried Corduan, "Transcendentalism: Hegel," in *Biblical Errancy: An Analysis of its Philosophical Roots* (Grand Rapids: Zondervan, 1981) 95.
[23] Ibid., 96.
[24] Nancy Pearcey, *Total Truth: Liberating Christianity from Its Cultural Captivity* (Wheaton, IL: Crossway, 2004) 155.

It's clear that, for Darwin, evolution was not so much a specific theory as a philosophical stance—a stance that could be described as, *any mechanism is acceptable, as long as it is naturalistic.* Darwinian evolution is not so much an empirical finding as a deduction from a naturalistic worldview.[25]

Charles Darwin did not originate the theory of biological evolution but he certainly popularized it. His theory of biological evolution by natural selection, described in *Origin of Species by Natural Selection* (1859), gave a scientific naturalistic explanation of origins without God. Darwin had no patience with a God-directed evolution. The deists had needed God for creation; now many rejected the biblical account of creation and concluded they didn't need God at all. At the end of *The Descent of Man* (1871) Darwin declares he did not believe man to be a direct creation of God. Darwin's championing of evolution promoted unbelief in God and the Bible. Evolution became a substitute god for many. A legacy of Darwinism is that anything considered scientific must be naturalistic.

The influence of Darwinism extended into many areas. Social Darwinism applied the concept of evolutionary, natural development (survival of the fittest) to religion, philosophy, economics, government, education, psychology, sociology, history, and other fields. Darwinism marks a significant turning point in intellectual history of western civilization.

Karl Marx (1818–1883) believed that only matter exists. Matter is capable of dynamic change and development. Matter became his god. He considered a personal God to be a human invention to ease suffering and explain life and death. The belief in religion arose out of class struggle. He boldly declared that religion was the "opiate of the masses" in that it suppressed any desire for social change in the present because of the hope of heaven. Marx and Engels in *Manifesto of the*

---

[25] Ibid., 170.

Communist Party stated, "Communism abolishes eternal truths, it abolishes all religion, and all morality."[26]

Marxism is a materialistic, atheistic form of economic socialism. Karl Marx advocated an atheistic economic approach to society. Marxism is a secularized version of the kingdom of God where each gives according to his ability and receives according to his need. Ownership of private property represents original sin. The classless society represents heaven on earth. Marxism presents a full-fledged atheistic worldview which promised to bring about a wonderful classless society. As a secular humanist, Marx believed his economic determinism would improve the social life of man.

Marxists preached their promises of a coming new world of justice, peace, and freedom. Sadly history records it produced state-sponsored atheism that resulted in brutal terrorism and totalitarianism. In the twentieth century, Stalin, Hitler, and others implemented the atheistic agenda. The twentieth century produced conclusive evidence of the failure of atheistic societies.

Søren Kierkegaard (1813–1855), a Danish Christian philosopher, reacted against Hegel's rationalism and idealism. He held that the individual was lost in the Hegelian dialectical system as the abstract became more important than the particular. Kierkegaard made individual choice supreme.

Doctrinally, Kierkegaard accepted Christian orthodoxy. He rightly insisted that one can't be a Christian without a passionate trust in Jesus. He exposed the shallowness of nominal Christianity. Rather than identifying Christianity with one's culture, he emphasized that those who follow Christ will face opposition from the world.

He considered any rational apologetic as shameless. Because he believed the gospel must always appear foolish to the

---

[26] Karl Marx and Friedrich Engels, *On Religion* (Moscow: Progress Publishers, 1976) 79.

world. By a "leap of faith" he accepted Christ's incarnation while affirming its absurdity. Kierkegaard held that the incarnation being an absolute paradox beyond human understanding can only be accepted by faith. While he accepted the Christian faith, his view of truth influenced many to minimize biblical authority and teaching.

Reason and history are irrelevant to Kierkegaard's subjective view of faith. He widened the gap separating the rational and historical basis from the content of faith. He wanted "to find a truth which is true for me."[27] He dismissed objectivity and reason as a way to know religious truth. He believed objective reasons or historical facts cannot provide grounds for faith in God. "Truth is subjectivity, an objective uncertainty held fast in an appropriation process of the most passionate inwardness."[28] He saw the essence of Christianity as passionate commitment. From his own experience he concluded that trying to live a good life by self-effort results in despair. However one can take a leap of faith into religious certainty.

Kierkegaard was not an unbeliever, but some unbelievers have used his philosophy of truth to justify their position. His existentialism led to neoorthodoxy and other subjective trends in modern theology. Many modern theologies reflect his opposition to any rational and historical apologetic.

According to Geisler, Kierkegaard's view of knowledge "grew out of the soil of Kantian agnosticism." Kant declared God to be unknowable by reason; Kierkegaard considered God paradoxical to reason. By a subjective act of will Kant came to moral reality; a move Kierkegaard called an "act of faith."[29] Although Kierkegaard believed the miracles of Jesus, he argued

[27] Søren Kierkegaard, *Diary of Søren Kierkegaard*, ed., Peter Rhode (New York: Citadel, 1971) 44.
[28] Søren Kierkegaard, *Concluding Unscientific Postscript* (Princeton: Princeton University Press, 1941) 182.
[29] Norman L. Geisler, "Philosophical Presuppositions," 327.

against basing faith on intellectual or historical evidence.[30] He left a legacy of separation of faith from reason and history and made faith a subjective leap.

Friedrich Nietzsche (1844–1900). Genius and tragedy characterize this German philosopher's life. A life of dissipation ending with years of insanity tarnished his brilliance. Little noticed in his century, his influence became greater in the twentieth century with its atheistic totalitarian regimes and its anti-movements.

He was skeptical of all traditional and accepted beliefs whether religious, social, scientific, or philosophical. He held that subconscious desires produce our beliefs and actions. The concept of God is a creation of weak humans imagining a supernatural world that doesn't exist. He denounced morality as a human creation intended to subvert the power of the strong. He scorned Christ and Christian morality as weak and decadent.

Nietzsche declared, "God is dead," affirming that modern man had killed him by rejecting the myth that God existed. A forceful writer, he pictured with painful vividness the brutal harshness of life in a world without God. Life in his nihilistic world had no purpose, value, meaning, or hope. More than most, he saw the logical consequences of atheism. In reality, God was not dead. But for Nietzsche truth was dead.

Nietzsche viewed human beings as shaped by the will to power. He proposed an Overman, a superior human, who would move beyond good and evil and create a new morality and who would dominate the world by force of his will. Hitler implemented Nietzsche's philosophy resulting in the horrors of the Holocaust and totalitarian aggression. Nietzsche's sister viewed Hitler as the embodiment of the Overman.

---

[30] Søren Kierkegaard, *Concluding Unscientific Postscript*, trans. By David F. Swenson and Walter Lowrie (Princeton: Princeton University Press, 1941) 25-48, 169-224.

Nietzsche saw psychological demands behind all language. A.F. Holmes says of Nietzsche, "This 'hermeneutic of suspicion', which interprets what people say and do in terms of subconscious desires, underlies much of postmodern subjectivism and relativism with its skepticism about truth claims generally."[31]

Literary brilliance, ironically, accompanied his life of dissipation. He made a lamentable but strong contribution to the development of atheistic unbelief, especially in existentialism and postmodernism.

Sigmund Freud (1856–1939), Austrian founder of psychoanalysis, provided for many a psychological rationale for disbelief in God. He viewed God as an illusion, a childish projection of wishful thinking growing out of human insecurity desiring an all-powerful Father. The concept of God is a human creation. For Freud, religious beliefs are "illusions, fulfillments of the oldest, strongest and most urgent wishes of mankind." As the father provides protection for the child, "Thus the benevolent rule of a divine Providence allays our fear of the dangers of life."[32] Feuerbach stated this wish fulfillment theory of the concept of God years earlier. We have already noted acceptance of this view by Marx and Nietzsche.

Purpose and meaning in life, Freud acknowledged, make sense only when based on a religious system. However, he viewed religion as a childish refusal to face reality, as neurotic and psychologically counterproductive. He regarded religion as infantilism and mass delusion.

Freud's psychoanalysis identified the libido, or sex drive, as the primary driving force in all of life. Our sex-saturated society with its almost universal acceptance of the view that the sex drive is what makes all things happen underscores the per-

---

[31] A.F. Holmes, "Nietzsche, Friedrich," in *New Dictionary of Christian Apologetics*, 496.

[32] Sigmund Freud, *The Future of an Illusion* (New York: Norton, 1961) 30.

vasive influence of Freud. Along with Darwin, he promoted the view that human beings are no more than higher animals.

Freud advocated the Oedipus complex—the boy's desire to replace his father—as the source of all neuroses. The sexually promiscuous, by making a god out of sex, live out Freud's idea of primal rebellion. Vitz states, "Man, not God, is now the consciously specified ultimate source of goodness and power in the universe. Humanistic philosophies glorify him and his 'potential' much the same way religion glorifies the Creator."[33]

A human being, according to Freud, is a collection of psychological forces, conditioned by one's social and physical environment. This determinism undermines personal responsibility. While many of his psychological views stand discredited, Freud's legacy lives on.

Jean-Paul Sartre (1905–1980). A French philosopher and novelist, Sartre became a leading twentieth-century existentialist atheist. Without God, no basis for meaning, truth, or morals exists. He said we are alone in an absurd and hopeless world, whose existence has no explanation. Life is absurd and unexplainable. We are free and responsible to be what we become. The greatest question for him was, "Why something exists instead of nothing existing?"

He was forlorn that God does not exist, but concluded that, because God does not exist, everything is permissible. Individuals are totally free to make themselves whatever they want and they are only responsible to themselves. Without God we have no ultimate standard of right and wrong. Believing objective morals do not exist, Sartre concluded, "It amounts to the same thing whether one gets drunk alone or is a leader of nations."[34] The individual has to take the responsibility of being his or her own god.

---

[33] Paul C. Vitz, *Faith of the Fatherless: The Psychology of Atheism* (Dallas: Spence, 1999) 14.

[34] Jean-Paul Sartre, *Being and Nothingness.* Last lines quoted by Geisler, *Baker Encyclopedia of Christian Apologetics,* 682.

As human beings, people become aware of themselves existing physically, then they define themselves by their choices and actions. No God created human beings, therefore no fixed human nature exists. Since it just "happens" that people exist, they must define themselves and create their own values and authenticate themselves through their choices. Sartre gave philosophical justification to the slogan, "Do your own thing." *Nausea,* the title of one of his books, describes living in an absurd world of "no exit" haunted with the fear of extinction.

Sartre's writings were highly popular in the mid-twentieth century. He became a "patron saint" for rebellious students in the 1960s. He influenced the existentialist movement and the social and sexual lawlessness in general culture. His revolutionary Marxist political theories led to many bloody killings.

In the further study of Christian apologetics, references to these thinkers will appear frequently. The purpose of this chapter is to give a general acquaintance with these influential men. We live today, not in the past. But understanding the ideas that have shaped our culture helps us better commend and defend Christian faith in our day.

Review Questions

1. Why does our culture lack a center?

2. From a Christian perspective what is unbelief?

3. Explain Descartes' concept of God.

4. What did Geisler say about Spinoza's legacy?

5. What reasons did Hume give for being skeptical of God and miracles?

6. Explain Kant's view of knowledge.

7. What is Kant's legacy in religion?

8. How did Darwin's thinking evolve in his view of God?

9. What did Kierkegaard mean by saying faith is a "subjective leap"?

10. What negative contributions has Kierkegaard made to modern theology?

11. What 20th-century political leader implemented Nietzsche's views?

12. Describe Nietzsche's world without God.

13. Summarize Freud's explanation of religion and its origin.

14. In what way has Freud contributed to our sex-saturated society?

15. According to Sartre, what consequences result if God does not exist?

Suggested Reading

Brown, Colin. *Philosophy and Christian Faith: An Introduction to the Main Thinkers and Schools of Thought from the Middle Ages to the Present Day*. Downers Grove, IL: InterVarsity, 1968. An introductory survey of the influence of modern philosophy upon Christian beliefs.

McGrath, Alister. *The Twilight of Atheism: The Rise and Fall of Disbelief in the Modern World*. New York: Doubleday, 2004. Challenges the assumption that the world is becoming more secular and demonstrates why atheism cannot provide the moral and intellectual guidance essential for coping with the complexities of modern life.

Sire, James W. *The Universe Next Door: A Basic Worldview Catalog*, 5th ed. Downers Grove, IL: InterVarsity, 2009. An excellent introductory overview of contemporary rival worldviews for the nonspecialist.

*"Take care, brothers, lest there be in any of you
an evil, unbelieving heart,
leading you to fall away from the living God."
"So we see that they were unable to enter
because of unbelief."*

Hebrews 3:12,19

5

Roots and Fruit of Unbelief

Roots and Fruit of Unbelief	"The natural parents of modern unbelief turn out to have been the guardians of belief. . . . It was religion, not science, or social change, that gave birth to unbelief. Having made God more and more like man—intellectually, morally, emotionally—the shapers of religion made it feasible to abandon God, to believe simply in man."[1]
Profile: Hitler, Stalin, and Mao—Why Unbelief Matters	
I. Roots of Unbelief	
A. Tradition and false teaching	
B. Unbelievers cite objections to faith	
1. Problem of evil and suffering	
2. Naturalistic science	James Turner

[1] James Turner, *Without God, Without Creed: The Origins of Unbelief in America* (Baltimore: The Johns Hopkins University Press, 1985) 260-261.

3. Projection of wish-fulfillment
4. Religious oppression
5. Religion as a natural phenomenon
6. No real evidence exists
C. Selfish Refusal
D. Behavior of Christians
II. Fruit of Unbelief
  A. Sinful disobedience
  B. Eternal lostness
  C. Loss of a basis for meaning and morality
	"Without God and the future life? How will man be after that? It means everything is permitted now."[2]
	
	Fyodor Dostoevsky
	
	"If God is dead, reason is dead. Morality is dead. Meaning is dead. Man is dead."[3]
	
	Francis Schaeffer

Profile: Hitler, Stalin, and Mao—Why Unbelief Matters

In their early years Hitler was a Roman Catholic, Stalin an Eastern Orthodox, and Mao a Buddhist. They turned from their religious backgrounds and conducted godless regimes responsible for murdering over 100 million people.

Some recent atheists defend atheism by blaming religion for these atrocities. They claim that Hitler was a Christian and that Stalin and Mao implemented political religions. In his ascent to power Hitler claimed God's approval for his political and military program not because of a Christian commitment but to rally support of the German people. He considered religion fit only for slaves and hated Christian ethics. The Nazis confiscated church property and closed Christian schools and organizations. The Nazi regime was a godless regime.

[2] Fyodor Dostoevsky, *The Brothers Karamazov* (New York: Vintage, 1991) 589.
[3] Francis A. Schaeffer in class lecture at Wheaton College, May 1967.

An atheistic attempt to abolish religion and morality stood at the center of Marxist Communism in both Russia and China. Communist leaders closed churches, murdered priests and believers. The program to eliminate religion included atheistic propaganda, education, and brutal force.

Hitler killed at least ten million people, including six million Jews. He implemented the unbelief of Darwin and Nietzsche. He believed "might makes right" and justified murdering those he didn't like in the interests of survival of the fittest and creating a master race.

Russian Communism under Stalin's leadership killed over twenty million in mass murders, firing squads, and starvation. Solzhenitsyn says the Russian Revolution "swallowed up some 60 million of our people."[4] The Chinese Communist regime under Mao Tze-tung was responsible for seventy million deaths.

Having no responsibility to God and no ultimate values or moral standards, these godless rulers used any means available to further their agenda. In their behavior they demonstrated the consequences of atheism and in the process discredited atheism. Unbelief does matter.

Ideas have powerful consequences. History gives us many examples. John Stott observes, "Every powerful movement has had its philosophy which has gripped the mind, fired the imagination and captured the devotion of its adherents." He mentions the examples of Hitler, Marx, and Mao.[5] Remembering the horrible fruit of unbelief should motivate Christian men and women to influence the world through the powerful ideas of Christian truth.

[4] Aleksandr Solzhenitsyn, "Men Have Forgotten God," *National Review* (July 22, 1983) 872.
[5] John R.W. Stott, *Your Mind Matters: The Place of the Mind in the Christian Life* (Downers Grove, IL: InterVarsity, 1973).

While many are convinced that God exists and Christianity is true, why is it that many others do not believe? If God's reality is so obvious, why does everyone not acknowledge the fact? This chapter will discuss reasons people choose not to believe in God and Christianity. The consequences that flow from unbelief will also be described.

Roots of Unbelief

Ideas have a history and a past. Many factors contribute to why people think the way they do. Until the Enlightenment most people in the western world believed in God and a generally Christian worldview. A significant percentage of today's population would be characterized as unbelieving. Several causes contribute to this situation. What are some of the reasons people have adopted unbelieving views?

Much unbelief is a result of tradition and false teaching. Many are raised in a cultural situation where teaching about the true God is absent and where they are taught against believing in God. In the fall of 1998 I taught modern history in Anglo-American College in Prague, Czech Republic. I asked one of my students if anyone was religious in his family. He said his grandmother was a Catholic, but she didn't go to church. He said no one was a believer in his family. He held his hands up to his mouth and blew through them and said, "Forty years of Communist teaching and no religion."

People from different cultures, whether they are Buddhists, Muslims, or Hindus, accept the traditional beliefs of their culture unless they are challenged in some way to consider another view. Many do not believe in God because they have been *taught* to believe in false gods and the doctrines of non-Christian religions.

Even in countries with a strong Christian past, we cannot take for granted that people are believers. Each generation teaches their traditions to the next generation. Frequently, Christian faith grows weak or is absent in the next generation. In some countries in the western world that have had a strong history of Christian belief, the majority no longer believe. The practice of living without God teaches unbelief to the next generation.

Some homes teach unbelief. John Clayton, a Christian teacher on Creation and science, in his essay, "Why I Left Atheism," related how his parents taught him atheism.[6] In *My Life Without God*, William Murray relates how his famous atheist mother, Madalyn Murray O'Hair, taught him atheism as a child.[7]

The media, public schools, and universities can be effective teachers of non-Christian worldviews. Charles Hodge in the nineteenth century predicted that secular public education would result in the "renunciation of allegiance to God" and "destruction to society."[8] The founders of the United States wanted to prevent any one religion being established as the state religion. They did not advocate freedom from religion, but freedom to choose one's own religion. Alas, current interpreters pervert the original position to mean separation of state from any expression of religion. This elimination of religion from public culture has furthered unbelief.

In the 1930s Germany had great universities and world-class culture. Soon after Hitler took control of Germany in January 1933, the Nazis had educational, medical, religious, and other professional leaders working with them. Germany's humanistic education and culture did not stop the program of genocide.

Unbelievers cite objections to Christian faith. As defenders of the faith, believers need to be prepared to answer their

[6] John Clayton, "Why I Left Atheism," **http://www.doesgodexist.org/AboutClayton/PastLife.html**.

[7] William Murray, *My Life Without God*, rev. and exp. (Eugene, OR: Harvest House, 1992).

[8] Archibald Alexander Hodge, *The Life of Charles Hodge* (New York: Charles Scribner's Sons, 1880) 409.

charges. Further study in apologetics will address these objections in detail. They will be briefly noted in this chapter.

Some Objections to Christian Faith Raised by Unbelievers

1. The existence of evil rules out an all-powerful and loving God.
2. Science can explain the world without God.
3. The belief in God resulted from a childish wish for a heavenly Father.
4. Religion is a hindrance to human progress and promotes oppression.
5. Religion is a natural phenomenon.
6. It is a leap in the dark with no real reason or evidence.

The problem of evil and suffering in the world is the most common objection to belief in a loving, personal God. Every worldview faces difficulties in explaining evil in the world, including the atheistic view. We will never answer all the questions that can be raised. However the Christian worldview—including creation, the fall, and redemption through God sacrificing himself on the cross—provides the most satisfactory explanation.[9]

As modern science has advanced and explained many of the mysteries of the physical universe, many conclude God is not needed. Naturalistic science has no room for the supernatural. The view that "If science can't prove it, it can't be true or real" supports much modern unbelief. This scientism has promoted the rejection of God, creation, miracles, the deity of

---

[9] See C.S. Lewis, *The Problem of Pain* (San Francisco: Harper/San Francisco, 1949, 1996); D.A. Carson, *How Long, O Lord? Reflections on Suffering and Evil*, 2nd ed. (Grand Rapids: Baker Academic, 2006); and Lynn Gardner, *Where Is God When We Suffer* (Joplin, MO: College Press, 2007) 41-54, 251-291.

Jesus, authority, the trustworthiness of the Bible, the reality of the soul, and the afterlife.[10]

Another objection is the psychological theory that wishful thinking created the concept of God. Following influential nineteenth-century thinkers, Freud popularized the view that belief in God resulted from a human need for heavenly security. Mankind wished such a God existed, so they created him out of their imagination. The illusion of God is a fulfillment of human desires.

Paul C. Vitz analyzed the lives of leading atheists in the light of Freud's projection theory of religion. In a biographical survey of the lives of these leading atheists, Vitz shows that disappointment in one's earthly father, whether through death, absence, or mistreatment frequently leads to a rejection of God.[11]

The charge that religion is merely a projection of wish thinking does not prove Christianity untrue. Neither does the view that atheism may be a projection of wish thinking prove atheism to be untrue. Wishing God to be real or wishing that God does not exist does not make either view true. A theory needs to be subjected to evidence. Does the evidence support the view of many intellectuals that belief in God is based on neurotic irrational wishes and immature needs? Does atheism and skepticism produce psychologically mature and well-ordered personalities?

Psychiatrist and professor of Psychiatry at Harvard Medical School, Dr. Armand M. Nicholi, Jr., conducted a research project interviewing Harvard University students who had

---

[10] See Nancy R. Pearcey and Charles B. Thaxton, *The Soul of Science: Christian Faith and Natural Philosophy* (Wheaton, IL: Crossway, 1994); Nancy Pearcey, *Total Truth: Liberating Christianity from Its Cultural Captivity* (Wheaton. IL: Crossway, 2004); and Phillip E. Johnson, *Darwin on Trial*, 2nd ed. (Downers Grove, IL: InterVarsity, 1993).

[11] Paul C. Vitz, *Faith of the Fatherless: The Psychology of Atheism* (Dallas: Spence, 1999).

undergone religious conversions while undergraduates. The study attempted to learn if these experiences were pathological (isolating and destructive) or if they were adaptive and constructive. Had their religious experience impaired or enhanced their functioning as a person? Nicholi concluded in his published results: Each subject described

> a marked improvement in ego functioning, [including] a radical change in life style with an abrupt halt in the use of drugs, alcohol, and cigarettes; improved impulse control, with adoption of a strict sexual code demanding chastity or marriage with fidelity; improved academic performance; enhanced self-image and greater access to inner feelings; an increased capacity for establishing "close, satisfying relationships"; improved communication with parents, though most parents at first expressed some degree of alarm over the student's rather sudden, intense religious interest; a positive change in affect, with a lessening of "existential despair"; and a decrease in preoccupation with the passage of time and apprehension over death.[12]

The evidence did not support the thesis that religious belief was a product of or produced psychologically maladjusted persons. Having a bad or absent father does not explain all unbelief any more than having a good father explains all belief. But in both cases it is often an important factor. Explaining the origin or occasion for a belief or unbelief does not decide the truth or falsity of that view. Other evidence must determine that.

Another objection to Christianity is the contention that religion brings oppression while unbelief brings freedom. The frequency of this charge has escalated since the Al Qaeda terrorist attacks in New York and Washington, September 11, 2001. Christopher Hitchens' book *God Is Not Great* carries the

---

[12] Armand M. Nicholi, Jr. *The Question of God: C.S. Lewis and Sigmund Freud Debate God, Love, Sex, and the Meaning of Life* (New York: The Free Press, 2002) 80.

subtitle, *How Religion Poisons Everything*. He argues that religion inspires cruelty and corrupts humanity and human progress by inciting violence and enslaving people.

Atheists contend that a secular view of culture resulted in a superior morality to that based on the belief in God. McGrath observes that the attitude of many in modern Europe has been that *"religion is an oppressor; atheism is a liberator."* For example, in eighteenth-century France atheism became attractive because the established church sided with the privileged. "Where the church is seen to be on the side of ordinary people, atheism has relatively little appeal."[13]

"Atheists regularly pointed to the poor human rights records of allegedly 'Christian' states in the past, such as Spain in the sixteenth century. Yet here were states [former Soviet Union] whose official ideology or 'established nonreligion' was atheism committing serious acts of violence, abuse, and oppression in the twentieth century—an age of supposed progress and enlightenment." McGrath continues, "The appeal of atheism as a public philosophy in the West largely came to an end in 1989 with the collapse of the Berlin Wall. Atheism, once hailed as a liberator, was now cordially loathed as an oppressor. . . . Where people enjoy their religion, seeing it as something life enhancing and identity giving, they are going to find atheism unattractive."[14]

Critics cite the Crusades and the Inquisition as a refutation of Christianity. These activities did not follow the spirit of Christ. The crimes and atrocities committed in the name of Christ stand in stark contradiction to the teaching of Christ and the NT (*Matt 5:38-48; Romans 12–14; Luke 23:24; Acts 8:60*). However, the crimes and cruel oppression of Nazi Germany and Russian and Chinese communism were based on the fun-

---

[13] Alister McGrath, "Challenges from Atheism," in *Beyond Opinion*, ed. by Ravi Zacharias (Nashville: Nelson, 2007) 25. Emphasis is in the original.
[14] Ibid., 26.

damental beliefs of Nazism and Communism. Darwin, Marx, and Nietzsche all justified and propagated violence.

While it does not justify violence by religions, Os Guinness says the secularist regimes have killed more people in the twentieth century than all of the religious persecutions in western history.[15]

Those who attack religion as being the cause of violence lump all activities claiming to be religious together. They fail to distinguish between false religion and true religion. Admittedly much evil has been done in the expression of false religion. However, that does not discredit true religion.

Some recent thinkers argue that religion is a natural product of the brain or of our DNA.[16] They contend that religion is a product of human adaptability. Religion arose because of its capacity to sustain cooperation within groups in the face of forces that threaten their unity. Mankind has invoked a super external agent with strategic information about human activity who doesn't require pay. The supposed punishment for non-cooperation is in an invisible afterlife. This external agent always watches—which results in more cooperation.

In an attempt to explain religion as a natural phenomenon is Dean Hamer's, *The God Gene: How Faith Is Hardwired into Our Genes*.[17] He argues that the inclination toward religious faith is basically due to our genes and may offer an evolutionary advantage by helping us deal with difficulties, reduce stress, prevent disease, and extend life. Jesse M. Bering claims to give empirical evidence that belief in a deity or an afterlife could be an evolutionarily advantageous byproduct of people's

---

[15] Os Guinness, *Unspeakable: Facing Up to Evil in an Age of Genocide and Terror* (San Francisco: HarperOne, 2005) 40.

[16] For an apologetic response to this "cognitive science of religion" (CSR), see Paul Copan, "Does Religion Originate in the Brain?" **http://equip.org/articles**.

[17] Dean Hamer, *The God Gene: How Faith Is Hardwired into Our Genes* (New York: Anchor Books, 2005).

ability to reason about the minds of others.[18] All of these attempt to explain religion's origin without acknowledging the reality of God.

Unbelievers claim that no real evidence exists to establish the religious worldview. Harris contends that religion is credulity because no valid reason or evidence exists for such faith.[19] They choose not to accept reasonable and historical evidence for the truth of Christianity because philosophically they are prejudiced against it.

Selfish refusal to believe in God is another cause of unbelief. Self-will is a desire to be independent of God and rule an individual's life keeping him or her from trusting God. Sinful human beings are at enmity with God (*Rom 8:7*). Preoccupation with the things of this world can make eternal things seem unreal. Even though they consider themselves to be impartial, human beings wanting to justify themselves love falsehood and resist the truth of God (*Matt 13:13-23*). Peter wrote that scoffers "deliberately overlook" the fact of creation by the Word of God (*2 Pet 3:3-6*). Paul said of the pagans *"For although they knew God, they did not honor him as God or give thanks to him. . . . They did not see fit to acknowledge God."* Because they deliberately refused God, He gave them up to wallow in their debased and ungodly practices (*Rom 1:21,28-32*).

Young people in their teen and college years often rebel against authority including religious authority. The attacks they have heard from scientists and biblical critics become easy excuses for unbelief without ever carefully studying both sides of the issue. Their real reason for adopting unbelief may be more a moral or spiritual issue than an intellectual one.

[18] Jesse M. Bering, "The Cognitive Psychology of Belief in the Supernatural," *American Scientist* 94 (March–April 2006) 142-149.
[19] Sam Harris, *The End of Faith: Religion, Terror, and the Future of Reason* (New York: W.W. Norton, 2004) 61-71.

They may enjoy shocking their elders with their new ideas and denials of the old ways.

Often an anti-Christian moral atmosphere at school or university—one that includes friends involved in drugs, drinking, and sexual immorality, and professors who ridicule believers—becomes a more dominant influence than home or church. An *environment* of unbelief may be the real cause of unbelief more than the *arguments* of unbelief. Prayer, Bible study, and Christian association can be crowded out. The university experience may expose and eliminate a secondhand faith. Many who were raised in a religious atmosphere never made a personal, intellectual decision to make the faith their own.

One can be angry with God blaming him for a horrible accident, tragic loss, or other disagreeable aspect in life. Arrogance and autonomy conflict with the humility and surrender demanded by Christian faith. Nietzsche said he hated God from his childhood. Postmodernist Richard Rorty admitted that the requirement of humility was a stumbling block for him in regard to Christian faith. Aldous Huxley said that a desire to be free to do as he pleased led to his choice of atheism. "I had motives for not wanting the world to have a meaning; consequently assumed that it had none. . . . For myself, the philosophy of meaninglessness was essentially an instrument of liberation, sexual and political."[20]

Behavior of Christians. Those claiming to be Christians are responsible for much unbelief. Bad examples of Christians have provided stumbling blocks to faith for many. Superstition, crime, division, and other sins in the name of Christ by professing Christians have caused the name of Christ to be blasphemed. It is difficult for the watching world to separate the perversions of Christianity from true Christianity.

[20] Aldous Huxley, *Ends and Means* (New York: Harper, 1937) 270f. Quoted in Michael Green, *Running from Reality* (Downers Grove, IL: InterVarsity, 1983) 82.

In studying the history of ideas one sees that great ideals soon become changed and corrupted. It is not surprising that Christianity, with its unique doctrine, its high morals, and simple institutions, would be changed and corrupted. Christ promises the church will never be destroyed. He does not promise that it would never become corrupted. Both Christ and the apostles predicted the coming of false teachers and a falling away (*Matt 7:15; Col 2:8,20-23; 1 Tim 4:1-4; 2 Pet 3:1-6*).

Jesus wants genuine love and unity in the lives of Christians. He prayed,

> I do not ask for these [apostles] only, but also for those who will believe in me through their word, that they may all be one, just as you, Father, are in me, and I in you, that they also may be in us, so that the world may believe that you have sent me. (*John 17:20-21*)

Discredit is brought upon the Bible when churches teach conflicting doctrines all claiming Bible support for their unbiblical teachings.

To the church's shame many Christians have adopted the culture of the world, loving the world more than loving God. James Turner in *Without God, Without Creed: The Origins of Unbelief in America* acknowledges the importance of science and social transformation, but he concludes that neither caused unbelief. To claim either produced unbelief distorts modern religious history. Turner continues, "Put briefly, unbelief was not something that 'happened to' religion. On the contrary, religion caused unbelief. In trying to adapt their religious beliefs to socioeconomic change, to new moral challenges, to novel problems of knowledge, to the tightening standards of science, the defenders of God slowly strangled Him."[21]

Turner gives an intellectual history of the fate of the idea of God. He shows "how the *available ideas* in the culture changed so

---

[21] Turner, *Without God, Without Creed*, xiii.

as to make unbelief viable." The changes brought about by science, economics, industrialization, and urbanization created a climate in which unbelief grew. "The purpose of this [his] book is simply to explain how it became possible for many people to say, 'I do not believe in God!' No more—and no less."[22]

> Yet, in the final analysis, these forces only raised new questions; it was religious leaders who gave the answers. If a pedestrian flings himself in front of a moving automobile, one does not usually charge the driver with responsibility for the ensuing smashup, even though without the car no disaster would have occurred. Responses to external pressures, not the pressures themselves, shaped belief—though no one should underestimate the strains on religion in a world growing modern. Change pushed the guardians of belief into confusion, often painful, dilemmas. Tradition offered no sure answers, yet answers had urgently to be found. In the end, the most influential church leaders tried to protect belief by making peace with modernity, by conceiving God and His purposes in terms as nearly compatible as possible with secular understandings and aims. A minority insisted that a transcendent God must utterly elude human grasp; their cause, their God seems too out of step, too remote. In the extreme case, the modernizers came close to making religion a thing of this world and creating a God in the image and likeness of man.[23]

Efforts to accommodate belief to the modern world resulted in new theologies such as the Social Gospel and evolutionary theologies.

> Yet attempts to modernize belief did often leave it exposed to the standards of judgment of a purely human criticism and made God morally and emotionally dispensable.
> The natural parents of modern unbelief turn out to have been the guardians of belief. . . . it was religion, not science

---

[22] Ibid., xiv.
[23] Ibid., 260.

or social change, that gave birth to unbelief. Having made God more and more like man—intellectually, morally, emotionally—the shapers of religion made it feasible to abandon God, to believe simply in man. [24]

The union of church and state has led to the secularization of the church and to the advance of unbelief. When one's taxes pay for the church and for Christian teaching, the result is that genuine belief and godly character and conduct are no longer requirements for Christian teachers and leaders. Christianity ceases to be a matter of personal conviction and commitment. History shows that in this arrangement the world leavens the church instead of the church leavening the world.

Fruit of Unbelief

Ideas have consequences. What we think and believe about God has eternal consequences. Our belief and relationship with God is our most important belief and relationship because it determines our purpose and meaning in life and our eternal destiny.

Unbelief results in sinful disobedience. Scripture warns, "Take care, brothers, lest there be in any of you an evil, unbelieving heart, leading you to fall away from the living God. But exhort one another every day, as long as it is called 'today,' that none of you may be hardened by the deceitfulness of sin" (*Heb 3:12-13*). B.F. Westcott commented, "Unbelief finds its practical issue in disobedience."[25]

Disobedience springs from unbelief. *Apistia* is the mental condition of unbelief and *apeitheia*, often translated disobedience, is the outward expression of unbelief. The children of Israel *"were unable to enter [the Promised Land] because of unbelief"* (*Heb 3:19*). *"Those who formerly received the good news failed*

---

[24] Ibid., 260-261.
[25] B.F. Westcott, *Commentary on Hebrews* (London: McMillan, 1920) on Hebrews 3:12.

to enter because of disobedience" (*Heb 4:6*). Unbelieving disobedience brings unwanted consequences.

Those who believe God is nonexistent, unknowable, or has not communicated with us, acknowledge no word from God to obey. Yet when people follow the god of Self they end up disobeying the true God of the universe.

Unbelieving disobedience brings one under the wrath of God. "And without faith it is impossible to please him, for whoever would draw near to God must believe that he exists and that he rewards those who seek him" (*Heb 11:6*). "For the wrath of God is revealed from heaven against all ungodliness and unrighteousness of men who by their unrighteousness suppress the truth" (*Rom 1:18*). Paul continued:

> And since they did not see fit to acknowledge God, God gave them up to a debased mind and to do what ought not to be done. They were filled with all manner of unrighteousness, evil, covetousness, malice. They are full of envy, murder, strife, deceit, maliciousness. They are gossips, slanderers, haters of God, insolent, haughty, boastful, inventors of evil, disobedient to parents, foolish, faithless, heartless, ruthless. Though they know God's decree that those who practice such things deserve to die, they not only do them but give approval to those who practice them. (*Rom 1:28-32*)

Unbelief grows out of a human desire for autonomy against the sovereignty of God—the desire to rule oneself instead of submitting to God's rule (*Rom 1:20-25; Ps 14:1; Isa 6:9-12; Jer 17:9*). Unbelief dominates the whole person, so the unbeliever needs to be reborn and become a new person (*John 3:3-13; 1 Cor 1:22-24; 2:12-16, 2 Cor 5:17; Gal 2:20*).

Sin and unbelief brings one under God's wrath and condemnation (*John 3:36; Rom 2:8; 11:20-24; Eph 2:2; 5:6*). Unbelief is sinful, evil, and results in one's being eternally lost. While not malicious, God's wrath is the personal reaction of his holy nature against sin. Pure holiness abhors ungodliness. God must reject sin.

A future day of reckoning and judgment is certain where the final verdict is given (*1 John 4:17; John 5:24-29; Acts 17:30*). Unbelievers cannot avoid the judgment of God (*Rom 2:2f; 5:16; 1 Cor 11:29,34*).

Our relationship with Christ determines our eternal destiny. Salvation in Christ releases us from God's wrath (*Rom 5:9; 1 Thess 5:9*). In God's eyes a marked division exists between those in Christ and those outside of Christ. This fact makes commending and defending the faith more crucial and urgent.

Unbelief in God results in the loss of a basis for morality and hope. Voltaire reportedly said, "Don't tell the servants there is no God, or they will steal the silver." Freud said religion was necessary to keep people from acting on their sexual and aggressive impulses.[26] Will Durant said that the common person will fall to pieces morally if he thinks there is no God. But "a man like me," said Durant, "I survive morally because I retain the moral code that was taught me along with the religion, while I have discarded the religion, which was Roman Catholicism." He said he was living on a shadow because he still operated on Christian ethics. "But what will happen to our children . . . ? We are not giving them an ethics warmed up with a religious faith. They are living on the shadow of a shadow."[27]

An atheist may have moral standards, but he or she cannot justify them. If no ultimate standard of goodness exists (God), then how do we know that hate, rape, murder are wrong?

Unbelief results in the loss of fellowship and favor of the infinite, personal God. Unbelief is a tragedy because it brings the loss of everything that really matters. If no ultimate Being exists and the universe is a cosmic accident, how can one prove a basis for purpose and meaning in life?

---

[26] Sigmund Freud, *Future of an Illusion*; and *Civilization and Its Discontents* (New York: Norton, 1961).

[27] Will Durant, *Chicago Sun Times* (24 August 1975) quoted by Norman L Geisler, *Baker Encyclopedia of Christian Apologetics*, 282.

Those who are without God are without hope (*Eph 2:12;*
1 Thess 4:13). Atheist Albert Camus admitted, "For anyone who is
alone, without God and without a master; the weight of days is
dreadful."[28] He believed the question of suicide was the only really serious philosophical question.[29] Ravi Zacharias, a native of
India, faced this question as he followed his atheism to its logical
conclusion. After two of his friends committed suicide, his
botched attempt to end his life landed him in a New Delhi hospital. While there he received a Bible and learned the gospel message. He testifies, "All I can say now is how grateful I am that Sam
Harris [atheist] was not my mentor or his tirade my inspiration,
for my life would have ended there and then."[30] Zacharias trusted Christ and for four decades has led others to trust in Christ.

Belief in the living God who acts in human affairs and
keeps his promises makes hope possible. Hope depends on
God, not on human personality, accomplishments, or circumstances. As Christians we have a responsibility to give nonbelievers a reason for a solid hope in Christ. We must not take
this privilege lightly.

A certain hope beyond death depends upon a confident
faith in God. The heart of Christian faith is faith in God who
raised Jesus from the dead (*1 Pet 1:21*). *"May the God of hope fill
you with all joy and peace in believing, so that by the power of the
Holy Spirit you may abound in hope"* (*Rom 15:13*). Our hope is in
God (*2 Cor 1:9-10; 1 Tim 4:10*) and in Christ (*1 Tim 1:1*). We can
have a living hope through the resurrection of Jesus from the
dead (*1 Pet 1:3*).

Unbelief is no trivial matter. Unbelief does matter. Commending and defending Christian faith becomes an urgent

---

[28] Albert Camus, *The Fall* (New York: Random House, 1956, 1984) 133.

[29] Albert Camus, *The Myth of Sisyphus and Other Essays* (New York: Vintage
Books, 1955) 1.

[30] Ravi Zacharias, *The End of Reason: A Response to the New Atheists* (Grand
Rapids: Zondervan, 2008) 27-28.

matter when we realize the seriousness of unbelief. When we witness to unbelievers we can urge them to ask themselves the following questions.

Personal Questions for the Unbeliever

1. Have I given careful study of the evidence for Christianity, or have I mainly looked for objections?
2. Would I be willing to make a complete change in my life if I conclude that Christianity is in fact true?
3. Have I allowed a wrong attitude or an inadequate approach to the issue to keep me from fairly evaluating the evidence?
4. Am I willing to study both sides of the issue?[31]

Review Questions

1. What connection exists between the atheism of the Nazi and Communist regimes and the atrocities committed?

2. Give examples of tradition and teaching accounting for unbelief.

3. List five unbelieving objections to Christian faith.

4. What does the evidence of atheists who have defective fathers say to the charge that belief in God is merely wish fulfillment?

5. How would you respond to the charge that religion causes oppression?

6. How do the Crusades and the Inquisition differ from the murderous regimes of the Nazis and Communists?

---

[31] Adapted from James D. Bales, *The Roots of Unbelief* (Kansas City, MO: Old Paths Book Club, 1948) 157.

7. Give Scriptures which show that some unbelief is a result of willful refusal to believe.

8. How has the behavior of some Christians been a cause of unbelief?

9. What does Turner mean when he says the "guardians of belief" made it possible for people to abandon belief in God?

10. Summarize the scriptural teaching about the consequences of unbelief.

11. Loss of belief in God results in the loss of meaning, morality, and hope. What evidence supports this statement?

Suggested Reading

McGrath, Alister. *The Twilight of Atheism: The Rise and Fall of Disbelief in the Modern World*. New York: Doubleday, 2004. A former atheist explains the appeal of atheism as well as what went wrong with the atheist dream. He exposes the flaws of atheism and sees it declining in influence. He predicts a renewal of faith in the twentieth-first century.

Turner, James. *Without God, Without Creed: The Origins of Unbelief in America*. Baltimore: The Johns Hopkins University Press, 1985. An intellectual history of the disbelief in God in America showing how unbelief became a viable option.

Vitz, Paul C. *Faith of the Fatherless: The Psychology of Atheism*. Dallas: Spence Publishing, 1999. Biographical survey of leading atheists' lives showing that disappointment with earthly fathers—whether through death, absence, or mistreatment—contributed to their rejection of God.

Foundations for
Apologetics

"Come now, let us reason together, says the LORD."
Isaiah 1:18

"You shall love the Lord your God with all your heart and with all your soul and with all your mind."
Matthew 22:37

6
Thinking

Thinking
Profile: Charles Malik—
  Redeeming the Soul
  and the Mind
I. Misuses of the Mind
  A. Intellectualism
  B. Anti-intellectualism
  C. The closed mind
  D. The corrupt mind
II. The Validity of Reason
  A. Creation
  B. Revelation
  C. Fallen reason
  D. Validity of logic
III. The Proper Use of the
  Mind
  A. Humility
  B. Honesty
	"Offering up our minds to God in all our thinking is a part of our praise."[1]
	          Os Guinness
	
	"Reason directs those who are truly pious and philosophical to honour and love only what is true, declining to follow traditional opinions, if these be worthless. For not only does sound reason direct us to refuse the guidance of those who did or taught anything wrong, but it is incumbent on the lover of truth, by all means, and if death be threatened, even before his own life, to choose to do and say what is right."[2]
	          Justin Martyr

[1] Os Guinness, *Fit Bodies, Fat Minds: Why Evangelicals Don't Think and What to Do about It* (Grand Rapids: Baker, 1994) 18.
[2] Justin Martyr, *The First Apology*, II.

117

C. Thinking Christianly about the world and life	"Once the life of reason is rejected, there is no reason why any one faith is better or worse than any other."[3] David Elton Trueblood

Profile: Charles Malik— Redeeming the Soul and the Mind

Lebanese Orthodox believer, professor, and diplomat, Charles Malik (1906–1987) delivered an important address at the dedication of the Billy Graham Center at Wheaton College in 1980. He asserted, "The problem is not only to win souls but to save minds. If you win the whole world and lose the mind of the world, you will soon discover you have not won the world. Indeed it may turn out that you have actually lost the world."[4]

He characterized as "self-worship" the rival non-Christian views in our intellectual world. He declared that the state of the mind in Western civilization is in trouble, demanding our urgent attention and action. Christians must take seriously the task of ordering young minds with sound principles. Malik warned evangelicals that "the greatest danger confronting American evangelical Christianity is the danger of anti-intellectualism." Being in a hurry to begin preaching the gospel, they "have no idea of the infinite value of spending years of leisure conversing

[3] Elton Trueblood, *A Place to Stand: A Practical Guide to Christian Faith as a Solid Point from Which to Operate in Contemporary Living* (New York: Harper and Row, 1969) 23.

[4] Charles Malik, "The Two Tasks," in *The Two Tasks of the Christian Scholar: Redeeming the Soul, Redeeming the Mind*, eds. William Lane Craig and Paul M. Gould (Wheaton, IL: Crossway Books, 2007) 63.

with the greatest minds and souls of the past, ripening and sharpening and enlarging their powers of thinking. The result is that the arena of creative things is vacated and abdicated to the enemy."[5] In order to be more effective in witnessing to Jesus Christ, "Evangelicals cannot afford to keep on living on the periphery of responsible intellectual existence."[6]

The influence of Malik's lecture lives on in evangelical thinkers. Os Guinness refers to it as an "incisive address."[7] Noll says the "acute wisdom" of his remarks serves as the "manifesto of a Christian intellectual to his friends in the faith."[8]

Malik challenged us to bring all our thinking into harmony with and obedience to Christ. "The critic in the final analysis is Jesus Christ himself." The question, "What does Jesus think?" is all that counts. Otherwise our thinking is "an exercise in fuzziness, in wobbly human effort, in subjectivist rationalism, in futility."[9]

Malik's son wrote about his father, "The most important and abiding feature of the man, the real clue by his own admission to his success and his positive influence was the strong faith in Jesus Christ" he learned from his grandmother.[10]

---

[5] Ibid., 63-64.

[6] Ibid., 64.

[7] Os Guinness, *Fit Bodies, Fat Minds*, 11.

[8] Mark A. Noll, *The Scandal of the Evangelical Mind* (Grand Rapids: Eerdmans, 1994) 25.

[9] Charles Habib Malik, *A Christian Critique of the University* (Downers Grove, IL: InterVarsity, 1982) 15-16, 23, 27.

[10] Habib C. Malik, "Foreword: Reflections on Charles Malik," in *The Two Tasks of the Christian Scholar* (Wheaton, IL: Crossway Books, 2007) 12.

Harry Blamires popularized the term "the Christian mind." The church is "rich in scholars" and "poor in thinkers," Blamires alleged. "The thinker challenges current prejudices. He disturbs the complacent. He obstructs the busy pragmatists. He questions the very foundations of all about him. . . . The thinker is a nuisance. . . . But the Church cannot do without thinkers."[11] The thinker distinguishes between right and wrong, being committed to decisive action. The Christian mind sees every area of life through the lens of Christian truth.

To emphasize thinking and reason goes against the grain of our culture. Reason is distrusted as a suspect contribution of the Enlightenment. Can we trust our minds? What is the right use of the mind? How do we misuse the mind? How can we defend the validity of reason? Are reason and faith compatible? How can one be a thinking Christian?

Since apologetics involves giving reasons for our faith, we need to understand the proper role of human reason and thinking. Because the Christian faith is rooted in a body of truth, we must affirm a valid approach to knowing before we can undertake the intellectual defense of the Christian faith. This chapter will examine the role of the mind by considering misuses of the mind, then defend the validity of rationality, and third, consider the proper use of the mind. Chapter 7 will address the topic of knowledge.

Misuses of the Mind

A popular slogan stated, "The mind is a terrible thing to waste." A valuable tool, the mind should not be minimized or misused. Effective defenders of the faith will avoid the following misuses of the mind.

Intellectualism. Intellectualism denotes an overconfidence in one's own mind. Before lecturing in his graduate church his-

---

[11] Ibid., 50.

tory class at Wheaton College in 1966, Dr. Earle Cairns read Jesus' words about loving God with all one's heart, mind, soul and strength. Before he prayed he made a brief application. "Some around here are so concerned to prove they are intellectuals that they just love their minds. Jesus wants us to love God *with* our minds."

Intellectualism is a form of idolatry. The worship of one's intellect displaces God from his rightful place. We should use our minds to gain knowledge and wisdom, but knowledge is not an end in itself. Education and learning can intoxicate us to think more highly of ourselves than we ought to think. But persons without formal education may also be guilty of making their own opinions their highest authority.

The Christian is "not to think of himself more highly than he ought to think but to think with sober judgment" (*Rom 12:3*). Destruction comes to those who are wise in their own eyes. *"Has not God made foolish the wisdom of the world? For since, in the wisdom of God, the world did not know God through wisdom, it pleased God through the folly of what we preach to save those who believe"* (*1 Cor 1:20-21*). God chose the seeming foolishness of Christ crucified to shame those who trusted in worldly wisdom (*1 Cor 1:22-29*).

Intellectual pride yields a wisdom that is "earthly, unspiritual, and demonic" and leads to "disorder and every vile practice" (*Jas 3:15-16*). We must guard our minds against an intellectual arrogance that trusts ourselves more than we trust God. Paul said, *"We destroy arguments and every lofty opinion raised against the knowledge of God, and take every thought captive to obey Christ"* (*2 Cor 10:4-5*).

Anti-intellectualism. Avoiding intellectualism, some swing to the opposite extreme. John Stott tells of a man who said, "Whenever I go to church . . . I feel like unscrewing my head and placing it under the seat, because in a religious meeting I never have any use for anything above my collar button."[12] A Neo-Pentecostal said his ultimate goal as a Christian was to stop using his mind and just follow the Holy Spirit's leading. But, how will he distinguish the leading of the Holy Spirit from that of an unholy spirit if he doesn't use his mind?

Bruce Lockerbie observes, "Too often Christians have shunned *thinking* at all in favor of *feeling*, contenting themselves with emotionalism borne along by experience, a 'feel-good' faith; what J. I. Packer has called 'jacuzzi Christianity,' based on warm, cozy, comfortable, familiar, complacent emotions, devoid of any thoughtful, intelligent, carefully reasoned faith."[13]

David Gill warns against "a mindless Christianity having to do only with our emotions or traditions. . . . Too often Christians check their minds at the door with their coats when they enter the church . . . and worse, check their Christianity at the door when they enter the university or business office."[14] "Mindless emotionalism or traditionalism, segmented, fragmented lives and ignorance disguised as simple faith are all terrible deformations of Christian discipleship."[15]

Elton Trueblood says we need to encourage the proper use of the mind to counter "discouragement produced by the preaching of anti-intellectualism."[16] This popular anti-intellectualism has arisen in response to a rationalism that thought reason could prove things absolutely. Trueblood continued:

---

[12] John R.W. Stott, *Your Mind Matters: The Place of the Mind in the Christian Life* (Downers Grove, IL: InterVarsity, 1973) 30.

[13] D. Bruce Lockerbie, *Thinking and Acting like a Christian* (Portland, OR: Multnomah, 1989) 14.

[14] David W. Gill, *The Opening of the Christian Mind: Taking Every Thought Captive to Christ* (Downers Grove, IL: InterVarsity, 1989) 31.

[15] Ibid., 30.

[16] Trueblood, *A Place to Stand*, 20.

But as so often occurs in the history of human thought, the tendency is to fall into an extreme even worse than the one that is being rejected. This has, in fact, occurred in our time. However bad some arid intellectualism has been, anti-intellectualism is worse, since it provides no antidote to either superstition or wish-thinking. If the tough-minded concern for evidence and for consistency is given up, there is no way to detect error, or even to distinguish between degrees of probability.[17]

Once the life of reason is rejected, there is no reason why any one faith is better or worse than any other. The pathetic fact is that the people who say they do not need to give reasons for the objective validity of the faith they espouse do not seem to realize how sad the consequences of their position are.[18]

The person who has become disillusioned by his inability to find satisfactory reasons often concludes that "careful reasoning has no value. By this step he succeeds in transferring the blame from himself and his own ineptitude; but he undermines, at the same time, any possibility of detecting error."[19] While deifying the mind is wrong, so is despising the mind which God gave us. We must seek a sensible balance between these extremes.

The Closed Mind. Closed minds refuse to reexamine their thoughts and opinions. Allan Bloom, in *The Closing of the American Mind*, insists that since Americans have accepted relativism with its denial of objective truth they have closed their minds to valid thinking.[20] When one is convinced that truth cannot be known, the mind remains empty and closed to the learning of truth.

---

[17] Ibid., 21.

[18] Ibid., 23.

[19] Ibid., 24.

[20] Allan Bloom, *The Closing of the American Mind* (New York: Simon and Schuster, 1987) 25.

In speaking of the Jews who read the OT with a veil over their minds, Paul said, *"Their minds were hardened"* (*2 Cor 3:14*). *"The god of this world has blinded the minds of the unbelievers, to keep them from seeing the light of the gospel of the glory of Christ, who is the image of God"* (*2 Cor 4:4*, see *2 Cor 2:11*). Isaiah spoke of those who refused truth, *"They know nothing, they understand nothing; their eyes are plastered over so they cannot see, and their minds closed so they cannot understand"* (*Isa 44:18*, NIV). Those who close their minds to truth remain imprisoned in their own thoughts. Thomas Aquinas observed, "It is the wisdom of the world that deceives and makes us foolish in God's sight."[21]

Paul describes those without God as futile in their minds. They are

> darkened in their understanding and alienated from the life of God because of the ignorance that is in them, due to their hardness of heart. They have become callous and have given themselves up to sensuality, greedily to practice every kind of impurity. (*Eph 4:18-19*)

A biased mind is a closed mind. Those who presuppose the impossibility of the supernatural and knowing objective truth have closed their minds. The Christian mind should be open to consider genuine knowledge and truth wherever he or she finds it.

Arrogant dogmatism is ugly whether seen in a Christian or a non-Christian. We must be relentless in our search for truth, all the while realizing we still have more to learn. One's mind may be blinded by a false worldview, conceit, or a sinful lifestyle.

The Corrupted Mind. Paul warns that we can have minds that are alienated, hostile, inflated, and corrupted. *"And you, who once were alienated and hostile in mind, doing evil deeds"* (*Col 1:21*). *"Let no one disqualify you, insisting on asceticism and worship of angels, going on in detail about visions, puffed up without*

---

[21] Thomas Aquinas, *Summa Theologica*, Part II, Question 46, Article 2.

reason by his sensuous mind" (Col 2:18). If one teaches contrary to the words of Jesus and godliness

> *he is puffed up with conceit and understands nothing. He has an unhealthy craving for controversy and for quarrels about words, which produce envy, dissension, slander, evil suspicions, and constant friction among people who are depraved in mind and deprived of the truth, imagining that godliness is a means of gain. (1 Tim 6:4-5)*

"As Jannes and Jambres opposed Moses, so these men also oppose the truth, men corrupted in mind and disqualified regarding the faith" (2 Tim 3:8). "See to it that no one takes you captive by philosophy and empty deceit, according to human tradition, according to the elemental spirits of the world, and not according to Christ" (Col 2:8).

Our minds are corrupted when sin and guilt have led us to deny truth, distort reality, and create self-justifying fantasies. When you fill your mind with immoral garbage and falsehood and practice sinful behavior your mind becomes corrupted and clear thinking becomes increasingly more difficult. Scripture frequently warns us against being deceived in our minds (*Rom 16:18; Eph 5:6; Col 2:4; 2 Thess 2:3; 2 Tim 3:13; Titus 1:10; 2 John 7*). In order to avoid these misuses of the mind, we need to understand the proper role and use of human reason.

The Validity of Reason

The Enlightenment glorified human reason, making it the ultimate standard of truth. Reason faced relentless assaults during the nineteenth and twentieth centuries. For the theological modernist, scientific naturalism and rationalism shaped what they accepted as true and reasonable. To combat this de-supernaturalized misrepresentation of Christianity, C.S. Lewis and others "set out to reason people into Christian belief. The Christian faith was presented as the only thing that made sense of life and the world."[22]

---

[22] Harry Blamires, *The Post-Christian Mind: Exposing Its Destructive Agenda* (Ann Arbor, MI: Servant, 1999) 15.

Increasingly during the twentieth and twenty-first centuries reason has been denied any validity and value in regard to religious knowledge. Harry Blamires recalls in the 1960s lecturing to students on philosophical and religious topics:

> One student suddenly said, forcefully and in a tone dismissive of the entire discussion, 'But this is the Age of Aquarius.' That was all. And the implication of the words became apparent. Reasoning about basic issues of life and death, of truth and falsehood, of goodness and evil, was no longer valid. There were no longer any intellectual landmarks or signposts by which such reasoning could be conducted.[23]

The New Age Movement and postmodernism hold vastly differing views of the nature of religious reality and experience, both, however, have denied reason a role in religious belief.

Some value reason in science and everyday life but eliminate it from religion. The area of ethics, values, and religion has been put in a category where only subjective, relative preferences and opinions exist. This attitude toward reason permeates the intellectual air of our day. It has infiltrated the thinking of church leaders as well as the popular mind of Christians.

Today's antireason mentality minimizes or rejects the role of the mind. Reason is dismissed from the interpretation of Scripture. Many contemporary thinkers reject a rational defense of Christian faith as "modernist rationalism." Since apologetics gives reasons for faith, we need to defend the validity of reason.

Creation. God created human beings in his image. God said, *"Let us make man in our image, after our likeness; and let them have dominion over the fish of the sea, and over the birds of the air, and over the cattle, and over all the earth, and over every creeping thing that creeps upon the earth"* (*Gen 1:26*). Gill says,

> One of the most distinctive characteristics of human existence is that we are capable of mental reflection and thought. We

---

[23] Ibid., 16.

are capable of self-transcendence (thinking about ourselves) through the use of our minds. We are not bound to a mechanical, unreflective obedience to instinct or conditioning. Rather, we can think about our actions and, still more remarkable, decide to go against our instincts or appetites. We are capable of amazing self-discipline, sacrifice, exertion, and even heroism in the face of various challenges. This is due in large part to the fact that we have been created with minds that can reflect and choose. We can transcend nature and culture; we do not always submit passively to our situations.[24]

We are created to think and communicate intelligently with God. *"Be not like a horse or mule, without understanding"* (**Ps 32:9**). The image of God includes intellectual capacity to have dominion over creation (**Gen 1:26**). Ability to reason is an aspect of human uniqueness. It distinguishes us from animals. God gave us reason as a tool for learning new information, in making judgments, in using things, and relating to other persons.

Carl F.H. Henry says the Christian Logos doctrine presupposes "an intelligible order or logos in things, an objective law which claims and binds man, and makes possible human understanding and valid knowledge. . . . The concept of the logos comprehends at once the interrelationship of thought, word, matter, nature, being and law."[25] "Christianity affirms that this world is a rational universe, that it is God's world; knowability of the universe is grounded in God's creation of man as a rational creature whose forms of thought correspond to the laws of logic subsisting in the mind of God, as well as to the rational character of the world as God's creation."[26] The eternal Logos created the universe and established the conditions of communication and logic. The ability to think, reason, and communicate is grounded in the Mind of God himself.

---

[24] Gill, *Opening of the Christian Mind*, 21-22.
[25] Carl F.H. Henry, *God, Revelation and Authority* (Waco: Word Books: 1979) 3:193.
[26] Ibid., 192.

Ronald Nash says,

> As the Logos of God, Jesus guarantees human rationality and certifies the ability of humans to understand the Word of God. The correspondence between the mind of God and the human mind (that is grounded in the Logos) makes possible a human understanding of the divine communication of truth.[27]

> Reason has an intrinsic relationship to God, it has cosmic significance. Christians believe the rational world is the projection of a rational God who objectifies His eternal thoughts in the creation and who endows the human creature, the apex of His creation, with the image of God which includes a structure of reason similar to God's own reason.[28]

Revelation. God "created men and women as creatures capable of knowing His mind and will and made information about His mind and will available in revealed truths."[29] God communicated with man and expected him to understand and respond rationally. Since God communicated with human beings through prophets, through his Son, through apostles, through the written Scriptures, this implies that we have the ability to know cognitively, to reason, and draw proper conclusions. He expected and still expects people to make a proper response to his communication. Solomon encourages us *"to know wisdom and instruction, to understand words of insight. . . . Let the wise hear and increase in learning, and the one who understands obtain guidance"* (*Prov 1:2,5*). *"Come now, let us reason together, says the* LORD*" (Isa 1:18)*.[30]

Fallen Reason. Some believe the Fall corrupted human reason, so it is now totally unreliable for understanding and

---

[27] Ronald H. Nash, *The Word of God and the Mind of Man: The Crisis of Revealed Truth in Contemporary Theology* (Phillipsburg, NJ: Presbyterian and Reformed, 1992) 68.

[28] Ibid., 69.

[29] Ibid., 14.

[30] See also *Ps 50:22; Prov 2:5,9; Isa 41:20; Dan 9:25; Hag 1:7; 2:15,18.*

believing the Bible and God. However the NT evangelists treated non-Christians as though they could still think. After the Fall, human reason has been impaired but not destroyed. The Fall did not obliterate the logical functioning of the mind. The influence of a sinful heart leads the mind to suppress information which the mind does not accept. The unbeliever may be intelligent, but when the mind is darkened and blinded, the person does not see what he or she *will* not see. Paul says the pagan should have known God from nature but chose willfully to remain ignorant of God (*Rom 1:19-32*).

Fallen men and women by their minds alone cannot reason to the content of the Christian faith. However, if they will, they can still think. Fallen persons know two plus two equals four. They can know whether a person is dead or alive. Those whose minds are open and seeking to know the truth can see the rationality of Christian faith. Jesus said, *"If anyone's will is to do God's will, he will know whether the teaching is from God or whether I am speaking on my own authority"* (*John 7:17*).

Validity of Logic. The rationalism of the Enlightenment held that human reason could by itself establish absolute truth. Because of the overconfidence in reason, the pendulum has now swung to subjectivism and relativism. Frequently today we hear that a rational defense of the faith is no longer effective.

In *Apologetics for a New Generation*, Sean McDowell cites these comments by young leaders,

- ✧ "We live in a postmodern era, so apologetics is not important anymore."
- ✧ "Young people no longer care about reasons for the existence of the Christian God. What matters is telling your narrative and being authentic."
- ✧ "New generations today no longer need 'evidence that demands a verdict' or a 'case for Christ."[31]

---

[31] Sean McDowell, *Apologetics for a New Generation: A Biblically & Culturally Relevant Approach to Talking about God* (Eugene, OR: Harvest House, 2009) 14.

Reason and logic are viewed by many as relics from the past. But as R.C. Sproul has said:

> Aristotle did not *invent* logic any more than Columbus invented America. All that Aristotle did was discover and define rules that were already in existence. Aristotle ascertained the necessary conditions for human beings to carry on meaningful conversations. He defined the proper relationships of propositions. He did not create the laws of logic; he merely articulated what was already there. These laws were placed in our minds by the Creator during the act of creation.[32]

The Enlightenment did not create reason; it produced a form of rationalism. We must rightly reject Enlightenment rationalism but that does not mean we must reject the proper use of reason. Thinking rationally does not make us a rationalist. Rationality has limitations but is valid when used properly. Christian thinkers through the centuries—Paul, Justin Martyr, Aquinas, John Wesley, C.S. Lewis, and others—have made good use of reason. Certainly we must avoid the misuse of reason. But the right use of reason has validity because God, not the Enlightenment thinkers, gave us reason. He expects us to use it as he intended.

The principles of logic describe correct thinking. We cannot prove these fundamental principles. However they are inescapable because their denial lands one in self-contradiction. The *law of identity* states that something is what it is and not something else. Something is identical with itself.

The *law of noncontradiction* states that A cannot be A and non-A at the same time and in the same sense. Nothing can both be and not be at the same time and in the same way. If something is true, then its contradiction is false. Those who deny the validity of this law assume it in order to deny it. To say the law of noncontradiction is false is to assume that it

---

[32] R.C. Sproul, *Defending Your Faith* (Wheaton, IL: Crossway, 2003) 37-38.

contradicts its opposite. Some theologians, postmodernists, and Emergent church bloggers argue that contradiction is the hallmark of truth. Sproul counters, "If contradiction is a hallmark of truth, then there is no way we can differentiate between right and wrong, good and evil, obedience and disobedience."[33]

Another principle or law of logic is the *law of excluded middle*. It's either A or non-A. Any factual statement and its denial cannot both be true. A proposition is either true or false, not halfway in between. Denial of this principle results in opposites both being true, which is absurd. Whatever something is, it must be either that or not that.

Logic is a tool describing careful and correct thinking. *Logic does not set up human reason as the highest authority*. It can help us avoid errors and false reasoning. By following its guidelines one can gain knowledge of reality. Reason is not the only valid source and test of knowledge but it is one source and a test of knowledge. The study of logic, the principles of clear and correct reasoning, and fallacies, errors in thinking, is valuable as one prepares to be a defender of the faith.

Those who try to reject the validity of human reason, use reason to try to refute reason. Attempts to establish irrationality assume rationality and therefore are unconvincing and self-refuting.

The Proper Use of the Mind

Humility. One cannot understand the appropriate use and limitations of human reasoning without an openness and reverence for God. *"The fear of the LORD is the beginning of knowledge"* (*Prov 1:7*). This requires a humble acknowledgment that God is the ultimate source and standard of all knowledge and truth. Job asked his friends *"From where, then, does wisdom*

---

[33] Ibid., 39.

come? And where is the place of understanding? . . . God under-
stands the way to it, and he knows its place. For he looks to the ends
of the earth and sees everything under the heavens. . . . And he said
to man, 'Behold, the fear of the Lord, that is wisdom, and to turn
away from evil is understanding" (*Job 28:20,23,28*). As human
beings we stand in awe before the infinite God, realizing our
limitations and finiteness. Humility does not mean you have to
deny that you know what you know. A humble defender of the
faith will not speak arrogantly, but will speak truth motivated
by a heart of love for God and people.

Christ is our example of humility. We are not to think
more highly nor more lowly of ourselves than we ought to
think (*Phil 2:1-11*). Peter said, *"Clothe yourselves, all of you, with*
humility toward one another, for 'God opposes the proud, but gives
grace to the humble'" (*1 Pet 5:5*). James said, *"Humble yourselves*
before the Lord, and he will exalt you" (*Jas 4:10*). James Sire
observes:

> For both Peter and James humility is not produced by compar-
> ing oneself to others or by self-abasement, saying to oneself,
> "Poor me! I'm just a worm." Humility is produced by seeing
> oneself in the light of who God is. . . . We believe as Christians
> that God is omniscient and that we, as much as we know, as
> much as God has told us in his Word, are finite and fallible in
> our knowledge. We should, therefore, keep our own develop-
> ing views of everything—God, human beings, nature, our-
> selves—in perspective. On any of these we could be wrong.[34]

Sire continues,

> We need to be confident enough in our beliefs to act but not
> so dogmatic about them that we do not allow them to come
> under scrutiny. We should recognize the inadequacy of our
> own understanding and the sinfulness of many of our actions
> and yet commit ourselves to kingdom actions with a vision of

---

[34] James W. Sire, *Discipleship of the Mind: Learning to Love God in the Ways We*
Think (Downers Grove, IL: InterVarsity, 1990) 20.

the city of God always in our sights. Jesus has gone before us through death.[35]

We need to give our minds to Jesus the Lord. Gill states,

The typical Christian mind is certainly not empty, but is underdeveloped and undervalued. Our Christian minds have too often been fearful, insecure and closed. My call is first of all to open the Christian mind toward God, inviting him to expand, invigorate and share our thinking toward the mind of Christ.[36]

G.K. Chesterton observes,

But what we suffer from to-day is humility in the wrong place. Modesty has moved from the organ of ambition. Modesty has settled upon the organ of conviction; where it was never meant to be. A man was meant to be doubtful about himself, but undoubting about the truth; this has been exactly reversed.[37]

William Lane Craig cautions us that apologetics, as a struggle of ideas,

tends to promote selfish ambition, arrogance, and competitiveness. . . . I think that pride is perhaps the most dangerous and insidious enemy that the Christian apologist will face. We may do good scholarly work, but if we are filled with vainglory, we shall undermine what we say by the way we are. Pride screams at people and pushes them away. It will undercut the message that we bring.[38]

We need to remember Paul's wise reminder, *"Knowledge puffs up, but love builds up. If anyone imagines that he knows something, he does not yet know as he ought to know"* (1 Cor 8:1-2).

---

[35] Ibid., 22.

[36] Gill, *Opening of the Christian Mind*, 13-14.

[37] G.K. Chesterton, *Orthodoxy: The Classic Account of a Remarkable Christian Experience* (Colorado Springs: WaterBrook Press, 1994, 2001) 38.

[38] William Lane Craig, "Advice to Christian Apologists," **http://www.reasonable faith.org/site/News2?page=NewsArticle&id=.**

Honesty. In addition to humility we must be consistently honest. A God-follower has a passion for truth. An honest person wants truth even when it hurts. Assuming the validity of the reasoning process an honest person wants to identify any fallacies in his or her thinking and reject all falsehoods. An honest person not only wants to know the truth but wants to live the truth. When people observe deceit and dishonesty in our words or life they will suspect falsehood in our message. Integrity is essential in those who would defend the truth of Christianity.

Wise apologists admit when they don't know the answer to a question or when they are mistaken. When we try to cover up our ignorance or mistakes we lose credibility for ourselves and for our message. Paul instructed Titus (and us), *"in your teaching show integrity"* (*Titus 2:7*).

Thinking Christianly about the World and Life. Harry Blamires challenges us to have a Christian mind, to think Christianly. We have a Christian mind when we have "a mind trained, informed, equipped to handle data of secular controversy within a framework of reference which is constructed of Christian presuppositions." He contrasts thinking secularly and thinking Christianly. "To think secularly is to think within a frame of reference bounded by the limits of our life on earth: it is to keep one's calculations rooted in this-worldly criteria. To think christianly [sic] is to accept all things with the mind as related, directly or indirectly, to man's eternal destiny as the redeemed and chosen child of God."[39]

Using our minds to the intended full potential involves seeking to answer all questions about God, man, and the world, from the perspective of the truth and wisdom of God. A Christian mind includes reason, will, and feeling. Christ calls

---

[39] Harry Blamires, *The Christian Mind: How Should a Christian Think?* (Ann Arbor, MI: Servant Books, 1963, 1978) 43-44.

for a total commitment of our whole being to him. Due to the speed and stress of modern life we often settle for fragmented, half-developed minds. Jesus said, *"And you shall love the Lord your God with all your heart and with all your soul and with all your mind and with all your strength"* (**Mark 12:30**). The word translated *mind* means "understanding, intelligence."[40]

Gill comments,

> Those well-meaning Christians who have worried about and warned against education, learning, and the exercise of the intellect have good reason. But nowhere does the biblical revelation tell us that the answer is mindless or thoughtless discipleship. The proper response to the misuse, deformity, pride, arrogance and error of the mind is not disuse but redemption and renewal. God created, and is redeeming, whole persons—body, soul, and spirit—not disembodied souls or mindless spirits.[41]

Christians in a pluralistic world can and must "develop unified Christian perspectives on their fields—and then to think, work and live as veritable salt and light in the midst of that world."[42]

Our thinking influences what we believe and how we live. *"Be transformed by the renewal of your mind"* (**Rom 12:2**). *"Let this mind be in you, which was also in Christ Jesus"* (**Phil 2:5**, KJV). *"Set your minds on things that are above"* (**Col 3:2**). Peter said we are to prepare our minds for action and be sober-minded (**1 Pet 1:13**). Our goal is to think like Jesus thought (**Phil 2:5; 1 Pet 4:1**).

Our sense of value, purpose, and direction in life is based on how we think. When Christ is the Lord of our mind, he brings a unity, richness, and fulfillment to our life. Gill says:

> It is also a fact that unthinking or fragmented individuals are more susceptible to degrading and destructive manipulation

---

[40] Bauer, Walter; W. F. Arndt, and F. W. Gingrich, *A Greek-English Lexicon of the New Testament and Other Early Christian Literature*, 2nd ed., revised by F. W. Gingrich and F. W. Danker (Chicago: University of Chicago Press, 1979) 187.
[41] Gill, *Opening of the Christian Mind*, 24.
[42] Ibid., 15.

by advertisers, propagandists and demagogues. A good preventative against the rise of authoritarianism, totalitarianism and other forms of manipulation is the development and nurture of individual men and women having coherent world views on the basis of which events, trends and people can be evaluated. Having a unified Christian mind, among other things, provides us with a sort of measuring stick to use in evaluating the ideas and phenomena which bombard us. No Christian mind, no measuring stick—chaos and uncertainty come instead.[43]

Our answers to the big questions make up our worldview. What is real? Who is God? Who are we as human beings? What is the world? How do we know what we know? How do we distinguish between truth and falsehood? How do we decide between right and wrong? How do we view history?[44] A Christian views all of life and the world from the viewpoint of biblical truth. We bring the tough questions in life to the study of the Bible. As we replace our misunderstandings and ignorance with truth, we grow as persons. We act on the truth and grow to maturity in Christ.

Our social and cultural context influences how we act and think about ourselves and society and how we understand Scripture. We need to give intellectual examination and analysis to our assumptions, our thinking, and our conclusions.[45]

God is the ultimate reality. He is our reference point for all meaning and understanding (*Isa 26:3*). "And the more closely we think God's thoughts after him with a truly active Christian mind, the better equipped we become to do all to his glory without intellectual compromise."[46]

Trueblood observes,

---

[43] Ibid.

[44] See James Sire, *The Universe Next Door*, 5th ed. (Downers Grove, IL: InterVarsity, 2009), for a discussion of these questions.

[45] Sire, *Discipleship of the Mind*, 24-25.

[46] Blamires, *The Christian Mind*, 20.

Part of the weakness of the Christian movement in our generation has been the relative lack of emphasis upon belief. There are three areas that must be cultivated if any faith is to be a living faith: the inner life of devotion, the intellectual life of rational thought, and the outer life of human service.[47]

The Christian mind is important in living and serving as a Christian.

Significance of the Mind in Christian Life and Service

✧ Evangelism and Apologetics—Shapes how we witness to our faith and how we defend Christian faith
✧ Theology and Discipleship—Guides us in learning and understanding God's truth
✧ Life and Worship—Essential to proper application of God's truth in our lives and an intelligent and appropriate response to God

---

The church moves toward irrelevancy, according to Paul Gould, "if the life of the mind is neglected inside the church and the truth of Christianity is not defended winsomely and rigorously outside the church."[48] Stott sees anti-intellectualism and intellectual laziness as negative and destructive. "They insult God, impoverish us and weaken our testimony. A responsible use of our minds, on the other hand, glorifies God, enriches us and strengthens our witness in the world."[49] *Thinking well enables us to glorify God.*

---

[47] Trueblood, *A Place to Stand*, 17-18.
[48] Paul M. Gould, "The Two Tasks Introduced," in *The Two Tasks of the Christian Scholar: Redeeming the Soul, Redeeming the Mind*, eds. William Lane Craig and Paul M. Gould (Wheaton, IL: Crossway Books, 2007) 19.
[49] Timothy Dudley-Smith, *John Stott: A Global Ministry, A Biography: The Later Years* (Downers Grove, IL: InterVarsity, 2001) 248.

Review Questions

1. What two tasks does Malik emphasize?

2. What does Malik say is the greatest danger facing evangelicals?

3. How does Blamires characterize thinkers?

4. List four misuses of the mind.

5. Summarize the dangers of intellectualism and anti-intellectualism.

6. How does a closed or corrupted mind affect our life?

7. Show the fallacies involved in viewing "faith" as totally separate from "reason."

8. State a case for the validity of human rationality.

9. How can we respond to the person who dismisses reason as modern, being a product of the Enlightenment?

10. How does creation relate to the validity of reason?

11. To what extent did the Fall affect reason?

12. What is the role of logic in thinking?

13. List three things essential to a proper use of the mind.

14. What elements are included in a developed Christian worldview?

Suggested Reading

Blamires, Harry. *The Christian Mind: How Should a Christian Think?* Ann Arbor: Servant Books, 1963, 1978. Contrasts the secular ways of thinking with thinking Christianly. Marks of the Christian mind are delineated.

Guinness, Os. *Fit Bodies and Fat Minds*. Grand Rapids: Baker Books, 1994. Boldly confronts evangelical anti-intellectualism's wanting faith without thought. Gives practical suggestions for thinking better and living wisely.

Moreland, J.P. *Love Your God with All Your Mind*. Colorado Springs: NavPress, 1997. Presents a logical case for the role of the mind in one's spiritual life. Challenges the reader to develop a Christian mind and use his or her intellect in the service of Christ.

Sire, James W. *Habits of the Mind: Intellectual Life as a Christian Calling*. Downers Grove, IL: InterVarsity, 2000. "The central goal of this book is to identify, describe and encourage those habits of the mind that are central to fulfilling our call to glorify God by thinking well."

Stott, John R.W. *Your Mind Matters: The Place of the Mind in the Christian Life*. Downers Grove, IL: InterVarsity, 1973. Explains why the mind is important for the Christian and how the mind relates to the practical aspects in the Christian life.

"And this is eternal life, that they know you the only true God, and Jesus Christ whom you have sent."

John 17:3

"I know whom I have believed, and I am convinced that he is able to guard until that Day what has been entrusted to me."

2 Timothy 1:12

7

Knowing

Knowing
 	
Profile: Ravi Zacharias—
    On Eastern versus
    Western Logic
  I. Nature of Knowledge
  A. Kinds of knowledge
    1. Propositional
       knowledge
    2. Knowledge by
       direct acquain-
       tance
    3. Skill or know-
       how knowledge
  B. Definition of
    knowledge—
    justified true belief
	"All men desire to know."
	
	Aristotle
	
	"Man is a creature who claims to know, who is deeply concerned to know more, and who is conscious of the need to distinguish between genuine and spurious knowledge. The moment we become truly aware of the possibility of error, in regard to either the objects or the processes of knowledge, we are forced, if we wish to be reasonable, to ask how genuine knowledge is possible."[1]
	
	David Elton Trueblood

[1] David Elton Trueblood, *General Philosophy* (New York: Harper and Row, 1963) 38.

C. Knowing External Reality
  1. Subjectivism—idealism
  2. Objectivism—realism
  3. Divided field of knowledge
  4. Negative views on knowledge
II. Postmodernism and Knowledge
  A. General characteristics
  B. Evangelical post-modernism
III. Basic Assumptions
  A. One's personal existence
  B. Reality of the external world
  C. Basic reliability of the senses
  D. Rationality of the mind
  E. Principle of causality
IV. Sources of Knowledge
  A. Senses
  B. Reason
  C. Intuition
  D. Authority
	"What should matter in matters of faith is knowledge, not merely sincere belief; good reasons for faith, not mere hunches; truth, not feelings. We can rightly say that Christianity is a knowledge tradition, meaning it is more than rituals or emotions. Christianity claims certain things can be known. The issues involved here cluster in the branch of philosophy called *epistemology*, the theory of knowledge."[2]
	
	Garrett J. DeWeese and
	J.P. Moreland

[2] Garrett J. DeWeese and J.P. Moreland, *Philosophy Made Slightly Less Difficult: A Beginner's Guide to Life's Big Questions* (Downers Grove, IL: InterVarsity, 2005) 54.

Profile: Ravi Zacharias on Eastern versus Western Logic

When Ravi Zacharias was speaking in California, a philosophy professor challenged him to speak the next night on "Why I Am Not a Hindu." The professor added that his class would attend and take him apart following the address. Zacharias said he would speak on "Why I Am a Christian" which would make clear why he was not anything else.

Zacharias recalls:

> As the lecture unfolded I could sense his discomfort, for I was touching upon the nerve of his worldview—the basic laws of logic and how they apply to reality. I began by establishing the law of noncontradiction, which contends that if a statement is absolutely contradictory, without qualification, the statement cannot be true. I continued by demonstrating that in the myriad postulations of Hinduism there are numerous contradictions, a fact admitted to by even some of its leading proponents. If the law of noncontradiction applies to reality and Hinduism is plagued by contradiction, then I concluded that, as a system, Hinduism is false.[3]

At the end of the lecture the man stormed to the front and exploded, "You don't understand the Eastern mind." He didn't see the irony of telling this to a man raised in India. Zacharias asked him to join him for lunch the next day.

The professor began, "Your biggest problem is that you don't understand Eastern logic." He explained that Western logic is either/or and based on the law of noncontradiction, meaning that if a statement was true its opposite was false. The Eastern way is both/and logic. He attempted to establish that the both/and logic was superior.

[3] Ravi Zacharias, *Can Man Live without God?* (Dallas: Word, 1994) 127.

"Dr. Zacharias," he declared, "when you see one Hindu affirming that God is personal and another insisting that God is not personal, just because it is contradictory you should not see it as a problem. The real problem is that you are seeing that contradiction as a Westerner when you should be approaching it as an Easterner. The both/and is the Eastern way of viewing reality."

Zacharias said, "Sir, are you telling me that when I am studying Hinduism I *either* use the both/and system of logic *or* nothing else?"

"Indeed, it does emerge," Zacharias said, "And as a matter of fact, even in India we look both ways before we cross the street—it is either the bus or me, not both of us."

After reporting this incident Zacharias states "Do you see the mistake he was making? He was using the either/or logic in order to prove the both/and. The more you try to hammer the law of noncontradiction, the more it hammers you."[4]

Human beings claim to know, want to know more, and want to distinguish between genuine knowledge and false knowledge. We need genuine knowledge to function in everyday life. We need to know where the food is for breakfast and where the bathroom is. We need to know what key will lock the house door and what key to use to unlock and start the car. And so it goes all day.

Is genuine knowledge possible? Can we know the external world? How do we know what we know? Can we live wisely without genuine knowledge?

Before we can commend and defend the truth of the Christian faith we have to be convinced that we have genuine

[4] Zacharias, *Can Man Live without God?* 126-129. See Winfried Corduan, *Reasonable Faith: Basic Christian Apologetics* (Nashville: B & H Publishers, 1993) 34.

knowledge about Christianity. This chapter will discuss the knowing process and the nature of knowledge. Chapters 8 and 9 will focus on truth and faith.

Nature of Knowledge

We gain knowledge through the proper operation (function) of the mind. Reason makes judgments about the information fed into the mind from the senses and imagination. Truth is a quality of propositions whose affirmations correspond with reality. Statements expressing a judgment may be either true or false. Arguments are valid or invalid. The mind can be knowing or ignorant. Objects may be real or imaginary. Epistemology is the study of knowledge—its sources, nature, and justification as truth. Metaphysics is the study of the nature of reality.

Kinds of knowledge. The term knowledge may refer to *propositional knowledge*—knowing that certain facts or states of affairs obtain. In a proposition the predicate affirms something about the subject. For example: This sandwich is a hamburger; Joe owns an old car. A second kind of knowledge is *experiential knowledge*—knowing something or someone because of direct personal experience. Ed experienced excruciating pain when burned over forty percent of his body. Jim knows what it is like to have bypass surgery. A third kind of knowledge may be called *skill or know-how knowledge*. Some people own a computer but lack the knowledge of how to successfully use it. A potter knows how to shape a pot from clay.[5]

Even though we make mental mistakes, our minds can make contact with the actual real world. Trueblood states, "What we know is not merely our ideas, but the real world, our ideas constituting our more or less accurate apprehension of

---

[5] J.P. Moreland and William Lane Craig, *Philosophical Foundations for a Christian Worldview* (Downers Grove, IL: InterVarsity, 2003) 72-73; and J.P. Moreland, *Kingdom Triangle: Recover the Christian Mind, Renovate the Soul, Restore the Spirit's Power* (Grand Rapids: Zondervan, 2007) 126-130.

the nature of the real world."[6] Realism is the view that we can know the real world external to our minds. Epistemological dualism is the view that accepts the distinction between knower and what is known.

We can know past events and objects and things near us as well as far away. The amazing thing about knowledge is that we can bridge the gap from our minds to other minds, between our minds and what we know. Knowledge can leap the bounds of time and geography.

In affirming the truth of Christianity we are dealing primarily with propositional truths: God exists; Jesus rose from the dead; the Bible is the Word of God. The affirmation of the truth of Christian faith involves an intellectual judgment and a decision that Christianity is grounded in facts and actually corresponds with reality. Christian faith does not stop with mere intellectual affirmation but issues in commitment and obedience.

The ultimate goal is not merely to know facts about God but to come to a personal relationship with him. For our knowledge of the founding facts of Christianity we depend upon those who had direct knowledge of Jesus and what he did. Evangelism, discipleship, leadership, and godly living involve know-how knowledge.

Definition of knowledge. When we know something we are acquainted with it and have an understanding of it. Knowledge is justified true belief. First, if we know something, we know that it is *true*. Second, knowledge involves true *belief* in the sense that one accepts and affirms that a proposition is true. Truth as a quality of a proposition means that what is affirmed corresponds with reality. The statement correctly describes actual reality. This is the correspondence theory of truth. The third aspect of knowledge is *justification*. Sufficient evidence

---

[6] David Elton Trueblood, *Philosophy of Religion* (New York: Harper and Brothers, 1957) 48.

establishes or justifies the truth of what is believed. It is reasonable to accept a belief as true on the basis or ground of good and sufficient evidence. Truth, belief, and justification are necessary conditions of knowledge.[7]

J.P. Moreland says, "In essence, *knowledge is the ability to represent things as they are on an appropriate basis of thought and experience.* . . . Knowledge provides truth about reality along with the skillful ability to interact with reality." To reject knowledge is to reject "the only appropriate ground for faith."[8]

Knowing something does not mean we know it with absolute certainty, meaning it is logically impossible to be wrong. This requirement "is too stringent and eliminates as knowledge many things that we do, in fact, know."[9] We know the external world exists.[10] We must recognize that our knowledge of it, while adequate, is not exhaustive, absolutely perfect, or omniscient.

When we affirm a knowledge claim, we, knowingly or unknowingly, assume a theory of knowledge. Implicit in that view of knowledge is a view of oneself as a knower, a concept about the reality of the world, a view of how one relates to the world and to other persons.

What Can We Know?

1. We have knowledge of bodies (having location and mass).
2. We have knowledge of minds other than our own.
3. As individuals we know our own minds.
4. We have knowledge of historical events.
5. We claim to know universals.
6. We can know God.   David Elton Trueblood[11]

---

[7] Moreland and Craig, *Philosophical Foundations*, 72-78.

[8] Moreland, *Kingdom Triangle*, 114. Emphasis is in the original.

[9] Ibid., 84-85.

[10] Dallas Willard, "How Concepts Relate the Mind to Its Objects: The 'God's Eye View' Vindicated," *Philosophia Christi*, Series 2, 1:2 (1999) 5-20.

[11] Trueblood, *General Philosophy*, 24-29.

Knowing External Reality

Subjectivism. In philosophy, idealism designates the view that reality is more akin to ideas than to things. Idealists believe objects do not exist apart from a knowing mind. External reality may be denied as actually physical or at least ascribed a status as a lesser kind of reality. They believe each person's view of reality is subjectively mediated so that one's view of reality is relative to the individual. They end up never being sure of what external reality actually is. Thinkers like Plato, Berkeley, and Hegel were idealists. This view is to be distinguished from idealism in the popular usage meaning the practice of forming ideals and living by them.

Postmodernists claim we are locked in our language which is shaped by our history and culture, and we don't have an objective picture of external reality. A neutral objectivity is attacked by postmodernists as impossible. Certainly as finite human beings we are subject to error in the knowing process. Stephen Evans distinguishes a totally neutral objectivity "from the honesty of the person who really cares about truth and is willing to respect contrary evidence. This kind of objectivity seems compatible with recognizing our human finitude and the ways in which our passions and assumptions can function as aids in the search for truth, rather than simply being distorting filters."[12]

Douglas Groothuis says, "Objective reality exists in its own right apart from human knowers; it is metaphysically objective and representable through true statements. However, our knowledge of truth is influenced by a number of subjective factors, such as our level of intelligence, background beliefs, personal interests and so on."[13]

---

[12] C. Stephen Evans, *Pocket Dictionary of Apologetics and Philosophy of Religion* (Downers Grove, IL: InterVarsity, 2002) 83.

[13] Douglas Groothuis, *Truth Decay: Defending Christianity against the Challenges of Postmodernism* (Downers Grove, IL: InterVarsity, 2000) 185.

Just because we are subject to errors in perception and judgment does not mean we cannot obtain objective knowledge of the external world. We don't have exhaustive or perfect knowledge of objects and events in the external world but we can have an adequate knowledge of their objective reality. While the human process of knowing the real world does not yield absolute certainty, we can know things about the world with a practical certainty.

Objectivism. Nancy Pearcey tells of dinner conversations about objective truth in the home of Udo and Debby Middelmann.

> It's a lesson we find ourselves learning, like it or not, from the time we are born, Udo would say. When a baby crawls to the edge of the crib and bumps his head against the wooden bars, he learns in a painful way that reality is objective. When a toddler tilts his high chair back until it falls to the floor, he learns that there is an objective structure to the universe. Reality does not bend itself to our subjective desires—a lesson that can be painful to learn even for adults. Thus we can confidently reject any philosophical position that leads to subjectivism. Why? Because it fails to account for what ordinary experience teaches us day by day. It is in tension with the data of experience.[14]

Trueblood states, "Philosophical realism of some sort is an instinctive faith, neither produced by argument nor destroyed by it, because it rests upon assumptions which no man can prove and which no man can really avoid."[15] Realism is the belief that actual entities exist apart from human knowers. Reality exists apart from a knowing mind. A real extra-mental, physical world does exist.

Naïve realism believes the senses give an exact picture of objective reality. As we gain more detailed knowledge we have

[14] Nancy Pearcey, *Total Truth: Liberating Christianity from Its Cultural Captivity* (Wheaton, IL: Crossway, 2004) 395.
[15] Trueblood, *Philosophy of Religion*, 50.

149

to modify the initial picture our senses report. For example, the railroad tracks appear to converge, but further investigation shows they do not. The earth appears to be flat, but when we fly around the earth we can know it is not flat.

The fact that our initial picture of external things may be incomplete does not mean that we can't have valid knowledge of things. Limited knowledge is not false knowledge. Our inability to know everything doesn't mean we can't know some things. We need an adequate realism. We do not have exhaustive knowledge of things but we can have an adequate knowledge. We can know that water is objectively real and we can take a drink and quench our thirst. This knowledge is sufficient for the ordinary purposes of life even though specialists can know much more. They can make a detailed analysis of the water listing all the component elements and the percentage of each in the water we are drinking.

Divided Field of Knowledge. For the last two hundred years many thinkers have accepted a divided view of knowledge. They limit objective knowledge to the rational, scientific realm of observable facts. Religion, morality, and the humanities, they allege, are known only through the individual's subjectivity and have nothing to do with reason or objective facts. In describing this divided-field thinking Francis Schaeffer calls the realm of facts and reasons, the lower story and the realm of values, morals, and religion, the upper story.[16]

Pearcey points out that after Kant, "The lower story became the realm of publicly verifiable *facts* while the upper story became the realm of socially constructed *values.*"[17] Religion and morality are viewed as merely creations of our subjective wishes and choices. These have no connection with history,

---

[16] Francis A. Schaeffer, *The God Who Is There*, 30th Anniversary Edition (Downers Grove, IL: InterVarsity, 1968, 1998).

[17] Pearcey, *Total Truth*, 106. Emphasis is in the original.

science, or reason. This approach to knowledge has enabled the contemporary person to view religion and morality as created by one's personal preference and choice having nothing to do with reason, facts, or objective reality.

Relativism rules when religion and ethics are quarantined from reason and objective truth. Philosopher Edmund Husserl asked why the highly educated state of modern Germany could so easily be led by leaders into terrible acts of barbarism. His answer was that the most important questions of human significance—meaning in life, God, the afterlife—were considered values not capable of objective knowledge.[18]

Negative views on knowledge. Views that reject genuine knowledge and objective truth challenge the relevancy and validity of apologetics. Relativism holds that all views can be true, even contradictory ones. In the light of the law of noncontradiction mutually contradictory statements or systems of thought cannot both be true.

Skepticism is the position that we can't know if anything is true. Hume was skeptical about rationally demonstrating any identity between the ideas in our minds and external reality and about discovering the truth about anything whatever. Claiming to know we can't know reality is contradictory. Doubting that any of our beliefs can be supported by adequate or sufficient evidence is itself a claim to knowledge.

Both relativism and skepticism are self-refuting and result in believing nonsense. Postmodernism declares we can't have a genuine knowledge of extra-mental material reality and we can't obtain objective truth. We will next address postmodernism's approach to knowledge.

---

[18] Edmund Husserl, *The Crisis of European Sciences* (Evanston, IL: Northwest University Press, 1970) 3-65.

Postmodernism and Knowledge

Postmodernists claim their views represent a new era in cultural and intellectual history and characterize themselves as *post*modernists. Postmodernism views itself as a replacement for Enlightenment modernism. Future history will indicate whether it is a new era in intellectual history or whether it is a trend or phase as existentialism was in the mid-twentieth century. In many senses we may view postmodernism as a variation and continuation of Enlightenment modernism with its rejection of external authorities and its emphasis on the knowing process being self-determined.

Modernism defined as a set of ideas consisting of rationalism, naturalism, and humanism has failed to produce the utopia it promised. Even if modernism, at least in its optimism, has been generally discredited, modernity consisting of the economic, technological, industrial, telecommunication revolution continues. Postmodernists certainly accept and utilize modern scientific technology so they haven't rejected modernity.[19]

Postmodernism includes a diversity of viewpoints, yet most postmodernists share general characteristics.

Postmodernism

"Reality, value, and truth are arbitrary conventions relative to different cultures."

Postmodernists reject:

(1) "Objective truth construed as correspondence with reality."

(2) "The rational objectivity of reason."

(3) "The reality of simply seeing and the human ability to be aware of and know reality directly, unmediated by 'conceptual schemes,' language, or their surrogates."[20]

---

[19] Os Guinness, *Fit Bodies, Fat Minds: Why Evangelicals Don't Think and What to Do about It* (Grand Rapids: Baker, 1994) 106.

[20] Moreland, *Kingdom Triangle*, 67.

Moreland describes philosophical postmodernism:

As a philosophical standpoint, postmodernism is primarily a reinterpretation of what knowledge is and what counts as knowledge. More broadly, it represents a form of cultural relativism about such things as reality, truth, reason, value, linguistic meaning, the self, and other notions. On a postmodernist view there is no such thing as objective reality, truth, value, reason, and so forth. All these are social constructions, creations of linguistic practices and, as such, are relative not to individuals but to social groups that share a narrative. Roughly, a narrative is a perspective such as Marxism, atheism, or Christianity that is embedded in the group's social and linguistic practices. Important postmodern thinkers are Friedrich Nietzsche, Ludwig Wittgenstein, Jacques Derrida, Thomas Kuhn, Michel Foucault, Martin Heidegger, and Jean-Francois Lyotard.[21]

Postmodernists reject metaphysical realism alleging that we can't have an accurate knowledge of objects and entities in the world. We can't know what the real world actually is because our senses do not give us an accurate picture of reality. They reject metaphysical realism in favor of a socially and linguistically constructed reality. They hold that we cannot have knowledge of a real world independent of language. We don't have epistemic access to an extralinguistic reality. Reality is within language and is shaped or constructed by language.

According to postmodernists we can't have objective knowledge. They reject "the myth of neutrality."[22] One's perspec-

---

[21] Moreland, "The Challenges of Postmodernism," in *Passionate Conviction: Contemporary Discourses on Christian Apologetics*, eds. Paul Copan and William Lane Craig (Nashville: B & H, 2007) 207-208.

[22] Brian McLaren states, "I think that most Christians grossly misunderstand the philosophical baggage associated with terms like *absolute* or *objective* (linked to foundationalism and the myth of neutrality). . . . Similarly, arguments that pit absolutism versus relativism, and objectivism versus subjection, prove meaningless or absurd to postmodern people." "Emergent Evangelism," *Christianity Today* (November 2004) 43-44.

tive shapes his or her beliefs and observations. "'Knowledge' is a construction of one's social, linguistic structures, not a justified, truth representation of reality by one's mental states."[23] Postmodernist Brad J. Kallenberg says, "Language does not represent reality, it constitutes reality."[24]

Postmodernism	Adequate Realism
Antifoundationalism—Rejects any foundationalism as wrong because it holds that basic beliefs yield absolutely certain knowledge.	Modest foundationalism— Some basic beliefs are defensible subject to refutation by further evidence.
Nonrepresentalism—We can't know what external objects actually are. We don't have epistemic access to reality.	Representalism—We can have an adequate knowledge of external objects. We do have epistemic access to reality.
Nonreferential theory of language—Linguistic signs refer to other signs not to the real world.	Referential theory of language—Language can refer to objects and states of affair in the real world.
Nonrealism—Rejects metaphysical realism. Reality is socially and linguistically constructed.	Realism—Objective reality exists apart from subjective beliefs or human language.
Reality is linguistic—Reality is within language and is shaped by language.	Nonlinguistic reality exists— Reality is outside language and is described by language.
Skepticism of facts— Objective facts do not exist but are actually subjective interpretations.	Verification of facts—Facts can be known supported by adequate evidence.

[23] Moreland, *Kingdom Triangle*, 78.
[24] Brad J. Kallenberg, *Ethics as Grammar* (Notre Dame, IN: University of Notre Dame Press, 2001) 234.

Reject or minimize science and the role of reason in religion.	Accept the role of both reason and science while recognizing their limitations.
Truth is made. Objective and universal truth does not exist.	Truth is discovered. We can know objective and universal truth.
Theory of truth—truth is defined as coherence or as useful results (coherentism or pragmatism).	Theory of truth—Truth is defined as correspondence with reality.
Authority for Christians is located in the believing community.	Authority for Christians is located in text of Scripture accepted as the Word of God.
Scripture is narrative, story, and functional.	Scripture is propositional expressed in all literary forms used by biblical writers.
A text means what the linguistic community says it means.	A text means what the author intends it to mean.

The theory of reality being linguistically constructed is flawed. An objective reality does exist apart from subjective beliefs or human language. A man who jumps from the thirty-fourth floor of a building can't construct reality by language so he won't be killed when he hits the pavement below. He will crash into the real world. We observe or experience objects or states of affairs before we use language to refer to them.[25] Reality is outside language and is described by language. We can have an adequate (not exhaustive) knowledge of external

---

[25] Scott Smith, "Hauerwas and Kallenberg and the Issue of Epistemic Access to an Extra-Linguistic Realm," in *Heythrop Journal*, XLV (July 2004) 305-326.

objects and states of affairs. We do have epistemic access to reality.[26]

Postmodernists allege truth is made, being constructed by each particular linguistic community. What is accepted as true is not true for all people in all places and does not describe objective reality.

Postmodernists operate in the everyday world as if they have objective truth about the real world. They think the hamburger is real and eat it. They get out of the way if a car is about to hit them. If in a crowded theater they would understand the announcement of "Fire" as having objective meaning, and they would flee for safety. George Will quoted novelist Walker Perry's definition of a deconstructionist as "an academic who claims that the meaning of all communication is radically indeterminate, but who leaves a message on his wife's answering machine requesting pizza for dinner."[27]

Postmodernists believe objective facts do not exist; we have only subjective interpretations. Rational arguments, historical facts, sense observations, and perceptions are marginalized or denied as having validity. When at the last second I see a baseball coming toward my head, then feel the throbbing headache, it borders on insanity to say I can't know and affirm the fact that I was hit in the head by a ball. I have knowledge of something that happened in the real world. It is little comfort to tell me that I can't know the fact that I hurt and that experiences such as suffering are linguistically determined. While I do not have exhaustive knowledge of what happened, I can know the objective fact that I was injured and in pain.

---

[26] R. Scott Smith, "Language, Theological Knowledge, and the Postmodern Paradigm," in *Reclaiming the Center: Confronting Evangelical Accommodation in Postmodern Times*, eds. Millard J. Erickson, Paul Kjoss Helseth, Justin Taylor (Wheaton, IL: Crossway, 2004) 109-133.

[27] George Will, "Editors Fail to Detect Essay Spoof," *The Joplin Globe* (31 May 1996).

To say that we cannot have knowledge of reality is itself a claim to know something about reality. Postmodernists also refute their own position when they give reasons for their views and cite facts and observations. We can know facts when they are supported by adequate evidence. We can know for a fact that a man was shot with a bullet because of the evidence—the testimony of eyewitnesses, the man's external puncture wound, the X-ray picture of the bullet imbedded in his body, and of course, the bullet, after its surgical removal.

Would you want a pharmacist who believed that language has no objective meaning ignoring the doctor's intended meaning in filling your prescription? Do you want a surgeon operating on you who believes there is no objective connection between the perception in his mind and the reality in your body?

If objectivity of meaning in a text is indeterminate, what would keep postmodernists from using texts to justify their own agenda. Postmodernist hermeneutics locates meaning in interpretation in the knowing subject. Gary Phillips comments, "Actually, the goal of exegesis is transformed from questions about what the text *meant* into how the text can be used to serve the new social agenda of the postmodernist."[28]

J.P. Moreland critiques postmodernism:

Postmodernism is self-refuting. Postmodernists appear to claim that their own assertions about the modern era, about how language and consciousness work, and so forth are true and rational; and they write literary texts and protest when people misinterpret the authorial intent in their own writings. In these and other ways postmodernism seems to be self-refuting.[29]

[28] Gary Phillips, "Religious Pluralism in a Postmodern World," in *The Challenge of Postmodernism*, ed. by David S. Dockery (Wheaton, IL: Victor Books, 1995) 260.
[29] Moreland, "The Challenges of Postmodernism," 208.

Scott Smith argues that postmodernists presuppose what they deny: that we can know the objective world.[30]

Our subjectivity and finiteness comes into play in the knowing process but that does not mean that objective truth does not exist. D.A. Carson was affirming that "true knowledge is possible, even to finite culture-based creatures." A postmodernist challenged his view. Carson interpreted everything she said as an ironic affirmation of objective truth. After a while she exploded in anger. He explained the point he was making:

> You are a deconstructionist, but you expect me to interpret *your* words aright. More precisely, you are upset because I seem to be divorcing the meaning I claim to see in your words from your intent. Thus, implicitly you affirm the link between text and authorial intent. I have never read a deconstructionist who would be pleased if a reviewer misinterpreted his or her work: thus *in practice* deconstructionists implicitly link their own texts with their own intentions. I simply want the same courtesy extended to Paul.[31]

Foundationalism is a theory of knowledge that holds that some truths serve as the basis and foundation for other truths. Beliefs must be grounded on basic or foundational beliefs. Cartesian foundationalism claimed that all beliefs can be deductively proved from absolutely certain first principles. In reacting against this overstated certainty of classical foundationalism postmodernists have accepted uncertainty as a virtue believing we can't have epistemological certainty or a foundation of basic beliefs. They have chosen coherentism or pragmatism as their theory of truth. Foundationalism has become a "whipping boy" among postmodernist Christians.[32] A denial

---

[30] R. Scott Smith, "Christian Postmodernism and the Internal Relation of Language and the World," in *Christianity and the Postmodern Turn*, ed. Myron Penner (Grand Rapids: Brazos, 2005).

[31] D.A. Carson, *The Gagging of God: Christianity Confronts Pluralism* (Grand Rapids: Zondervan, 1996) 102-103.

[32] Kevin DeYoung and Ted Kluck, *Why We're Not Emergent: (By Two Guys Who Should Be)* (Chicago: Moody Press, 2008) 70.

of a basic foundation for the knowing process leads to epistemological relativism. I agree with J.P. Moreland and Garrett
DeWeese that Grenz and Franke in *Beyond Foundationalism* have
prematurely reported the demise of foundationalism.[33]

A modest foundationalism (also called weak or minimalist
foundationalism or the fallibilist version of foundationalism) is
more realistic than the denial of foundationalism.[34] It is not necessary that all our beliefs are necessary truths or empirically
demonstrable. Some of our core beliefs serve as first principles,
not being derived from other beliefs or cultures or persons.
Groothuis lists two principles: "1. There are essential truths of
logic that are necessary for all intelligible thought and rational
discourse. . . . The law of noncontradiction and excluded middle. . . . 2. There are also basic forms of reasoning that are non-
negotiable and are universally valid; they are not matters of
contingent social construction or personal taste."[35]

Not the text of Scripture but the contemporary community of believers following the Spirit's appropriation of Scripture
becomes the locus for theology. Stanley Grenz and John Franke
write, "As we noted earlier, it is not the Bible as a book that is
authoritative, but the Bible as the instrumentality of the Spirit;
the biblical message spoken by the Spirit through the text is
theology's norming norm."[36] The task of theology, they say, is
"to express communal beliefs and values as well as the mean-

---

[33] J.P. Moreland and Garrett DeWeese, "The Premature Report of Foundationalism's Demise," in *Reclaiming the Center: Confronting Evangelical Accommodation in Postmodern Times*, eds. Millard J. Erickson, Paul Kjoss Helseth, and
Justin Taylor (Wheaton, IL: Crossway, 2004) 81-107. See Stanley J. Grenz,
and John R. Franke, *Beyond Foundationalism: Shaping Theology in a Postmodern
Context* (Louisville, KY: Westminster John Knox, 2001).

[34] Groothuis, *Truth Decay*, 175-178; Millard J. Erickson, *Truth or Consequences:
The Promise & Perils of Postmodernism* (Downers Grove, IL: InterVarsity, 2001)
257-261; Moreland and Craig, *Philosophical Foundations*, 118-121.

[35] Groothuis, *Truth Decay*, 176-177.

[36] Grenz and Franke, *Beyond Foundationalism*, 69.

ing of the symbols of the faith community."[37] The authority of Scripture is diminished and downgraded because no longer are the church's beliefs grounded in authoritative Scripture accepted as the Word of God inspired by God's Spirit.

Using various labels such as *emerging* or *postconservative*, these thinkers follow postmodernist motifs. Persons in this category include Brian McLaren, Stanley Grenz, Robert Webber, and Nancey Murphy. They represent their views as new, fresh, and relevant in contrast to outdated, reactionary, rationalistic historic orthodoxy. They prefer stories and narrative over propositions and doctrine. They are uncomfortable with biblical inerrancy, historical-grammatical hermeneutics, and salvation exclusively through Christ. They see validation or verification of Christianity in community, and spiritual experiences, not in rational apologetics.

Basic Assumptions

On a practical level in our everyday life we operate on the basis of certain assumptions. Knowledge involves some basic faith leaps. Foundationalism is the view that some beliefs form the basis or foundation for learning other truths. Following postmodernist epistemologies, leaders in the emerging church and the postconservative movements reject foundationalism.[38]

Classical foundationalists such as Descartes held certain basic beliefs as self-evident and indubitably certain. This overstates the case. Some basic beliefs may be said to be indubitable. The fact that other basic beliefs do not qualify as indubitable does not mean we should reject that knowledge has a foundation of basic beliefs. To reject all foundationalism is "throwing out the baby with the bathwater."

---

[37] Ibid., 231.

[38] See J. P. Moreland and Garrett DeWeese's "The Premature Report of Foundationalism's Demise," in *Reclaiming the Center: Confronting Evangelical Accommodation in Postmodern Times*, Millard J. Erickson, Paul Kjoss Helseth and Justin Taylor, eds. (Wheaton: Crossway Books, 2004) 81-107.

We end in skepticism and subjectivism when at least a modest foundationalism is not acknowledged. We cannot prove these fundamental beliefs absolutely, and it is possible to question each of them philosophically. Yet even those who believe they have successfully proved them false still seem to employ them in their everyday choices and actions thus refuting their own position. G.K. Chesterton says, "The man who begins to think without the proper first principles goes mad; he begins to think at the wrong end."[39]

Geisler and Zukeran state, "*First principles* of knowledge are self-evident (obvious) truths, and they form the foundation of all knowledge. Since a principle is that from which everything else in its order flows, first principles of knowledge are those basic premises from which all else follows in the realm of knowing."[40]

The following basic assumptions are essential to the knowing process.

1. *One's personal existence.* One would have to exist in order to deny his or her existence. Without this basic belief no further knowledge or discussion would be possible.

2. *Reality of the external world.* A material world exists independent of our knowing minds. The doctrine of creation gives the basis for believing in the reality of the external world. From our earliest childhood, when we fell, we knew we hit a physical reality and we knew that an external reality actually existed. Idealism holds that the world is an illusion or a projection of the mind. Idealists hold that reality is more akin to ideas than to physical things. However in everyday life we treat things as having an objective reality independent of anyone

[39] G.K. Chesterton, *Orthodoxy: The Classic Account of a Remarkable Christian Experience* (Colorado Springs: WaterBrook Press, 1994, 2001) 31.
[40] Norman L. Geisler and Patrick Zukeran, *The Apologetics of Jesus: A Caring Approach to Dealing with Doubters* (Grand Rapids: Baker Books, 2009) 66.

perceiving them. In the common matters of life we are realists. The idealists who believe that the world is an illusion still eat food and move away when someone tries to hit them. Most human beings assume that the physical world outside of their minds actually exists.

Whether people affirm religious faith or not, we all assume the reality of the external world. Human beings have an instinctive belief that they have direct experiences of an independent material universe and knowledge of other minds. Trueblood states, "No man really doubts the external world any more than he doubts his own existence."[41]

3. *Basic reliability of the senses.* Of course our senses may distort reality or be deceived due to disability or disease. But the accurate function of one person's senses corrects the distortion in another's sense perceptions. Our senses are limited and fallible, but they are not useless. We use devices such as telescopes and microscopes to enhance our senses but they do not replace them. Our senses do not provide exhaustive knowledge of objects. Our eyes cannot detect the atoms in a baseball. But our sense perception is adequate to inform us when the ball comes toward our eye so we can duck our head.

We cannot prove for certain that our senses provide valid information about the external world. However, we assume the basic reliability of our senses every day of our life. To deny sense perception is to deny any valid knowledge of anything outside of ourselves.

4. *Rationality of human reason.* Those who insist that human beings are irrational betray their case by using reason as they attempt to prove irrationalism. The law of noncontradiction is a fundamental principle in rational thought. Something cannot both be and not be at the same time and in the same sense. This does not mean an object cannot have more than one

---

[41] Trueblood, *Philosophy of Religion*, 50.

attribute. A box may be both big and black. But it cannot both exist and not exist at the same time. To affirm the truth of a contradiction is to deny truth. Logic must be assumed in correct thinking and meaningful communication. Mathematical principles are inherent in the orderliness of the world and are recognized by human reason. One cannot deny objective truth without assuming the principle of noncontradiction.

5. *Principle of causality.* Events have cause and effect relationships. An event is an effect with an antecedent cause or causes. As a strict empiricist, Hume said that since cause and effect relationships are not observed by sense perception we cannot have knowledge of cause and effect relationships. However, Hume could not deny it consistently in his life. He got out of the way of a carriage about to run over him. It is true that the law of causality cannot be proven absolutely by reason or by the senses. But to deny causality is to deny all valid scientific knowledge and is to affirm that events are not related to each other in an arbitrary world.

These five basic assumptions are made by people in everyday life, by most modern scientists, and even by those who deny them. Assumptions are basic beliefs forming starting points and a foundation for one's thinking. In practice all people make these assumptions every day whatever their religious orientation. The Christian who believes in an all-wise, all-powerful God who created the world and made man in his image has a better intellectual basis for accepting these assumptions than does the non-Christian who believes this world is merely a product of an accidental collision of atoms. Rejection of God as Creator leaves one without a solid intellectual foundation for these basic assumptions.

Sources of Knowledge

We gain information about the real world from several sources. These sources are not totally isolated from one another but are interrelated. A combination of them is often utilized in the knowing process. One of the frequent errors of philosophers is to affirm that all knowledge comes through only one source of knowledge.

1. *Senses.* We know what we see, taste, hear, smell, and touch. Our senses furnish our minds with factual information. Sense data is a valid kind of knowledge but it is not the only valid source of knowledge. Empiricism holds that all or most knowledge comes through sense experience.

2. *Reason.* Reason is the human faculty which makes judgments and can evaluate those judgments to see if they are valid or not. Our minds process and organize information provided by our senses. Our minds enable us to handle facts and draw conclusions about those facts. Logic and math involve the study of knowledge derived from reasoning. Rationalism affirms that all knowledge or most knowledge comes through reason alone. Rationalists believe by reasoning alone we can discover certain knowledge that could under no sense be wrong. Rationalism accepts no belief as true if it is not proved by reason. While reason provides some knowledge, it is an error to conclude that reason alone provides all knowledge. The role of reason in relationship to faith will be pursued in Chapter 9.

3. *Intuition.* Insights may come into our minds not directly from sense data or logical reasoning. Intuition is a direct awareness of something in one's inner consciousness. It is an immediate insight or apprehension or cognition without being an obvious rational inference. This may be called a feeling knowledge or a "hunch." It may be actually subconscious reasoning. Intuition as a source of knowledge is very limited and must be checked by reason and the senses. Mysticism is the view that knowledge is gained through inner personal experience transcending reason and sense experience. Mystery does exist in the knowing process. While acknowledging the

noncognitive, we must not rule out our cognitive knowledge of reality.

4. *Authority*. We gain knowledge from an authority when someone in a position to know tells us something that we have not directly experienced ourselves: we accept their testimony. Authority as a source of knowledge is the acceptance of testimony from a reliable source that is in a position to have true knowledge. Scientists accept the testimony of fellow scientists on many matters. They do not repeat all experiments themselves. We learn the identity of our own fathers by testimony. While it is possible to refute paternity by DNA testing, the number of people who actually seek this proof is very small indeed. The overwhelming majority accept the identity of their father by faith in testimony. Persons who reject testimony as a valid source of knowledge cut themselves off from all history and from all knowledge except their own thinking and their own experience—a very narrow area of knowledge indeed.

Authoritarianism blindly accepts what the authority says. We must, however, reject authoritarianism which says that authority is the only source of knowledge. We have a right as knowers to evaluate the credentials of the authority. Jesus did not demand blind acceptance of his authority. He told the Jews, *"If I am not doing the works of my Father, then do not believe me; but if I do them, even though you do not believe me, believe the works, that you may know and understand that the Father is in me and I am in the Father"* (John 10:37-38).

Sources of Knowledge	Theories of Knowledge
Senses	Empiricism
Reason	Rationalism
Intuition	Mysticism
Authority	Authoritarianism

While we don't have absolutely certain and exhaustive knowledge of objects in the real world, we can have adequate knowledge of objects. We gain this kind of knowledge in every-day experience. I am not defending naïve realism—"Only a few thousand stars exist because that's all I can see." We do need a sensible reasonable realism. In the knowing process we assume a functional, workable realism. We assume certain basic beliefs as a foundation in the knowing process. While not defending the strong Cartesian form of foundationalism which insists on absolute certainty, as knowers we employ a modest foundationalism.

As human beings we can gain reliable knowledge about the real world. Human knowledge may be essentially accurate as far as it goes but does not yield absolute certainty. It is not exhaustive but is adequate when justified by sufficient evidence. Douglas Groothuis says, "Objective reality exists in its own right apart from human knowers; it is metaphysically objective and representable through true statements. However, our knowledge of truth is influenced by a number of subjective factors, such as our level of intelligence, background beliefs, personal interests and so on."[42]

God has given us evidence as a basis for our knowledge and trust in him. As finite human beings we can know certain and absolute truth that he has chosen to reveal to us in the Scriptures. Our role as apologists is to reassure believers in their Christian knowledge and convince seekers and skeptics that they can know God, Christ, and the core truths in God's great story of redemption.

---

[42] Groothuis, *Truth Decay*, 185.

Review Questions

1. Define the law of noncontradiction. Demonstrate that it is not limited to Western logic.

2. Discuss the importance of genuine knowledge to the study of apologetics.

3. Briefly define: reason, truth, epistemology, and metaphysics.

4. Describe three kinds of knowledge. Apologetics deals mostly with which one?

5. Define knowledge.

6. How does the idealist view the external world?

7. How does a realist view the external world?

8. What is meant by the divided field of knowledge?

9. Give a summary of the key characteristics of postmodernism's view of knowledge and reality.

10. What is meant by the postmodernist claim that reality is socially and linguistically constructed?

11. In what ways is postmodernism self-refuting?

12. How have postmodernist concepts influenced evangelicals in the emergent and postconservative movements?

13. List names of postmodernist evangelicals.

14. Explain foundationalism. What form of foundationalism is advocated in this book?

15. List the five basic assumptions we make in the knowing process in everyday life.

16. List and explain four sources of knowledge.

17. Contrast having absolutely certain knowledge with having adequate knowledge of reality.

Suggested Reading

DeWeese, Garrett J., and J.P. Moreland. *Philosophy Made Slightly Less Difficult: A Beginner's Guide to Life's Big Questions.* Downers Grove, IL: InterVarsity, 2005, 53-78. The chapter on epistemology deals with kinds of knowledge, nature of knowledge, and skepticism.

Erickson, Millard J., Paul Kjoss Helseth, and Justin Taylor, eds. *Reclaiming the Center: Confronting Evangelical Accommodation in Postmodern Times.* Wheaton, IL: Crossway, 2004. Strong response to the evangelical postconservative and postmodernist reinterpretation of Christianity.

Erickson, Millard J. *Truth or Consequences: The Promise and Perils of Postmodernism.* Downers Grove, IL: InterVarsity, 2001. In-depth analysis of the intellectual roots of postmodernism and prominent postmodernist thinkers. Critique and constructive response.

Groothuis, Douglas. *Truth Decay: Defending Christianity against the Challenges of Postmodernism.* Downers Grove, IL: InterVarsity, 2000. Critique of postmodernism's view of truth and defense of absolute, objective, and universal. Constructs a solid, biblical understanding of truth and relates it to apologetics.

Moreland, J.P., and William Lane Craig. *Philosophical Foundations for a Christian Worldview.* Downers Grove, IL: InterVarsity, 2003, 71-170. Philosophical study of rationality, skepticism, justification, and theories of truth. A careful assessment of postmodernism.

"You will know the truth,
and the truth will set you free."
John 8:32b

"I am the way, the truth and the life."
John 14:6

8

Knowing Truth

Knowing Truth
Profile: Aleksandr
  Solzhenitsyn—Passion
  to Tell the Truth
I. Rejection of Truth as
  Objective and
  Absolute since the
  Enlightenment
II. Postmodernism and
  Truth
  A. Challenges to
    Christianity
  B. Postmodernism's
    view of truth
III. Biblical View of Truth
	"The tragedy of our situation today is that men and women are being fundamentally affected by the new way of looking at truth, and yet they have never even analyzed the drift which has taken place."[1]
	<div align="right">Francis A. Schaeffer</div>
	"One word of truth shall outweigh the world."[2]
	<div align="right">Aleksandr Solzhenitsyn</div>
	"Truth prevails for those who live in truth."[3]
	<div align="right">Vaclav Havel</div>

[1] Francis A. Schaeffer, *The God Who Is There*, 30th Anniversary Edition (Downers Grove, IL: InterVarsity, 1968, 1998) 25.
[2] Aleksandr Solzhenitsyn in his speech accepting the Nobel Prize in 1974.
[3] Vaclav Havel, the motto of the Charter 77 Movement. See his *Living in Truth* (London: Faber and Faber, 1989).

A. Conformity to reality and in opposition to error
B. Personal—Rooted in God
C. Propositional—Objective truth is knowable.
D. Truth is absolute and universal.
E. Truth is exclusive.
IV. Nature of Truth
A. Theories of truth
B. The objectivity of truth
C. The subjectivity of truth
V. Tests of Truth
A. Correspondence
B. Coherence
C. Pragmatic
VI. Practical Certainty

"Truth is one of the simplest, most precious gifts without which we would not be able to handle reality or negotiate life. . . . Truth matters supremely because in the end, without truth there is no freedom. . . . Our overarching life-task will be clear—to seek the truth, speak the truth, and live the truth."[4]

Os Guinness

Profile: Aleksandr Solzhenitsyn— Passion to Tell the Truth

The life of Aleksandr I. Solzhenitsyn (1918–2008), a courageous Russian writer, demonstrates the power of truth. While a teenager he became a Marxist communist. His service as an officer in the Soviet army was halted by his arrest and an eight-year imprisonment for criticizing Stalin in a letter to a friend. In prison he began to question the validity of the Marxist goal of creating a good society by social condi-

[4] Os Guinness, *Time for Truth: Living Free in a World of Lies, Hype & Spin* (Grand Rapids: Baker Books, 2000) 13, 14, 19.

tioning and gradually accepted the Christian views of his childhood.

In 1952 a large lump in his groin was diagnosed as cancer. He endured a painful operation. David Aikman describes his experience:

> The discovery of cancer, a murder almost weekly in the camp, the trauma of the operation, and finally the brutal death of a man who had spoken fervently and with kindness to Solzhenitsyn just hours earlier: all these coalesced in Solzhenitsyn's mind. There was no Damascus Road experience, no blinding revelation, but a slow, inexorable plumbing of life's greatest depths and the discovery there of a truth for which he had not been consciously searching.[5]

Solzhenitsyn states,

> In the intoxication of youthful success I had felt myself to be infallible, and I was therefore cruel. In the surfeit of power I was a murderer, and an oppressor. In my most evil moments I was convinced that I was doing good, and I was well supplied with systematic arguments. And it was only when I lay there on rotting prison straw that I sensed within myself the first stirrings of good. Gradually it was disclosed to me that the line separating good and evil passes not through states, not between classes, not between political parties either—but right through every human heart—and through all human hearts.[6]

Instead of essential human goodness he acknowledges the sinfulness of every person. He realizes the futility of a selfish life based on materialism.

[5] David Aikman, "One Word of Truth: A Portrait of Aleksandr Solzhenitsyn," in *Unriddling Our Times: Reflections on the Gathering Cultural Crisis*, ed. Os Guinness (Grand Rapids: Baker Books, 1999) 89.
[6] Quoted from the *Gulag Archipelago* in ibid., 90.

In prison he composed and memorized his writings in his mind. After his release in 1953, he remained in exile. He taught school during the day and wrote at night, burying his writings in bottles in his yard. In a few months his cancer returned, threatening him with only weeks to live. "All that I had memorized in the camps ran the risk of extinction together with the head that held it." He continues, "I did not die, however. With a hopelessly neglected and acutely malignant tumor, this was a divine miracle; I could see no other explanation. Since then, all the life that has been given back to me has not been mine in the full sense: it is built around a purpose. . . ."[7]

His *The Gulag Archipelago*, detailed the horrors of communist prisons as "a massive indictment of all Russians, holding them accountable for the accumulated crimes of the state."[8] After a copy was seized by the KGB he published his work in Paris in 1973. He wrote to express universal moral values. "Underlying all his work is the sense that he was called by God to record for history the terrible sacrifices of his fellow citizens. He let nothing stand in the way of this mission. As his life matured and his challenges became greater, he seemed to gain strength not only to pursue his writings but also to express openly his faith and his moral values."[9]

A passion for truth consumed Solzhenitsyn. He writes, "For the writer intent on truth, life never was, never is (and never will be!) easy: his like have suffered every imaginable harassment."[10] "I entered into the inheritance of every mod-

---

[7] Alonzo L. McDonald, "The Writer Underground," in *Character Counts: Leadership Qualities in Washington, Wilberforce, Lincoln, and Solzhenitsyn*, ed. Os Guinness (Grand Rapids: Baker Books, 1999) 147.

[8] Ibid., 141.

[9] Ibid., 143.

[10] Aleksandr I. Solzhenitsyn, "The Oak and the Calf," in *Character Counts*, 145.

ern Russian writer intent on the truth: I must write simply to ensure that it was not all forgotten, that posterity might someday come to know of it."[11]

He explains, "From dawn to dusk the correction and copying of *Gulag* went forward; I could scarcely keep the pages moving fast enough." He feared the intervention of the KGB, and then all would be lost. He said he could have enjoyed himself, ". . . but my duty to the dead permitted no such self-indulgence. They are dead. You are alive: Do your duty. The world must know *all about it*."[12] "All my life I had been tortured by the impossibility of speaking the truth aloud. My whole life had been spent hacking my way to an open space where I could tell the truth in public. . . . I have never doubted that the truth would be restored to my people. I believe that we shall repent, that we shall be spiritually cleansed, that the Russian nation will be reborn."[13]

He believed in God and testified to his Christian faith. He appealed for a church not spiritually subordinate to the power of the state that would aim at restoring the purity of primitive Christianity. G.R. Houston writes, "It may be argued with some justification, therefore, that Aleksandr Solzhenitsyn remains, at the time of writing, the greatest living literary apologist for the Christian faith."[14]

Ravi Zacharias states, "Prior to entering the core of Christian defense, the first step is to cross two major hurdles. The first one deals with the very method of how we arrive at

---

[11] Ibid., 146.

[12] Ibid., 155.

[13] Ibid., 160.

[14] G.R. Houston, "Solzhenitsyn, Aleksandr," in *New Dictionary of Christian Apologetics*, eds. W.C. Campbell-Jack and Gavin McGrath (Downers Grove, IL: InterVarsity, 2006) 676.

the truth for any religion, and the second examines whether truth can indeed be exclusive."[15]

Jesus told Pilate that he had come into the world to bear witness to the truth. We cannot hear the tone of Pilate's voice but he may have had an air of detached skepticism and a shrug of his shoulders as he responded, *"What is truth?" (John 18:38)*. Skepticism and cynicism about truth is alive and well in the twenty-first century. What has happened to truth?

Os Guinness observes,

> Truth, in fact, is said to be "dead"—or put more carefully, truth is relative, subjective, "socially constructed," and cul- turally determined; anything but objective, absolute, and uni- versal. The result is politics by power plays in which "might makes right" and the one with the better lawyers, spinmeis- ters, muckrakers, and rumormongers wins. Do we seriously believe such a sea change had no consequences?[16]

Apologetics is concerned with a reasoned defense of the truth of Christianity. If truth does not exist, then apologetics has no purpose. Is truth understood in terms of what is per- sonally satisfying and socially useful? Or is Christianity objec- tively true for all people? Is faith a subjective self-validating experience regardless of the object or content of the faith? Does faith have an intellectual element of truth?

During the Enlightenment of the seventeenth and eigh- teenth centuries questions about knowledge and truth took center stage in intellectual discussions. The rationalists stressed human reason as the only source and test of truth. The empiricists stressed sense experience as the source and test of truth. The romantics emphasized the individual's feel- ings as the key to life. Out of this debate many decided that the objective scientific method was the model for establishing all knowledge. Mohler states:

---

[15] Ravi Zacharias, *Can Man Live without God?* (Dallas: Word, 1994) 123.

[16] Os Guinness, "This Too Shall Pass," in *Unriddling Our Times*, 118-119.

The problem with the Enlightenment was the totalitarian imposition of the scientific model of rationality upon all truth, the claim that only scientific data can be objectively understood, objectively defined, and objectively defended. The loss in the wake of this modernist agenda was huge. It left Western culture with little more than a materialist worldview. However, in such a world of mere naturalistic materialism, what can truth possibly mean?[17]

Rejection of Truth as Objective and Absolute since the Enlightenment

Several philosophies of the last two hundred years have challenged the concept of truth as objective and absolute. Romanticism in the early nineteenth century grounded truth in one's subjective feelings, evident in the British Romantic poets—Wordsworth, Coleridge, Byron, Keats, and Shelly. A German philosopher, Hegel, while he was an ardent rationalist, saw truth as a developing, dialectical process. He saw truth as the unfolding of the World Spirit. America's primary contribution to modern philosophy, pragmatism, denies any concept of absolute truth saying that when an idea works it becomes true. James, Pierce, and Dewey, developers of pragmatism, based their ideas on Darwinian evolution. They viewed truth as an evolutionary development, the "survival of the fittest" of ideas. Existentialism, in both its religious and atheistic forms, denies objective truth holding that truth is subjectivity, being determined by the individual authenticating his or her existence.

Relativism holds that truth is not correspondence with external reality but truth is dependent upon the individual or culture and changes as the situation changes. Allan Bloom stated in his *The Closing of the American Mind*, "There is one thing a professor can be absolutely certain of: almost every student entering the university believes, or says he believes, that truth is rela-

---

[17] R. Albert Mohler, "Truth and Contemporary Culture," in *Whatever Happened to Truth?* ed., Andreas Köstenberger (Wheaton, IL: Crossway, 2005) 56.

tive."[18] Subjectivism is the view that individual preference determines truth. Conventionalism holds that truth is whatever a group or culture accepts as true for them for pragmatic reasons.

Pluralism, as used by many today, holds that all views are equally true. The New Age Movement and others hold that all spiritual ways are equally valid. John Hick and Joseph Campbell have given philosophical and popular expression that all roads are true. Advocates of postmodernism are saying that truth in an objective or absolute sense, independent of the mind of the knower, does not exist. Valid objective or universal truths do not exist. Truth does not describe objective reality, but rather is a social construction of the cultural community.

Rejection of Truth as Objective and Absolute

Romanticism—Truth is based in feelings.

Hegelian Idealism—Truth is expressed in the dialectical unfolding of the World Spirit.

Pragmatism—Survival of the fittest of ideas, what works becomes true.

Existentialism—Truth is subjectivity.

Relativism—Truth changes with the situation.

Pluralism—All views are equally true.

Postmodernism—Truth in an objective, universal, or absolute sense does not exist. Truth is only a linguistic construction of society.

Many in today's society have no love or passion for truth because they no longer believe in truth. They prefer the mental fencing that keeps ultimate decisions at arm's length. When people believe nothing can be known for certain and nothing is objectively and universally true, it is easier to rationalize whatever behavior they choose.

---

[18] Allan Bloom, *The Closing of the American Mind* (New York: Simon and Schuster, 1987) 25.

The essential question is not "Does Christianity contain truths?" but rather "Is Christianity true?" Is it objectively true—that is, true for all people, in all places, regardless of their circumstances? Do the affirmations of biblical, historical Christianity correspond to the reality that actually exists? How can we know Christianity is true? Before these questions can be answered, it is important to ask, "Can we know what is true?"

Postmodernism and Truth

A serious flaw in the postmodernist agenda is the denial of objective, absolute truth and the correspondence theory of truth. It is not language or belief that makes a proposition true; reality makes it true or false. Moreland and Craig argue, "Those who reject the correspondence theory either take their own utterances to be true in the correspondence sense or they do not. If the former, then those utterances are self-defeating. If the latter, there is no reason to accept them, because one cannot take their utterances to be true."[19]

According to postmodernists, truth is made, not discovered. Truths are particular to a linguistic community and are not objective or universal. Yet postmodernists make universal claims and sweeping generalizations in their widely published books telling those outside their particular community that their linguistic method will enable us to see things rightly. They have replaced a correspondence definition of truth with coherence or pragmatism.

Some of the most serious challenges to Christian faith come not from the enemies of the faith but from friends. Postmodernism, adopted by many evangelicals, rejects the idea of objective truth and undermines the rational defense of historic Christianity. In the accompanying sidebar Albert Mohler identifies some of the challenges postmodernism poses to Christians.

---

[19] J.P. Moreland and William Lane Craig, *Philosophical Foundations for a Christian Worldview* (Downers Grove, IL: InterVarsity, 2003) 140.

Challenges Postmodernism Presents to Christians

"(1) The *deconstruction of truth* means that truth is no longer considered to be universal in scope, but rather relative and subjective. Truth is not absolute or objectively real, but rather socially constructed, a mere human convention subject to change.

"(2) The *death of the meta-narrative* ensues in the notion that all comprehensive accounts of truth, meaning, and existence, equally binding for everyone, are cast aside. . . . Truth is localized. . . . Truth has no global reach or validity.

"(3) The *demise of the text,* including the text of Scripture, follows. If all truth is local, and all meaning is subjective, no text can claim absolute authority or command universal acceptance.

"(4) Another result of the demise of the notion of absolute truth is 'the *dominion of therapy.*' Once the notion of objective, absolute truth has been abandoned, all that remains is fulfilling the desire to be as comfortable as possible.

"(5) There is a commensurate *decline in authority*, not merely of biblical authority, but of any authority and the notion of authority itself.

"(6) The final result is the *displacement of morality*. If there is no absolute truth, there is no firm basis for morality, and prevailing notions of morality become nothing but a person's or group's oppressive exercise of his or her personal beliefs to dominate others."

Albert Mohler[20]

Writers such as Brian McLaren, Stanley Grenz, Leonard Sweet, and Nancey Murphy are reinterpreting Christianity along postmodernist lines. Evangelical publishers publish and promote their works. Groothuis observes,

There is little recognition of the profoundly unbiblical and irrational nature of postmodernism and the threat it poses to the

---

[20] Mohler, "Truth and Contemporary Culture," 13.

articulation and defense of Christian truth. Nevertheless, many writers are claiming that since our society is postmodern (more pluralistic, less idealistic and less tolerant of absolute truth-claims), the church and apologetics must bend in this direction as well.[21]

Truth becomes a casualty. John Caputo says, "The truth is that there is no truth."[22] Philip Kenneson declares, "There's no such thing as objective truth and it's a good thing, too." He says,

I *don't believe* in objective truth. . . . One can defend objective truth or relativism only by assuming that it is possible for human beings to take up a 'view from nowhere'; since I don't believe in 'views from nowhere,' I don't believe in objective truth or relativism. Moreover, I don't want *you* to believe in objective truth or relativism either, because the first concept is corrupting the church and its witness to the world, while tilting at the second is wasting the precious time and energy of a lot of Christians.[23]

Postmodernists claim the belief in absolute and objective truth and certainty about a truth claim constitutes Enlightenment modernism. Truth can't be objective because the perspective of our social and linguistic community colors all we consider knowledge. Because we can't attain absolutely certain knowledge, they conclude we can't have objective and absolute truth.

Unfortunately the denial of absolute truth is self-refuting. The rejection of absolute truth is an affirmation of an objective,

---

[21] Douglas Groothuis, "Facing the Challenge of Postmodernism," in *To Everyone an Answer: A Case for the Christian Worldview*, eds., Francis J. Beckwith, William Lane Craig, and J.P. Moreland (Downers Grove, IL: InterVarsity, 2004) 239.

[22] John D. Caputo, *Radical Hermeneutics* (Bloomington: Indiana University Press, 1987) 156.

[23] Philip Kenneson, "There's No Such Thing as Objective Truth, and It's a Good Thing, Too," in *Christian Apologetics in the Postmodern World*, eds. Timothy R. Phillips and Dennis L. Okholm (Downers Grove, IL: InterVarsity, 1995) 156. Emphasis is in the original.

absolute, and universal truth claim. The assertion that all truth claims are socially constructed is in fact a truth claim.

William Lane Craig notes the self-defeating nature of postmodernism, "If postmodernist claims are objectively true, then those claims are themselves the mere products of social forces and so are not objectively true. Of course, if postmodernist claims are not objectively true, then they are just the arbitrary opinions of certain people that we are free to ignore."[24]

Postmodernism's view of truth results in the death of truth. If truth is dead then, as Francis Schaeffer said, God is dead and man is dead. When objective truth cannot be known and absolute moral values are rejected, the unique value of human beings is lost. True freedom is lost and all social relationships are reduced to power struggles by various social groups.

Os Guinness identifies "telltale fingerprints" of postmodernism: "the rejection of truth and objective standards of right and wrong, the leveling of authorities, the elevation of the autonomous self as the sole arbiter of life and reality, the equalizing of cultures, the promotion of image over character, the glorifying of power."[25]

A society that rejects moral restraints will end in chaos and decay. Affirming the validity of all cultural values will end in self-destruction. When objective standards for right and wrong are rejected, the only thing left to settle differences is power. When spirituality is divorced from truth, what restraint is there on the kingdom of evil? What is to restrain the oldest power struggle of all—the selfish human will rebelling against a holy God? Without accountability to truth, religion becomes baptized paganism.

---

[24] William Lane Craig, "A Classical Apologist's Response to Cumulative Case Apologetics," in *Five Views on Apologetics*, ed. Steven B. Cowan (Grand Rapids: Zondervan, 2000) 182-183.

[25] Guinness, *Time for Truth*, 52.

Postmodernist evangelicals see the essence of Christianity as narrative and community-based spiritual experience rather than God revealing himself through historical facts, doctrinal truths, and verbal revelation. Rather than establishing beliefs on an authoritative Bible they draw upon the Bible, as filtered through Christian tradition, culture, and the experience of God's community. Not the text of Scripture (we have only interpretations) but the contemporary community of believers following the Spirit's appropriation of Scripture becomes the locus for theology.[26] They diminish and downgrade the authority of Scripture. While criticizing those who worship the Bible more than Christ, they have chosen to honor God's Word less than Christ did.[27]

Some emergent writers substitute mystery for knowability of God. Humility is defined as uncertainty and certainty is arrogance. Doubt becomes the essence of faith.

The metaphysical and epistemological skepticism of postmodernism makes it difficult to gain knowledge from the God outside of us, who has revealed truth in words to us. It is an approach to spirituality that encourages people to know the god within rather than the God who stands outside us and has spoken to us. In spite of the talk of community it lends itself to a gathering with others where each person finds and creates his or her own truth based on one's own experience. Given their epistemological skepticism and antirealism how can they draw understanding from others in their community? They

---

[26] Stanley J. Grenz, and John R. Franke, *Beyond Foundationalism: Shaping Theology in a Postmodern Context* (Louisville, KY: Westminster John Knox, 2001) 69, say "It is not the Bible as a book that is authoritative, but the Bible as the instrumentality of the Spirit; the biblical message spoken by the Spirit through the text is theology's norming norm." See McLaren, *A New Kind of Christian* (San Francisco: Jossey-Bass, 2001) 50; and Rob Bell, *Velvet Elvis: Repainting the Christian Faith* (Grand Rapids: Zondervan, 2005) 54.

[27] Kevin DeYoung and Ted Kluck, *Why We're Not Emergent: (By Two Guys Who Should Be)* (Chicago: Moody Press, 2008) 81.

ultimately choose what they will believe. The Enlightenment ideal of the autonomous self with no external limitations sadly continues.

The adoption of contemporary thought forms runs the risk of losing the permanent truth of Christianity. In reviewing a book by Stanley Grenz, D.A. Carson comments, "But it does not seem to have struck him that, just as thoughtful Christians should not permit their epistemology to be held hostage by modernism, so they should not permit their epistemology to be held hostage by postmodernism."[28] The accommodation of Christianity to the postmodern spirit of our culture produces a version of Christian faith that is no longer the Christianity of the Scriptures.

Postmodernism fails to be accountable to truth and reality. J.P. Moreland says, "Postmodernism is the cure that kills the patient, the military strategy that concedes defeat before the first shot is fired, the ideology that undermines its own claims to allegiance."[29] British philosopher Roger Scruton advises us, "The man who tells you truth does not exist is asking you not to believe him. So don't."[30]

Biblical View of Truth

While the Bible does not give a formal definition of truth, it does speak authoritatively concerning the nature of truth. Even though some scholars try to contrast Hebrew and Greek concepts of truth, there is a unity of the biblical concept of

---

[28] D.A. Carson, "Domesticating the Gospel: A Review of Grenz's Renewing the Center," in *Reclaiming the Center: Confronting Evangelical Accommodation in Postmodern Times*, eds. Millard J. Erickson, Paul Kjoss Helseth, and Justin Taylor (Wheaton, IL: Crossway, 2004) 55.

[29] J.P. Moreland, "Postmodernism and Truth," in *Reasons for Faith: Making a Case for the Christian Faith*, eds. Norman L. Geisler and Chad V. Meister (Wheaton, IL: Crossway, 2007) 126.

[30] Quoted in Garrett J. DeWeese and J.P. Moreland, *Philosophy Made Slightly Less Difficult: A Beginner's Guide to Life's Big Questions* (Downers Grove, IL: InterVarsity, 2005) 53.

truth. The OT word for truth (*emeth*) conveys the ideas of faith-fulness and conformity to fact. The word is used in contrast with that which is erroneous and deceitful. The NT word for truth (*aletheia*) expresses the idea of conformity to reality and opposition to error and falsehood.[31] Nicole summarizes the biblical view of truth as involving "factuality, faithfulness, and completeness."[32] The biblical understanding of truth assumes the correspondence view of truth.

The Biblical Concept of Truth

1. Truth is revealed by God.
2. Objective truth exists and is knowable.
3. Christian truth is absolute in nature.
4. Truth is universal.
5. The truth of God is eternally engaging and momentous, not trendy or superficial.
6. Truth is exclusive, specific, and antithetical.
7. Truth, Christianly understood, is systematic and unified.
8. Christian truth is an end, not a means to any other end.

Douglas Groothuis, *Truth Decay*[33]

The Jews and Christians did not originate truth but received it from God who revealed it to them. A personal God has disclosed to mankind who he is and his will for us.

Truth in Scripture has a personal, relational dimension. Truth is embodied in God—the Father, the Son, and the Holy Spirit—and revealed by God. The Lord is a *"God of truth"* (*Ps*

---

[31] Roger Nicole, "The Biblical Concept of Truth," in *Scripture and Truth*, eds. D.A. Carson and John Woodbridge (Grand Rapids: Zondervan, 1983) 290-295.

[32] Ibid., 296.

[33] Douglas Groothuis, *Truth Decay: Defending Christianity against the Challenges of Postmodernism* (Downers Grove, IL: InterVarsity, 2000) 65-81.

31:5, NASB). *"I the LORD speak the truth"* (*Isa 45:19*). God is true (*Rom 3:4; 1 Thess 1:9; Heb 10:22*). The fullness of grace and truth came through Jesus Christ (*John 1:17*). Jesus encourages those who believe in him to abide in his Word and they would *"know the truth, and the truth will set you free"* (*John 8:32*). In contrast to the devil who *"has nothing to do with the truth, because there is no truth in him,"* Jesus says, *"I tell the truth"* (*John 8:44-45*). Jesus is the way, the truth and the life (*John 14:6*). The Holy Spirit is *"the Spirit of truth"* (*John 14:17; 15:26; 16:13*) and he would guide the apostles into all truth (*John 16:13*). God's Word is truth (*John 17:17; 2 Tim 2:15*). Jesus came into the world *"to bear witness to the truth"* (*John 18:37*). He prays, *"And this is eternal life, that they know you the only true God, and Jesus Christ whom you have sent"* (*John 17:3*). Jesus is *"Faithful and True"* (*Rev 19:11*).

Truth is personal and propositional. God has revealed objective truth about himself which is knowable. Moreland states, "When we affirm that the Bible is a revelation from God, we do not simply assert that God as a person is known in and through it. We also mean that God has revealed understandable, objectively true propositions. . . . God has revealed truth to us and not just Himself."[34]

Groothuis says,

> The claim that God has revealed himself to us presupposes objective truth as the cognitive content of revelation. God is the source of objective truth about himself and his creation. . . . Objective truth is truth that is not dependent on any creature's subjective feelings, desires or beliefs. . . . God's truth is not dependent upon any individual's or group's experiences or interpretations, however strongly felt or culturally entrenched they may be.[35]

---

[34] J.P. Moreland, *Love Your God with All Your Mind* (Colorado Springs, CO: NavPress, 1997) 45.

[35] Groothuis, *Truth Decay*, 67.

Truth is absolute and universal. God's truth is not tentative, relative, nor revisable. His truth is absolute because he is infinite, absolute, and unchanging in his nature. Some point to Einstein's theory of relativity as a reason for challenging the concept of absolute truth. Groothuis states, "According to Einstein's theory of relativity, the speed of light is an absolute limit in physics; nothing can travel faster. For this reason, Einstein almost called his model idea 'the theory of invariance.' He named it 'the theory of relativity' not because everything is relative but because things are relative to what is invariant or absolute, namely, the speed of light."[36]

Absolute truth is objective truth established by God himself and the reality he created. We do not make it, we discover it. It is not dependent upon how humans came to know or believe it.

The absolute truth of God's Word is not subject to human correction or change. Affirming the absoluteness of God's truth does not mean we understand it perfectly or we can prove it absolutely. We can spend a lifetime learning and growing in the knowledge of God's truth and never plumb the depth of the riches of His wisdom.

The gospel is universal in that it applies to all people everywhere. Christ is the only way of salvation for all (*Acts 4:12*). Every church, everywhere is under his headship (*Eph 1:21-22*). At the appropriate time all men everywhere will acknowledge Christ (*Phil 2:6-11*). Christ's kingdom is not limited to specific communities but is for all the peoples of the world (*Matt 28:18-20*).

Groothuis says, "God's truth is not provincial, parochial or partial; it is universal in scope and application. Yet it also allows for unique cultural expression and the creative individ-

---

[36] Ibid., 69. See Paul Johnson, *Modern Times: The World from the Twenties to the Nineties*, rev. ed. (New York: HarperCollins, 1991) 1-5.

uality of people made in the divine image and redeemed through the Lamb."[37]

Truth is exclusive. When Elijah confronted the false prophets on Mt. Carmel he made clear the exclusive nature of truth. *"How long will you go limping between two different opinions? If the LORD is God, follow him: but if Baal, then follow him"* (*1 Kgs 18:21*). Either Jehovah is Lord or he is not Lord.

Jesus affirms the exclusivity of truth. *"No one can serve two masters, for either he will hate the one and love the other, or he will be devoted to the one and despise the other. You cannot serve God and money"* (*Matt 6:24*). *"No one comes to the Father except through me"* (*John 14:6b*). Peter says, *"And there is salvation in no one else, for there is no other name under heaven given among men by which we must be saved"* (*Acts 4:12*). Scripture contrasts truth from falsehood. John draws a sharp antithesis between *"the Spirit of truth and the spirit of error"* (*1 John 4:6*).

Scripture frequently warns of those who distort and pervert God's revealed truth with lies and false teaching (*Jer 8:8; Matt 7:15; 24:11,24; 1 John 4:1-6*). Those who advocate a false gospel face the judgment of God (*Gal 1:6-9*). Paul insists that his gospel was not of human origin, but he received it by revelation of Jesus Christ (*Gal 1:11-12*).

C.S. Lewis wrote in a letter to Dom Bede Griffiths, "Your Hindus certainly sound delightful. But what do they *deny?* That has always been my trouble with Indians—to find any proposition they would pronounce false. But truth must surely involve exclusions?"[38]

Christians are accused of being intolerant because we believe that God's truth is universally and exclusively true. One is not intolerant because he or she believes and says falsehood is falsehood. Tolerance traditionally has meant allowing others

---

[37] Groothuis, *Truth Decay*, 73.

[38] C.S. Lewis, *Letters of C. S. Lewis*, ed. W.H. Lewis (London: Bles, 1966) 267.

to hold opinions different from one's own yet without compromise of one's own convictions. The new meaning of tolerance, adopted by many in our society, means accepting all views as equally true. This is a redefinition of tolerance and truth arising from and resulting in relativism and pluralism. It stands in stark contrast to the biblical view of respect for others and of truth.

Some object to propositional truth claiming that Christianity is not about propositions but about personal relationships. Relationships however depend upon communication in words and statements. Relationships depend upon trust. Trust depends upon truth expressed in words and statements.

Nature of Truth

Theories of truth. How do we determine whether or not a statement is true? The *correspondence theory of truth* holds a statement or belief is true if what is affirmed corresponds or matches things as they actually are. A true statement correctly describes objective reality. Facts determine the truth or falsity of a statement or belief. This view assumes the basic laws (principles) of logic: identity, noncontradiction, and excluded middle. These assumptions are undeniable and unavoidable and are based on the nature of God who made reality.

Statements or propositions may be true or false. Declarative statements assert something about reality. A proposition is what the declarative statement asserts or means. The truth or falsity of propositions does not depend on belief, individuality, preference, or taste. A statement is true when the proposition in the statement corresponds with objective reality. Note the distinction between truth and validity. A valid argument follows the principles of correct reasoning. The conclusion of a valid argument may be true or false, depending on the truth or falsity of the premises.

Douglas Groothuis states:

The correspondence view of truth entails that propositional or declarative statements are subject to verification and falsification. A statement can be proven false if it can be shown to disagree with objective reality. . . . statements are true or false by virtue of their relationship to what they attempt to describe, this makes possible the marshaling of evidence for their veracity or falsity.

Therefore, Christians—who historically have affirmed (whether implicitly or explicitly) the correspondence view of truth—believe that there are good historical reasons to believe that Jesus Christ rose from the dead in space-time history, thus vindicating his divine authority (see Rom 1:4; 1 Cor 15:1-11). "And if Christ has not been raised, our preaching is useless and so is your faith. More than that, we are then found to be false witnesses about God, for we have testified about God that he raised Christ from the dead" (1 Cor 15:14-15). Without the correspondence view of truth, these resounding affirmations can only ring hollow. Therefore, the correspondence view of truth is not simply one of the many options for Christians. It is the only biblically and logically grounded view of truth available and allowable. We neglect or deny it to our peril and disgrace. Truth decay will not be dispelled without it.[39]

Coherence theories of truth hold that a statement or belief is true if it is internally coherent. Truth is defined as logical consistency. This definition of truth fails because some beliefs are internally consistent yet they are false, for example, a good fiction story. While coherence has a role as a test of truth, it must be rejected as a theory and definition of truth.

Another theory of truth is the *pragmatic theory of truth*. A belief is true if it produces beneficial results. Truth is made not discovered. An idea becomes true when it works to produce desired results. It can become false when it does not work. This view imports some baggage. It assumes one already knows what are good results and what will happen in the long run.

---

[39] Douglas Groothuis, *Truth Decay*, 110.

Another problem for pragmatism is that some false beliefs have some beneficial outcomes.

The pragmatic theory of truth must be rejected. Good results do not make a belief true. Again a distinction must be made between the pragmatic definition of truth and the pragmatic test of truth. The evidence of experience and results can be useful in certain cases as a test of truth. Christianity produces beneficial results because it is true. It is not true because it produces beneficial results.

Groothuis concludes that we must reject coherence and pragmatic theories of truth and accept the correspondence theory of truth.

> A set of beliefs may be internally coherent and not match reality. A set of beliefs may produce some good outcomes (at least in this life) and fail to connect with reality in important ways. A culture may construct beliefs that connect with reality in important ways. A culture may construct beliefs that grant it meaning and significance—e.g., the idea that if one perishes in an Islamic jihad one goes directly to paradise—yet those beliefs may be false in the light of the facts. We are, then, left with the reality of the truth—truth that is recalcitrant and resistant to any coercion. Christians, of all people, must swear allegiance to the notion that truth is what corresponds to reality—and we must do so unswervingly whatever the postmodern winds of doctrine may be blowing in our faces. Whenever postconservative evangelicals depart from the correspondence view of truth—which is both biblical and logical—and thus sink into the postmodernist swamps of subjectivism, pragmatism, or constructivism, they should be lovingly but firmly resisted. Nothing less than the integrity of our Christian witness is at stake.[40]

The Objectivity of Truth. Objective truth can be known. Truth never changes. New information may cause us to give up

---

[40] Douglas Groothuis, "Truth Defined and Defended," in *Reclaiming the Center*, 79.

old ideas about something, but the new information only brings us closer to what was objectively true all along. Truth concerns an objective "thereness." Contrary to pragmatic and postmodernist views, truth is *discovered* not made or created. We learn that something is true. Truth does not change when conditions change. In the last one hundred years many movements have insisted on the subjective nature of truth as changeable.

C.S. Lewis argues for objective value:

> The doctrine of objective value [is] the belief that certain attitudes are really true, and others really false, to the kind of thing the universe is and the kind of things we are. . . . Because our approvals and disapprovals are thus recognitions of objective value or responses to an objective order, therefore emotional states can be in harmony with reason (when we feel liking for what ought to be approved) or out of harmony with reason (when we perceive that liking is due but cannot feel it). No emotion is, in itself, a judgement: in that sense all emotions and sentiments are alogical. But they can be reasonable or unreasonable as they conform to Reason or fail to conform.[41]

C.S. Lewis in *The Great Divorce*, describes a dream. An apostate bishop from hell takes a tour to the edge of heaven. A Bright Person appeals to him to repent and believe, "I will bring you to the land not of questions but of answers, and you shall see the face of God." The Spirit tells him that one in heaven can experience truth. "I will bring you where you can taste it like honey and be embraced by it as by a bridegroom. Your thirst shall be quenched. . . . I will bring you to Eternal Fact, the Father of all other facthood." In hell the fallen bishop shaped his truth by his desires but nothing satisfied. In heaven, objectivity reigns. Things there are real and cannot be twisted and

---

[41] C.S. Lewis, *The Abolition of Man* (New York: Simon & Schuster, 1966) 32-33.

distorted to one's desires. The people in heaven are called solid people. He finds the objective truth of heaven stifling preferring hell with its questions without answers.[42]

Shirley MacLaine, New Age advocate, rejects the objectivity of truth: ". . . not only was the truth relative, but it kept changing. One person's truth was not another person's . . . there are so many truths, one just as valid as the other."[43] If all truths are equally true, they are in fact all equally false.

While objective, absolute, universal truth does exist, no human being understands it perfectly or completely. Subjectivity is involved in our coming to know the truth.

The Subjectivity of Truth. A statement describing reality is true for all persons in all times and places. Subjectivity is involved in how a truth is understood, accepted, and appropriated. Truth concerns what actually is or what has happened. While truth is objective and absolute, our understanding of that truth is affected by subjective factors. Our understanding of truth may be limited, partial, and incomplete.

When Jesus rose from the dead, an *objective* event happened in time and space. But many subjective factors influenced the disciples as they came to an understanding of this truth. The empty tomb had not convinced them of the truth of the resurrection. The report of the women who had seen Jesus was likewise discounted by the apostles. Only when they saw Jesus in bodily life did they accept the truth that he had risen from the dead. The truth did not change, but their understanding of the truth was influenced by their naturalistic thinking.

In *Taran Wanderer*, a children's story written by Lloyd Alexander, Taran is a pigkeeper who does not know who his parents are. He wants to marry a princess but he must estab-

---

[42] C.S. Lewis, *The Great Divorce* (New York: Macmillan, 1946) 36-38.
[43] Shirley MacLaine, *Don't Fall off the Mountain* (Toronto: Bantam Books, 1971).

lish his family history first before he is eligible to marry her. He is visiting about the matter with a witch named Orddu.

"Parentage?" said Orddu. "Nothing easier. Choose any parents you please. Since none of you has ever known each other, what difference can it possibly make—to them or to you? *Believe what you like. You'll be surprised how comforting it is.*"

"*I ask no comfort,*" replied Taran, "*but the truth, be it harsh or happy.*"[44]

C.S. Lewis says, "Comfort is the one thing you cannot get by looking for it. If you look for truth, you may find comfort in the end: if you look for comfort you will not get either comfort or truth—only soft soap and wishful thinking to begin with and, in the end, despair."[45]

Groothuis states:

Objective reality exists in its own right apart from human knowers; it is metaphysically objective and representable through true statements. However, our knowledge of truth is influenced by a number of epistemologically subjective factors, such as our level of intelligence, background beliefs, personal interests and so on. . . . No one is neutral, since we have a set of subjective dispositions and unique experiences. However, one may come to know objective truth as one sincerely applies the proper procedures of knowing.[46]

Our goal should be to overcome any subjective hindrances and to learn objective truth as fully as possible.

Groothuis summarizes:

The biblical emphasis on objective truth does not minimize the imperative to make God's truth subjectively and existentially one's own; rather, it sharpens and deepens the need for authentic personal experience. Believing in objective truth

---

[44] Lloyd Alexander, *Taran Wanderer* (New York: Holt, Rinehart and Winston, 1967) 28.

[45] C.S. Lewis, *Mere Christianity* (New York: Macmillan, 1952) 25.

[46] Groothuis, *Truth Decay*, 185.

does not mean one is neutral or detached concerning that truth. Truth matters mightily, particularly the saving and sanctifying truth of the gospel. Biblical faith involves assent to true doctrine (derived from biblical revelation) as a necessary element of saving faith and growth in Christ, but it also demands trust and commitment to the flaming truths to which one has given assent. The objective truth must be subjectively appropriated.[47]

Tests of Truth

Statements making truth claims must be evaluated to see if they are actually true descriptions of reality. Tests of truth enable us to examine statements for their truth value.

Ravi Zacharias suggests three tests for truth claims— "(1) logical consistency, (2) empirical adequacy, and (3) experiential relevance."[48] "These three tests provide such a high degree of confidence that as they are applied to a system of belief, truth or falsehood can be established. The truth claims of Christianity, Hinduism, Buddhism, Islam, or atheism must *all* meet these tests."[49] Geisler adds undeniability as a test for truth and unaffirmability as a test for falsehood.[50]

Three tests of truth will be discussed. Not all of them are applicable in testing every truth claim.

1. *Correspondence.* Does the statement correspond to external reality? Some statements can be easily checked by this test. For example, a statement asserting that there are ten people in a certain room at a certain time. The persons in the room can be counted in order to test the accuracy of the statement. We need to investigate all the relevant factual reality we can in order to determine the truth of a belief or statement. We use

---

[47] Ibid., 68.
[48] Ravi Zacharias, *Can Man Live without God?* 123.
[49] Ibid., 123-124.
[50] Norman Geisler, *Christian Apologetics* (Grand Rapids: Baker Book House, 1976) 141-145.

the correspondence test of truth frequently everyday, and it is perhaps the most useful test of truth. But some statements are very difficult to verify using this test, for example, the triune nature of God.

2. *Coherence.* Is the statement logically consistent? When a limited number of facts are available, a false statement may seem plausible. But overall, when all facts are in, truth will be logically consistent. A true statement will not contradict itself. Contradiction and inherent logical inconsistency can refute the truth-claims of a belief or statement.

3. *Pragmatic.* Does it work? In areas where there is no absolute standard one can experiment and find whatever works. When one's car will not start, you experiment until you find what is wrong and what will make it operate properly. But in morality and areas where objective standards operate the pragmatic test must be rejected. Murder, adultery, or suicide must not be tried just to see if they work. It would be utterly unwise to kill oneself to see if there is life after death.

Complete skepticism—truth is unknowable—is self-defeating. It refutes itself because it is an affirmation of a truth claim—that we can't know truth.

The view that metaphysics is perspectival is problematic. If it means that we have human limitations as we seek to know the truth of a worldview or a proposition, it has some merit. If it means we can't know reality because we only know our perspective, then it seems to be an incipient agnosticism preventing knowledge of objective reality. It also becomes self-defeating if one claims that the statement itself stands outside of being perspectival.[51]

---

[51] Arthur Holmes, *Faith Seeks Understanding* (Grand Rapids: Eerdmans, 1971), 46f. I profited from Dr. Holmes's course in Epistemology but I could never fully accept his view of metaphysics being perspectival.

Practical Certainty

Absolute certainty and mathematical proof is unavailable for many things, including worldviews. We can't prove there will be a tomorrow. We cannot absolutely prove we will survive an operation. We cannot prove absolutely the existence of God in the same way we can prove two plus two equals four. We cannot demonstrate mathematically the resurrection of Christ. We have convincing evidence as a basis for the Christian faith, but we do not have absolute proof.

Several kinds of evidence converging and pointing to the same conclusion has a cumulative effect in producing a practical certainty for Christian faith. Seth Wilson observed, "We can have a practical certainty that Pike's Peak is not a hole in the ground and go out and jump in."

On the basis of adequate factual and rational evidence we can have a moral and practical certainty that Christianity is true. We can have a solid basis for accepting the reality and veracity of God. This absolute and infinite God tells us the truth about that which he chooses to reveal. Even though we are finite and fallible, we have access to infinite and infallible truth. God is our ultimate authority. We should accept what he says about any subject. For example, he is the only valid authority for what happened at creation and we should accept what he has revealed.

Truth in an ultimate sense resides in God. If there is a God, he is the ultimate source and standard of truth. He is described as a God of truth (*Isa 65:16; Jer 10:8,10; 1 Thess 1:9; John 3:33; 17:3*). Jesus said, *"I am the truth"* (*John 14:6*; see also *John 1:9,14; 15:1; Rom 9:1; Eph 4:21; Col 2:3; Rev 5:14; 19:11*).

God is the ultimate reality. He is the absolute, the infinite being. Finite human beings can only know the infinite God because He made us in His image and chose to communicate with man. He made the external world. He created human beings with senses and reason as equipment for knowing. The principle of noncontradiction and the principle of causality are woven into the fabric of the world and human reason. We can use our senses and reason to know a box weighs ten pounds. But to know the truth about our origin, ultimate moral values and standards, our purpose and meaning in life, and our final destiny, we must look to God who is Truth.

We can know him who is Truth (*John 14:6; 17:3; 1 John 5:20*). We can know God's truth that he has divinely revealed (*John 17:17*). In defending Christian faith we must not club people over the head with truth but rather combine grace with truth. Paul reminds us to speak the truth in love (*Eph 4:15*). As Stott says we should be "neither truthless in our love, nor loveless in our truth, but holding the two in balance."[52]

Review Questions

1. Describe Solzhenitsyn's conversion to Christ from communism.

2. Explain Solzhenitsyn's passion for truth.

3. Why is truth important for apologetics?

4. How does Mohler summarize the Enlightenment worldview?

5. List and briefly define views in the last two hundred years that have rejected truth as objective and absolute.

6. What is the essential question for apologetics concerning truth and Christianity?

7. List six challenges postmodernism presents to Christians.

---

[52] John R.W. Stott, *Christ the Controversialist* (Downers Grove, IL: InterVarsity, 1970) 19.

8. List four writers interpreting Christianity along the lines of postmodernism.

9. Why does Kenneson say he does not believe in objective truth?

10. Summarize postmodernism's view of truth.

11. List characteristics of the biblical view of truth.

12. Identify the source of absolute, objective truth.

13. Explain what is meant by saying truth is absolute and universal.

14. Give Bible examples of truth being exclusive.

15. Contrast the traditional and recent uses of the word *tolerance*.

16. State and defend the correspondence theory of truth.

17. State the coherence and pragmatic theories of truth. What weaknesses of these theories are given?

18. How does our subjectivity enter in to our acceptance of truth? Does that deny the objectivity of truth?

19. Explain three tests of truth.

20. Contrast absolute certainty with practical certainty.

Suggested Reading

Cowan, Steven B., and James S. Spiegel. *The Love of Wisdom: A Christian Introduction to Philosophy*. Nashville: B & H Academic, 2009. Useful discussion of logic, truth, and epistemology.

Groothuis, Douglas. *Truth Decay: Defending Christianity against the Challenge of Postmodernism*. Downers Grove, IL: InterVarsity, 2000. See also Douglas Groothuis, "Truth Defined and Defended." In *Reclaiming the Center: Confronting Evangelical*

Accommodation in Postmodern Times. Pp. 59-79. Eds. Millard J. Erickson, Paul Kjoss Helseth, Justin Taylor. Wheaton, IL: Crossway, 2004. Defends truth as objective, absolute, and universal. Strong critique of postmodernism and defense of the correspondence theory of truth.

Köstenberger, Andreas, ed. *Whatever Happened to Truth?* Wheaton, IL: Crossway, 2005. Four evangelical scholars defend the truth of God's revelation in Christ and in the Bible exposing the inadequacies of postmodernism and the evangelical accommodation to it.

Lindsley, Art. *True Truth: Defending Absolute Truth in a Relativistic World.* Downers Grove, IL: InterVarsity, 2004. Upholds absolutes without absolutism. Shows that relativism is self-refuting.

MacArthur, John. *The Truth War: Fighting for Certainty in an Age of Deception.* Nashville: Thomas Nelson, 2007. Strong defense of truth challenging a generation that no longer believes truth can be known.

Moreland, J.P. "Postmodernism and Truth." In *Reasons for Faith: Making a Case for the Christian Faith.* Pp. 113-126. Eds. Norman L. Geisler and Chad V. Meister. Wheaton, IL: Crossway, 2007. Defends the correspondence theory of truth and exposes confusions in the postmodernist view of truth.

Pearcey, Nancy. *Total Truth: Liberating Christianity from Its Cultural Captivity.* Wheaton, IL: Crossway, 2004. Updates Schaeffer's cultural analysis and a defense of the truth of the Christian worldview.

Pressley, Johnny. "The Nature of Truth." In *A Humble Defense: Evidence for the Christian Faith.* Pp. 197-211. Ed. by Mark Scott and Mark Moore. Joplin, MO: College Press, 2004. Responds to postmodernism by affirming truth as objective with an absolute standard and based on sufficient knowledge.

"Faith is a confident assurance of that for which we hope, a conviction of the reality we do not see."

Hebrews 11:1 (Weymouth)

"But you, beloved, build yourselves up in the most holy faith."

Jude 20

9

Believing

Believing	"Faith is the assurance of the heart in the adequacy of the evidence."[1]

Profile: Josh McDowell—
  From Skepticism to
  Faith
	Josh McDowell

I. What Is Faith? A. Intellectual content B. Mental assent C. Personal trust	"Faith uses reason, and reason cannot succeed in finding truth without faith."[2]
	Norman Geisler

II. Faith and Knowledge
 A. Faith involves
  knowledge
 B. Not based on ex-
  haustive knowledge
	"For that which is above the human reason we believe only because God has revealed it."[3]

	Thomas Aquinas

[1] Josh McDowell, *Evidence That Demands a Verdict: Historical Evidences for the Christian Faith* (San Bernardino: Campus Crusade for Christ, 1972) 4.
[2] Norman L. Geisler, *Baker Encyclopedia of Christian Apologetics* (Grand Rapids: Baker Books, 1999) 239.
[3] Thomas Aquinas, *Gentiles*, 1.9.

| III. Faith, Facts, and Feelings
  A. Faith without a factual basis is false
  B. Faith based on facts results in feelings
  C. Not based on feelings alone
  D. Feelings result from faith; they do not establish faith
IV. Faith and Reason
  A. Reason without faith
  B. Faith without reason
  C. Faith before reason
  D. Faith based on reasonable evidence
V. Faith and Trust
  A. Faith as confidence
  B. Faith as commitment | "A man can believe only what he holds to be true."[4]

J. Gresham Machen

"Faith must be based on reasons, and the reasons must be good ones."[5]

Richard L. Purtill

"Christianity is based on evidence. It is reasonable faith. Christian faith goes beyond reason, but not against it."[6]

Paul Little |

Profile: Josh McDowell—From Skepticism to Faith

A college teacher challenged Josh McDowell (1939–), "Don't buy everything you're told. Examine these areas for yourself."

His English teacher asked if he had decided on a topic for his term paper. He replied, "I plan to do a serious historical study which will—once and for all—refute Christianity as nothing but meaningless fables."

[4] J. Gresham Machen, "Christianity and Culture," in *J. Gresham Machen: Selected Shorter Writings*, ed. by D.G. Hart (Phillipsburg, NJ: P & R Publishing, 2004) 403.
[5] Richard L. Purtill, *Reasons to Believe* (Grand Rapids: Eerdmans, 1974) 75.
[6] Paul Little, *Know Why You Believe*, 3rd ed. (Downers Grove, IL: InterVarsity, 1988) 20.

Once he went forward in a church, but nothing special happened. He thought all religious people were just fooling themselves that it was real. He didn't see how any intelligent person could believe the myth of the resurrection of Jesus. "Most Christians I've met are duds," he told a classmate in a coffee shop.

A group of Christian students frustrated him because he could not discern what made them different. He asked one of the girls what changed her life. "Jesus Christ," she replied.

"Oh, for heaven's sake, don't give me that garbage!" he snapped back. He apologized for his rude answer but made clear his disgust with the church and religion.

A student in the group asked, "Is it true that you're working on a paper to refute Christianity?" After Josh said he was, the student continued, "Have you ever intellectually examined the claims of Jesus Christ?" They challenged Josh, and he agreed to honestly investigate Christianity searching for the truth.

As he began to research, he realized he had an antisupernatural philosophical bias. To be honest he had to objectively consider the evidence. He decided to examine the historical testimony for Christianity to see if it met the tests for reliable history. He discovered compelling evidence for the fact of the resurrection of Jesus. He became convinced that it was one of the best-established facts of history. Josh recalls, "My mind told me Christianity was true on the one hand, and my will said, 'Don't admit it.' . . . I knew I had to get Jesus off my mind or go out of my mind!" On December 19, 1959, he accepted Christ as his Lord. He asked Christ to forgive him and change his life. The change in his life enabled him to win his alcoholic father to Christ. Instead of going to law school he attended seminary.

He says the evidence showed him Christianity was true. When he realized God's love for him shown through Christ's death, he accepted Christ. "If I hadn't considered whether the claims of Christianity were true, I would never have considered its message. So for me, apologetics had to come before I exercised faith."

Josh has spoken to more than seven million young people in eighty-four countries, including seven hundred university and college campuses. His *Evidence That Demands a Verdict* and *More Than a Carpenter* state clearly and forcefully evidence for the Christian faith. He also speaks on "Maximum Sex" and "Why Wait?" giving positive reasons for abstaining from sexual intimacy until marriage.[7] For over forty years the primary focus of his ministry has been defending the faith by presenting evidence to skeptics and seekers alike.

When the Sunday school teacher asked, "What is faith?" a young boy answered with a popular misconception, "Believing something you know isn't true."[8] H.L. Mencken also misunderstood faith when he defined faith as "an illogical belief in the occurrence of the improbable."[9] Keith Lockitch expresses the secularist mistaken idea of faith, "[There is an] essential difference between reason and faith. In reason, one accepts only conclusions one can prove to be true—conclusions based

---

[7] Joe Musser, *JOSH: The Excitement of the Unexpected* (San Bernardino: Here's Life Publishers, 1981) 34-41; Martha Millhouse, "Josh McDowell—Where There's a Will," in *Ambassadors for Christ: Distinguished Representatives of the Message throughout the World* (Chicago: Moody Press, 1994) 320-325; Josh McDowell, *The Resurrection Factor* (San Bernardino: Here's Life Publishers, 1981) 113-120; Christy Tennant, "Josh McDowell on Defending the Bible," *Bible Study Magazine* (Nov & Dec 2008) 11-14.

[8] Paul Little, *Know Why You Believe*, 13.

[9] Quoted by Terry Miethe, *Living Your Faith* (Joplin, MO: College Press, 1993) 24.

on sensory evidence and logical inference from such evidence. Faith, on the other hand, is belief unsupported by facts and logic—the blind embrace of ideas despite an absence of evidence or proof."[10] Atheist Sam Harris contends that religious faith is "credulity" being without evidence, *"unjustified* belief."[11]

Faith is not believing without evidence. It is not opposed to reason. Such misunderstandings as these make it necessary to clarify the real nature of faith. Faith is commonly misunderstood as a private matter only. Nancy Pearcey says, "Faith is often reduced to a separate add-on for personal and private life—on the order of a private indulgence, like a weakness for chocolates—and not an appropriate topic in the public arena."[12]

What Is Faith?

Since apologetics seeks to establish the truth of the Christian faith, we must be clear what we mean by faith. Authentic faith includes three elements: intellectual content (*notitia*), mental assent (*assensus*), and personal trust (*fiducia*). Apologetics seeks to establish the intellectual content of Christian faith, endeavors to secure assent to that body of truth and to the reality of God and Christ, and encourages personal commitment, trust, and obedience to the Lord.

Intellectual content. Christian faith has content. It is not just the act of believing. Beliefs are convictions based on reasons or evidence. Christian faith has a body of truth and a focus on the person of God as its content. The Hebrews writer says we must believe that God is, and that he is a rewarder of

---

[10] Keith Lockitch, "Reader Rebuttal: Creationism," *The Orange County Register* (December 11, 2005) editorial section. Quoted in J.P. Moreland and Klaus Issler, *In Search of a Confident Faith: Overcoming Barriers to Trusting in God* (Downers Grove, IL: InterVarsity, 2008) 16.

[11] Sam Harris, *The End of Faith: Religion, Terror, and the Future of Reason* (New York: W.W. Norton, 2004) 17, 19, 65. Emphasis in original.

[12] Nancy Pearcey, *Total Truth: Liberating Christianity from Its Cultural Captivity* (Wheaton, IL: Crossway Books, 2004) 99.

his followers (*Heb 11:6*). A saving faith in Christ accepts His claim to be Savior, Christ, Lord, and Son of God and that he died for our sins and rose from the dead to guarantee our hope.

Mental and heartfelt assent. One can give bare intellectual assent without trust and commitment but that is an inadequate faith (*Jas 2:19*). Genuine faith must include mental assent and emotional acceptance of the content believed. A robust faith has unqualified and wholehearted agreement with the truth or person believed.

Personal trust and commitment. Any faith without trust and commitment is incomplete and inadequate. Commitment follows conviction. Faith involves our whole being—mind, emotions, and will. Trust and reliance upon God result in a life of obedience and faithfulness to him.

Apologetics does not coerce the will. It removes obstacles preventing assent and trust. It provides evidence of the truth to be believed. The Holy Spirit works on the heart through the evidence. Each person chooses to surrender his or her self to trust and obey Christ as their Lord and Savior.

Faith Includes
Intellectual content
Mental and heartfelt assent
Personal trust and commitment

In common usage the word faith means many things. In regard to how we know things, faith means the acceptance of testimony by an authority about a matter where we do not have direct sense experience. In every area of life we gain knowledge by accepting testimony. Faith is not limited to religion. When we accept a statement as true on the basis of someone's testimony, we accept it on faith. We accept by faith the meteorologist's statement that it is 75 degrees Fahrenheit at 3:00 p.m. when we do not check the thermometer ourselves.

Much human knowledge comes from authorities we accept by faith. We accept testimony as valid knowledge in history, news reporting, and in much of our scientific knowledge. If the authority or witness tells the truth, the information is just as true for the person who accepts it by faith as it is for the original witness. It is just as true as if the person who believed the testimony had experienced the fact directly.

Those who deny faith as a valid means of knowledge overlook what they accept by faith. Kreeft and Tacelli state, "No human being ever existed without some faith. We all know most of what we know by faith; that is, by belief in what others—parents, teachers, friends, writers, society—tell us. Outside religion as well as inside it, faith *and* reason are roads to truth."[13]

We accept by faith statements made by trusted authorities on matters outside our personal experience. Because of misinformation, we should not accept blindly and uncritically everything we hear or read. Authority is a valid source of knowledge when by faith we accept testimony based on good evidence. Faith is trust based on adequate evidence. Carnell defined faith as the "resting of the soul in the sufficiency of the evidence."[14]

All people take their basic assumptions about the nature of the world by faith. Our philosophy of life, our worldview, is an act of faith. Atheism is accepted by faith just as theism is.[15] The belief that the world originated by chance and developed naturally by process of evolution is as much a faith as the belief that a personal God created the world. It is a confidence that goes beyond the demonstrated evidence.

---

[13] Peter Kreeft and Ronald K. Tacelli, *Pocket Handbook of Christian Apologetics* (Downers Grove, IL: InterVarsity, 2003) 15. Emphasis in original.

[14] Edward J. Carnell, *An Introduction to Christian Apologetics*, 4th ed. (Grand Rapids: Eerdmans, 1952) 82.

[15] Norman Geisler and Frank Turek, *I Don't Have Enough Faith to Be an Atheist* (Wheaton, IL: Crossway Books, 2004) 7-32.

The NT describes faith as *"a confident assurance of that for which we hope, a conviction of the reality which we do not see"* (**Heb 11:1**, Weymouth translation). In the spring the farmer plants seed corn in the ground in faith, hoping for a harvest in the fall—a harvest he cannot yet see with his eyes. A patient who submits to brain surgery has faith that the surgeon will successfully perform the operation even though it is impossible to know absolutely for certain that it will be a success.

J.D. Thomas said of *Hebrews 11:1*: "The meaning of the above passage is simply that faith takes us beyond reason and gives us a certitude, an assurance and a confidence concerning those things we have accepted and have committed ourselves to—beyond what our reason and our senses are able to certify."[16]

Faith trusts in someone or something. The various aspects or dimensions of faith include an understanding of what is believed, an assent to the propositional truth believed, trust and reliance on the person believed, and a willingness to act in obedience to what we believe. What we believe in is the object of faith. We must distinguish this from the act of believing. A Christian believes what God has revealed in his Word and ultimately God himself as the supreme focus and object of our faith. Christian faith includes emotional assurance, confident trust, and volitional obedience to God. Genuine faith issues in actions. What we believe shapes our lives. What we believe guides our values, goals, choices, and actions.

Moreland and Issler write, "Three key synonyms for *faith* are *confidence, trust,* and *reliance.* To have faith in a real estate agent is to have confidence in the agent, to trust and rely on her."[17] They state, *"Faith is trusting what we have reason to believe is true."*[18] John Stott defines faith as "a reasoning trust, a trust

---

[16] J.D. Thomas, *Facts and Faith* (Abilene, TX: Biblical Research Press, 1965) I:249-250.
[17] Moreland and Issler, *In Search of a Confident Faith,* 17.
[18] Ibid., 18. Italics in the original.

which reckons thoughtfully and confidently upon the trustworthiness of God."[19] C.S. Lewis defines faith as "the power of continuing to believe what we once honestly thought to be true until cogent reasons for honestly changing our minds are brought before us."[20]

A genuine faith includes faithfulness. Paul says some have made *"shipwreck of their faith, . . . will depart from the faith, . . . have denied the faith, . . . having abandoned their former faith"* (*1 Tim 1:19; 4:1; 5:8,12*). Those *"who have swerved from the truth"* are *"upsetting the faith"* of others (*2 Tim 2:17-18*). Those who oppose the truth *"are corrupted in mind and disqualified regarding the faith"* (*2 Tim 3:8*). Apologetics not only seeks to lead people to Christian faith but also seeks to nourish and strengthen the faith of believers.

We will next examine more in detail how faith relates to knowledge, feelings, and facts.

Faith and Knowledge

The NT depicts faith as knowing, accepting, and obeying the truth (*Titus 1:1; 2 Thess 2:13; 1 Pet 1:22*).

Faith involves knowledge. Faith and knowledge are not opposites. Faith is based on some knowledge and is also a source of some knowledge. All knowledge involves some faith and valid faith must be based on some knowledge. We reject the false view that faith is totally subjective and scientific knowledge is totally objective.

E.J. Carnell said, "If faith is not related to knowledge and truth, it is meaningless."[21] Charles Hodge stated, "Faith is limited by knowledge. We can believe only what we know, i.e.,

---

[19] John Stott, *Your Mind Matters: The Place of the Mind in the Christian Life* (Downers Grove, IL: InterVarsity, 1973) 36.

[20] C.S. Lewis, "Religion: Reality or Substitute?" in *Christian Reflections*, ed. Walter Hooper (Grand Rapids: Eerdmans, 1967) 42.

[21] Carnell, *Introduction to Christian Apologetics*, 66.

what we intelligently apprehend. If someone announces a proposition to us in an unknown language we can affirm nothing about it. We can neither believe nor disbelieve it."[22] J. Gresham Machen affirmed, "All true faith involves an intellectual element; all faith involves knowledge and issues in knowledge."[23] J.D. Thomas said that knowledge is a "precondition of faith . . . faith cannot exist in the absence of an intellectual acceptance of some type of propositional statement. . . . A person would not be willing to sit in a chair unless he were intellectually convinced that a chair was there."[24]

We must have some knowledge of a person before we trust him or her. We must have some knowledge about God before we trust him. *"And without faith it is impossible to please him, for whoever would draw near to God must believe that he exists and that he rewards those who seek him"* (**Heb 11:6**). We can't trust a God we believe to be nonexistent or untrustworthy.

Richard Swinburne asserts that a major aspect of faith

> . . . is belief—that or *propositional belief.* The man who has faith in God . . . believes that there is a God and believes certain propositions about him. The faith which the Christian religion commends is *basically faith in a person or person, God (or Christ)* characterized as possessing certain properties and having done certain actions; and secondarily perhaps in some of the deeds which he has done, and the good things which he has provided and promised.[25]

Jesus says we are to "receive the kingdom of God like a child" (**Mark 10:15**). This did not mean that faith is a subjective leap, empty of intellectual content. A child trusts his mother because of the many times she has cared for and met the

---

[22] Quoted by Carnell, ibid., 66.

[23] J. Gresham Machen, *What Is Faith?* (Grand Rapids: Eerdmans, 1925) 40.

[24] J.D. Thomas, *Facts and Faith*, 1:259.

[25] Richard Swinburne, *Faith and Reason* (Oxford, Eng.: Clarendon Press, 1981) 3, 104, 124. Emphasis in the original.

child's needs. A child's faith is not independent of knowledge because the child does not trust a person he or she considers untrustworthy. Terry Miethe states, "The faith that makes the child willing to jump [into his father's arms] is based on the child's intimate knowledge of his parents. The child *knows* that he can trust his father to catch him because he has experienced his father's care and love."[26]

Moreland and Issler say,

> In the contemporary understanding, faith and reason are polar opposites such that as one gains evidence or knowledge about something, the room for faith vanishes, and, indeed, there is no need for faith. After all, no one (allegedly) needs to exert faith in the claim that water is H_2O or that gravity keeps us anchored to the ground. But, the argument continues, one needs faith in religions or moral claims because there is no knowledge that these claims are true, no evidence either way for them. But we can see that if faith is essentially *trust* and *confidence*, its proper exercise crucially requires reasons, evidence, and knowledge.[27]

D. Martyn Lloyd-Jones, commenting on the Sermon on the Mount, states, "Faith according to our Lord's teaching in this paragraph, is primarily thinking; and the whole trouble with a man of little faith is that he does not think . . . his thought is being controlled by something else. . . . That is not thought; that is the absence of thought, a failure to think."[28]

Genuine faith has intellectual content. It is not a mindless leap or trust apart from knowledge. Christian faith has a factual, historical, intellectual basis. Faith without a basis in objective truth is not Christian faith. The NT evangelists called men and women to an intelligent faith.

---

[26] Miethe, *Living Your Faith*, 30.

[27] Moreland and Issler, *In Search of a Confident Faith*, 18.

[28] D. Martyn Lloyd-Jones, *Studies in the Sermon on the Mount* (Grand Rapids: Eerdmans, 1970) 2:129.

Biblical faith is a personal response to the God outside who has spoken and acted on our behalf. For those marketing Christianity as therapeutic self-help, faith becomes individualistic and self-focused. Divorced from knowledge, faith can become believing in the god within. Believing in one's self-created spirituality replaces a relationship with the God of the Bible.

Not based on exhaustive knowledge. Faith is not based on exhaustive knowledge. Exhaustive knowledge is not available to finite human beings. We do not have total knowledge of our friends, of ourselves, or of God. "But partial knowledge is not necessarily false knowledge; and our knowledge of God on the basis of His revelation of Himself is, we hold, true as far as it goes."[29] "When people insist on complete understanding before they believe, they elevate their minds to the level of a god. . . . Minds like ours don't have what it takes to be our own gods or to comprehend the existence of a real God. In fact, a god we could understand would not be a god worth having."[30] C.S. Lewis says faith gives "assent to a proposition which we think so overwhelmingly probable that there is a psychological exclusion of doubt although not a logical exclusion of dispute."[31]

Faith, Facts, and Feelings

Frequently the relationship between faith, facts, and feelings is confused. Faith is based on facts and results in feelings.

Faith without factual basis is false. The superiority of the Christian faith rests in its factual basis. Clark Pinnock clearly underscores this point:

---

[29] J. Gresham Machen, *What Is Christianity?* (Grand Rapids: Eerdmans, 1951) 254-255.

[30] Josh McDowell and Thomas Williams, *In Search of Certainty* (Wheaton, IL: Tyndale House, 2003) 121.

[31] C.S. Lewis, "On Obstinacy in Belief," in *The World's Last Night and Other Essays* (New York: Brace Jovanovich, 1955) 16.

That the gospel rests upon an objective historical foundation is a priceless asset in this world in which there is a cafeteria of clues as to the meaning of the universe. The basis on which we rest our defense of the gospel consists of evidence open to all investigators. The non-Christian has no right to disregard the gospel because it is a matter of fact. The historical foundations of the gospel, especially the resurrection itself, comprise a powerful incentive and challenge to our secular contemporaries to consider Christ and His claims on their lives.[32]

Paul emphasizes the factual foundation of faith by arguing *"If Christ has not been raised, your faith is futile, and you are still in your sins"* (*1 Cor 15:17*). A faith unsupported by facts is false.

Atheist Sam Harris acknowledges that faith must have an evidential basis. "To believe that God exists is to believe that I stand in some relation to his existence *such that his existence is itself the reason for my belief.* There must be some causal connection, or an appearance thereof, between the fact in question and my acceptance of it. In this way, we can see that religious beliefs, to be beliefs about the way the world *is*, must be evidentiary in spirit as any other."[33] "There is no way around the fact that we crave justification for our core beliefs and believe them only because we think such justification is, at the very least, in the offing."[34]

He, however, refuses to accept the evidences for Christianity.

Faith based on facts results in feelings. Alexander Campbell discussed the relationship of facts, faith, and feelings.

Facts must precede either knowledge or belief. An event must happen before it can be known by man—it must be known by some before it can be reported to others—it must be report-

[32] Clark Pinnock, *Set Forth Your Case*, rev. ed. (Chicago: Moody Press, 1971) 66.
[33] Harris, *End of Faith*, 63.
[34] Ibid., 66.

ed before it can be believed, and the testimony must be confirmed, or made credible, before it can be relied on.

Something must be done before it can be known, reported, or believed. Hence, in the order of nature, there is first the fact, then the testimony, and then the belief. A was drowned before B reported it—B reported it before C believed it, and C believed it before he was grieved at it. This is the unchangeable and universal order of things as respects belief.[35]

Billy Graham preached a sermon on "Facts, Faith, and Feeling." He insisted that the proper order must be faith based on facts resulting in the right feelings. The witness of the early Christians focused on facts. They "pointed away from their experiences to the evidences that a divine Saviour had entered history, a fact amply attested by the bodily resurrection."[36]

Not based on feelings alone. A novelist wrote that one should never inquire into why one believes in supernatural religion. He gave his reason, "Though believers will give you a good deal of prose on the subject, the subject is always touchy, fruitful of offense or anger; because the awkward truth usually is that they have no reason, they just feel like believing."[37] For many today life is a series of experiences and emotions without any serious thought about rational or moral justification.

In this age of subjectivism, many have based their faith on emotion. "I know it is true because I can feel it in my heart." "I know I am saved because I feel I am saved." "I know God is real because he feels so close to me." But feelings can mislead. Just because a patient feels that he does not have cancer is no proof that he does not have cancer. James Orr observed, "A religion based on mere feeling is the vaguest, most unreliable, most

---

[35] Alexander Campbell, *The Christian System* (Cincinnati: Standard Publishing, 1830) 8-14.

[36] Pinnock, *Set Forth Your Case*, 75. See chapters 11 and 12 in this book.

[37] Quoted by Joel Nederhood, "The Source of Faith," in *The Radio Pulpit* (February, 1969) 14:17.

unstable of all things. A strong, stable, religious life can be built upon no other ground than that of intelligent conviction."[38]

Dallas Willard states, "Feelings are a primary blessing *and* a primary problem for human life."[39] Feelings are essential to life and can be healthy or destructive. For those led only by their feelings *"their god is their belly"* (*Phil 3:19*). We should never allow our feelings to govern us. We should not deny our feelings but direct them by our spiritual heart in the light of reality.

Feelings result from faith; they do not establish faith. Proper feelings result from truth; they do not establish truth. Edward Carnell expressed it this way, "Proper feeling . . . follows upon the establishment of the truth of the law of God. Truth establishes feelings; feelings do not establish truth."[40] Willard says, "Feelings have a crucial role in life, but they must not be taken as a *basis* for action or character change. That role falls to insight, understanding, and conviction of truth, which will always be appropriately accompanied by feeling."[41]

A philosophy professor from a Christian college was speaking at a banquet. His wife sat next to a Hindu from India. She testified to the Hindu, "The reason I know Christianity is true is because it gives me peace in my heart."

The Hindu gentleman replied, "You know, that's why I'm a Hindu!"

Now what can she say? Basing one's faith only on feelings leaves the person without an outside reference point in external reality that would be objective evidence demonstrating the reality of one's faith. Clark Pinnock rightly asserts, "Experience alone is too flimsy a base on which to rest the

---

[38] James Orr, *The Christian View of God and the World* (New York: Scribner's Sons, 1893) 20.

[39] Dallas Willard, *Renovation of the Heart: Putting on the Character of Christ* (Colorado Springs: NavPress, 2002) 117.

[40] Carnell, *An Introduction to Christian Apologetics*, 88.

[41] Willard, *Renovation of the Heart*, 138.

Christian system. The mere fact that a psychological event has taken place in one's brain cannot establish the truthfulness of the gospel."[42] Zacharias says, "We are fashioned by God to be thinking and emotional creatures. The emotions should follow reason, and not the other way around."[43]

John Stott writes "The contemporary craze for denigrating the mind and enthroning experience is in reality a subtle mode of 'worldliness' (because it is taken over from secular existentialism), and that God intends *truth* (His own revealed truth) to be the criterion of experience and to set our hearts on fire."[44] Stott wrote this in 1972. If he were writing it today he would say postmodernism instead of existentialism.

C.S. Lewis believed in mysticism. However he made clear a mystical experience did not validate religion. True religion gives value to mysticism.

Rationalism determined what early twentieth-century liberals could not believe (miracles, etc.). Their subjective experience became the basis for what they did believe about Christianity. In the mid-twentieth century several theological spin-offs of existentialism interpreted the faith from the viewpoint of subjective experience. In the twenty-first century religious postmodernists base faith on experience while minimizing or denying intellectual content and rational and historical basis.

Personal experience and emotions are important. The Christian faith is not true because it gives one peace and joy. It brings peace and joy because it is true. Such feelings are the fruit not the basis of faith. They confirm the truth of Christianity but feelings alone cannot constitute the initial establishment of Christian truth.

---

[42] Pinnock, *Set Forth Your Case*, 69.

[43] Ravi Zacharias, "An Apologetic for Apologetics," in *Beyond Opinion*, ed. Ravi Zacharias (Nashville: Thomas Nelson, 2007) xv.

[44] Timothy Dudley-Smith, *John Stott: A Global Ministry, A Biography: The Later Years* (Downers Grove, IL: InterVarsity, 2001) 187. Emphasis in the original.

Faith and Reason

The relationship between faith and reason has long been a matter of controversy. It is important because the conclusion we reach about this matter shapes our apologetic method. A look at various views will be instructive.

Reason without faith. This position rejects acceptance of testimony as a valid source of knowledge. This rationalism holds that reason is the only or at least primary source of knowledge. Atheist, George Smith sees the conflict between Christian theism and atheism at its essence as a conflict between faith and reason. He says,

> Reason and faith are opposites, two mutually exclusive terms: there is no reconciliation or common ground. Faith is belief without, or in spite of, reason. Explicit atheism is the consequence of a commitment to rationality—the conviction that man's mind is fully competent to know the facts of reality, and that no aspect of the universe is closed to rational scrutiny. Atheism is merely a corollary, a specific application, of one's commitment to reason.
>
> I will not accept the existence of God, or any doctrine, on faith because I reject faith as a valid cognitive procedure. The particular content or object of faith—whether it be gods, unicorns, or gremlins—is irrelevant in this context. The statement, "I will not accept the existence of God on faith" is derived from the wider statement, "I will not accept anything on faith." Thus, explicit atheism is primarily an epistemological position: if reason is one's only guide to knowledge, faith is necessarily excluded. If theistic doctrines must be accepted on faith, theism is necessarily excluded. A rational man will be without theistic belief, and therefore atheistic.[45]

He rejects miracles or anything which does not fit his naturalist reasoning. Rationalism, inadequate as it is, is a dogmatic, narrow-minded view which ignores the vast abundance of

---

[45] George H. Smith, *Atheism: The Case against God* (Los Angeles: Nash, 1974) 98.

factual data and valid information available through reliable witnesses. Christian faith is not rationalism. Neither is it irrational or contrary to reason.

In his attack on religious faith atheist Sam Harris says, "The truth is that religious faith is simply *unjustified* belief in matters of ultimate concern—specifically in propositions that promise some mechanism by which human life can be spared the ravages of time and death." He sees faith as credulity without the constraints of "reasonableness, internal coherence, civility, and candor." He accuses those with religious faith of ignorance, claiming they "disregard the facts of this world out of deference to the God who lurks in his mother's and father's imaginations."[46]

The Christian world, according to Harris,

> will not stoop to reason when it has no *good* reasons to believe. If a little supportive evidence emerges, however, the faithful prove as attentive to data as the damned. This demonstrates that faith is nothing more than a willingness to await the evidence—be it the Day of Judgment or some other downpour of corroboration. It is the search for knowledge on the installment plan: believe now, live an untestable hypothesis until your dying day, and you will discover that you were right.[47]

Faith without reason. It is popular today to divorce faith from reason. Many insist that reason cannot establish matters relating to ethics, religion, and values. They view matters of faith as personal and private while matters of reason are public. This view holds that a subjective part of man can make a valid response of faith which is separated from rational consideration and often contradictory to the world of reason and fact. This subjectivism is unacceptable because it opens the door to any superstition or foolishness. It provides no objective basis

---

[46] Harris, *End of Faith*, 65. Emphasis is in the original.
[47] Ibid., 66.

for distinguishing a true faith from a false faith. It destroys faith by making it unrelated to objective reality. Elton Trueblood said, "Revelation must be tested by reason for the simple reason that there are false claims to revelation."[48]

Faith before reason. According to this view man must assume or presuppose God. Then after believing in God his reason is free to see that Christian faith makes sense. Frequently this view emphasizes the depravity of man and the necessity of a miraculous regeneration by the Holy Spirit before one can believe. Many orthodox believers accept this presuppositional view. But it falls short because it argues in a circle. It assumes what it tries to establish. Fideism holds that one must assume or presuppose God rather than be able to come to faith in God based on reasons or evidences. Presuppositionalists, following Van Til, reject any common ground between Christian and non-Christian. They only present a negative apologetic of judgment to non-Christians. They affirm that nonbelievers are incapable of accepting and believing spiritual truth without the supernatural enablement of the Holy Spirit.

Why should we believe the reasons given for accepting presuppositionalism or fideism when fideists allege reasons are useless as a basis for faith? Using reasons to prove we shouldn't use reason is self-refuting. Believers should be able to present convincing evidence for faith in Christianity to non-Christians because the apostles presented reasons and evidences to unbelievers in persuading them of the truth of the gospel.

Faith based on reasonable evidence. Both reasoning and believing have a part to play in Christian faith. God himself called on people to test his revelation to see if it had the evidence of having come from him (for example, *Isaiah 41* and *Deuteronomy 18*). Jesus didn't say, "Just believe. Accept what I say." He said,

---

[48] David Elton Trueblood, *Philosophy of Religion* (New York: Harper and Brothers, 1957) 32.

"If I don't do the works of God, don't believe me" (*John 10:37*, paraphrase). The apostles appealed to the facts about Christ as a reasonable basis for a faith committed to Christ. Reason does not coerce faith, but Christian faith is not unreasonable.

Faith and Trust

Reason doesn't force the will. One can know good reasons why something is true, yet he or she refuses to act on this truth. Many persons acknowledge good reasons why they should quit smoking, but they continue to smoke. Many refuse to believe in Christianity in spite of good reasons to believe. Faith requires more than reasons and evidence. Genuine faith requires an act of the mind and will to accept and trust.

Faith as confidence. Mere assent is not full-bodied faith. Simple agreement with a truth or a person is not genuine faith. The demons believe and tremble (*Jas 2:19*). They accept as true that Jesus is the Son of God, but they do not submit in trusting obedience to Christ. The children of Israel said they believed that God was able to bring them into the Promised Land (*Numbers 14*), but their actions showed that they did not trust him to do so (*Hebrews 3*).

Faith as an avenue of knowledge is acceptance of information on the basis of testimony from another on a matter where we do not have direct knowledge. Faith confidently accepts the statement as true. Mere acceptance of the truth of a statement is not the same as trusting the person who makes the statement.

Faith as commitment. Faith reaches a higher level when confidence is expressed in commitment and trusting obedience. *Belief that* is confirmed by *belief in*. The highest level of faith is trust and reliance on a person in whom we trust. Saving faith involves confidence in the reality and truthfulness of God and Christ which issues in absolute commitment and submission in obedience to Christ as Lord.

McDowell and Williams write,

Reason cannot comprehend the concept of an intelligent being who has neither beginning nor end. But when reason examines the evidence, it can accept the concept of God as a rational necessity because nothing less will account for the existence of matter, life, and order. Based on this rational necessity, reason can rightly direct the mind to take the step beyond comprehension into belief.[49]

Norman Geisler notes,

Evidence of truth should precede faith. No rational person steps in a [sic] elevator without some reason to believe it will hold him up. No reasonable person gets on an airplane that is missing part of one wing and smells of smoke in the cabin. People deal in two dimensions of belief: *belief that* and *belief in*. *Belief that* gives the evidence and rational basis for confidence needed to establish *belief in*. Once *belief that* is established, one can place faith *in* it. Thus, the rational person wants evidence that God exists before he places his faith in God. Rational unbelievers want evidence that Jesus is the Son of God before they place their trust in him.[50]

Douglas Groothuis summarizes, "Christian faith involves both intellectual assent (*fides*) and personal trust (*fiducia*); in fact, the latter is logically dependent on the former for its rationale."[51]

Walter Hooper watched C.S. Lewis peacefully approach death. Hooper commented, "You know, you really do believe all the things you've written."

Lewis responded, "Of course! That's why I wrote them."[52]

---

[49] McDowell and Williams, *In Search of Certainty*, 122.

[50] Norman L. Geisler, *Baker Encyclopedia of Christian Apologetics*, 38.

[51] Douglas Groothuis, *Truth Decay: Defending Christianity against the Challenges of Postmodernism* (Downers Grove, IL: InterVarsity, 2000), 142.

[52] Charles Huttar, ed., *Imagination and the Spirit* (Grand Rapids: Eerdmans, 1971) 339.

Review Questions

1. What convinced Josh McDowell of the truth of Christian faith?

2. Describe the secularist's misunderstanding of faith.

3. Identify and briefly explain three elements in authentic faith.

4. How is faith a source of gaining knowledge?

5. How does *Hebrews 11:1* describe faith?

6. Give three definitions of faith. Which do you feel is most helpful?

7. Show how a genuine faith must have a basis in knowledge.

8. Cite a Scripture reference showing that faith without a factual basis is false.

9. Give an example showing the sequence of faith, facts, and feelings.

10. What are the dangers of basing faith only on emotion?

11. What important role do feelings and experience play in regard to faith?

12. Identify four positions in regard to faith and reason.

13. Refute the view of a person who claims to accept nothing on faith.

14. Which view do you accept—faith before reason or faith based on reasonable evidence—and why?

15. Show the importance of trust and commitment in genuine faith.

Suggested Reading

Geisler, Norman L. "Faith and Reason," *Baker Encyclopedia of Christian Apologetics*. Grand Rapids: Baker Books, 1999. Discussion of the relationship of faith and reason.

Howe, Thomas A., and Richard G. Howe. "Knowing Christianity Is True: The Relationship between Faith and Reason." In *To Everyone an Answer*, pp. 23-36. Downers Grove, IL: InterVarsity, 2004. Discusses the relationship between knowledge, reason, truth, and faith.

Machen, J. Gresham. *What Is Faith?* pp. 13-11. Grand Rapids: Eerdmans, 1925. Stresses the factual basis and the intellectual aspect of faith in answering the subjectivism of liberalism.

Montgomery, John Warwick. *Faith Founded on Fact: Essays in Evidential Apologetics*, pp. ix-42. Nashville: Thomas Nelson, 1978. "Can Faith Rest on Fact?" and "The Place of Reason in Christian Witness."

Moreland, J.P., and Klaus Issler. *In Search of a Confident Faith: Overcoming Barriers to Trusting in God*. Downers Grove, IL: InterVarsity, 2008. Drawing upon biblical, philosophical, and experiential data, the authors write to increase the reader's trust and confidence in God.

The Practice of
Apologetics

"But in your hearts regard Christ the Lord as holy, always being prepared to make a defense to anyone who asks you for a reason for the hope that is in you, yet do it with gentleness and respect."

1 Peter 3:15

"Contend for the faith that was once for all delivered to the saints."

Jude 3

10

Reasons for Apologetics

Reasons for Apologetics	"A century ago our task was to edify those who had been brought up in the Faith: our present task is chiefly to convert and instruct infidels."[1]
Profile: From Opposing Giving Reasons for Faith to Giving Reasons for Faith	
I. Objections to Apologetics	C.S. Lewis
A. Truth does not need to be defended	"There is communication, because there is a God who created us with the ability to communicate and understand, and who communicates to us. There is logic and rationality, because we are created
B. Christian faith is a matter of life and experience not lifeless facts or reasons	

[1] C.S. Lewis, "Christian Apologetics," in *God in the Dock: Essays on Theology and Ethics*, ed. Walter Hooper (Grand Rapids: Eerdmans, 1970) 94.

C. Christian faith is verified by subjective response, not by reason or history

D. Objective truth does not exist

E. It is wrong to look to miracles for evidence

F. All we need is faith. We don't need reasons for faith

G. Apologetics usurps the work of the Holy Spirit

H. Apologetics converts no one

I. Apologetics is not used in the Bible

II. Reasons for Apologetics

A. To obey biblical command and example

B. To honor and glorify God

C. To remove obstacles to faith for nonbelievers

D. To confirm the faith of believers

E. To equip Christians to defend their faith

in the image of God to rule the world, which requires understanding. We have reason for hope, and reason to be positive about our capacity both to understand and to be understood. So, even though our opponents might insist that a rational argument cannot operate upon them, or that linear discussion is not relevant, we can still have confidence that our rational argument can affect their minds. Even if popular wisdom tells us that no-one will be convinced by propositional apologetics, that the only thing people will react to is stories, Christians know that propositions can be convincing. We believe in a God who communicates both through propositions and history."[2]

K.R. Birkett

---

[2] K.R. Birkett, "Christian Apologetics: Is It Viable in a Post-Christian Culture?" in *New Dictionary of Christian Apologetics*, eds. W.C. Campbell-Jack and Gavin McGrath (Downers Grove, IL: InterVarsity, 2006) 31.

Profile: From Opposing Giving Reasons for Faith to Giving Reasons for Faith

Mark Mittelberg tells about two of his fellow graduate students who were philosophy of religion students in graduate school. They contended that apologetic arguments were ineffective in reaching nonbelievers. Since non-Christians start with secular presuppositions, they can never rationally "get to God from non-God." Mittelberg wondered why then they were spending so much time studying apologetics.

In exasperation he asked his friends separately if their view of what a nonbeliever could and could not understand was based on their reading alone or was it based on actual conversations with unbelievers. He states, "Both of these guys, at separate times and locations, hung their heads and acknowledged what I'd suspected—that, no, they had never really talked to any non-Christians to try out their answers on them. They'd been so convinced by certain professors and books that it wouldn't do any good, they hadn't tried."

A couple of years later Mittelberg visited one of these men who was then in a doctoral program in philosophy. The friend said his studies were going well. When the discussion turned to how he was getting along sharing his faith, he looked sheepish. He admitted that when he faced challenges to his faith from his atheistic professors, "It seems to make a lot of sense to actually give them reasons and answers for what we believe."[3]

Mittelberg observes:

Somehow being around people with genuine spiritual doubts and confusion helps us regain our bearings and

---

[3] Mark Mittelberg, "An Apologetic for Apologetics," *Reasons for Faith: Making a Case for the Christian Faith*, eds. Norman L. Geisler and Chad V. Meister (Wheaton, IL: Crossway, 2007) 22-23.

reminds us of our mission: to bring the truth of the gospel to bear so that real people—people in our families and in our neighborhoods, people we know at work or at school, people who are like us as well as those who are very different from us, people on the other side of the town, the county, the country, and the world—will believe and receive Christ.[4]

Does apologetics represent an unspiritual dependence upon human wisdom? Is it irrelevant academic philosophizing? Can apologetics play an important role in the evangelization of unbelievers and in strengthening faith and building spiritual maturity in believers?

Sean McDowell desiring to be biblically grounded and culturally relevant has wrestled with the challenge of postmodernism and the changes in our culture for the past fifteen years. He asks, "What does this *really* mean for ministry today? Certainly, as postmoderns like to emphasize, story, image, and community are critical components. But does it follow that we downplay reason, evidence, and apologetics? Absolutely not! . . . apologetics is more important than ever."[5]

In this chapter answers will be given to the objections that are raised against apologetics. I am giving an apologetic for apologetics. Objections to apologetics prove ineffective. Good reasons call us to commend and defend the truth of the Christian faith.

Objections to Apologetics

Critics express many objections to apologetics. Christianity, they say, ought not to be defended. Zacharias observes that many in Christian leadership

---

[4] Ibid., 23.

[5] Sean McDowell, *Apologetics for a New Generation: A Biblically & Culturally Relevant Approach to Talking about God* (Eugene, OR: Harvest House, 2009) 15.

. . . question the method and the impact of apologetics as it has been customarily used—or should I say misused? We hear it almost as a refrain: Doesn't apologetics focus on the intellect while abandoning the heart? Doesn't apologetics diminish the authority of the Bible itself while exalting reason? Doesn't apologetics end up displacing the role of the Holy Spirit in bringing conviction to the heart? Isn't it a discipline that feeds the pride of the individual? Don't we ultimately accept things by faith? When these queries are added up, apologetics is at best an illegitimate child in the household of faith and at worst a rogue who plunders the wealth of the faithful.[6]

When we carefully analyze the objections to defending Christian faith we can see they are unconvincing. Here are some arguments against apologetics.

Truth does not need to be defended. It can take care of itself. The following quotation attributed to Spurgeon has been used by those who reject apologetics: "Defend the Bible? I would as soon defend a lion!" It is held that the Bible should be preached and taught but needs no defense. *Hebrews 4:12, "The word of God is living and active,"* is given to support this view. Truth, it is alleged, can take care of itself.

Did the truth take care of itself against the attacks of unbelieving theologians and philosophers that left Europe largely without faith today? Did truth take care of itself when Hitler and Stalin advanced and exercised their dictatorial rule? False teachings have left many in America without faith as well. How can truth be distinguished from falsehood if there is no rational evidence and defense of the truth? Without reasons and evidence to establish something as true, we have no good reason to accept it as truth.

---

[6] Ravi Zacharias, *Is Your Church Ready? Motivating Leaders to Live an Apologetic Life,* eds. Ravi Zacharias and Norman Geisler (Grand Rapids: Zondervan, 2003) 21.

Christian faith is a matter of life and experience not lifeless facts or reasons. Theological liberals rejected apologetics, viewing Christianity as a matter of experience and ethics, not based on objective, historical events. Acceptance of a postmodernist view of knowing rejects a rational approach to truth opting for experience as a validation of spirituality. When Christianity is interpreted as an experience unrelated to its historical origin it loses its uniqueness and can be made to mean most anything.

Experience does not establish truth. We may have a sensation of falling down some steps. It may be a dream or it may in fact be happening. Personal experience must be interpreted by truth. A true understanding of our experience is the one that corresponds to reality. We need rational evidence to establish truth so we can know that our Christian experience is not fictional mysticism but rather solid reality.

When Lee Strobel was researching for his book, *The Case for Christ*, a respected theologian told him, "People don't care about historical evidence for Jesus anymore. They're more persuaded by experience and community than facts and reason." Yet his book has been a phenomenal best seller. Strobel reports that the largest group of persons influenced to become Christians by his book are sixteen to twenty-four-year-olds.[7] People still want to know if the gospel is true.

Christian truth is verified by subjective response not by reason or history. Those who reject the correspondence view of truth holding rather to a subjective view of truth generally reject rational apologetics. Existentialist, Neo-Orthodox, and postmodern thinkers reject apologetics because they base truth on subjective experience. The increase of subjectivism, relativism, and pluralism in the last two centuries has led to the devaluation of reason and to the denial of objective truth. This type of thinking has contributed to the rejection of apologetics by non-Christians and some Christians as well.

---

[7] Sean McDowell, *Apologetics for a New Generation*, 16.

Those who reject reason often quote Pascal's statement, "The heart has reasons, which reason does not know." Trueblood declares them mistaken because:

> Pascal, being himself an unusually keen rationalist, is not their ally. When he contrasts the reasons of the heart with the reasons of the head he is not denying reason, but instead seeking to show the necessity of the involvement of the entire person. In saying that reason, as ordinarily understood, is not all there is, he is not denying but rather supplementing it, 'We know truth,' he said, 'not only by the reason, but also by the heart.' Pascal would have been the last man to make a defense of unreason.[8]

Arnold Lunn reasons, "No irrationalist is consistent for, if he were, he would be forced to deduce from his own premises the conclusion that all that is of interest about his conviction that objective value is unobtainable is the irrational influences which led him to this conclusion."[9] Genuine Christian faith includes a subjective response, but faith does not exclude logical reasoning or evidence.

Zacharias states, "The one who argues against apologetics ends up using argument to denounce argument."[10] To those who insist that we can't argue people into the kingdom, I answer that we can give them reasons to believe.

Paul's statement, *"The world did not know God through wisdom"* (*1 Cor 1:21*) is used to support this objection. Paul does not mean that God cannot be known by human reason. He says the person who has not heard the gospel who doesn't acknowledge God is *"without excuse"* because of the obvious evidence for God's existence (*Rom 1:19-20*). Knowing God from

---

[8] Elton Trueblood, *A Place to Stand* (New York: Harper & Row, 1969) 30.
[9] Arnold Lunn, "An Apology for Apologetics," *Christian Counter-Attack*, Arnold Lunn and Garth Lean, eds. (New Rochelle, NY: Arlington House, 1969) 117.
[10] Ravi Zacharias, "An Apologetic for Apologetics," *Beyond Opinion: Living the Faith We Defend*, ed. by Ravi Zacharias (Nashville: Thomas Nelson, 2007) xi.

the evidence in nature is not a saving knowledge. We come to a saving knowledge of God only through Christ. The NT has abundant examples of giving reasons and evidence for believing Jesus is the Christ, the Son of God. See chapters 11 and 12.

Christian apologists do not claim to prove God in the sense of demonstrating with mathematical certainty. We do have adequate evidence, beyond a reasonable doubt, that God does in fact exist and Christianity is true.

Objective truth does not exist. Postmodernists (and those influenced by them) in recent times have declared rational, historical apologetics to be irrelevant because truth or meaning does not exist. We are told that rational and linear thought is out of date. Gutenberg is dead! Digital reigns. Images have replaced words as the medium of communication. It is very common today to hear popular church leaders say we cannot give reasons for faith because today's generation has rejected reason. They say what we must do is to tell stories. They say that metanarratives or worldviews claiming to be universally true are meaningless.

Are the postmodernists' universal statements to be accepted as true? Aren't they claiming that it is universally true that reason and science must be rejected while declaring that no universal truths exist? Though they claim to reject reason and words; they use words and reason to try to convince us. They give us their apologetics without good reason. The Enlightenment did not create reason, which now must be rejected. Many in the Enlightenment taught a rationalism which must be rejected. God gave us reason and appealed to rational evidences. Christ and the apostles appealed to reasons and evidence to establish the truth about Christ. We must follow the example of Christ and the apostles instead of the modern voices denying the validity of reason and the existence of objective truth.

It is wrong to look to miracles as evidence because Jesus rebuked those who sought for signs. The Jewish leaders stubbornly refused to believe in Jesus in spite of his many miracles. They ignored what he had done and insisted he do a sign on their demand. Carson notes, "Jesus was not a trained seal, happy to do tricks on cue."[11] It is arrogant for finite human beings to dictate to God what evidence would be convincing to them. Jesus said, *"An evil and adulterous generation seeks for a sign, but no sign will be given to it except the sign of the prophet Jonah" (Matt 12:39).* Jesus wasn't saying signs can't be a basis for faith. He offers the sign of his resurrection (*Matt 12:40*). Miracles are offered as evidence for believing (*Matt 9:6-7; 11:4-5,21-23; Mark 2:10-11; Luke 7:22; John 5:36; 10:24-25,37-38; 14:10-11; 15:24; 20:31; Acts 2:22; Heb 2:3-4*). Frequently in the Bible signs are given to establish the reality of God and the authority of his messengers.

All we need is faith. We don't need reasons for faith. The only way this objection carries any weight is for faith to be understood as blind faith or a self-created force or power one can generate. Saving faith is not empty faith. Those who have faith in faith consider gospel history and doctrinal truth irrelevant. Faith must have content. A saving faith in Jesus must include believing he died on the cross and rose from the dead (*Rom 10:9; 1 Cor 15:1-19*). Believing in a false Christ or a false gospel will not save (*Gal 1:6-9; Matt 7:15-23*). Christian faith must be based on truth.

Apologetics usurps the work of the Holy Spirit. Extreme Calvinists see apologetics as competing with the Holy Spirit. They see faith as produced by the Holy Spirit alone and claim the Bible is self-authenticating. How do we know the Bible is the Word of God instead of the Book of Mormon or the Qur'an? Mormons use the "burning breast" argument. Read the book of

---

[11] D.A. Carson, *God with Us: Themes from Matthew* (Ventura, CA: Regal Books, 1985) 73.

Mormon and see if it moves you. We would not accept the word of Mormons or Muslims who say their books are inspired and self-authenticated. We would demand evidence.

The Holy Spirit does not make evidence unnecessary. Carnell said, "The Spirit of God draws men *through* the convicting power of evidence."[12] The Spirit of Truth works through evidence addressed to minds to reach people. The evidence does not save. It does provide a basis so the person who is willing to believe can believe.

Machen said,

> Argument alone is quite insufficient to make a man a Christian. You may argue with him from now until the end of the world; you may bring forth the most magnificent arguments—but all will be in vain unless there is one other thing: the mysterious, creative power of the Holy Spirit in the new birth. But because argument is insufficient, it does not follow that it is unnecessary. Sometimes it is used directly by the Holy Spirit to bring a man to Christ. But more frequently it is used indirectly. A man hears an answer to objections raised against the truth of the Christian religion, and at the time when he hears it he is not impressed. But afterwards, perhaps many years afterwards, his heart at last is touched: he is convicted of sin; he desires to be saved. Yet without that half-forgotten argument he could not believe; the gospel would not seem to him to be true, and he would remain in his sin. As it is, however, the thought of what he has heard long ago comes into his mind; Christian apologetics at last has its day; the way is open, when he will believe he can believe because he has been made to see that believing is not an offense against truth.[13]

Apologetics converts no one. While apologetic arguments do not convince everyone, it is not true that no one is converted by

---

[12] Edward Carnell, *Introduction to Christian Apologetics*, 4th ed. (Grand Rapids: Eerdmans, 1952) 8. Emphasis in original.

[13] J. Gresham Machen, "Christian Scholarship and Evangelism," *Selected Shorter Writings: J. Gresham Machen*, ed. by D.G. Hart (Phillipsburg, NJ: P&R Publishing, 2004) 144-145.

apologetics. Many examples can be given where apologetics was a handmaiden in bringing nonbelievers to Christian faith. Many, including Augustine, C.S. Lewis, Frank Morison, Francis Schaeffer, Josh McDowell, Nancy Pearcey, and Lee Strobel have testified that apologetics helped bring them to Christ. C.S. Lewis says most of the people he knew who had accepted Christianity as adults had been influenced by an argument for theism.[14]

Apologetics is not used in the Bible. Apologetics is used in the Bible. Chapter 11 and 12, in describing NT apologetics, will demonstrate this objection to be false.

Reasons for Apologetics

Giving a reason for our Christian faith and hope is an expression of loving God with our minds. It presents to unbelievers the truth of the Christian faith and confirms and strengthens the faith of believers. We will consider five good reasons for commending and defending the faith.

To obey biblical command and example. Jesus healed the paralyzed man (*Mark 2*) as an evidence that he had the authority to forgive sins. Hazen points out,

Jesus' goal on this occasion and on many that followed (e.g., Mt 11:2-5; Lk 7:18-23; Jn 3:2; 5:31-36; 10:38; 15:24-25) was to help those in attendance have good reason to "know" that he had authority from God and, by implication in the case of the paralytic, that he was the divine Son of God. Jesus provided reasons to believe through many different means, the most dramatic of which were miracles done in public as authentication of his message, identity and authority. Of course Jesus' prediction of his death and resurrection (Mt 12:39-40; Lk 11:29-30; Jn 2:18-22; etc.) which he overtly labeled *"the sign"* to a wicked generation, took this to the highest level.[15]

---

[14] Lewis, *God in the Dock,* 173.

[15] Craig J. Hazen, "Defending the Defense of the Faith," in *To Everyone an Answer,* eds. Francis J. Beckwith, William Lane Craig, and J.P. Moreland (Downers Grove, IL: InterVarsity, 2004) 38-39.

Jesus demonstrated the truth of his message and his identity over and over again using nearly every method at his disposal, including miracle, prophecy, godly style of life, authoritative teaching *and* reasoned argumentation.[16]

J.P. Moreland points out,

Scripture commands us to defend the faith and gives us several examples of such activity. . . . The Old Testament prophets often appealed to the facts of history, prophecy, creation, or providence to reason with other nations. . . . In the New Testament, Jesus authenticated his own credentials by urging people to consider his works. He met honest questions with evidence, as is seen in his encounter with Thomas. In Acts, Paul reasoned with unbelievers and gave evidence for the gospel by appealing to creation and the facts surrounding Jesus' life and resurrection. Jude 3 and 1 Peter 3:15 explicitly command us to contend for the faith by giving a rational answer to those who question our faith.[17]

Defending the faith is a command not a suggestion. (See *Phil 1:27; Eph 6:11,13; 1 Tim 6:20; 2 Tim 4:7; Titus 1:9.*)

Clark Pinnock says, "The earliest believers called men to an intelligent faith. They pressed boldly the claims of Jesus Christ as they had been dramatically verified by the fact of the resurrection."[18] "Paul, John, and Peter seemed almost obsessed with offering evidence, testimony and argument at every turn in order to establish the truth of the gospel message."[19]

To those who advocate we should not defend the faith but only propagate it, Machen says, "Christianity that avoids argument is not the Christianity of the New Testament. The New Testament is full of argument in defense of the faith. . . . Every-

---

[16] Ibid., 39.

[17] J.P. Moreland, *Scaling the Secular City: A Defense of Christianity* (Grand Rapids: Baker, 1987) 11-12.

[18] Clark Pinnock, *Set Forth Your Case*, rev. ed. (Chicago: Moody Press, 1971) 8.

[19] Hazen, "Defending the Defense of the Faith," 40.

where the New Testament meets objections fairly and presents the gospel as a thoroughly reasonable thing."[20]

Church elders must be able to exercise an apologetic ministry, *"He must hold firm to the trustworthy word as taught so that he may be able to give instruction in sound doctrine and also to rebuke those who contradict it"* (**Titus 1:9**). *"And the Lord's servant must not be quarrelsome but kind to everyone, able to teach, patiently enduring evil, correcting his opponents with gentleness. God may perhaps grant them repentance leading to a knowledge of the truth"* (**2 Tim 2:24-25**).

To honor and glorify God. In setting forth the truth and beauty of Christianity we exalt God. Apologetics is not seeking to glorify the apologist by winning an argument. It is not a game of one-upmanship. When so many ignore God, deny him, dishonor him, misrepresent him, and even blaspheme and defame him—we who love truth and the living God must defend and proclaim the truth about God. We cannot be indifferent to the slurs and slanders against our God. We honor God when we stand up for his truth.

To remove obstacles hindering non-Christians from believing in Christ. Many have rejected Christ because of ignorance of the gospel, because the facts of Christianity have been misrepresented to them, or because of their false presuppositions. Apologetics seeks to remove any barriers which unbelievers use as a basis for their unbelief. If Christians are silent to the attacks against Christianity made by the enemies of God, then many will think that these attacks are valid. Christianity loses by default in this case. Christians need to answer the objections offered by critics so that if persons continue to disbelieve it will be a choice of unbelief rather than a stumbling block based on misinformation. The presentation of Christian evidences and

---

[20] J. Gresham Machen, *What Is Christianity?* (Grand Rapids: Eerdmans, 1951) 127.

apologetic arguments is evangelistic in that it seeks to remove the intellectual barriers to Christian faith and to provide a basis for an intelligent saving faith.

Arnold Lunn comments that in spite of the antirational mood of our age, it is "the duty of those who are capable of effectively stating the rational case for Christianity to continue to use the reason God gave them in defense not only of God but also of reason itself."[21] He continues,

> Fortunately the number of those who can be influenced by rational argument is far greater than the more timid of our Christian defeatists suspect. Every experienced apologist knows from his own personal contacts, in person or by letter, that the rational case for Christianity is an important, and in many cases the most important factor in the conversion of sceptics and also, be it noted, in the preventing the perversion of doubting Christians.[22]

Presenting reasons for faith is not sufficient to convert one, but neither is it unnecessary. By removing obstacles and hindrances we open the way to faith for those who are willing to believe. We want to convince unbelievers of the truth of Christianity and bring them to a commitment to the One who is the Way, the Truth and the Life.

J.P. Moreland said, "Apologetics can help remove obstacles to faith and thus aid unbelievers in embracing the gospel. . . . Ambassadors for Christ are not excused from the responsibility of defending the gospel. The Spirit can use evidence to convict men of the truth of the proclamation."[23]

Some intellectual objections are only a smokescreen to hide a moral rebellion against God (*Rom 1:20-21,25,28*). Paul Little states:

---

[21] Lunn, "An Apology for Apologetics," 118-119.

[22] Ibid., 119.

[23] Moreland, *Scaling the Secular City*, 12.

The moral issue always overshadows the intellectual issue in Christianity. It is not that man *cannot* believe—it is that he *will* not believe. Jesus pointed the Pharisees to this as the root of the problem, "Ye *will* not come to me." He told them, "That ye might have life" (Jn 5:40). He makes it abundantly clear that moral commitment leads to a solution of the intellectual problem. "If any man *will* (wants to) do His will, he shall *know* of the doctrine, whether it be of God or whether I speak of myself" (Jn 7:17). Alleged intellectual problems are often a smoke screen covering moral rebellion.

A student once told me I had satisfactorily answered all his questions. "Are you going to become a Christian?" I asked. "No," he replied. Puzzled, I asked, "Why not?" He admitted, "Frankly, because it would mess up the way I'm living." He realized that the real issue for him was not intellectual but moral.[24]

We need to remove the excuses for not believing or repenting, realizing that we cannot force either faith or repentance.

An important hindrance keeping many from accepting Christian faith is ignorance of Christianity. They do not know the essentials of Christianity and have not studied an effective apologetic for Christianity. Commending and defending Christian faith requires correcting misunderstandings of Christianity and clearly stating basic Christianity. C.S. Lewis emphasized the need for an intelligent defense of the faith observing that

> to be ignorant and simple now—not to be able to meet the enemies on their own ground—would be to throw down our weapons, and to betray our uneducated brethren who have, under God, no defence but us against the intellectual attacks of the heathen. Good philosophy must exist, if for no other reason, because bad philosophy needs to be answered.[25]

[24] Paul Little, *Know Why You Believe*, 3rd ed. (Downers Grove, IL: InterVarsity, 1988) 18.
[25] C.S. Lewis, *The Weight of Glory* (Grand Rapids: Eerdmans, 1949) 50.

Machen said, "Controversy of the right sort is good; for out of such controversy, as Church history and Scripture alike teach, there comes the salvation of souls."[26] History refutes the idea that the church will not grow in times of controversy. The Protestant Reformation and the First and Second Great Awakenings demonstrate this. Lost people can only know the saving truth when believers stand up and share that truth.

Apologetics does not save people. It is not the basis of salvation. But it can play a vital and valuable role in preparing the person's mind and heart so he or she can believe the gospel.

To confirm the faith of believers. Learning Christian evidences and apologetics can bring reassurance to believers. As those who have inherited Christianity as a family faith mature, they come to a point where they need to make their beliefs their own. Accepting Christianity on an emotional or social basis makes one vulnerable at a time when he or she questions whether it is really true or not. Reexamining why we believe does not mean rejecting everything about our faith. It does mean searching for answers to our questions. Can we have intelligent reasons for believing Christianity is true? Becoming convinced that our Christian faith is valid and true issues in a robust faith and vibrant spiritual maturity.

Many Christians are troubled in their faith by the charges and objections of the critics as well as doubts that arise in their own hearts. It can be a real strength and relief to learn that the objections can be answered and non-Christian positions can be shown to be invalid. It is no sin to doubt, but we must ask our honest questions and find answers. It is worse to suppress doubts because of fear because unresolved doubts can become termites eroding the foundation of our faith. We must show Christians that the attacks of the critics against God, Christ,

---

[26] J. Gresham Machen, *What Is Faith?* (Grand Rapids: Eerdmans, 1925) 42-43.

and the Bible are not true. Love compels us to rescue those who have a weakened and wounded faith.

Moreland says, "Apologetics can strengthen believers in at least two ways. For one thing, it gives them confidence that their faith is true and reasonable; therefore, apologetics encourages a life of faith seeking understanding. Further, apologetics can actually encourage spiritual growth."[27] The teaching of Christian apologetics can help believers see the world with a Christian worldview rather than through secular eyes.

Enemies of the faith are within the Christian movement as well as on the outside. We must answer legitimate questions, refute error, and show the invalidity of critical attacks. We must confront in love those who are slipping into dangerous compromises in their faith. Giving a reasonable factual basis for faith can help rescue those whose faith has been shaken.

What the Study of Apologetics Can Do for Believers

✧ It helps us grow in understanding our own beliefs as we learn about the evidence, the Bible, and other belief systems in the effort to help our friends move toward Christ.

✧ It gives us clarity on what we believe, much as a final test in school helps us pull together all that we've learned—or should have learned—during the semester.

✧ It gives us confidence concerning why we believe what we believe as our faith stands up to scrutiny and challenges.

✧ It gives us spiritual stability, preventing us from being *"tossed back and forth by the waves, and blown here and there by every wind of teaching . . ."* (Eph 4:14).

✧ It matures us in our faith and helps shape us for leadership in the church as ones who can *"encourage others by sound doctrine and refute those who oppose it"* (Titus 1:9).

✧ It expands our capacity to *"love . . . God . . . with all [our] mind . . ."* (Matt 22:37).

Mark Mittelberg[28]

---

[27] Moreland, *Scaling the Secular City*, 12.
[28] Mittelberg, "An Apologetic for Apologetics," 23.

To equip Christians to defend their faith. Recently best-selling books by atheists Christopher Hitchens, Sam Harris, and Richard Dawkins have attacked Christian faith. Sean McDowell says, "Their writings have wreaked havoc on many unprepared Christians. This has taken place while many inside the church have neglected the need to defend the faith intellectually."[29]

You may not be troubled by the objections of unbelievers, but many are. You should prepare yourself as best you can to help those Christians and non-Christians alike who have intellectual problems. Those you save may be members of your own household.

Tools and methods should be given to Christians to help them defend their faith. We need to help believers defend what they believe. Give them resources to enable them to help those troubled by the hostile voices. See chapter 16 on Practical Uses of Apologetics.

A few years ago Donald McGavran warned,

Standardless pluralism challenges not only the entire missionary enterprise, but also all Christian churches here in the United States and throughout the world. . . . Indeed, Christians everywhere have such a large stake in the battle that they ought to understand what is going on. Christian colleges and seminaries should provide their students with a reasoned defense of the Christian position. Churches should educate their members in today's danger.[30]

The study of apologetics should include preparation for answering current objections to Christianity. Tim Keller in *Reason for God* gives clear and convincing responses to the following current objections to Christian faith. After completing *Commending and Defending Christian Faith* as introductory study of apologetics, additional study should include answers to such objections.

---

[29] Sean McDowell, *Apologetics for a New Generation*, 16.
[30] Donald McGavran, *The Clash between Christianity and Culture* (Washington, DC: Canon Press, 1974) 15.

Current Objections to Christianity

1. There can't be just *one* true religion.
2. How could a good God allow suffering?
3. Christianity is a straitjacket.
4. The church is responsible for so much injustice.
5. How can a loving God send people to hell?
6. Science has disproved Christianity.
7. You can't take the Bible literally.

Tim Keller, *Reason for God*[31]

Popular books by atheists, for example Christopher Hitchens and Richard Dawkins, have emphasized the injustice and cruelty caused by religion. Because of the publicity given to these atheists, many mistakenly think their objections are valid. We need to educate believers to challenge atheists with the facts of atrocities conducted by atheists. The atheist regime of Stalin and other Russian communists murdered some fifty million people. Also, Mao Tse Tung in the cultural revolution in China, and Pol Pot's killing fields in Cambodia. We must ask the hard questions that expose the bankruptcy of unbelief. It does not produce the paradise that John Lennon envisioned in his famous song "Imagine." Those who do not believe in God have no way to motivate and produce self-discipline in people to behave decently and morally.

Christian believers are continually under attack from naturalistic science. We need to help Christians know that no new scientific facts refute Christianity, yet several discoveries are devastating to naturalism. Attacks on Christianity are often old objections in new dress. Those who commend and defend Christian faith must continue to study and prepare to answer the objections that are being currently voiced.

---

[31] Tim Keller, *The Reason for God* (New York: Dutton, 2008) 3-114.

K.R. Birkett contends that Christian apologetics is viable in a post-Christian culture:

> Non-Christians are frequently surprised by how substantial the Christian philosophy is. The secular media provide little idea about what Christianity says and generally assume it is just as weak as any other answer. We practise Christianity in the midst of misunderstanding and misinformation, in which our beliefs are seen at worst immoral and at best outdated. It is our task, our powerful, convincing task, to demonstrate otherwise.[32]

The objections to apologetics are not valid. We have important and compelling reasons for commending and defending Christian faith. We need to make sure we conduct our apologetics to glorify God and to extend the kingdom of our Lord Jesus Christ.

Review Questions

1. What change occurred in the thinking of Mittelberg's friend described in the Profile?
2. Give examples in history when truth did not take care of itself.
3. Explain the relationship between experience and truth.
4. Why does subjectivism lead to the rejection of apologetics?
5. Some say Pascal opposed rational apologetics. How did Trueblood respond to that view?
6. Does a Christian's subjective response to Christ rule out a rational basis?
7. Show that Paul is not against apologetics.

[32] Birkett, "Christian Apologetics," 34.

8. Explain the postmodernist rejection of rational apologetics.

9. Explain why Jesus sometimes refused to do signs and at other times emphasized his signs.

10. Why is blind faith insufficient?

11. Respond to the charge that apologetics usurps the work of the Holy Spirit.

12. Give examples of persons who testify that apologetics helped them come to Christian faith.

13. List five reasons for apologetics.

14. Quote a NT verse commanding defending the faith.

15. What apologetic role is stated as part of the elder's responsibility?

16. How does apologetics honor and glorify God?

17. Apologetics doesn't coerce faith, but how can it help unbelievers come to faith?

18. C.S. Lewis says good philosophy must exist for what reason?

19. In what ways does apologetics prove beneficial to believers?

20. What are the seven current objections to Christianity listed by Tim Keller?

Suggested Reading

Birkett, K.R. "Christian Apologetics: Is It Viable in a Post-Christian Culture?" *New Dictionary of Christian Apologetics*, 29-34. Eds. W.C. Campbell-Jack and Gavin McGrath. Downers Grove, IL: InterVarsity, 2006. Discusses the nature of apologetics needed in our largely post-Christian culture.

Geisler, Norman L. *Baker Encyclopedia of Christian Apologetics.* Grand Rapids: Baker Books, 1999. "Apologetics, Need for," 37-41. God commands apologetics and the world needs it. Objections to apologetics are answered.

Hazen, Craig J. "Defending the Defense of the Faith." In *To Everyone an Answer,* 37-46. Ed. by Francis J. Beckwith, William Lane Craig, and J.P. Moreland. Downers Grove, IL: InterVarsity, 2004. Documents biblical use of apologetics and answers objections to apologetic engagement.

Lewis, C.S. *God in the Dock.* Grand Rapids: Eerdmans, 1970. Essay on "Christian Apologetics" (89-103) insists that Christians must uphold the truth and not twist Christian beliefs to fit the current fashion of thinking.

Mittelberg, Mark. "An Apologetic for Apologetics." In *Reasons for Faith: Making a Case for the Christian Faith,* 17-26. Ed. by Norman L. Geisler and Chad V. Meister. Wheaton, IL: Crossway, 2007. Emphasizes the need for apologetics motivated by the love for God and for people.

Trueblood, David Elton. *A Place to Stand,* 13-36. New York: Harper and Row, 1969. Insists on a rational defense of Christianity and criticizes subjectivism's copout on apologetics.

Zacharias, Ravi. "An Apologetic for Apologetics." In *Beyond Opinion: Living the Faith We Defend,* xi-xx. Ed. by Ravi Zacharias. Nashville: Thomas Nelson, 2007. We need to live what we defend. Apologetics is seeing things God's way, and it is not only for experts.

*"If I am not doing the works of my Father,
then do not believe me; but if I do them,
even though you do not believe me, believe the works,
that you may know and understand that
the Father is in me and I am in the Father."*

John 10:37-38

*"For we did not follow cleverly devised myths when we
made known to you the power and coming of our Lord
Jesus Christ, but we were eyewitnesses of his majesty."*

2 Peter 1:16

11

New Testament Apologetics: Jesus and Peter

New Testament Apologetics: **Jesus and Peter** Profile: John Stott—Christ and Scripture Introduction: Old Testament Apologetics I. Apologetics of Jesus A. Appeal to testimony B. Appeal to miracles C. Appeal to his resurrection	"Anyone who makes a truth claim—to say nothing about a claim to absolute truth (John 14:6)—must provide evidence for that claim. Jesus does exactly that, and in so doing, he provides a pattern for apologetics that is of great value to the contemporary defender of the Christian faith."

D. Appeal to prophecy
E. Use of reasoning
F. Refutation of false views
G. The evidence of his life
II. Apologetics of Peter
  A. Peter's preaching and teaching in the book of Acts
  B. Peter's exhortations in his letters
	"Jesus is an evidentialist, not a fideist, in that he believes in the use of evidence to convince others of the truth of his claims."[1]
	<div align="right">Norman L. Geisler &
	Patrick Zukeran</div>
	"The purpose of studying His [Jesus'] controversies is to make sure that the principles on which He took His stand are those which we are seeking to maintain today."[2]
	<div align="right">John R. W. Stott</div>

Profile: John Stott—Christ and Scripture

John Stott, British preacher and evangelical church leader, wrote *Basic Christianity*, that has two million copies in print, to help searchers know the truth of Christianity. He suggests starting one's inquiry with the person of Christ for two reasons. One reason is "essentially Christianity is Christ." He continues:

Secondly, if Jesus Christ can be shown to have been a uniquely divine person, many other problems begin naturally to be solved. The existence of God is proved and the character of God is revealed if Jesus is divine. Again, questions touching man's duty and destiny, the life after death, the purpose and authority of the Old Testament and the meaning of the cross begin to be answered

[1] Norman L. Geisler and Patrick Zukeran, *The Apologetics of Jesus: A Caring Approach to Dealing with Doubters* (Grand Rapids: Baker Books, 2009) 13, 25.
[2] John R.W. Stott, *Christ the Controversialist* (Downers Grove, IL: InterVarsity, 1970) 49.

because Jesus taught about these things, and His teaching must be authoritative if His person is divine.[3]

He does not ask the seeker to begin assuming the Gospels are inspired Scriptures but accepting them as historical documents. He identifies the divine claims of Jesus and then marshals evidence to establish his deity.

Stott based his belief in the Bible as God's word written on the authority of Christ. He believed it is right and reasonable to submit to the authority of Scripture. He writes,

> First, to accept the authority of the Bible is a Christian thing to do. It is neither a religious eccentricity, nor a case of discreditable obscurantism, but the good sense of Christian faith and humility. It is essentially "Christian" because it is what Christ himself requires of us. The traditional view of Scripture (that it is God's word written) may be called the "Christian" view precisely because it is Christ's view.[4]

> The ultimate issue in the question of authority concerns the lordship of Christ. "You call me 'Teacher' and 'Lord,'" he said, "and you are right, for so I am" (John 13:13). If Jesus Christ is truly our teacher and our lord, we are under both His instruction and His authority. We must therefore bring our mind into subjection to Him as our teacher and our will into subjection to Him as our lord. We have no liberty to disagree with Him or to disobey Him. So we bow to the authority of Scripture because we bow to the authority of Christ.[5]

As we seek to commend and defend Christian faith we must make sure we are advocating the truth about Jesus Christ and are faithful to what he taught about Scripture.

[3] John R.W. Stott, *Basic Christianity* (Grand Rapids: Eerdmans, 1958) 7, 20-21.
[4] John R.W. Stott, *Understanding the Bible* (Glendale, CA: Regal Books, G/L Publications, 1972) 202.
[5] Ibid., 203. See Timothy Dudley-Smith, *John Stott: The Making of a Leader, A Biography: The Early Years* (Downers Grove, IL: InterVarsity, 1999) 354-357.

The apologetics of the OT provides the background for the apologetics of the NT. God himself introduced miracles and fulfilled prophecy as evidence of his reality and as credentials verifying a messenger as a spokesman for God.

When God wanted Moses to deliver the Israelites from Egypt, Moses protested, *"But behold, they will not believe me or listen to my voice, for they will say, 'The LORD did not appear to you.'"* God turned Moses' rod into a serpent and then back to a rod *"that they may believe that the LORD, the God of their fathers, the God of Abraham, the God of Isaac, and the God of Jacob, has appeared to you"* (*Exod 4:1,5*). God sent the plagues as divine manifestations to convince Pharaoh and the Egyptians of his reality. *"By this you shall know that I am the LORD. . . . the Egyptians shall know that I am the LORD"* (*Exod 7:17; 14:4*).

In the contest between Elijah and the prophets of Baal on Mount Carmel the evidence of miracle distinguished the true God from the false god. Elijah asked the people, *"How long will you go limping between two different opinions? If the LORD is God, follow him, but if Baal, then follow him"* (*1 Kgs 18:21*). Elijah instructed that two bulls be killed and each one placed on an altar. *"You call on the name of your god and I will call on the name of the LORD; and the God who answers by fire, he is God"* (*1 Kgs 18:24*).

After the prophets of Baal failed, Elijah said, *"O LORD, God of Abraham, Isaac and Israel, let it be known this day that you are God in Israel. . . . Answer me, O LORD, answer me, that this people may know that you, O LORD are God"* (*1 Kgs 18:36-37*). God sent fire from heaven to consume the bull and the altar. The people acknowledged, *"The LORD, he is God; the LORD, he is God"* (*1 Kgs 18:39*).

Fulfilled predictive prophecy validated a true prophet. A prophecy that did not come to pass identified a false prophet (*Deut 13:1-5; 18:14-22; Isa 41:20; 48:3-5; Ezek 6:7*).

God's spokesmen declare that the power and revelation of the living God distinguishes him from lifeless and powerless pagan gods. The Lord of history controls the destinies of men and nations. God knows what will come to pass in the future but the idol knows nothing about the future. The prophets refute false gods. Isaiah taunts the pagan gods to tell the future *"that we may know that you are gods."* He asked them to act so that *"we may be dismayed and terrified."* But because they were lifeless, Isaiah concludes, *"Behold, you are nothing"* (**Isa 41:23-24**). Habakkuk comments about speechless idols, *"Woe to him who says to a wooden thing, Awake; to a dumb stone, Arise! Can this teach? Behold, it is overlaid with gold and silver, and there is no breath at all in it"* (**Hab 2:19**).

Bernard Ramm summarizes the OT apologetic, "God's action in history, God's revelation through his prophets, and God's creation and control of the universe are the criteria that show Him to be the living Lord, whereas the pagan gods and idols are speechless, powerless, and helpless."[6] The OT provides the background and basis for NT apologetics.

Those who seek to be defenders of Christianity need to look to the NT to learn how the Christian faith was confirmed and defended by Jesus, the apostles, and early preachers. In the next two chapters I will investigate NT apologetics: its purpose, emphasis, and approach. This chapter will focus on the apologetics of Jesus and Peter. Chapter 12 will discuss the apologetics of Paul and others. As God's Word the NT should be our standard for faith and practice. We need to study the NT teaching and examples to find guidance for the practice of apologetics today.

F.F. Bruce observes that the main lines of argument used by apologists in the early centuries of the church were already present in the first century. He said that a study of the apologetics of the NT "will help us to discover lines along which the defence of the gospel and other forms of Christian witness

---

[6] Bernard Ramm, "Apologetics, Biblical," in *The International Standard Bible Encyclopedia*, ed. by Geoffrey Bromiley (Grand Rapids: Eerdmans, 1979) 1:190.

should be conducted in our own day, when necessary allowances have been made for the differing situations of the first and twentieth [now twenty-first] centuries."[7] J.K.S. Reid said that looking at the apologetic elements in the NT helps us see the "justification and the continued validity of apologetics."[8]

Avery Dulles observes:

Unlike the apologists of the next centuries, the NT writers do not engage in arguments with unbelievers or vacillating believers as to why one should be a Christian. . . . it is sufficient to affirm at the outset that a careful study of the NT throws considerable indirect evidence on the way in which the infant Church carried out her apologetical encounter with Judaism, with paganism, and with deviant tendencies that arose within the Christian community. This is apparent from the apologetically significant themes that are present, in a diffused way, throughout the New Testament.[9]

Apologetics of Jesus

Christ as Lord stands at the heart of Christianity. His approach to commending and defending Christian faith should be a model for us as we follow him. Geisler and Zukeran observe,

Those who oppose apologetics in favor of a leap of faith without evidence will be disappointed in Jesus. Nowhere does he call on anyone to make an unthoughtful and unreasoned decision about his or her eternal destiny. Everywhere Jesus demonstrates a willingness to provide evidence for what he taught to every sincere seeker.[10]

Appeal to testimony. After Jesus healed the lame man at the pool of Bethesda, the Jews challenged his claims because he

---

[7] F.F. Bruce, *The Defense of the Gospel in the New Testament*, rev. ed. (Grand Rapids: Eerdmans, 1977) viii.
[8] J.K.S. Reid, *Christian Apologetics* (Grand Rapids: Eerdmans, 1969) 15.
[9] Avery Dulles, *A History of Apologetics* (San Francisco: Ignatius Press, 2005) 1.
[10] Geisler and Zukeran, *The Apologetics of Jesus*, 11.

healed on the Sabbath. They charged Jesus with blasphemy because he made himself equal with God (*John 5:18*). Jesus responded by making clear his divine claims:

✧ He does what the Father does,
✧ He gives life to whom he pleases,
✧ He is the Judge of human destinies,
✧ To honor the Father one must honor him, and
✧ He gives eternal life to those who hear and believe his word (*John 5:19-24*).

Jewish law required two or three witnesses (*Deut 19:15*). In his speech in *John 5:31-47*, Jesus cited the testimony of John the Baptist (*vv. 33,35*), his own works (*v. 36*), God the Father (*vv. 36-38*), the OT Scriptures (*v. 39*), and Moses (*vv. 45-46*) as evidence validating his divine claims.

John the Baptist's testimony was that Jesus was *"the Lamb of God who takes away the sin of the world! . . . I have seen and have borne witness that this is the Son of God"* (*John 1:29,34*). In appealing to his works he may have meant his whole ministry but certainly he referred to his miraculous signs. God used miracles as credentials to validate his message and messengers. At Jesus' baptism the voice of God declared, *"This is my beloved Son, with whom I am well pleased"* (*Matt 3:17*; cp. *Mark 1:11; Luke 3:22*). Later at the transfiguration the Father also testified of the Son (*Matt 17:5; Luke 9:35*). As God's plan of redemption developed in OT history, it was punctuated with prophecies pointing forward to the coming Christ. Jesus fulfilled the Law and the prophets (*Matt 5:17*). He concluded his case by appealing to Moses, *"If you believed Moses, you would believe me; for he wrote of me. But if you do not believe his writing, how will you believe my words?"* (*John 5:46-47*).

Leon Morris quotes Ryle's comment, "Nowhere else in the Gospels do we find our Lord making such a formal, systematic, orderly, regular statement of His own unity with the Father,

His divine commission and authority, and the proofs of His Messiahship, as we find in this discourse."[11]

After Jesus claimed to be the Light of the world, the Jews reject his words because they said he was testifying on his own behalf (*John 8:13*). Jesus affirmed he is telling the truth (*John 8:14*). But he does appeal to the testimony of God (*John 8:19,54*). Jesus said, *"You seek to kill me, a man who has told you the truth that I heard from God"* (*John 8:40*). In contrast to the lying nature of the devil, Jesus told the truth. He questioned, *"Which one of you convicts me of sin?"* (*John 8:46*). His sinless life backed up his claims. He shocked the Jews by saying that Abraham rejoiced to see his day (*John 8:56*).

"Witness is a pivotal concept in John's Gospel and the reason for this is clear: the signs Jesus performed are thoroughly attested by many witnesses; therefore, these miracles cannot be simply dismissed or explained away."[12]

Appeal to miracles. A miracle is an event in the external world, worked by the direct power of God, intended as a sign. The disciples believed in Jesus as a result of the miracle of changing the water into wine (*John 1:11*). Nicodemus told Jesus, *"We know that you are a teacher come from God, for no one can do these signs that you do unless God is with him"* (*John 3:2*).

Friends brought a paralyzed man to be healed. They lowered the man on a pallet through a hole in the roof in front of Jesus. Jesus announced to the man, *"My son, your sins are forgiven."* The Pharisees considered it blasphemy because only God can forgive sins. But how could you tell that his sins were forgiven? The man still looked the same. So they could *"know that the Son of Man has authority on earth to forgive sins"* Jesus healed the paralyzed man and sent him home (*Mark 2:1-10*).

---

[11] Leon Morris, *The Gospel according to John* (Grand Rapids: Eerdmans, 1971) 311.

[12] Geisler and Zukeran, *The Apologetics of Jesus*, 38.

"Jesus used physical miracles, visible to the senses to demonstrate His spiritual authority."[13]

Geisler and Zukeran state, "Christ's miracles demonstrated that what he claimed about himself was true and that God's confirming hand was on the message he preached. Jesus performed a vast array of miraculous signs that demonstrated him to be God incarnate and confirmed his authority over every realm of creation."[14] He manifested supernatural knowledge (*John 1:43-51; 4:1-38*), supernatural power over nature (*Matt 14:13-21; 15:29-39; Luke 5:1-11; 8:22-25; John 6:16-24*), sickness (*Matt 8:1-4; Mark 10:46-52; John 4:43-54; 5:1-15; 9:1-12*), demons (*Matt 8:28-34; Mark 9:14-32; Luke 8:26-39; 9:37-45*), and death (*Mark 5:21-43; Luke 7:11-17; and John 11*).

While in prison, John the Baptist questioned, *"Are you the one who is to come or shall we look for another?"* Jesus reassured John that indeed he was the Coming One by citing the evidence of the miracles predicted by Isaiah (*Matt 11:2-6; Luke 7:18-23; Isa 35:4-6 and 61:1*). Here Jesus appealed to both miracles and prophecy.

When the Jews asked Jesus to tell them plainly if he were the Christ, he pointed to the evidence of his miracles. *"I told you, and you do not believe. The works that I do in my Father's name bear witness about me"* (*John 10:25*). Because he claimed, *"I and the Father are one"* they took up stones to stone him. He answered, *"I have shown you many good works from the Father; for which of them are you going to stone me?"* They respond, *"It is not for a good work that we are going to stone you but for blasphemy, because you, being a man, make yourself God"* (*John 10:32-33*).

Jesus emphasized, *"If I am not doing the works of my Father, then do not believe me; but if I do them, even though you do not believe me, believe the works, that you may know and understand that the Father is in me and I am in the Father"* (*John 10:37-38*).[15]

---

[13] Lynn Gardner, *Christianity Stands True* (Joplin, MO: College Press, 1994) 65.

[14] Geisler and Zukeran, *The Apologetics of Jesus*, 33.

[15] See the following passages on the evidential purpose of miracles: *Matt 11:21-23; John 5:36; 14:10-11; 15:24; 20:31*.

Even after they saw his miracles many refused to believe. John records, *"Though he had done so many signs before them, they still did not believe in him. . . . Nevertheless, many even of the authorities believed in him"* (*John 12:37,42*). A miracle does not coerce or guarantee that one will believe, but it provides rational evidence for faith. Jesus' miracles demonstrated the truth of his claims for those who were willing to believe. "The defense of and appeal to Jesus's miracles remains to date the most effective evidence for the deity of Christ."[16]

Appeal to his resurrection. The resurrection of Christ is undoubtedly his greatest miracle. The OT predicted the resurrection of Jesus (*Ps 16:10; 22:14-18; Isa 52:13–53:12; Dan 9:24-27; Zech 12:10*). On several occasions Jesus predicted his resurrection (*Matt 12:38-40; 16:1-4; 17:9,22-23; 20:18-19; Mark 8:31-32; 9:31; 10:33-34; Luke 9:22; John 2:18-22; 10:18*).

Early in his ministry after cleansing the temple Jesus told the Jews, *"Destroy this temple, and in three days I will raise it up."* John editorially explained, *"But he was speaking about the temple of his body. When therefore he was raised from the dead, his disciples remembered that he had said this, and they believed the Scripture and the word that Jesus had spoken"* (*John 2:18-22*).

When asked about a sign, he pointed to his resurrection as his ultimate sign and identifying credential. *"No sign will be given to it except the sign of the prophet Jonah. For just as Jonah was three days and three nights in the belly of the great fish, so will the Son of Man be three days and three nights in the heart of the earth"* (*Matt 12:39-40*).

Even though Jesus had on several occasions informed his disciples of his upcoming death and resurrection, the apostles were skeptical of the first reports. Jesus personally appeared to his disciples several times in different locations to certify the fact of his resurrection (*Matthew 28; Mark 16; Luke 24; John*

---

[16] Geisler and Zukeran, *The Apologetics of Jesus*, 63.

20–21; Acts 10:41-42). His personal appearances to them convinced them of the certain reality of the resurrection and became a basis for appeal to others to believe in Jesus as the Son of God.

Appeal to prophecy. The question of Jesus' identity occupies center stage in his ministry. Was he the Messiah promised in the OT? Was he in fact God in the flesh? Jesus presents evidence of prophecy as evidence for believing in his divine claims and authority.

Jesus read from *Isaiah 61* when he spoke in his hometown of Nazareth. He made clear that he was the fulfillment of Isaiah's prophecy. John Stott describes this dramatic moment in the synagogue: "He closed the book, returned it to the synagogue attendant and sat down, while the eyes of all the congregation were fastened on Him. He then broke the silence with the amazing words, 'Today this scripture has been fulfilled in your hearing.' In other words, 'Isaiah was writing about me.'"[17]

Jesus explained to the travelers on the road to Emmaus that his sufferings and death constituted an essential part of God's plan for glorifying his servant (*Luke 24:26-27*). He told his disciples that his death and resurrection fulfilled the OT (*Matt 26:31-35,54; Luke 24:25-27,44*). William Craig summarizes, "Jesus appealed to miracles and to fulfilled prophecy to prove that his claims were true (Luke 24:24-27; John 14:11)."[18]

Use of reasoning. Philosopher Dallas Willard observes, "He [Jesus] constantly uses the power of logical insight to enable people to come to the truth about themselves and about God from the inside of their own heart and mind."[19] Jesus used the fundamental principles of logic in his presentation and defense of truth.

---

[17] Stott, *Basic Christianity*, 23.

[18] William Lane Craig, *Reasonable Faith: Christian Truth and Apologetics*, 3rd ed. (Wheaton, IL: Crossway Books, 2008) 47.

[19] Dallas Willard, "Jesus the Logician," *Christian Scholars Review* (Summer 1999) 610.

The law of noncontradiction states that, if a statement is true, then its contradiction is false. Jesus assumed this principle in contrasting true with false prophets (*Matt 7:15; 24:24*). He rebukes those who reject truth and choose error.

The law of the excluded middle states a proposition cannot be both true and false. This principle underlies this statement of Jesus, "*Whoever is not with me is against me*" (*Matt 12:30*).

Geisler and Zukeran affirm:

> The use of reason and logic were essential to the apologetics of Jesus. Using carefully reasoned arguments, he dismantled the arguments of his opponents and pointed out their errors in thinking. Exposing contradictions and fallacies in logic were the methods he employed. Since reason and logical arguments were a part of Jesus's defense, the apologist and all Christians today should make this an area of study as they engage in the battle of ideas.[20]

John Stott appeals to the apologetics of Jesus as a guide. "Evangelical Christianity is biblical, original, fundamental Christianity. . . . This faith is the true faith of Christ, as He taught it to His apostles and especially as He defended it against its opponents and detractors."[21] Stott says we should study how Jesus handled controversies "to make sure that the principles on which He took His stand are those which we are seeking to maintain today."[22]

Responding to the naturalism of the Sadducees, Jesus advocated the supernaturalism of resurrection religion (*Matt 22:23-33*). In debates with the Pharisees concerning authority he held that Scripture is divine, tradition is human; Scripture is obligatory, tradition is optional; Scripture is supreme, tradition is subordinate (*Mark 7:1-13*). "He affirmed Scripture's sufficiency without the addition of any binding traditions, and its

---

[20] Geisler and Zukeran, *The Apologetics of Jesus*, 76.

[21] John Stott, *Christ the Controversialist*, 8.

[22] Ibid., 49.

supreme authority by which all traditions must be judged. And the foundation on which He built these two truths is the divine origin and inspiration of Scripture, tradition being the word of men, but Scripture the Word of God."[23]

A case for the Bible being the Word of God can be made from the teachings of Jesus. He taught that the OT was historically true, inspired by God, authoritative and prophetic (*Mark 12:36; Luke 24:44; John 10:35*). He also promised Holy Spirit inspiration to the apostles (*John 14:26; 15:26; 16:13*). The apostles claimed that inspiration (*1 Thess 2:13*), and the early church recognized the inspiration of the apostles.[24]

Christ's Case for His Unique Identity and Authority

Appeals to the OT Scriptures as the authoritative Word of God (*Matt 4:4; 22:31; Mark 7:9,13; 12:36; John 10:35*).

Cites fulfillments of OT prophecies in demonstrating his Messiahship (*Matt 25:56; 26:54-59; Mark 9:12-13; 14:21; Luke 4:21; 16:29-31; 22:37; 24:21,25-27,44-47; John 5:39*).

Points to his miraculous signs as credentials for his claims (*Matt 9:6-7; Mark 2:10; Luke 7:22; John 5:36; 10:37-38; 14:10-11; 15:24*).

Uses logic and penetrating questions to expose unbelieving attacks (*Matt 12:22-30; 22:23-46*).

His resurrection from the dead constitutes the greatest sign (*Matt 12:39-40; 16:21; 17:12,22-23; 20:17-19; 28:1-20: Mark 8:31-9:1; 16:1-20; Luke 9:22-27; 24:1-53; John 2:18-22; 20:1-21:25*).

---

[23] Ibid., 76.

[24] This argument is developed in these sources: John Wenham, *Christ and the Bible*, 3rd ed. (Grand Rapids: Baker, 1994); Lynn Gardner, *Christianity Stands True* (Joplin, MO: College Press, 1994); Kenneth Kantzer, "Christ and Scripture," *His* reprint; John R.W. Stott, *The Authority of the Bible* (Downers Grove, IL: InterVarsity, 1999); John R.W. Stott, *Understanding the Bible*, 181-205; J. Norval Geldenhuys, *Supreme Authority* (Grand Rapids: Eerdmans, 1953); H.N. Ridderbos, *The Authority of the New Testament Scriptures* (Philadelphia: Presbyterian and Reformed, 1963).

Careful study of the Gospels strengthens one's personal faith in Christ. It also provides valuable instruction for one who seeks to communicate and defend the faith. McGrath reminds us, "The Gospels record encounters between Jesus and individuals that are clearly of help in seeing how best to present the person and work of Jesus Christ to one's culture."[25]

Apologetics of Peter

J.K.S. Reid affirms, "Apologetic activity is built into the foundations of the apostolic witness."[26] Avery Dulles states:

> Factual memories, dogmatic reflections, and apologetic arguments became so intertwined in the apostolic preaching that it would be artificial to try to draw a line between them. To the minds of believing Christians, the events themselves bore witness to the divine mission of Jesus, interpreted the meaning of His career, and served to clear up the doubts and difficulties that might arise in the minds of those called to believe. To some degree, therefore, apologetics was intrinsic to the presentation of the kerygma.[27]

The early preachers proclaimed Jesus as Messiah, Savior, and Lord and backed up these claims by stressing fulfilled prophecy and the resurrection.

In *Acts* we find apologetics practiced by the apostles and others. McGrath observes, "Here is material that is explicitly apologetic in nature. In a series of addresses and incidents Paul and others directly interacted with the ideas and concerns of a number of major social groups. . . . The apologetic approaches illustrated in Acts led to conversions with each of these groups [the Jews, the Greeks, and the Romans]."[28] As we seek to give

---

[25] Alister E. McGrath, "Evangelical Apologetics," *Bibliotheca Sacra* 155 (January–March 1998): 9-10.

[26] Reid, *Christian Apologetics*, 15.

[27] Dulles, *A History of Apologetics*, 2. Both proclamation and defense are found in these sermons: Acts 2:14-40; 3:12-26; 4:8-12; 5:29-32; 10:34-43; 13:13-41.

[28] McGrath, "Evangelical Apologetics," 10.

witness to our faith, valuable principles can be gained from studying how the apostles proclaim and defend Christianity.

"But Peter" introduces the apostolic response to the naturalistic interpretation of the miraculous events on the day of Pentecost (*Acts 2:14*). J.S. Reid says, "What Peter rose to do was to defend the faith, and from that time on the defence of faith has unceasingly been undertaken and faithfully discharged."[29] The first Christian sermon was an apologetic commending and defending Christian faith.

Peter explained the unusual events of the Day of Pentecost as fulfilling OT prophecies (*Acts 2:14-21*). He then presented evidence that demonstrated that the crucified Jesus, now risen, is God and Messiah (*Acts 2:16-36*). Peter:

- ✧ Appealed to miracles: *"Jesus of Nazareth, a man attested to you by God with mighty works and wonders and signs that God did through him in your midst, as you yourselves know"* (*Acts 2:22*).
- ✧ Emphasized the resurrection: *"God raised him up, having loosed the pangs of death, because it was not possible for him to be held by it"* (*Acts 2:24*).
- ✧ Showed the fulfillment of Messianic prophecy: David (*Psalm 16*) prophetically *"foresaw and spoke of the resurrection of Christ"* (*Acts 2:31*). His appeal to prophecy gave power and significance to his evidence.
- ✧ Claimed eyewitness testimony: *"This Jesus God raised up, and of that we all are witnesses"* (*Acts 2:32*).
- ✧ Concluded: *"Let all the house of Israel therefore know for certain that God has made him both Lord and Christ, this Jesus whom you crucified"* (*Acts 2:36*).
- ✧ Called for repentance and baptism in accepting the salvation Jesus offers (*Acts 2:38*).

---

[29] Reid, *Christian Apologetics*, 16.

In addressing Jews Peter made his case for belief in Christ by stressing fulfilled prophecy, miracles, and especially the resurrection of Christ. William Craig calls Peter's sermon in *Acts 2* "a model apologetic for Jews" showing them that Christianity is true.[30]

Alister McGrath echoes this sentiment:

> Peter's apologetic was directly related to themes that were important to and comprehensible by a Jewish audience. The expectation of the coming of the Messiah was (and remains) significant for Judaism. Peter did several interesting things for his Jewish audience. First, he demonstrated that Jesus meets the specific expectations of Israel. Second, he appealed to authorities (prophetic passages in the Old Testament) that carried weight with his Jewish audience. Third, he used language that would readily have been accepted and understood by his hearers. For example he referred to Jesus as 'Lord and Christ.' No explanation is offered or necessary. These were terms well familiar to those Jews. What was new about Peter's message was his emphatic insistence that *Jesus* is both God ('Lord') and Messiah ('Christ'), evidenced by His resurrection from the dead.[31]

Peter set Christ's death and resurrection in the context of OT messianic prophecies and God's activity in human history.

The apostles not only affirmed the historical fact of the resurrection; they explained the significance of both Jesus' death and resurrection. His death makes possible our salvation. His resurrection assures us of its validity. McGrath points out that these two events stand at the center of God's dealings with humanity. "As Peter showed, the resurrection of Jesus is the culmination of the many factors leading to the conclusion that He is 'both Lord and Christ.' Christians need to do more than simply prove that Jesus died on a cross and rose again.

---

[30] Craig, *Reasonable Faith*, 57.

[31] Alister E. McGrath, "Apologetics to the Jews," *Bibliotheca Sacra* (April–June 1998) 134.

They need to convey the significance of those facts for the fallen, lost world."[32]

McGrath applies Peter's approach to our witness to Jews today:

Christians should explain the gospel in terms that make sense to their audiences. . . . Peter's approach in Acts 2 stands as a landmark on how to present the gospel to Jews. To summarize his sermon in a few words, 'Jesus is the Messiah; the resurrection proves it.' . . . The issue of the messiahship of Jesus remains of critical importance in Christian apologetics to Jewish audiences. At the center of the divide between Judaism and Christianity is the figure of Jesus. Is He the Messiah? What are Jewish messianic beliefs and expectations, and on what are they based?[33]

Several obstacles stood in the way of Jews accepting Jesus as Messiah. The leaders of the Sanhedrin rejected him and condemned him for blasphemy. His death on a cross marked him with a curse (*Deut 21:23*).

In his sermon in *Acts 3* Peter stressed the resurrection, the prophet's prediction of the sufferings of Christ, and Moses' prediction of a coming prophet like unto himself (*Acts 3:15-22*). The apostles *"proclaimed in Jesus the resurrection from the dead"* and emphasized God raised him from the dead (*Acts 4:2,10*). As eyewitnesses they boldly spoke what they *"had seen and heard"* (*Acts 4:19-20*). *"And with great power the apostles were giving their testimony to the resurrection of the Lord Jesus"* (*Acts 4:33*).

When reprimanded for not obeying the officials' command not to speak about Christ, Peter and the apostles answered,

We must obey God rather than men. The God of our fathers raised Jesus whom you killed by hanging him on a tree. God exalted him at his right hand as Leader and Savior, to give repentance to Israel and forgiveness of sins. And we are witnesses to these things, and

[32] Ibid.
[33] Ibid.

so is the Holy Spirit, whom God has given to those who obey him. (Acts 5:29-32)

In his first letter Peter grounded our new life and hope on the resurrection. *"He [God] has caused us to be born again to a living hope through the resurrection of Jesus Christ from the dead"* (1 Peter 1:3).

Peter encouraged Christians to be ready with their defense to respond to the opposition they can expect to encounter. *"In your hearts regard Christ the Lord as holy, always being prepared to make a defense to anyone who asks you for a reason for the hope that is in you; yet do it with gentleness and respect"* (1 Peter 3:15). Rather than fearing the unbelievers, the Christian must offer a defense because of a deep reverence and confident obedience to Jesus as the supreme authority. The Greek word translated "reason" or "defense" is *apologia* from which we get the word apologetics. It denotes an answer given in reply to a charge brought against an individual, or an argument justifying a claim. *Apologia* was used to describe a legal brief defending a person charged with some crime. Socrates gave an *apologia* when charged with atheism and corrupting the youth of Athens.

Peter Davids says:

> Both 'make a defense' (Acts 25:16; 26:2; 2 Tim. 4:16) and 'question' (Rom. 4:12; 1 Pet. 4:5) can indicate formal legal or judicial settings, but they were also used for informal and personal situations (Plato, *Pol.* 285e and 1 Cor. 9:3; 2 Cor. 7:7 respectively). The 'always' and 'to all' in this passage indicates that the latter is in view. Rather than fear the unbelievers around them, Christians, out of reverence to Christ, should be prepared to respond fully to their often hostile questions about the faith.[34]

When questioned as to why we believe and hope in Christ, we need to be able to state reasons why we believe. Preparation is necessary for presenting an effective witness. Peter's instruc-

---

[34] Peter H. Davids, *The First Epistle of Peter* (Grand Rapids: Eerdmans, 1990) 131-132.

tion is obeyed by both a formal apologetic as well as by informal answers to questioners. I.H. Marshall states that Peter implies that "the aim of the answering is evangelistic—the conversion of the opponents."[35]

Peter gave firsthand, eyewitness testimony, *"For we did not follow cleverly devised myths when we made known to you the power and coming of our Lord Jesus Christ, but we were eyewitnesses of his majesty"* (*2 Pet 1:16*). He then referred to the divine approval Jesus experienced on the Mount of Transfiguration. He affirmed the divine authority of Scripture by stating that the prophets *"moved by the Holy Spirit spoke from God"* (*2 Pet 1:21*).

Peter asked his readers to:

Remember the predictions of the holy prophets and the commandment of the Lord and Savior through your apostles, knowing this first of all, that scoffers will come in the last days with scoffing, following their own sinful desires. They will say, "Where is the promise of his coming? For ever since the fathers fell asleep, all things are continuing as they were from the beginning of creation." For they deliberately overlook this fact, that the heavens existed long ago, and the earth was formed out of water and through water by the word of God, and that by means of these the world that then existed was deluged with water and perished. But by the same word the heavens and earth that now exist are stored up for fire, being kept until the day of judgment and destruction of the ungodly. (2 Pet 3:2-7)

Peter affirmed the basis of faith in Christ and Scripture. He also encouraged an apologetic response to both seekers and skeptics.

As Jesus and Peter gave their defense, the focus was on the person of Christ. Both appealed to the OT prophecies, Christ's miracles, and the resurrection as credentials for Jesus' claim to be Savior, Lord, and Son of God.

---

[35] I. Howard Marshall, *1 Peter* (Downers Grove, IL: InterVarsity, 1991), 116.

Review Questions

1. Summarize Stott's defense of the authority of Scripture from the authority of Christ.

2. What evidence in the OT verified the reality of God and certified his messengers?

3. Why should Christian apologists study NT apologetics?

4. Instead of viewing faith as a leap of faith, what kinds of evidence did Jesus give people as a basis for believing in him?

5. List the five witnesses Jesus appealed to in *John 5* in defense of his claim to be God.

6. Give Scriptural evidence showing that Jesus referred to his miracles as evidence of his deity.

7. What is the importance of his resurrection in Jesus' apologetics?

8. Give Scriptural evidence that Jesus cited fulfillment of OT prophecies as evidence for faith.

9. Survey Jesus' use of reason and logic in defending the truth.

10. Why should we study how Jesus handled controversy?

11. How is defense (*apologia*) involved in preaching (*kerygma*)?

12. Summarize the apologetic of Peter's sermon in *Acts 2*.

13. McGrath says Peter did what three things in addressing a Jewish audience?

14. Explain in your own words what *1 Peter 3:15* means.

Suggested Reading

Bruce, F.F. *The Defense of the Gospel in the New Testament*, rev. ed. Grand Rapids: Eerdmans, 1977. Brief, well written. May still be the best summary available of New Testament apologetics.

Geisler, Norman L., and Patrick Zukeran. *The Apologetics of Jesus: A Caring Approach to Dealing with Doubters.* Grand Rapids: Baker Books, 2009. Readable discussion of apologetic teaching, methods, and practices of Jesus. Presents the various ways he defended who he was and why he came.

Stott, John. *Christ the Controversialist.* Downers Grove, IL: InterVarsity, 1970. This is a study of how Jesus defended truth in conversations on the following issues: religion, authority, Scripture, salvation, morality, worship, responsibility, and ambition. These issues continue as live issues and the position Jesus held on each one is the position we should hold today.

"I hold you in my heart, for you are all partakers with me of grace, both in my imprisonment and in the defense and confirmation of the gospel. . . . I am put here for the defense of the gospel."

Philippians 1:7,16

12

New Testament Apologetics: Paul and Others

New Testament Apologetics: Paul and Others	"Paul was a living apologetic for Christ."[1]
Profile: F.F. Bruce—Defending Truth with Love	A. T. Robertson
I. The Apologetics of Paul	"Luke . . . had explicit apologetic purposes in the construction of his Gospel (Luke 1:1-4). . . . Luke's book of Acts begins by mentioning the 'many convincing proofs' Jesus has given his followers to confirm the truth of the resurrection (Acts 1:3)."[2]
A. To the Jews	
B. To the Gentiles	
C. To Roman officials	
D. Paul's commitment to defending the faith	
II. The Apostles as Apologists	Craig J. Hazen

[1] A.T. Robertson, *Paul's Joy in Christ* (Nashville: Broadman Press, 1959) 47.
[2] Craig J. Hazen, "Defending the Defense of the Faith," in *To Everyone an Answer: A Case for the Christian Worldview*, eds. Francis J. Beckwith, William Lane Craig, and J.P. Moreland (Downers Grove, IL: InterVarsity, 2004) 41.

A. Matthew B. John III. Apologetics of Others 　A. Stephen 　B. Mark 　C. Luke 　D. Hebrews 　E. Jude IV. NT Principles for 　Apologetics	"But in polemic and apologetic, as in every form of Christian witness, the object must always be to commend the Savior to others. A victory in debate is a very barren thing compared with the winning of men and women to the cause of Christ. If at times we are inclined to forget this, the Christian apologists of the first century will refresh our memories."[3] 　　　　　　　　　　F.F. Bruce

Profile: F.F. Bruce—Defending Truth with Love

Biblical scholar, F.F. Bruce (1910–1990), wrote "more than fifty books, numerous translations and editions, hundreds of essays and literally thousands of reviews." W.W. Gasque writes, "Bruce towered over British biblical scholarship for fifty years. He commended a moderate, intelligent and contemporary evangelicalism to his academic colleagues and he set an example of scholarship, balance, integrity, humility and ecumenicity for his evangelical brothers and sisters to follow."[4]

Bruce states, "I should not find the career of a Bible teacher so satisfying as I do if I were not persuaded that the Bible is God's word written. The fact that I am so persuaded means that I must not come to the Bible with my own preconceptions of what the Bible, as God's word writ-

---

[3] F.F. Bruce, *The Defense of the Gospel in the New Testament*, rev. ed. (Grand Rapids: Eerdmans, 1977) viii.

[4] W.W. Gasque, "BRUCE, Frederick Fyvie," in *Biographical Dictionary of Evangelicals*, Timothy Larson, ed., (Downers Grove, IL: InterVarsity, 2003) 88.

ten, can or cannot say. It is important to determine, by the canons of grammatical, textual, historical and literary study, what it actually does say."[5]

When people asked about Bruce's theological position he often asked what particular passage they had in mind. Then he would explain how he understood that passage. He claimed to be an unhyphenated evangelical. He held his views because he believed them to be true, not because of any party or theological tradition.

"Bruce's knowledge of the Bible was prodigious. He seemed to have had the whole Bible, both in the original languages and in several translations, committed to memory."[6] "His natural way to think of everything was in reference to the general flow of Scripture. He did not think topically, but according to chapter and verse. His mind was fundamentally exegetical."[7]

C.F.D. Moule states, "I know of no better example of uncompromising truthfulness wedded to that most excellent gift of charity."[8] He had a reputation of being mild and restrained in criticizing others. He treated others as he wanted to be treated. Bruce says,

> Where someone deliberately sets himself to subvert the morals of those who are young or easily influenced, or to undermine their faith in God, no language is too severe to condemn such wickedness. . . . Where I consider that someone is wrong, I have no hesitation in saying so, and I try to show why I consider him to be wrong (remembering that it is I who may be mistaken).

---

[5] F.F. Bruce, *In Retrospect: Remembrance of Things Past* (Grand Rapids: Eerdmans, 1980) 311.

[6] Gasque, "BRUCE," 86.

[7] Ibid., 87.

[8] On the dust jacket of F.F. Bruce, *In Retrospect*

> Whether my disagreement springs from a difference in basic presuppositions or from a difference of judgment about the significance of the evidence at some point, no one can reasonably object to being disagreed with. But the way in which the disagreement is expressed could certainly be objectionable.[9]
>
> In discussion of issues he says contempt and impugning another's motives have no part. He set a high standard for those who would commend and defend Christian faith.
>
> His *The New Testament Documents: Are They Reliable?* (1943; 1960), *The Books and the Parchments* (1950), and *Jesus and Christian Origins outside the New Testament* (1974), deal with evidence for the Bible's trustworthiness. His two commentaries on Acts and other NT commentaries, and his history of the early church, *The Spreading Flame* (1953), and *The Defense of the Gospel in the New Testament* (1977), all contribute much to our understanding of NT apologetics.

In surveying the last two thousand years of western civilization (outside of Christ), it would be hard to find a person who has had greater influence than Paul. We can learn valuable insights from the way he worked with unbelieving Jews and pagan Greeks and Romans to build and defend faith in Christ.

The Apologetics of Paul

Paul initially opposed and attacked those who affirmed the truth of Christianity, yet after acknowledging Jesus as the Messiah and the Son of God, he became a fearless defender of the faith. After Jesus appeared to him on the road to Damascus, he believed and was baptized into Christ. Immediately he went into the Damascus synagogues proclaiming *"Jesus, saying,*

---

[9] F.F. Bruce, *In Retrospect*, 301.

'He is the Son of God'" and *"proving that Jesus was the Christ"* (*Acts 9:20,22*). Paul *reasoned, proved,* and *persuaded* as he declared the truth of the gospel (*Acts 17:2-4,17; 18:4; 19:8,11*).

To the Jews. Paul stood on common ground with the Jews with his belief in the OT Scriptures and the anticipation of the Messiah. In Antioch of Pisidia Paul addressed his message to *"Men of Israel and you who fear God"* (*Acts 13:16*). His Jewish audience consisted of natural born Jews and God-fearers, probably proselytes who were Gentile converts to Judaism. Paul surveyed OT history showing how Jesus fulfilled the OT prophecies (*Acts 13:16-40*).

Paul reasoned with the Jews in the synagogue at Thessalonica that the death and resurrection of Jesus was in fulfillment of the Scriptures thus demonstrating that he was the Christ (*Acts 17:1-4*). After Athens he preached in Corinth *"testifying to the Jews that the Christ was Jesus"* (*Acts 18:5*). At Ephesus he *"powerfully refuted the Jews in public, showing by the Scriptures that the Christ was Jesus"* (*Acts 18:28*). In defense of the faith to the Jews Paul regularly appealed to the OT Scriptures.

Bruce observes, "To Jews, who already know that God is one, and that He is the living and true God, the gospel proclaims that Jesus is the Christ, but pagans must first be taught what Jews already confess regarding the unity and character of God."[10]

To the Gentiles. To non-Jews common ground was found in the evidence of God in the created universe. In Lystra Paul pointed to the handiwork of God in nature to show the existence of God. When the people wanted to worship Paul and Barnabas, Paul said,

> Men, why are you doing these things? We also are men, of like nature with you, and bring you good news, that you should turn from these vain things to a living God, who made the heaven and

---

[10] F.F. Bruce, *The Book of Acts* (Grand Rapids: Eerdmans, 1954) 293.

the earth and the sea and all that is in them. In past generations he allowed all the nations to walk in their own ways. Yet he did not leave himself without witness, for he did good by giving you rains from heaven and fruitful seasons, satisfying your hearts with food and gladness. (Acts 14:15-17)

Paul's sermon in Athens (*Acts 17*) is an expanded example of his approach to pagans. F.F. Bruce said,

Here Paul does not quote Hebrew prophecies quite unknown to his hearers; the direct quotations in this speech are quotations from Greek poets. But he does not descend to the level of his hearers by arguing from "first principles" as one of their own philosophers might. His argument is firmly based upon the Biblical revelation of God, echoing throughout the thought, and at times the very language, of the Old Testament Scriptures. Like the Biblical revelation itself, his argument begins with God the Creator of all and ends with God the Judge of all.[11]

The Greek philosophers thought Paul spoke of foreign divinities when he mentioned Jesus and the resurrection. They may have thought the resurrection was the name of a female deity. Since they loved to discuss new ideas they asked Paul to speak to them of his new teaching. The word "Areopagus" can refer to an administrative body of people in Athens or it can refer to Mars Hill itself. *Acts 17:19* may mean that he was brought before the council that was meeting on Mars Hill. Paul declared,

Men of Athens, I perceive that in every way you are very religious. For as I passed along, and observed the objects of your worship, I found also an altar with this inscription, "To an unknown god." What therefore you worship as unknown, this I proclaim to you. The God who made the world and everything in it, being Lord of heaven and earth, does not live in temples made by man, nor is he served by human hands, as though he needed anything, since he himself gives to all mankind life and breath and everything. And he

---

[11] F.F. Bruce, *The Book of Acts*, rev. ed. (Grand Rapids: Eerdmans, 1988) 354-355.

made from one man every nation of mankind to live on all the face of the earth, having determined allotted periods and the boundaries of their dwelling place, that they should seek God, in the hope that they might feel their way toward him and find him. Yet he is actually not far from each one of us, for "In him we live and move and have our being"; as even some of your own poets have said, "For we are indeed his offspring." Being then God's offspring, we ought not to think that the divine being is like gold, or silver, or stone, an image formed by the art and imagination of man. The times of ignorance God overlooked, but now he commands all people everywhere to repent, because he has fixed a day on which he will judge the world in righteousness by a man whom he has appointed; and of this he has given assurance to all men by raising him from the dead. (Acts 17:22-31)

Paul did not assume his audience knew the one true God of Israel. He built a bridge by making several points of contact with his audience. He mentioned their interest in religion and the altar to an unknown God (*Acts 17:22-23*). In ignorance they worshiped an unknown god. He proceeded to make known the true God. This Creator and Lord of the universe can't be contained in buildings or shrines made by human hands (*Acts 17:24*). He has given life to every person. Since we are his offspring we naturally seek to find him (*Acts 17:25-28*). "The God who is known indirectly through His creation can be fully known in redemption."[12] He is near and can be known through the resurrection of Christ which assures us that as his offspring we all need to turn to him because we are accountable to him (*Acts 17:30-31*).

F.F. Bruce's Outline of Paul's Mars Hill Speech

I. Doctrine of God
   A. "God is the Creator of universe and all that is in it."
   B. "God does not inhabit shrines which human hands have built."

---

[12] Alister E. McGrath, "Apologetics to the Greeks," *Bibliotheca Sacra* (July-September 1998) 262.

C. "God requires nothing from his creatures."
II. Doctrine of Man
A. "Man is one."
B. "Man's earthly abode and the course of the seasons have been divinely ordained for his benefit."
C. "God's purpose in making these arrangements was that man might seek and find Him."
D. "God's desire that men should seek and find him is the more natural because they are his offspring, and he aids them in the attainment of his desire by his nearness to them. Our need to seek and find God is natural because we are His offspring."
E. "Paul issues a call to repentance."[13]

H. Wayne House comments on Paul's speech to the Athenians:

What we need to understand about the Pauline strategy and methodology is that he took them from the known to the unknown, from the partly correct thinking they possessed to thinking that was enlightened by the Scripture, even though he never quoted it. He never belittled the Athenians, though verse 16 tells us he was deeply troubled by the town full of idols, saying that he recognized that they were very religious (*not* superstitious).[14]

Paul is a forerunner of Christian apologists in his approach to the Gentiles. His example should be a model for us as we reach out to those in an increasingly pagan society. Though Paul used their interests, concepts, and authorities, he brought them to the fundamental facts of Christianity. He did not compromise the integrity of biblical truth.

---

[13] F.F. Bruce, *The Defense of the Gospel*, 41-47.
[14] H. Wayne House, "A Biblical Argument for Balanced Apologetics: How the Apostle Paul Practiced Apologetics in Acts, (Acts 14:8-18; 17:16-34)" in *Reasons for Faith: Making a Case for the Christian Faith*, eds., Norman L. Geisler and Chad V. Meister (Wheaton, IL: Crossway, 2007) 71.

F.F. Bruce states, "The idea, popular with many preachers, that his determination, when he arrived in Corinth, to 'know nothing' there 'except Jesus Christ and him crucified' (1 Cor 2:2), was the result of disillusionment with the line of approach he had attempted in Athens, has little to commend it."[15] Stott adds, "His firm 'decision' to preach nothing but Jesus Christ and him crucified was taken because of the anticipated challenges of proud Corinth, not because of his supposed failure in Athens. Besides, as Luke shows in his narrative, Paul did not change his tactic in Corinth, but continued to teach, argue and persuade (18:4-5)."[16] Bock notes that "nothing about what Paul does or says is viewed negatively or as a failure."[17]

Paul started with the one true God—personal Creator, Ruler and Sustainer of all. Bock says,

> Paul appeals to the appreciation of God through the creation as a bridge to the idea of looking for the expression of God's will and plan, an idea Paul will now develop. God will not be discovered through nature alone, even though nature does at least show us that God is not like humanity (vv. 28-29). One must come to grips with God's revelation, as Paul will emphasize in verses 30-31."[18]

After introducing the creator God, Paul then moved to the uniqueness of Christ. Even though God is near, he will be found only through knowing how he has acted on behalf of those he created. The resurrection of Christ proves that all people will stand before Jesus as Judge. Upon the mention of the resurrection, the crowd rudely interrupted. "The speech came to a halt."[19] No doubt Paul would have taught concerning the cross if he had been given the opportunity. Luke record-

---

[15] F.F. Bruce, *Acts*, rev. ed., 344.

[16] John R.W. Stott, *The Message of Acts* (Downers Grove, IL: InterVarsity, 1990) 290.

[17] Darrell L. Bock, *Acts* (Grand Rapids: Baker, 2007) 572-573.

[18] Ibid., 567.

[19] Ibid., 588.

ed what was no doubt the beginning of Paul's speech before the crowd stopped him and did not allow him to complete his presentation of the gospel.

Paul used the religious interest of the Athenians as a bridge to lead them to consider the truth of God. Alister E. McGrath states, "The entire episode illustrates the manner in which Paul is able to exploit the situation of his audience without compromising the integrity of faith."[20] McGrath continues:

> Paul's Areopagus sermon also illustrates the New Testament tendency to mingle *kerygma* (preaching) and *apologia* (apologetics) as two aspects of a greater whole. Unfortunately the proclamation of the gospel and its reasoned defense are often separated. Kerygmatic theology is detached from apologetics for methodological reasons, yet in the New Testament both are essential components in proclaiming Christ. The New Testament brings the two together in a creative and productive interplay; to proclaim the gospel is thus to defend the gospel, just as defending the gospel is proclaiming the gospel.[21]

Earlier sermons in Acts by other apostles also combine proclamation and apologetic (*Acts 2:14-40; 3:12-26; 4:8-12; 5:29-32; 10:34-43; 13:13-41*).

Paul was not a product of some Roman rationalistic educational system or just a pre-Enlightenment rationalist who sought to "own" or "control" the gospel by his human logic, but was part of the line of spiritual descendants of Jesus who loved others enough to offer them reasons to follow Jesus.

In witnessing to our faith we need to understand the background and worldview of those to whom we speak. McGrath states, "The apologist needs to know his or her audience, speak its language, and share its common flow of life."[22] Effective apologetics is not a one-method-fits-all matter.

---

[20] Alister E. McGrath, *Intellectuals Don't Need God and Other Modern Myths* (Grand Rapids: Zondervan, 1993) 29.

[21] McGrath, "Apologetics to the Greeks," 265.

[22] McGrath, *Intellectuals Don't Need God*, 29.

Bock observes, "Paul directly engages the current culture. He does so with the attitude that although his argument challenges the way people are living, his message stresses the gospel as an invitation into a new life and seeks points of contact with such desires as already exist in people he evangelizes." Paul commends and defends the faith in a manner and level appropriate to those he encounters. Though he disapproves of their lifestyle and worldview, "He knows how to confront but does so honestly and graciously. Both message and tone are important in sharing the gospel. Here Paul is an example of both."[23]

Paul declared the pagans guilty for rejecting the truth about God available to them in nature. *"For what can be known about God is plain to them. For his invisible attributes, namely his eternal power and divine nature, have been clearly perceived, ever since the creation of the world, in the things that have been made. So they are without excuse"* (**Rom 1:19-20**). From nature alone all people, including fallen persons, can know that God exists. In spite of this available knowledge of God, sinful humanity exchanges *"the truth about God for a lie"* (**Rom 1:25**).

The NT does not present formal theistic proofs and does not develop a complete natural theology. However it affirms that the evidence in the created universe points to an eternal power and deity. Kenneth Kantzer observed,

> In Romans 1:20 Paul presented data which, ever since the creation of the world, are sufficient, as data, to lead man to a knowledge of God's eternal power and of His essential deity. Romans 2:14 and 15 explicitly assert, that, apart from any knowledge of special revelation, man would still know the moral law and his obligation to God. The entire point of these passages is that the evidences are valid and, because of this, man can be justly condemned. He ought to see, and if he does not see, it is only because he *will* not see.[24]

---

[23] Bock, *Acts*, 573.

[24] Kenneth Kantzer, "The Communication of Revelation," in *The Bible: The Living Word of Revelation*, ed. by Merrill C. Tenney (Grand Rapids: [cont.]

The person without the Bible who refuses the knowledge of God and deifies the creature stands justly condemned "for failing to see what the evidences clearly point to and what he very well could see if he were only willing." In spite of the fall and the curse, the evidence of God has remained available. "Sufficient light now shines so that man could see God if he only would."[25]

The evidence of the universe demands belief in God. Kantzer summarizes,

> These facts lie in the areas commonly designated by the terms cosmological, theological, moral, and revelational. The type of argumentation is strictly inductive. From the data available in the physical nature (Romans 1 and Psalm 19), from the evidence of history (Acts 14, 17), and from the facts of moral consciousness (Romans 2:14, 15) man ought to be able to draw the conclusion, coherent only with these bodies of data, namely the existence of a supreme being properly called God, to whom we are morally responsible. . . . the whole of the data is adequate to establish the existence of deity.[26]

To Roman officials. Rather than using a theological or philosophical approach Paul employed a practical approach in answering Roman officials. Roman authorities viewed sedition as a serious crime. Paul defended Christians as respecting social and political rules. He identified Christians as a grouping within Judaism as Roman authorities viewed Judaism as a legal religion (*Acts 18:12-16*). Jewish opponents frequently created conflict between the Romans and the Christians (*Acts 13:50; 14:5; 17:6-7*). Before the mob in Jerusalem (*Acts 22:3-21*) and before Agrippa (*26:4-29*) Paul made his defense not of himself, but he gave his personal testimony in defense of the truth of

---

Zondervan, 1968) 64. See also Kantzer's foreword to *Christianity Stands True* by Lynn Gardner (Joplin, MO: College Press, 1994) 12-13.

[25] Kantzer, "The Communication of Revelation," 66-67.

[26] Ibid., 65-66.

Christianity. F.F. Bruce calls Paul's speech before Agrippa "the crowning apologia for his own missionary career."[27]

McGrath notes,

> The most important of Paul's speeches in Acts that deal with Christianity in the eyes of the Roman authorities are recorded in Acts 24–26. Recent studies have shown the way these speeches conform to patterns well known in the legal proceedings of that period. . . . [Forensic speeches] would include a refutation of the specific charges being brought against the accused."[28]

In his speech before Governor Felix (*Acts 24:10-21*), Paul responded to the charges brought against him by the orator Tertullus (*Acts 24:1-8*).

> In the view of many scholars Paul followed with great skill the "rules of engagement" laid down by Roman legal custom as he subjected Tertullus's accusations to a point-by-point refutation. Paul stressed the continuity between his own beliefs and those of the Jews who had accused him, particularly regarding the Scriptures and the resurrection. But most significant is his appeal to Roman rules of evidence; his accusers (some Asian Jews) were not present to witness against him.[29]

In his speech before King Agrippa (*Acts 26:1-23*) Paul mentioned Agrippa's competence in Judaism (*Acts 26:2-3*). His accusers had misrepresented both Paul and his gospel (*Acts 25:7,15,18-19*). "Paul's strategy was to set out clearly what he believed."[30] Those to whom we defend the gospel often have distorted ideas of it, so it is crucial that we make clear what true Christianity is.

Paul's commitment to defending the faith. Some hold that apologetics is only presented to individuals hostile to, doubtful

---

[27] Bruce, *Acts*, rev. ed., 24.

[28] Alister E. McGrath, "Apologetics to the Romans," *Bibliotheca Sacra* (October–December 1998) 390.

[29] Ibid., 391.

[30] Ibid.

of, or at least ignorant of the Christian faith. However apologetics can reassure and strengthen the faith of believers. Though addressed to Christians Paul's letters include apologetics. He emphasized the basis for believing the fundamentals of Christian faith. To Christians he frequently and vigorously defended his apostolic authority and the authority of the Word of God. *"Am I not an apostle? Have I not seen Jesus our Lord?"* (*1 Cor 9:1*). To the Galatians he wrote, *"Paul an apostle—not from men nor through man, but through Jesus Christ and God the Father, who raised him from the dead"* (*Gal 1:1*; see also *Galatians 1, 2* and *2 Cor 10–13*). *"All Scripture is breathed out by God"* (*2 Tim 3:16*).

Paul warned about following human wisdom instead of the wisdom of God. He claimed special revelation for the apostles. The Holy Spirit guided their words so that they convey the truth God wanted communicated (*1 Cor 2:10-13*). Paul affirmed the divine origin of his gospel, *"For I did not receive it from any man, nor was I taught it, but I received it through a revelation of Jesus Christ"* (*Gal 1:12*). To the Thessalonians he wrote, *"And we also thank God constantly for this, that when you received the word of God, which you heard from us, you accepted it not as the word of men, but as what it really is, the word of God, which is at work in you believers"* (*1 Thess 2:13*).

Paul upheld the deity of Jesus on the basis of fulfilled prophecy and his resurrection from the dead (*Rom 1:1-4*). To those who rejected the resurrection of the dead he pointed them to the resurrection of Christ in affirming that the good news centered in the death and resurrection of Jesus (*1 Cor 15:3-8*). The Christian has assurance and hope because Christ rose from the grave (*1 Thess 4:13-18*). In his last letter Paul urged, "Keep remembering Jesus Christ, risen from the dead [miracle], descended from David [fulfilled prophecy], as preached in my gospel" (*2 Tim 2:8*, literal translation).

Paul used his imprisonment as an opportunity to make an *apologia* for the truth of the gospel. He said the Philippians were partakers *"in the defense and confirmation of the gospel"* (*Phil 1:7*). Defense here means "removing obstacles" and confirmation conveys the idea of "direct advancement and establishment of the Gospel."[31] Later in the chapter he stated, *"I am put here for the defense of the gospel"* (*1:16*). In the words of A.T. Robertson, "Paul was a living apologetic for Christ."[32]

Paul opposed any worldview that omits or diminishes God. To those influenced by Greek philosophy causing them to question the reality of Jesus' body, he warned, *"See to it that no one takes you captive by philosophy and empty deceit, according to human tradition, according to the elemental spirit of the world, and not according to Christ. For in him the whole fullness of deity dwells bodily"* (*Col 2:8-9*).

Apologetic has both offense and defense. Paul explained, *"For the weapons of our warfare are not of the flesh but have divine power to destroy strongholds. We destroy arguments and every lofty opinion raised against the knowledge of God, and take every thought captive to obey Christ"* (*2 Cor 10:4-5*). He exposed the inadequacy and invalidity of human worldly thinking. We must repudiate any ideas contrary to God's truth because of our allegiance to Christ as the Lord of our lives.

The Apostles as Apologists

The apostles stand behind the Gospels either as authors or sources. Each Gospel has an apologetic motive. Matthew demonstrated that Jesus is the Messiah *"the son of David, the son of Abraham"* (*Matt 1:1*). Mark presented *"Jesus Christ, the Son of God"* (*Mark 1:1*). Luke provided an orderly, accurate account of the origins of Christianity (*Luke 1:1-4*). John's purpose was to establish in his readers a saving faith in Jesus as the Christ, the Son of God (*John 20:31*).

---

[31] J.B. Lightfoot, *Epistle to the Philippians* (Grand Rapids: Zondervan, 1956; repr. of 1913 ed.) 85.

[32] Robertson, *Paul's Joy in Christ*, 47.

In the twentieth century form critics explained the origin of the Gospels as developed in a period of anonymous community transmission with the final form many strata removed from the original eyewitnesses. This type of criticism undermined the apologetic nature of the Gospels. Richard Bauckham challenges this view, affirming of the Gospels,

> They embody the testimony of the eyewitnesses, not of course without editing and interpretation, but in a way that is substantially faithful to how the eyewitnesses themselves told it, since the Evangelists were in more or less direct contact with eyewitnesses, not removed from them by a long process of anonymous transmission of the traditions.[33]

The Gospels were written within the living memory of the eyewitnesses who report the events and the significance of those events.[34] Bauckham argues that the link between the Jesus who actually lived in history and the Gospels is "the continuing presence and testimony of the eyewitnesses, who remained the authoritative sources of their traditions until their deaths." Bauckham continues:

> Gospel traditions did not, for the most part, circulate anonymously but in the name of the eyewitnesses to whom they were due. Throughout the lifetime of the eyewitnesses, Christians remained interested in and aware of the ways the eyewitnesses themselves told their stories. So, in imagining how the traditions reached the Gospel writers, not oral tradition but eyewitness testimony should be our principal model.[35]

Eyewitness testimony stands as a valuable witness in establishing a case in law courts, in history, and in everyday life.

Matthew. The first Gospel provides information that will help Jewish converts answer the objections they no doubt reg-

---

[33] Richard Bauckham, *Jesus and the Eyewitnesses: The Gospels as Eyewitness Testimony* (Grand Rapids: Eerdmans, 2006) 6.
[34] Ibid., 7.
[35] Ibid., 8.

ularly heard from hostile Jews. Matthew's Gospel provides ammunition for Christians to answer Jewish attacks. Dulles says, "Matthew's pervasive use of prophetic texts with assertions of their fulfillment in the life of Jesus is obviously designed to prove to rabbinic readers that Jesus is, as the Church claims, the divinely promised Messiah."[36]

Donald Guthrie states the apologetic purpose of Matthew's Gospel:

> He purposes to show that the major events in the life of Jesus took place in fulfillment of prophecy. . . . However Jewish many of Matthew's emphases are, his main target is to show Christianity as much more comprehensive than Judaism. Here was Old Testament fulfillment in the widest possible sense. . . . In all probability there was an apologetic purpose behind this Gospel. It would have answered many questions about our Lord which may well have been raised against Him by calumnists. The infancy story, for instance, would answer any charge of illegitimacy against Jesus. The descent into Egypt and the subsequent return to Nazareth would account for the residence in Nazareth rather than Bethlehem. The same might be said of the apologetic character of some of the details in the resurrection narrative which are peculiar to Matthew (*e.g.*, the story of the bribing of the guard, which would refute any allegation that the disciples had stolen the body of Jesus).[37]

R.V.G. Tasker says of Matthew's Gospel, "The author is most concerned to establish the truth that the earthly history of Jesus, in its origin and its purpose, and in the actual manner of its unfolding was the activity of God Himself, who was therein fulfilling His own words spoken by the prophets. . . . In many respects the Gospel of Matthew might be called an early Christian apology."[38]

---

[36] Avery Dulles, *A History of Apologetics*, 2nd ed., (San Francisco: Ignatius Press, 2005) 18.

[37] Donald Guthrie, *New Testament Introduction*, 4th ed. (Downers Grove, IL: InterVarsity, 1990) 32-33.

[38] R.V.G. Tasker, "Matthew, Gospel of," *New Bible Dictionary*, 3rd ed., ed. by I. Howard Marshall, A. Millard, J.I. Packer, and D.J. Wiseman (Downers Grove, IL: InterVarsity, 1996) 740-741.

The Passion narrative in all four Gospels "reveals an increasing preponderance of apologetical motifs. This is apparent, first, in the growing insistence that every detail unfolds 'as it was written' in the Old Testament."[39] Coming from a village in Galilee posed a problem to Jews who expected the Messiah to be born in the city of David, Bethlehem. Both Matthew and Luke make it clear that, though Jesus spent his childhood in Nazareth, he was born in Bethlehem. "The manner in which the birth stories are told, especially in Matthew, indicates a strongly apologetic concern."[40]

John. Convincing evidence points to the apostle John as *"the disciple Jesus loved"*[41] as the author. The writer claims to be an eyewitness, *"This is the disciple who is bearing witness about these things, and who has written these things, and we know that his testimony is true"* (*John 21:24*). The testimony of witnesses figures prominently in John's Gospel (*John 1:14-16,34; 3:10-13,32; 19:35*) as well as in his letters (*1 John 1:1-5; 4:11-16; 3 John 12*).

In spite of speculation about why the fourth Gospel was written, our clearest clue is John's stated purpose, *"Now Jesus did many other signs in the presence of the disciples, which are not written in this book; but these are written that you may believe that Jesus is the Christ, the Son of God, and that believing you may have life in his name"* (*John 20:30-31*). Leon Morris sees in this statement an evangelistic aim, "that people may believe."

> Faith is fundamental, and John longs to see people believe. He has not tried to write an impartial history; he is avowedly out to secure converts. He is bearing witness to those great events in which God has acted for humanity's salvation. For he is sure that God has acted, and that his action is to be seen in Jesus Christ. John does not think of faith as a vague trust, but as something with content. . . . Faith means believing that—.

---

[39] Dulles, *History of Apologetics*, 6.
[40] Ibid., 7.
[41] Bauckham, *Jesus and the Eyewitnesses*, 358-411.

Here he singles out two things in faith's content. The one is that Jesus is the Christ, that is, the Messiah, the long-expected one. The other is that he is the Son of God. We take these two as more or less identical, but the Jews of the day did not. The Messiah was not expected to stand in that very close relationship to the Father of which John speaks. John's conception of messiahship is fuller and richer than that of contemporary Judaism . . . . The combination of terms indicates the very highest view of the Person of Jesus, and it must be taken in conjunction with the fact that John has just recorded the confession of Thomas that hails Jesus as "My Lord and my God." There cannot be any doubt but that John conceived of Jesus as the very incarnation of God.[42]

Thompson states,

The Gospel [of John] intends to present Jesus to second and subsequent generations of believers, those who did not 'see the signs' but have the Gospel's written account of them (20:30-31: 'these are written'). By making clear who Jesus is and the salvation that he offers, the Gospel intends to encourage and strengthen believers in their faith in Jesus as the Messiah and Son of God."[43]

John's Gospel helps believers continue to believe.

John often cited OT predictions of events: the unbelief of the Jews (John 12:38-40), Judas's betrayal (John 13:18), the parting of Jesus' garments and casting lots for his robe (John 19:24), and his bones not being broken (John 19:36). In the fourth Gospel it is clear that Jesus hears the words of the Father (John 3:34; 7:16; 8:26; 12:49-50). God's authoritative testimony is seen in Jesus' testimony (John 3:11; 5:31; 7:7; 8:14,18; 18:37).

Dulles observes that John:

---

[42] Leon Morris, The Gospel according to John, rev. ed. (Grand Rapids; Eerdmans, 1995) 755-756.

[43] M.M. Thompson, "The Gospel of John," in Dictionary of Jesus and the Gospels, eds. Joel B. Green, Scot McKnight, I. Howard Marshall (Downers Grove, IL: InterVarsity, 1992) 372.

records the Christian witness in a way calculated to appeal to men looking for light in the Hellenistic world at the close of the first century. The universal significance of Christ as the light and savior of the world is clearly brought out. The Word who enlightens everyone (1:9) becomes flesh to save the world (3:17; 4:42) and is raised up in order to draw all human beings to Himself (12:32). His redemptive purposes extend not only to the Jewish nation but to all the scattered children of God (11:52), including the other sheep not of Israel's fold (10:16).[44]

The apostles fulfilled the role of apologist-evangelists in their speaking and writing. We can learn from them the importance of tailoring our defense to meet the actual needs of those to whom we speak while always pointing to Christ.

The Apologetics of Others

Stephen. Before the Sanhedrin Stephen made a defense of Christianity as the only true way to worship God (*Acts 7:2-53*). He insisted that the presence of God is not limited to any land or building, even the temple. He gave a panoramic review of Hebrew history showing how it leads up to the coming of Christ. Stephen did not give a personal defense seeking his acquittal. As John Stott observes, "Stephen's speech was not so much a self-defense as a testimony to Christ. His main theme was positive, that Jesus the Messiah had come to replace the temple and fulfil the law, which both bore witness to him."[45] He delivered, in F.F. Bruce's words, "a defense of pure Christianity as God's appointed way of worship; Stephen is a precursor of the later Christian apologists, especially those who defended Christianity against Judaism."

Bruce continues, "Another theme of the speech becomes a regular feature in later anti-Judaic apologetic—the insistence

---

[44] Avery Dulles, *A History of Apologetics*, 2nd ed., 22-23.
[45] Stott, *The Message of Acts*, 141.

that the Jewish people's refusal to acknowledge Jesus as Messiah was all of a piece with their attitude to God's messengers from the beginning of their national history."[46] The Jewish leaders were the persons guilty of subverting the Law of Moses.

The martyrdom of Stephen is a prototype of an important type of apologetic in the centuries to come—the apologetic of martyrdom. Willingness to die for a truth communicates a powerful message. The gentle spirit of Stephen lovingly praying for his murderers also gives testimony to the love of Christ. This picture never left the mind of the brilliant persecutor who held the coats that day—Saul of Tarsus. When Christ appears to him on the road to Damascus, the Lord tells him, *"It is hard for you to kick against the goads"* (*Acts 26:14*). Perhaps remembering the death of Stephen was one of those goads.

Mark. Mark introduced his Gospel, *"The beginning of the gospel of Jesus Christ, the Son of God"* (*Mark 1:1*). Ralph Martin says of the purpose of Mark's Gospel, "He is saying to his contemporaries, and to us if we will but hear it, that the Galilean poet-preacher, the ex-carpenter turned prophet, the strange Man on his cross is none other than the risen Lord and a living power in His church in every age."[47]

Mark highlighted the identity of Jesus by frequent reminders in the story (*1:11,25,34; 3:11; 5:7; 8:27-29; 9:7; 14:61-62; 5:39*) as he made his case that Jesus is indeed the *"Messiah, Son of God."* His action-packed narrative documented the evidence: defeat of Satan, healing all manner of sickness, raising the dead, casting out demons, feeding the hungry, forgiving sinners, silencing the objections of the scribes and Pharisees, and strengthening the wavering faith of his disciples.

R. A. Guelich summarizes Mark's purpose,

---

[46] Bruce, *The Book of Acts*, rev. ed., 130.

[47] Ralph Martin, *Mark, Evangelist and Theologian* (Grand Rapids: Zondervan, 1972) 16.

He wanted to address a community under duress, a duress that may well have given rise to questions about who Jesus really was and the nature of the kingdom he had come to inaugurate. This Gospel offered a renewed basis for their faith, made clear the trials and tribulations along the journey of that faith, and offered the hope of the kingdom future when the harvest, the full-grown mustard tree, the resurrection and the consummation of God's salvation would make all things right.[48]

Dulles states, "The event of the Resurrection, toward which the whole Gospel ineluctably moves, signifies the triumph of Jesus's power over all the forces of evil—sin, sickness, death, blindness, and unbelief. . . . In narrating his sublime history Mark furnishes abundant materials for the defense of the Christian faith."[49]

Luke. The *Gospel of Luke* and the book of *Acts* form a two-part apologetic work fulfilling Luke's stated purpose *"to write an orderly account for you, most excellent Theophilus, that you may have certainty concerning the things you have been taught"* (*Luke 1:3-4*). This formal literary preface affirmed Luke's intention of providing a factual history of the origins of Christianity. Luke conducted thorough, accurate research and wrote a well-organized account of the historical origins of Christianity (5 B.C. to A.D. 62).

Scholars have questioned the accuracy of some statements in Luke–Acts, but today, Luke's reliability is widely acknowledged. After being taught that Luke's writings were unhistorical, William Ramsay spent over thirty years in archaeological research. He concluded, "Luke's history is unsurpassed in respect of its trustworthiness."[50] Luke wrote

---

[48] R.A. Guelich, "Gospel of Mark," in *Dictionary of Jesus and the Gospels*, 524.

[49] Avery Dulles, *A History of Apologetics*, 2nd ed., 17.

[50] William Ramsay, *The Bearing of Recent Discoveries on the Trustworthiness of the New Testament* (Grand Rapids: Baker Book House, 1911) 79. See Norman Geisler, "Historicity of Acts," in *Baker Encyclopedia of Christian Apologetics* (Grand Rapids: Baker Books, 1999) 4-8.

with a sense of history in which Jesus is the central focus in God's saving activity in human history (*Luke 1:78-79; 2:11; 19:10; 22:19-20; 24:46-49; Acts 1:8; 2:36; 4:10-12; 17:30f.*).

I.H. Marshall summarizes,

Luke's purpose was to give an historical account which would form the basis for a sound Christian faith on the part of those who had already been instructed, perhaps imperfectly and incompletely, in the story of Jesus. Throughout the preface there is a stress on the historical accuracy of the material presented."[51]

Josh McDowell states, "I think the Gospel of Luke is probably one of the greatest apologetic pieces of all time."[52]

Hazen states the apologetic purpose of Luke's prologue.

He highlights the importance of eyewitness testimony, careful investigation and accurate reporting all with an eye toward helping his reader, Theophilus, to know "the certainty" of the things he had been taught (Lk 1:1-4). Luke's book of Acts begins by mentioning the "many convincing proofs" Jesus had given his followers to confirm the truth of the resurrection (Acts 1:3).[53]

Bock expresses a central purpose for Luke's Gospel, "Luke's desire is to assure Theophilus, or anyone who reads his Gospel, of the truth of the apostolic teaching about Jesus."[54] "Luke's Gospel, as his preface made clear, is a reassurance that through Jesus one *can* know God and experience life as God designed it."[55] One of the functions of apologetics is to reassure believers that Christianity is actually true. This encourages faithfulness and perseverance. Luke showed God's faithfulness

---

[51] I. Howard Marshall, *Commentary on Luke* (Grand Rapids: Eerdmans, 1978) 40.

[52] Quoted in Christy Tennant, "Josh McDowell on Defending the Bible," *Bible Study Magazine* (November and December 2008) 14.

[53] Hazen, "Defending the Defense of the Faith," 41.

[54] Darrell L. Bock, *Luke 1:1–9:50* (Grand Rapids: Baker Books, 1994) 67.

[55] Darrell Bock, *Luke* (Downers Grove, IL: InterVarsity, 1994) 30.

to his promises and plan which comes to fulfillment in Christ who offers salvation to all, including Gentiles. Jesus stands at the center of God's pattern of promise and fulfillment as he came to seek and save the lost (*Luke 19:10*). The historical truth about Christ validates the offered salvation in God's gracious mission for all peoples.

In his two-part work Luke traced Jesus' saving ministry and its spread through the early church. Christians encountered opposition wherever they went (*Acts 28:22*). Luke recorded for us the responses Christians gave to these objections. Bruce calls Luke "the first Christian historian" and "the first Christian apologist."[56]

First-century Apologetic Prototypes

Defense against paganism — Christianity is true; paganism is false

Defense against Judaism — Christianity is the fulfillment of true Judaism

Defense against Roman political accusations — Christianity is innocent of any offense against Roman law

F. F. Bruce[57]

F.F. Bruce comments on the political challenges Christians faced,

> When we examine the way in which Luke develops his narrative, we can hardly fail to be struck by his apologetic emphasis, especially in the second volume. He is concerned to defend Christianity against the charges which were popularly brought against it in the second half of the first century. We must recognize that in the eyes of those who set some store by law and order in the Roman Empire Christianity started off

---

[56] F.F. Bruce, *The Acts of the Apostles*, 3rd revised. and enlarged. ed. (Grand Rapids: Eerdmans, 1990) 22.
[57] Ibid.

with a serious handicap. Its Founder had admittedly been condemned to death by a Roman governor on a charge of sedition. And the movement which he inaugurated seemed to be attended by tumult and disorder wherever it spread, both in the Roman provinces and in Rome itself. Luke sets himself to reduce this handicap, or rather to remove it altogether.[58]

Bruce summarizes Luke's role as an apologist,

Luke is, in fact, the pioneer among Christian apologists, especially in that form of apologetic which is addressed to the civil authorities to establish the law-abiding character of Christianity. But other forms of apologetic are represented in the course of his work, particularly in some of the speeches of Acts. Thus, Stephen's defense is the prototype of Christian apologetic over against the Jews, designed to demonstrate that Christianity and not Judaism is the true fulfillment of the Word of God spoken through Moses and the prophets and that the Jews' rejection of the gospel is consistent with their rejection of the divine message brought to them by earlier messengers. Paul's address to the Athenian court of the Areopagus is one of the earliest examples of Christian apologetic to pagans, designed to show that the true knowledge of God is given in the gospel and not in the idolatrous vanities of paganism. His farewell address at Miletus to the elders of the Ephesian church is partly apologetic; he replies by implication to some criticisms voiced against him within the Christian community.[59]

Hebrews. As Augustine's *City of God* gives a philosophy of history for those coping with reconciling the fall of Rome and the truth of Christianity, the epistle of Hebrews provides a philosophy of history for Jewish Christians who lived through the era of the destruction of the temple. The author emphasizes the superiority of Christianity as it superseded the OT dispensation. The eternal has replaced the temporary. The *"removal of*

---

[58] F.F. Bruce, *The Book of Acts*, rev. ed., 20.
[59] Ibid., 13.

things that are shaken" was necessary so that *"the things that cannot be shaken may remain" (Heb 12:27).*

J.K.S. Reid states, "The apologetic offered is that Christianity fits into a framework already constructed in the Old Testament. Here is an early form of the argument from prophecy that constitutes so important an element in later Apologetics."[60] Reid says of all books in the NT canon, "the Epistle to the Hebrews is the clearest example of sustained apology for the Christian faith."[61] A.B. Bruce says of the book of Hebrews, "It may be regarded as the most important contribution to the apologetics of Christianity contained in the New Testament. . . . a sustained attempt to meet in a comprehensive spirit the difficulties of the Christian faith as these presented themselves to the minds of Hebrews."[62] He subtitled his commentary on Hebrews "the first apology for Christianity."

Jude. In response to those who were subverting and denying the faith, Jude urged his readers to "contend for the faith that was once for all delivered to the saints" *(Jude 3).* Christians are to defend the body of belief that the apostles taught which is normative for the church. Michael Green states,

> Apostolic teaching, not whatever be the current theological fashion, is the hallmark of authentic Christianity. The once-for-allness of the apostolic "faith" is inescapably bound up with the particularity of the incarnation, in which God spoke to men through Jesus once and for all. And simply because Christianity is a historical religion, the witness of the original hearers and their circle, the apostles, is determinative of what we can know about Jesus. We cannot get behind the New Testament teaching, nor can we get beyond it, though we must interpret it to each successive generation. Jude would agree with 2 John 9, 10 that the man whose doctrine outruns

---

[60] Reid, *Christian Apologetics,* 27.

[61] Ibid., 28.

[62] A.B. Bruce, *Apologetics* (New York: Charles Scribner's Sons, 1892) 2.

the New Testament witness is to be rejected. The test of progress is, for him, faithfulness to the apostolic teaching about Christ (cf. 1 Tim. vi. 20, 2 Tim. i. 13,14).[63]

Green observes that the word for *contend* emphasizes "that the faith will be costly and agonizing; the cost of being unfashionable, the agony of seeking to express the faith in a way that is really comprehensible to contemporary man."[64]

The cultural and intellectual world of the first century differs in significant ways from our contemporary world. Yet as we give our witness for Christ, we can follow relevant principles from the apologetics practiced in the NT.

New Testament Principles for Apologetics

1. The NT gives both commands and examples for defending the faith.
2. Appeal to miracle and prophecy may appropriately be made as evidence for faith.
3. Even though formal theistic proofs are not developed in the NT, evidence of God's handiwork in nature can be presented as it was to non-Jews.
4. The primary thrust of Christian apologetics centers in Christ's claims to be Messiah, Lord, Savior, and God in flesh and in the credentials which support his claims, especially his resurrection.
5. The NT does not make strict distinctions between preaching (*kerygma*), teaching (*didache*), and defense (*apologia*) or between apologetics and evangelism.
6. Apologetics involves both commending and defending the faith. We must give a positive case for the truth of Christianity as well as answering the attacks brought against the faith.

---

[63] Michael Green, *The Second Epistle General of Peter and the General Epistle of Jude* (Grand Rapids: Eerdmans, 1968) 159.
[64] Ibid., 160.

7. We must expose the bankruptcy of non-Christian world-views.
8. We must understand the interests and needs of our audience and shape our defense in light of the authorities and line of argument most persuasive to them.
9. Speak the truth with love. Commend and defend the faith with gentleness and respect.

Review Questions

1. Compare and contrast Paul's apologetic to the Jews with his approach to non-Jews.

2. What points of contact did Paul make in his sermon on Mars Hill? How did Paul engage his culture?

3. Summarize Bruce's outline of Paul's Mars Hill speech.

4. What is Kantzer's position on the role in apologetics of the evidence in the natural universe?

5. Apologetics can benefit believers. Explain.

6. Briefly state the apologetic purpose of each Gospel.

7. State Bauckham's position on the Gospels as eyewitness testimony.

8. Identify some Jewish objections to Jesus being the Messiah that are answered in Matthew's Gospel.

9. What does Morris list as the two things John wants readers to believe about Jesus?

10. In what two ways does Bruce say Stephen is a precursor of future apologists?

11. Bruce identified three types of defenses in the book of Acts. Identify them and the basic response given.

12. How may the book of Hebrews be seen as a philosophy of history?
13. Briefly state the nine principles for apologetics drawn from the NT.

Suggested Reading

Bruce, F.F. *The Book of Acts*, rev. ed. New International Commentary of the New Testament. Grand Rapids: Eerdmans, 1988; and *The Acts of the Apostles: The Greek Text with Introduction and Commentary*, 3rd ed. Grand Rapids: Eerdmans, 1990, and Wipf & Stock, 2000. Excellent commentaries giving attention to the apologetic nature of the speeches in Acts.

Bruce, F.F. *The Defense of the Gospel in the New Testament*, rev. ed. Grand Rapids: Eerdmans, 1977. Brief, well written. May still be the best summary available of New Testament apologetics.

McGrath, Alister E. "Apologetics to the Jews," *Bibliotheca Sacra*, 155:618 (April–June 1998): 131-138; "Apologetics to the Greeks," *Bibliotheca Sacra*, 155:619 (July–September 1998): 259-265; "Apologetics to the Romans," *Bibliotheca Sacra*, 155:620 (October–December 1998): 387-398.

"And they have conquered him by the blood of the Lamb and by the word of their testimony, for they loved not their lives even unto death."

Revelation 12:11

13

History of Apologetics: AD 96–450

History of Apologetics: AD 96–450	"Not surprisingly, therefore, no apologist from previous centuries or generations precisely fills the prescription that might be written for a present-day apologetic. But a careful reading of the old masters in the field reveals that the same basic problems continually recur and that it is almost impossible to say anything substantially new. In such a time as our own, when many Christians find it especially difficult to articulate the reasonableness of their faith, it can be particularly profitable to review the record of the past."[1]
The Early Church (96–450)	
I. Second and Third Centuries	
A. Justin Martyr	
B. Athenagoras	
C. Irenaeus	
D. Tertullian	
E. Origen	
II. Fourth and Fifth Centuries	
A. Eusebius	
B. Athanasius	
C. Augustine	Avery Dulles

[1] Avery Dulles, *A History of Apologetics*, 2nd ed. (San Francisco: Ignatius Press, 2005) xx-xxi.

"In every age, Christians have sought to address the issues of their day by 'translating' timeless truths into contemporary language. They have commended the ancient faith by using up-to-date terms understood by the people around them. The trick is to find a language that communicates effectively *without* compromising the gospel in the process."[2]

Nancy R Pearcey

Letter to Diognetus—Little Known Apologetic

Scholars have used these terms—"pearl," "noblest," and "brilliant"—to describe this short yet powerful apologetic. The style of the letter demonstrates the classical training and literary skill of the unknown author. Near the end of the second century this joyful believer defended Christian faith to Diognetus, a prominent pagan. In 1453 an Italian student found our sole manuscript in a fish shop under a pile of wrapping paper. Thankfully copies had been made before the manuscript burned in 1870 in a fire in the Franco-Prussian War.[3]

The letter answered Diognetus's questions as he wanted "to know what God Christians believed in, and what sort of cult they practice which enables them to set so little store by this world, and even to make light of death itself." He expressed curiosity about "the warm fraternal affection they

[2] Nancy R. Pearcey, *Total Truth: Liberating Christianity from Its Cultural Captivity* (Wheaton, IL: Crossway, 2004) 296. Emphasis in the original.

[3] Maxwell Staniforth, *Early Christian Writings* (New York: Penguin Group, 1968) 137.

all feel for one another."[4] The fact that Christians genuinely loved one another amazed the pagans.

Responding to Diognetus's question about God, the author stated, "I pray God the Author of both our speech and hearing, to grant me such use of my tongue that you may derive the fullest benefit from listening to me, and to you such use of your ears that I may have no cause to regret having spoken."[5]

The author exposed the folly of pagan idolatry. He urged them to look "with your intelligence" at their gods accepted as divine. They are only stone, brass, wood, silver, iron, and earthenware. They are "nothing but dumb, blind, lifeless things, without sense, without movement, rotting and decaying" "Do you really call these things gods?" You worship them and become like them, but Christians are not subject to such gods.

He distinguished between Christian worship and Jewish worship pointing out that God no longer wanted sacrifices. The Christians' God is not a product of human imagination. "The Almighty Himself, the Creator of the universe, the God whom no eye can discern, has sent down his very own Truth from heaven, His own holy and incomprehensible Word, to plant it among men and ground it in their hearts."[6] God has revealed himself and he is not fire or water as pagans asserted.

God revealed himself through the incarnation of his Son. The Son, through whom all things were created, came "as God" to earth to reveal God. God does not hate us or reject us but shows his mercy. Our writer explained:

[4] *Letter to Diognetus* 1, translated by Staniforth, *Early Christian Writings*, 142-151.
[5] Ibid.
[6] Ibid., 7.

He bore with us, and in pity He took our sins upon Himself and gave His own Son as a ransom for us—the Holy for the wicked, the Sinless for sinners, the Just for the unjust . . . For was there, indeed, anything except His righteousness that could have availed to cover our sins? In whom would we, in our lawlessness and ungodliness, have been made holy, but in the Son of God alone? O sweet exchange! O unsearchable working! O benefits unhoped for!—that the wickedness of multitudes should thus be hidden in the One holy, and the holiness of One should sanctify the countless wicked![7]

Apologetics must address the mind and the heart.

The question of Diognetus about why Christians loved each other is answered. God loved people. He made them in his image with the ability to reason and sent his Son to them. He promised them his kingdom. "Once you have grasped these truths, think how your joy will overflow, and what love you will feel for Him who loved you so."[8] Christians love one another because of God's love demonstrated in his Son. Their love for one another verifies the reality of God in heaven.[9]

He cited the evidence that Christians were willing to be morally different from their culture and were willing to die for their faith. Christians refuse to expose their children on the garbage dump. They stood out because they refused to participate in sexual immorality. "Any Christian is free to share his neighbour's table, but never his marriage-bed."[10]

They show love to all men—and all men persecute them. They are misunderstood, and condemned; yet by suffering death they are quickened into life. They are poor, yet making many rich; lacking all things, yet having all things

[7] Ibid., 9.
[8] Ibid., 10.
[9] Ibid.
[10] Ibid., 5.

in abundance. They are dishonoured, yet made glorious in their very dishonour; slandered, yet vindicated. They repay calumny [i.e., slander] with blessings, and abuse with courtesy. For the good they do, they suffer stripes as evildoers; and under the strokes they rejoice like men given new life. Jews assail them as heretics, and Greeks harass them with persecutions; and yet of all their ill-wishers there is not one who can produce good grounds for his hostility.[11]

He mentions the faithfulness of martyrs who died by fire and by wild beasts as proof of the truth of their faith.

Lessons for Apologists from the Letter to Diognetus

✝ Pray for the person you are seeking to win to faith.
✝ Give honest answers to questions.
✝ Reason alone is not enough. Point to God's revelation.
✝ Christ's death is central in making our witness.
✝ Love in practice gives power to our testimony.[12]

Christians today face unbelieving attacks from philosophy, religion, science, and culture. Apologists have responded to similar attacks throughout the history of the church. An understanding of the history of apologetics can enhance one's effectiveness as an apologist. Avery Dulles, author of the important *A History of Apologetics*, says,

Most apologists are shamefully ignorant of the history of their own discipline, and for this reason they overlook important distinctions that have been worked out over the centuries and fail to build on the best achievements of the past. The history

---

[11] Ibid., 5:11-17.
[12] Michael Haykin, *Defence of the Truth: Contending for the Faith Yesterday and Today* (Webster, NY: Evangelical Press, 2004) 29.

of apologetics holds a certain fascination because it exhibits the Christian faith confronting a whole succession of cultures, religious and secular. The unchanging gospel gives unity to apologetics, but the variety of cultures makes each era unique.[13]

The purpose of this chapter is to briefly introduce leading apologists in the early history of the church and how they met the challenges of their day. The truth of Christianity does not change but cultures do. Each age faces new threats as well as old ones. It is instructive to observe how each apologist addresses and answers his culture's assumptions and attacks.

Second and Third Centuries

After Nero (37–68), the Roman authorities viewed Christianity as an unlawful religion. Pagans accused Christians of the following:

- ✧ *Atheism.* Christians rejected the Greco-Roman gods. From the perspective of the pagan culture, believing in only one God was the same as none.
- ✧ *Cannibalism.* Pagans misunderstood Jesus' statements about the Lord's Supper.
- ✧ *Incest.* The pagans concluded this must be the reason for their secret meetings and the *holy kiss.*
- ✧ *Novelty.* Christians were charged with creating a new religion that rejected all past traditions.
- ✧ *Treason.* The Romans interpreted the Christians' refusal to participate in emperor worship and the culture's religious practices as disloyalty to the government.

The early apologists answered these unjust charges and appealed to Roman officials for civil toleration of the Christian religion. They exposed the absurdities in pagan mythology and

[13] "The History and Purpose of Apologetics—An Interview with Avery Cardinal Dulles, S.J.," by Carl E. Olson, **http://ignatiusinsight.com/features2005/print 2005/carddullesint_july05.html**.

argued that human aspirations were best fulfilled in Christianity and demonstrated by the moral lives of Christians.

Justin Martyr (100–167), leading Christian apologist of the second century, was born of pagan parents in Palestine and died a Christian teacher in Rome. Before becoming a believer he studied Stoicism, Aristotelianism, Pythagoreanism, and Platonism.

One day while Justin stood beside the Aegean Sea, an old man approached him and asked, "Does philosophy produce happiness?"

Being a philosopher Justin responded, "Absolutely and it alone."

After much discussion the man said Plato could not answer many questions, but Christianity was a true philosophy that could answer all questions. The prophets inspired by the Holy Spirit prophesied the birth of Jesus and declared truth. He asked Justin to beg God to open to him "the gates of light." Justin said he never saw him again but "a flame was kindled in my soul."[14] Justin discovered in Christianity "the only sure and useful philosophy" being convinced that it fulfilled the highest aspirations of the philosophers.

Many Jews rejected the divinity of Christ. Some mixed their Judaism with Greek philosophy. Justin's *Dialog with Trypho the Jew* (130), an apologetic to convince Jews of the messiahship of Jesus, showed how the Law of Moses prepared for Christ and the gospel and marshaled the evidences of fulfilled prophecy. He addressed the emperor in his *First Apology* (150–155) and addressed the Roman Senate in *Second Apology* (155–161). He wrote both after incidents of martyrdom. Because the criminal charges against Christians were false he sought toleration for Christians under Roman law, insisting they did not deserve the persecution inflicted on them. He believed that if

---

[14] Justin Martyr, *Dialog with Trypho the Jew*, 3, 7-8.

Christians did not speak up, they bore guilt for the ignorance of the pagans.[15]

In *First Apology* Justin refuted the popular charges against Christianity, such as atheism, novelty, and being political liabilities. He emphasized the high moral character of Christians as a strong positive apologetic. He saw the biblical religion as the oldest and truest philosophy. Jesus, the unique Son of God, fulfilled the prophecies in the OT and manifested supreme excellence of character. Though impressed with Socrates, Justin clearly stated that his faith was not in Socrates but in Christ. Any wisdom found by the philosophers came from the divine Logos and the Hebrew Scriptures. Uneducated believers have access to great wisdom in the Bible.[16]

Justin defended the bodily resurrection of Jesus answering those who considered the resurrection appearances as only spiritual. The apostles "were by every kind of proof persuaded that it was Himself, and in the body, they asked Him to eat with them, that they might thus still more accurately ascertain that He had in verity risen bodily."[17]

Responding to critics' reasons for rejecting Christianity Justin gave a rational apologetic. Eusebius described him: "Justin in philosopher's garb served as an ambassador of the word of God."[18] Some wrongly conclude that Justin was a rationalist. Geisler says, "Justin was far from a rationalist in his use of reason. He believed firmly in the superiority and necessity of divine revelation. However, there is no doubt that Justin, like classical apologists after him, used reason to explain and defend Christian faith."[19]

---

[15] Justin Martyr, *First Apology*, 3.

[16] Ibid., 60.

[17] Justin Martyr, "Fragments of the Lost Work of Justin on the Resurrection," 9, quoted in A. Roberts and J. Donaldson, eds., *The Ante-Nicene Fathers*, vol. 1, 298.

[18] Eusebius, *Church History*, 4.11.

[19] Norman L. Geisler, *Baker Encyclopedia of Christian Evidences* (Grand Rapids: Baker Books, 1999) 396.

In 167 Justin and six others were beaten and beheaded for the crime of being Christians and refusing to sacrifice to Roman gods.[20] He spoke to three cultures—the Greco-Roman paganism of his background, the Greek-speaking Judaism of the Diaspora (many of their methods he employed but their conclusion he rejected), and the advancing Christian mission.

Athenagoras (d. ca. 185), a Christian philosopher of Athens, Greece, was an articulate apologist of the second century. His defense of the faith before Marcus Aurelius was clear and strong. Athenagoras thoroughly destroyed each of the standard charges against Christians—incest, cannibalism, and atheism—and then offered positive reasons for Christian beliefs. Responding to the charges of immorality he defended the purity of Christians contrasted with the immoral behavior of pagan gods—eating their own children, incest with mothers or sisters, and adultery with other deities and humans. He cited the Christians' respect for human life by forbidding abortion. He described their love for their neighbors and their enemies.[21]

Early tradition said that Athenagoras was originally a philosopher who intended to write against Christianity. While studying the Scriptures preparing to refute them, the "all-holy Spirit" changed him and he became a teacher of the faith and a brilliant Christian apologist.[22]

He addressed his apology, The *Embassy* (also called *The Plea*), to the emperor Marcus Aurelius (176). Russ Bush says,

> The *Embassy* of Athenagoras is probably the finest single apologetic work from the period of the early church. He appears to be well acquainted with the leading ideas of the current philosophies, and he may be properly characterized as sharing the essential and pervading spirit of the age—

---

[20] Russ Bush, *Classical Readings in Christian Apologetics: A.D. 100–1800* (Grand Rapids: Zondervan, 1983) 1–3.

[21] Athenagoras, *The Embassy*, chapter 11.

[22] Bush, *Classical Reading in Christian Apologetics*, 31.

eclecticism (not following any one system exclusively but selecting good elements from more than one system).[23]

He drew ideas from Plato, Stoics, Neo-Pythagoreans. He respected reason but recognized its limitations. Reason alone could not come to a full knowledge of God; that could be obtained only through revelation.

He believed that the Bible was the Word of God inspired by the Holy Spirit. Against atheists and polytheists he defended the existence, unity, and triune nature of God. He saw God as the eternal Creator and matter as created and temporal.

B.P. Pratten observes that his works reveal a "practiced pen and a richly cultured mind. He is by far the most elegant, and certainly at the same time one of the ablest, of the early Christian Apologists."[24] "Athenagoras had that unusual ability to tie everything together, express himself clearly, and use language that catches the imagination of the reader."[25] He emphasized the elements of Christianity most easily commended to the pagan world. He pled for civil toleration asking the rulers to stop persecuting Christians.

Irenaeus (120–202/3), a Greek raised in Asia Minor, became an important theologian in the second century. He studied under Polycarp, bishop of Smyrna, who received instruction from the apostle John. Irenaeus read many of the Greek authors and most of the early Christian works. He came to Lyons in southern Gaul as a missionary, later serving as bishop there. "His evangelistic spirit is clearly seen in his apologetic writings."[26] He viewed himself as a faithful transmitter of the apostles' teaching. He referred to it as the "rule of

---

[23] Ibid., 32.

[24] B.P. Pratten, "Introductory Note to the Writings of Athenagoras," in *The Ante-Nicene Fathers*, vol. 2, eds., A. Roberts and J. Donaldson.

[25] Bush, *Classical Readings in Christian Apologetics*, 33.

[26] Ibid., 64.

faith" and "the word of Christ" in answering false teachers. He defended the NT canon and the teaching of the apostles. He stated "as a fundamental principle that all Christian teaching must be in harmony with that teaching of the Apostles, that is the Twelve and Paul."[27]

He taught a "soul-making" view of suffering as developing humans into all they were meant to be. The bishop before him had been martyred, nevertheless Irenaeus feared heresy more than death. He wrote a five-volume work *Against Heresies*[28] (185), a systematic refutation of Gnosticism, which in his day was the most serious intellectual challenge to the Christian faith.

Gnosticism includes a variety of second- and third-century heretical viewpoints. Edwin Yamauchi states, "Fundamental to clearly Gnostic systems was a dualism that opposed the transcendent God and an ignorant demiurge (often a caricature of the OT Jehovah). . . . The material creation, including the body, was regarded as inherently evil."[29] Divine souls trapped in a material body could only be released and find salvation through a special knowledge (*gnosis*) known only to the elect. Most denied Christ's incarnation.

Gnostics reinterpreted Christianity through the lens of false philosophy. Apologists have through the centuries had to discern when Christianity was being corrupted by false philosophy. Defenders of the faith have arisen to alert the church to the danger and have endeavored to refute the false worldview.

Irenaeus said the Gnostics began with an incorrect view of creation and evil. They wrongly viewed matter as evil and failed to distinguish between the Creator and the creation. He

---

[27] Irenaeus, *Against Heresies*, III, preface.

[28] *Refutation and Overthrow of Gnosis, Falsely So Called* was the full name of the work.

[29] E.M. Yamauchi, "Gnosticism," in *Dictionary of New Testament Background*, eds. Craig A. Evans & Stanley E. Porter (Downers Grove, IL: InterVarsity, 2000) 416. See pages 414-418 for clarification of varieties of Gnosticism.

refuted Valentinian and Marcion, Gnostic leaders. He strongly defended fundamentals such as the equality of the Son with the Father, the existence of only one God, the creation of all things by the word of God, the fall of man, redemption, the actual historical incarnation of Christ, and his bodily resurrection—all supported by the authority of the Scriptures.

His apologetic *Demonstration of the Apostolic Preaching* emphasized the OT prophecies for the messiahship of Jesus. He considered the NT as Scripture on a par with the OT and defended the four Gospels. He believed the churches of apostolic foundations preserved the apostolic teaching. He stressed the uniqueness of the God of the Bible, as well as the authority and reliability of the apostles' teaching. He viewed the incarnation as the culmination of God's dealings with mankind in bringing salvation and unity to the human race.

Tertullian (ca. 160–225). Tertullian's legal knowledge and skill in rhetoric made him an influential Latin Christian leader in the Western church. A native of Carthage, North Africa, he was raised a pagan. He later practiced law in Rome where he accepted Christianity in the 190s. He became a presbyter in the church in Carthage. A few years before his death he joined with Montanism. The founder and some leaders claimed direct revelations. They protested the formalism and worldliness of the church and advocated withdrawal from the world as preparation for the coming advent. There is some debate whether or not he returned to the orthodox church before his death.

Bush describes him, "He argued for Christianity by appealing to the absurdity of persecution, to the authority of Scripture, and to the factual evidence that supports orthodox faith. His brilliance and his versatility made him a powerful apologist for Christianity in the days of the late second century."[30]

---

[30] Bush, *Classical Readings in Christian Apologetics*, xv.

Everett Ferguson calls his *Apology* (197) "the greatest Latin apologetic for Christianity before Augustine."[31] He skillfully responded to the social and political attacks on Christians insisting they were condemned without investigation. He asked why all kinds of deities are lawful except the God of the Christians? The good lives of Christians demonstrate the truth of Christianity. He stressed their unconditional love for one another. Persecution failed because Christians continued to believe even when threatened with death. "The more we are cut down by you, the more in number we grow; the blood of Christians is seed."[32] Martyrdom became an apologetic for the Christian faith.

He asked, "What indeed has Athens to do with Jerusalem? What concord is there between the Academy and the Church?"[33] In the context he argued that heresy, like philosophy, resulted from a search for truth apart from God's revelation. He said that one could find truth in the churches that taught the Scripture. Scripture presents the truth of Christ formulated by the church into a rule of faith. He felt Christians did not need philosophy in the sense of seeking truth apart from revelation. He did not totally reject reason and philosophy since he gave a rational defense of the faith.

He spoke of the self-attesting Christ speaking in the Bible. "After Jesus Christ we have no need of speculation, after the gospel no need of research, when we come to believe, we have no desire to believe anything else; for we begin by believing that there is nothing else which we have to believe."[34]

He said the crucifixion of Christ "is credible because it is unlikely."[35] This is often translated "I believe because it is

---

[31] Everett Ferguson, *Church History, Volume One: From Christ to Pre-Reformation* (Grand Rapids: Zondervan, 2005) 127.

[32] Tertullian, *Apology*, 50.

[33] Tertullian, *Prescription against Heretics*, 7.

[34] Ibid.

[35] Tertullian, *On the Flesh of Christ*, 5.

absurd." He did not use the Latin word for absurd meaning *logically contradictory* but a word meaning *foolish*. It was foolish and impossible only to unbelievers (*1 Cor 1:18*). He was not defending an apologetic method of irrationalism or anti-intellectualism. He argues that the utter improbability of essential Christian claims indicates that they were not invented by humans.

In his *Against Marcion*, Tertullian made clear that he considered Christian faith to be rational.[36] While he stressed God's revelation in the human soul, he also acknowledged "We are worshippers of one God, of whose existence and character Nature teaches all men."[37] His fiery nature and vigorous prose resulted in strong statements. He described Marcion as a "mouse . . . who has gnawed the Gospels to pieces."[38]

Modalistic Monarchians believed that God the Father and God the Son were one, only differing in their mode of appearance. James North summarizes Tertullian's view:

[Tertullian] insisted that the Father is God, the Son is God, and the Holy Spirit is God; yet there are not three gods, but one. His formula was to understand this as one substance (one Being) in three persons. In so doing, he safeguarded the uniqueness of each of the three figures of the Godhead; at the same time he defended the basic position of monotheism.[39]

Alexandria, Egypt, became a center for Christian theology with a philosophical slant in the third century. Clement of Alexandria (c. 150–c. 214) became the head of the catechetical school in 190. He set Christian thought in the context of the philosophical thought of the day, considering philosophy a tutor to bring the Greeks to Christ. His apologetic *Encouragement* gracefully appealed to his readers to become followers of

---

[36] Tertullian, *Against Marcion*, 1,23-25.
[37] Tertullian, *To Scapula*, 2.
[38] Tertullian, *Against Marcion*, 1.1.
[39] James North, *A History of the Church: From Pentecost to the Present* (Joplin, MO: College Press, 1983), 95.

Christ. He was conversant with classical culture. He emphasized the Logos of God as the true source of knowledge and freedom in his responses to Gnosticism, polytheism, and dualism. Ferguson says,

> Clement reconciles the supreme goodness of God with evil in the world by distinguishing between what God causes and what happens without his providence, by affirming that God can transform evil into good, by noting God's use of evil as a chastisement and by pointing out that it was free will that introduced evil into the world. The goal for human beings is to be joined to God by participating in his goodness.[40]

He used allegorical language in his appeal to intellectuals of his day.

Origen (c.185–c. 254). Raised in a Christian family, he studied under Clement of Alexandria becoming his successor as a teacher of his school at the age of eighteen. His *Against Celsus* refuted the anti-Christian charges made by the Platonist philosopher Celsus in his book, *The True Doctrine* (Logos) which attempted to discredit Christianity. Ambrose, one of Origen's converts, asked Origen to answer it. In the preface Origen proposed to answer fully every objection. While long and somewhat tedious, Everett Ferguson calls *Against Celsus* "the greatest Greek apology for Christianity."[41]

Many consider Celsus the strongest intellectual opponent of biblical Christianity in the early centuries. He argued as a Jew and as a pagan philosopher. He alleged Christians borrowed doctrine and morality from others and accepted many foolish things. If Jesus really was divine why would he have to go into hiding into Egypt? Why would a god allow himself to be betrayed by friends and then be killed by soldiers? His fol-

---

[40] Everett Ferguson, "Clement of Alexandria," in *New Dictionary of Christian Apologetics*, eds., W. C. Campbell-Jack and Gavin McGrath (Downers Grove, IL: InterVarsity, 2006) 160.

[41] Everett Ferguson, "Origen," in *New Dictionary of Christian Apologetics*, 516.

lowers were only tax gatherers and sailors, men of worthless and untrustworthy character. They welcomed wicked and ignorant people. He said Jesus was a sorcerer and denied any good evidence for the resurrection. He objected to Christians making exclusive claims to truth and charged that they had introduced a new religion detrimental to society. Origen replied to these charges.[42]

Origen answered charges about the irrationality of Christians and lack of historical foundations for Christianity. He emphasized the change in conduct Christ produces in contrast with paganism and cited Christians' willingness to investigate to learn truth, and the moral purity of Christ and his followers. In spite of rejecting many Roman values he argued that their higher morality benefited Rome.

Celsus said Christians and Jews attack each other on trivial things. They differ on whether the savior had already come or not. He saw no reason to believe that a god would come to earth because he would have to change from best to worst which a god could not do. Because Jesus was historically insignificant, he could not have been the divine son of God, the savior of the world.[43]

North states, "Origen effectively silenced this [Celsus'] kind of attack on Christian faith."[44] Dulles comments, "Adopting a direct and logical style Origen pursues each argument to its ultimate conclusion. . . . He is perhaps the first apologist who seems prepared to take on any objection that can be urged against the Christian faith, whether from the standpoint of history, of philosophy, or of the natural sciences."[45]

Origen was the most prolific Christian writer before Augustine. In addition to being an apologist he produced the first

---

[42] Origen, *Against Celsus*, Book II: chapters. xlviii–lxvii.

[43] Ibid., Book IV: chapters xiv–lxxix; and Book VII: chapters liii–lvii.

[44] North, *A History of the Church*, 100.

[45] Avery Dulles, *A History of Apologetics*, 2nd ed., 46.

systematic theology, wrote biblical commentaries and ser-mons, engaged in textual criticism, and developed principles of Christian education. Many of his controversial views were not accepted by Christian orthodoxy: allegorical interpretation, eternal generation and subordination of the Son, preexistence of souls, spiritualizing of the resurrection body, and universal salvation. Origen moved to Caesarea in 232 and continued teaching. He was imprisoned and tortured in 251 in the Decian persecution and died in 254.

Fourth and Fifth Centuries

Eusebius of Caesarea (260–339). Origen left his consid-erable library to Pamphilus and his student Eusebius. This library became the foundation for Eusebius's important church history, *Ecclesiastical History* (325). Eusebius quotes Papias and early Christian writers giving independent testimony to tradi-tional authors, the early date, and historical value of the Gospels.[46] Eusebius wrote two major apologetic works. In *Preparation for the Gospel* (314) he refuted Porphyry's philosophical case against Christianity by showing the absurdities of pagan-ism's pantheism and the superiority of the Hebrew faith. The *Demonstration of the Gospel* (320) gave a rational, historical response to Porphyry's critique of Jesus' miracles and resur-rection. He focused on the moral superiority of Christ, his mir-acles, and fulfillment of prophecy. He defended the credibility of the apostles arguing that the view they were deceivers did-n't make sense in light of their mutual agreement and willing-ness to die for a lie they created.

Eusebius answered some common objections: Jesus' disci-ples and the Gospels were unreliable erroneous witnesses; Jesus was just one of many miracle workers in the ancient world; and Christians disparaged reason gullibly taking Christianity on faith

---

[46] Eusebius, *Ecclesiastical History*, III, 39; V, 20.

alone. He stressed the biblical text itself, especially fulfilled prophecy. He argued that the lives of Christians demonstrated the truth of the Christian faith, notably as they faced persecution.

Athanasius (298–373). Being raised in Alexandria, Egypt, he was well educated in Greek classics, philosophy, theology, and in biblical knowledge. He wrote two major apologetic works before the Council of Nicea (325). In *Against the Heathen* he built a natural theology on the order and harmony of the universe. *The Incarnation of the Word* defends the incarnation arguing that if Jesus was less than God he could not have been the Redeemer. He stressed the cross and the resurrection. To Jews he emphasized fulfillment of prophecy. To unbelieving Gentiles he gave evidence of the truthfulness of Christian claims. In speaking of the second coming of Jesus, Athanasius called persons to repent and believe in Christ.

Edgar and Oliphint say that Athanasius's *The Incarnation of the Word of God* is "one of the great masterpieces of patristic writing."[47] He attacked Jewish and Gentile unbelief and made a positive case for Jesus being God himself coming in flesh to save mankind.

At the Council when he was twenty-seven, he championed the view of the eternal deity of Jesus against Arius who affirmed that there was a time when Jesus did not exist. Arius taught Jesus had a beginning by a creative act of God. He also believed that Jesus was of a different substance or essence from the Father being subordinate to the Father. By virtue of his obedience to the Father Jesus was divine. But he was not deity.

Athanasius argued that if Jesus was less than deity he would not be the savior of mankind. He believed the issue of man's eternal salvation hinged on the view of the nature of Christ and his relationship with the Father. Christ was coequal,

---

[47] William Edgar & K. Scott Oliphint, *Christian Apologetics: Past & Present, Volume 1: To 1500* (Wheaton: Crossway, 2009), 174.

coeternal, and coessential with the Father. The issue struck at the very heart of Christianity and salvation. The council accepted Athanasius's view as the orthodox view. This victory was short-lived. For the next half-century the battle continued between orthodox believers and Arians. Athanasius suffered exile five times for his views.

After the Council he wrote *Apology against the Arians* and other apologetic writings. His writings provide classical statements of orthodox Christianity. In *Festal Letter 39* (367) he listed the twenty-seven books in our present NT canon, our earliest exact list. He stated, "In these alone is the teaching of true religion proclaimed as good news. Let no one add to these or take anything from them."[48]

Augustine (354–430). Bernard Ramm says of Augustine:

> Outside of the apostolic circle it is difficult to find a man with a greater stature than that of Augustine, bishop of Hippo. He was a mystic, saint, preacher, administrator, scholar, theologian, controversialist, philosopher, historian, letter writer, commentator, teacher, and author. This great genius created the philosophy of history with his *City of God* and introspective religious literature with his *Confessions*. The roots of our modern university curriculum stem from his work, *On Christian Doctrine*. He is the chief parent of medieval mysticism, monasticism, and scholasticism. He dominated the theology of the Middle Ages as its greatest authority. The Reformers claimed that they were doing nothing more or less than returning to Augustine.[49]

Augustine was born near Carthage in North Africa to a pagan father and a Christian mother. They sent him to a school at age twelve where he adopted a pagan lifestyle. At sixteen he went to Carthage where he studied rhetoric, Latin classics, and

---

[48] Quoted in Everett Ferguson, *Church History, Volume One, From Christ to Pre-Reformation* (Grand Rapids: Zondervan, 2005) 119.

[49] Bernard Ramm, *Varieties of Christian Apologetics* (Grand Rapids: Baker Book House, 1961) 147.

Greek philosophy. Plato's idealism impressed him. Seeking to find a resolution to the problem of evil, he was intrigued with dualism which viewed the soul as imprisoned in an evil body. However, he later rejected dualism. For years he cohabited with a concubine and fathered a son.

In 384 he moved to Milan where he taught rhetoric. He came to see ultimate reality as spiritual and not material. Human philosophy did not provide ultimate answers or satisfy his quest for certainty. Through reading the Bible he became convinced that the grace of God could save him from his sins. While in Milan the sermons of Ambrose and the prayers of his mother influenced him. In 386 at the age of thirty-three Augustine professed faith in Christ and Ambrose baptized him the next year.

His *Confessions* (401), a classic of spiritual autobiography, gave his personal testimony of how he lived away from God and how he became a believer and found forgiveness. Augustine defended the worthiness and majesty of God.

His distrust in the senses led him to seek inner assurance for his faith. Truth is not found in the senses but in the inner world. "Do not go outside, come back into your very own self, truth dwells in the inner man."[50] Dulles observes, "The point of departure for Augustine's apologetic is subjective and psychological rather than objective and systematic."[51]

The doubter possesses knowledge and thus has truth. "Everyone who knows that he is in doubt about something knows the truth, and in regard to this he is certain."[52] He agreed with the rationalist in the sense that he held the test of truth lies in the mind and not the senses. Truth is that which is consistent and does not violate the law of noncontradiction. These basic principles of thought are impressed upon the mind

---

[50] Augustine, *The True Religion*, XXXIX, 72.
[51] Avery Dulles, *History of Apologetics*, 2nd ed., 75.
[52] Augustine, *The True Religion* XXIX, 73.

by God, "for it exists eternally in the reason of things, and has its origin with God."[53]

In 388 he returned to Africa, where in 395 he was consecrated as the new bishop of Hippo. He wrote apologetic answers to the Manicheans, the Pelagians, and the Donatists.

Believing human reason can establish the existence of God by arguments, his *The Free Choice of the Will* gave a theistic argument for the existence of God from truth. Our minds acknowledge absolute truths such as our self-evident existence and mathematical truths (2 + 2 = 4), but we did not cause them. An independent, unchanging Mind must be the source for these truths. "Behold, there is He wherever truth is known."[54] However, he is not a rationalist in natural theology because he believed one must be illuminated by God in order to gain positive knowledge of God.

The Goths under their king Alaric sacked Rome in 410. Being the first time a foreign army had been at Rome's gates in over 600 years, this event sent shock waves through the empire. Many concluded that the gods were angry because Rome had accepted Christianity and this setback would not have happened if Rome had remained pagan. In response to this charge Augustine wrote *The City of God* (413–426).[55]

Books 1–10 attacked paganism, refuting the view that polytheistic worship ensures worldly prosperity. He recounted the fall of many pagan nations where their gods did not prevent these catastrophes. Rome was an earthly city subject to decline. Its fall did not refute Christianity. Rome fell, but Christianity lives on because it is an eternal city.

He developed a philosophy of history in Books 11–22 that interpreted human events from a total perspective. God gives us both temporal and spiritual blessings that the Roman gods

[53] Augustine, *On Christian Doctrine*, II, 32.

[54] Augustine, *Confessions*, IV, 12

[55] Augustine, *Retractions*, 2.43.

could not give. Those who live for self make up the city of earth. They love only themselves and do not see the total perspective. Persons in the city of God love God and others and have an eternal perspective.[56]

Those in both cities live in the world and continue in conflict. Regardless of what happens in this temporal world, the Christian as a part of the eternal City of God can continue to trust and be faithful to the sovereign God of the universe. The outcome of history rests in the hands of the eternal God. In the end of time God will give people what they love most—sharing his presence or eternal separation from him. Standing at a significant crossroads of history, Augustine called people to be a part of the City of God as the old classical civilization crumbled beneath their feet.

Edgar and Oliphint characterize *The City of God*:

> What we have, therefore, in this *magnum opus* is a clear apologetic, a defense of the Christian faith. It is a defense applied to a very specific occasion. Even so, the general principles that Augustine is able to advance and develop, as he argues for the heavenly citizenship of every Christian, are themselves applicable across the spectrum of the church's history.[57]

Sometimes Augustine sounded like the basis of faith was unquestioned divine authority as if reason had no part in justifying Christian belief. An important part of Augustine's influence was his emphasis on faith seeking understanding. Yet although he accepted the Scriptures as absolutely authoritative and inerrant, he did not see it as self-authenticating. People needed signs, specifically miracle and prophecy, which are credentials establishing the authority of Scripture. He viewed knowledge of the past as based on authority. We believe it is true based on testimony. "Since for Augustine the historical evidence for miracle and prophecy lay in the past, it was in the realm of authori-

---

[56] Augustine, *The City of God*, XIV, 28.
[57] Edgar and Oliphint, *Christian Apologetics*, 259.

ty, not reason. . . . Therefore, he turns to the present miracle of the church as the basis for accepting the authority of Scripture."[58] Avery Dulles states, "In his apologetical works, Augustine, mirroring the route he had followed in his own religious pilgrimage, frequently argued to the truth of Christianity on the basis of the concrete reality of the Catholic Church."[59]

Augustine died in 430 having set forth a comprehensive Christian worldview as a Christian Platonist. In the light of his influence on Catholicism, Protestantism, and modern philosophy, few thinkers have had a more significant influence on western history.

The affirmation of the full humanity and deity of Jesus by the Council of Chalcedon (451) and by Leo in his *Tome* (451) represented significant triumphs for Christian apologetics.

The early patristic apologists contended that the books of Moses gave the best account of creation and argued that pagan religions led to moral decay. To the Jews they presented the testimony of messianic prophecies. In their apologetic they emphasized the change in the hearts and lives of believers.

Many in this era drew upon Platonism in developing their worldview. The faithfulness of martyrs and the political support for Christianity (Constantine's conversion) contributed to the advance of Christianity. Eusebius and Augustine in their apologetic related Christianity to the big picture of world history. Edgar and Oliphint remind us, "Courageous, erudite, and also deeply spiritual, the apologetics of the Fathers continue to inspire their successors down to the present."[60] Through the periods of persecution the church persisted because of the faithfulness of believers who refused to deny the faith even on threat of death.

---

[58] William Lane Craig, *Reasonable Faith: Christian Truth and Apologetics*, 3rd ed. (Wheaton, IL: Crossway, 2008) 31.

[59] Dulles, *History of Apologetics*, 78.

[60] Edgar & Oliphint, *Christian Apologetics*, 18.

The Early Church (96–450)	
Apologists and Their Principal Works	**Primary Threat**
Justin Martyr (100–167), *First Apology*	Civil and social pagan charges
Dialog with Trypho the Jew	Jewish unbelief
Athenagoras (d. ca. 185), *The Embassy* and *Apology*	Civil and social pagan charges
	Atheism and polytheism
Irenaeus (115–202), *Against Heresies* and *Demonstration of the Apostolic Preaching*	Gnosticism
Tertullian (160–220), *Apology* and *Against Marcion*	Civil and social pagan charges
	Gnosticism
Origen (c. 185–ca. 254), *Against Celsus*	Greek philosophy
Eusebius (ca. 260–ca. 340), *The Preparation of the Gospel* and *Proof of the Gospel*	Pagan pantheistic philosophy
Athanasius (298–373), *Against the Heathen* and *Incarnation of the Word*	Arianism
Augustine (354–430), *Confessions* and *The City of God*	Accusation that Christians caused the fall of Rome

Review Questions

1. What lessons can apologists learn from *Letter to Diognetus*?

2. List and explain the charges leveled against Christians in early church history.

3. Name and state the purpose of Justin Martyr's apologetic to the Jews and to the emperor.

4. What positive comments were made about Athenagoras as an apologist?

5. Define Gnosticism and summarize the defense made by Irenaeus to the Gnostics.

6. What aspects of Tertullian's apologetic did you agree with and what did you not agree with?

7. State the charges Celsus made against Christianity and summarize how Origen answered him.

8. What did Arius believe about Jesus and how did Athanasius respond?

9. What did Ramm say about the importance of Augustine?

10. What charge did Augustine answer in *The City of God*? Why is this book significant?

11. Which two apologists put Christianity in the context of world history?

Suggested Reading

Bush, L. Russ. *Classical Readings in Christian Apologetics: A. D. 100–1800*. Grand Rapids: Zondervan, 1983. Brief introductions and selected readings from major Christian apologists through 1800.

Dulles, Avery. *A History of Apologetics*, 2nd ed. San Francisco: Ignatius Press, 2005. Major work by a Catholic. Most extensive and up-to-date history of apologetics available in English.

Edgar, William, and K. Scott Oliphint. *Christian Apologetics: Past & Present, A Primary Source Reader, Volume 1: To 1500*. Wheaton, IL: Crossway, 2009. A collection of classic pre-Reformation apologetic sources with brief introductions.

Ramm, Bernard. *Varieties of Christian Apologetics*. Grand Rapids: Baker, 1961. Summarizes the apologetics of nine thinkers arranged under systems stressing subjective immediacy, natural theology, and revelation.

Reid, J.K.S. *Christian Apologetics*. Grand Rapids: Eerdmans, 1969. A brief history of apologetics from the perspective of a neo-orthodox theologian.

> *"Blessed is the man who remains steadfast under trial, for when he has stood the test he will receive the crown of life, which God has promised to those who love him."*
>
> **James 1:12**

14

History of Apologetics: AD 450–1805

Apologetics "consists of the positive declaration of this gospel in the face of the facts and circumstances with which it is confronted and by which it is often opposed. Apologetics engages with confessed enemies of Christianity outside, defending it against the ignorance, misunderstanding and defamation of unbelief. It engages with the wreckers from within, defending the Gospel against heresy that would ruin or disable it. And it engages more generally in expounding the faith so that it may secure a fair hearing, knowing that it is equally important to emphasize that reason is not the whole of faith and that faith is not tenable in utter defiance of reason. Apologetics not only defends but also commends the faith."[1]

J.K.S. Reid

Profile: Mortimer Adler—The Journey from Pagan Philosopher to Christian Believer

Even though he grew up with an Orthodox Jewish father, Mortimer Adler (1902–2001) never accepted the Jewish faith. He recounted, "It was through my study of philosophy, not through religious observances and rituals, that I became interested in God—as an object of thought, not as an object of love and worship. . . . When I graduated from college at twenty and started to conduct Great Books seminars with Mark Van Doren, I first came into contact with the Treatise on God in the *Summa Theologica* of Thomas Aquinas."[2] The "intellectual austerity, integrity, precision and brilliance of that book" intrigued and excited his mind initiating a philosophical study of theology.[3] This interest resulted in a book he wrote in 1980, *How to Think about God: A Guide for the 20th-Century Pagan*. He wrote it as a pagan to pagans. But it was an important step in his conversion from being a philosophical theologian to becoming a religious believer.

In 1932 Adler joined the American Catholic Philosophical Association. "Without becoming a Roman Catholic, I had become a Thomist in philosophy as a result of my intensive

[1] J.K.S. Reid, *Christian Apologetics* (Grand Rapids: Eerdmans, 1969) 13-14.
[2] Mortimer J. Adler, "A Philosopher's Religious Faith," in *Philosophers Who Believe: The Spiritual Journeys of 11 Leading Thinkers*, ed. Kelly James Clark (Downers Grove, IL: InterVarsity, 1993) 205.
[3] Ibid.

study of the *Summa theologica* of Thomas Aquinas."[4] He attended Episcopalian services with both his first wife and his second but did not convert to Christianity until 1984.

From 1943 to 1978 he worked on improving the arguments for the existence of God, being dissatisfied with Aquinas's five ways of proving God's existence. He came to the conclusion that purely philosophical reasoning merely affirmed the existence of God but did not bring one to belief in a good God who loves his creatures, who answers our prayers and forgives our sins.

> I therefore concluded by saying that the soundest rational argument for God's existence could carry us only to the edge of the chasm that separated the philosophical affirmation of God's existence from religious belief in God. What is usually called "a leap of faith" is needed to carry anyone across the chasm. But the leap of faith is usually misunderstood as being a progress from having insufficient reasons for affirming God's existence to a state of greater certitude in that affirmation. That is not the case. The leap of faith consists in going from the conclusion of a merely philosophical theology to a religious belief in a God that has revealed himself as a loving, just and merciful Creator of the cosmos, a God to be loved, worshiped and prayed to.[5]

As he thought about God, he wanted to know which of the world religions had the best claim to being true. During a prolonged illness in 1984, by the gift of grace, he made the leap of faith across the chasm to believing, worshiping, and praying to the good, loving, and merciful God. He said, "Here after many years of affirming God's existence and trying to give adequate reasons for that affirmation, I found myself

[4] Ibid., 208.
[5] Ibid., 215.

believing in God and praying to him."[6] While Father Howell was praying for him, Adler prayed silently, "Dear God, yes, I do believe, not just in the God my reason so stoutly affirms, but the God to whom Father Howell is now praying, and on whose grace and love I now joyfully rely."[7]

He confessed that he still did not understand many things and maybe would never understand them but those things did not matter. He concluded, "I feel secure in my rational affirmation of God's existence and of my understanding of the chasm between that philosophical conclusion and belief in God. I thank God for the leap of faith that enabled me to cross that chasm."[8]

The Middle Ages (450–1517)

During the Middle Ages in much of Europe the rejection of Christianity made one a social and cultural outcast. Avery Dulles notes that in this period the struggle of Christianity "was not with the old pagans or the young barbarians but with other races that had a rich cultural heritage of their own."[9]

In the Middle Ages, apologists answered the objections of Jews and Muslims. Jews lived in the west and practiced Judaism. To the Jews the apologists stressed Messianic fulfillment of OT prophecies. The Arabs presented a military and religious challenge in the East. The Jews and the Muslims received the most attention from apologists during this time. Apologists such as Anselm and Aquinas emphasized the rational grounds for Christian faith as they endeavored to strengthen the faith of Christians and prepare them to defend their faith to others.

---

[6] Ibid., 216.

[7] Ibid.

[8] Ibid., 221.

[9] Avery Dulles, A History of Apologetics, 2nd ed. (San Francisco: Ignatius Press, 2005) 91.

Beginning in the seventh century the church especially in the East faced the advances of Islam. Islam gained control of much of the Eastern Empire being turned back by Emperor Leo III as late as 718. The march of Islam was stopped in the west at Tours in 732. They wiped out the church in North Africa and put the Eastern church under Muslim political control. Between the death of Mohammed (632) and the defeat at Tours (732) the Arabs took over half of what had been the Roman Empire and held political control of at least half of what had been the Christian world: Syria, Persia, Asia Minor, Palestine, Egypt, northern Africa, Spain, central Asia.

Latourette states,

> As was expected, nearly everywhere the Arab conquests were followed by extensive defections to Islam. Occasionally, but infrequently, these were accomplished by force. Some were from the conviction that the Moslems were right in proclaiming Mohammed to be the true prophet of God and to have a later and higher revelation than Christianity. The conviction was reinforced by the military victories, but they appeared to prove that Islam was under the peculiar favour of God. Many moved over to Islam from quite mundane reasons: from the worldly standpoint it was better to be identified with the ruling class.[10]

As Muslim forces advanced in some cases, they were welcomed as liberators from the Byzantine emperor. Ferguson states,

> The rapid expansion of Islam in lands where Christianity had first taken root (Palestine, Syria, Egypt) demonstrates how superficial the Christianization had become. The people had been harassed by doctrinal controversies and sectarianism. Many persons' Christianity was bound up with former pagan beliefs and practices, prayers to the saints, reverence for Mary, and use of amulets and other features of magic.[11]

---

[10] Kenneth Scott Latourette, *A History of Christianity* (New York: Harper and Row, 1953) 289.

[11] Everett Ferguson, *Church History, Volume One: From Christ to Pre-Reformation* (Grand Rapids: Zondervan, 2005) 334.

Ferguson identifies the various responses apologists made to the challenge of Islam:
- ✧ Islam was a Christian heresy.
- ✧ Islam was God's judgment on the shortcomings of the church.
- ✧ Islam was an imitation of the true religion.[12]

Christian apologists emphasized Jesus, not Muhammad, fulfilled the OT prophecies and worked miracles. Christianity spread by preaching, while Islam conquered with the sword.

"The first writer to articulate a Christian apologetic in Arabic was Theodore Abu Qurrah (c. 745–c. 825), whose work was more designed to keep Christians from being influenced by Islam than to try to convert Muslims."[13] He wrote *God and the True Religion*. He used an allegory in discussing choosing between religious claims.

> A certain king, he narrates, had a son who had never seen him. In a foreign land the son fell ill and sent to his father for medical advice. Several messages came, one from the father, the others from the latter's enemies. The son, assisted by the advice of a doctor, scrutinized each message from the point of view of what it indicated about the author, the understanding of the disease, and the reasonableness of the proposed remedy, and he accepted the prescription that best satisfied all three criteria. Applying the allegory to the choice of a religion, Abu Qurrah tried to show that Christianity presents the most plausible idea of God, exhibits the fullest understanding of humanity's actual religious needs, and prescribes what appear to be the most appropriate remedies.[14]

Later Aquinas summarized and gave reasons for Christian faith preparing missionaries going to the Muslims. He contrasted Jesus and Muhammad in regard to fulfilled prophecies and miracles and in the way the religions were spread.

---

[12] Ibid., 335.

[13] Ibid., 336.

[14] Dulles, *A History of Christian Apologetics*, 2nd ed., 94.

Medieval Scholasticism, led by thinkers like Anselm and Aquinas, synthesized Greek philosophy with the teachings of the Bible and early Christian writers. Anselm is known as the father of medieval Scholasticism. The Scholastic theologians applied critical reasoning to matters of faith. They intended to show the reasonableness of Christian truth. They felt the need to give reasons for believing that God exists by demonstrating that belief is more rational than disbelief.

Anselm of Canterbury (1033–1109), an Italian, wrote most of his books while an abbot at a Benedictine monastery in Normandy (1063–1078). Later he became Archbishop of Canterbury in 1093. Royal efforts to reduce ecclesiastical power and Anselm's reform efforts resulted in a rocky relationship between the kings of England and this gentle and humble man.

As a realist he followed Plato and Augustine in believing universals existed before creation. He set forth his view of faith and reason in this statement—"For I do not seek to understand that I may believe, but I believe in order to understand."[15] Some conclude that Anselm presupposed Christian faith and rejected a rational apologetic. G.L. Isaac states,

> It has been argued that Anselm sets forward his arguments for God's existence, not to convince non-believers but to aid believers in their comprehension of the faith. This also is a misreading of Anselm's intentions, for the arguments were intended as rational proofs to convince unbelievers even though they started as meditations that originated in faith. Anselm makes this very clear in the first chapter of the *Monologion* where he insists that even someone of moderate intelligence could be convinced of most of the truths regarding God by reason alone without recourse to the Bible.[16]

---

[15] Anselm, *Proslogium*, Chapter I.

[16] G.L. Isaac, "Anselm," *New Dictionary of Christian Apologetics*, eds. W. C. Campbell-Jack and Gavin McGrath (Downers Grove, IL: InterVarsity, 2006) 79.

He used formal logic to demonstrate the truths of the faith. In *Cur Deos homo?* (Why did God become man?) Anselm defended the rationality of the Christian faith. He argued that "in proving that God became man by necessity . . . you [can] convince both Jews and Pagans by the mere force of reason."[17] His view of the atonement as satisfying God's justice replaced the view that Christ's death was a ransom paid to the devil. The God-Man by his death, as our sacrifice, paid the debt humans could not pay.

His *Monologion* (1076) tried to prove the existence of God by rational reflection alone apart from supernatural revelation. Here he developed a form of the cosmological argument (from effect to cause)—from goodness, from perfection, and from existence itself for the existence of God.

In *Proslogion* (1078), originally called *Faith Seeking Understanding,* he sought for an argument that "would require no other for its proof than itself alone." He developed his ontological argument—"a simple and conclusive argument" as "proof of the existence of God."[18] He argued that perfection implies existence. A being than which no greater can be conceived must exist. The idea of a perfect supreme being in people's minds must correspond to his objective existence.

Even though Anselm discussed faith in intellectual terms—as belief not trust—he wrote his books from a perspective of meditation and prayer. His rationalism was not in opposition to revelation. Edgar and Oliphint say, "He was convinced that there was no disharmony between revelation and reason; to appeal to the truth gleaned by the latter is consistent with truth given in the former. Reason *alone,* for Anselm, meant the *right use* of reason."[19] Reason and faith led to the same conclusion.

---

[17] Anselm, *Cur Deos homo?* 2.22.

[18] Anselm, *Proslogion,* 19, v.

[19] William Edgar and K. Scott Oliphint, *Christian Apologetics: Past & Present, Volume 1: to 1500* (Wheaton, IL: Crossway, 2009) 367.

His approach appealed to idealists and rationalists like Descartes and Leibniz. Aquinas and those with an empirical approach rejected Anselm's apologetic. Reformed theologians liked his view that faith precedes understanding. This approach that you must believe in order to understand stands in the Augustinian tradition.

Kenneth Boa and Robert Bowman describe the intellectual situation of thirteenth century Europe:

> In the thirteenth century Christian Europe was shaken by the rediscovery and distribution of the philosophical works of Aristotle and the strong impetus given to the Aristotelian worldview by the very capable Spanish-Arab philosopher Averroes [1126–1198]. The growing influence of Averroist thought in European universities led to a crisis for Christian thought. Some scholars at the universities were embracing an uncritical Aristotelianism, while others, especially high-ranking church officials, uncritically condemned anything Aristotelian.[20]

The new scientific vision independent of biblical imagery created a spiritual crisis as the influence of the spiritual theology of Augustine was waning. Albertus Magnus (Albert the Great) gave a philosophical response to this challenge in his *On the Unity of the Intellect against Averroes*. He attempted to reconcile Christianity and Aristotle. His disciple, Thomas Aquinas, surpassed his teacher in harmonizing Christianity and Aristotle.

Thomas Aquinas (1225–1274), an Italian Dominican theologian and philosopher, became the strongest voice of scholasticism. He was a prayerful scholar who spent his life in teaching and writing. The Arabs perpetuated Aristotle's influence by preserving his writings. New translations of his works made an impact on intellectuals. Many feared that abandoning Platonism and accepting Aristotle would lead to materialism. To

---

[20] Kenneth D. Boa and Robert M. Bowman, Jr., *Faith Has Its Reasons: An Integrative Approach to Defending Christianity*, 2nd ed. (Waynesboro, GA: Paternoster, 2005) 19.

those ready to abandon Christian faith in the light of Aristotle's philosophy, Aquinas came as a knight to their rescue. He created a synthesis of Christian theology and Aristotelian philosophy. Christians could believe the Bible and the Church *and* Aristotle. The Bible and the Church were authorities in matters of faith. Aristotle was the authoritative source for natural knowledge.

Aquinas "made a persuasive impact on the intellectual world. . . . Aquinas made it possible for those who were strongly influenced by Aristotle's views to remain Christians without sacrificing philosophical consistency."[21]

Aquinas's *Summa Contra Gentiles* (1264) is considered the greatest apologetic work in the Middle Ages. Some manuscripts bear the title, *On the Truth of the Catholic Faith against the Errors of the Unbelievers.* One early source said he wrote this apologetic manual to equip missionaries to defend Christianity to intellectual Muslims. He also intended to counteract the growing influence of Averroism in Europe. Avery Dulles says, "The *Summa* is an all-embracing apologetical theology drawn up with an eye to the new challenge of the scientific Greco-Arabic worldview."[22]

In *Summa Contra Gentiles* Aquinas distinguished between truths of faith and truths of reason. Truths of faith—the trinity, the incarnation, and the way of salvation—surpass the capability of human reason and can be known only through revelation. Natural reason cannot prove these truths. They are accepted by faith on the authority of Scripture. They are truths of faith because they can't be proven or demonstrated by empirical facts or reasoning with absolute certainty. They go beyond and transcend reason, but they do not contradict reason. Reason can show the invalidity of objections to these beliefs.

---

[21] Russ Bush, *Classical Readings in Christian Apologetics* (Grand Rapids: Zondervan, 1983) 273.

[22] Dulles, *A History of Christian Apologetics*, 114.

Truths of reason can be established by reason and natural resources alone, for example, the existence and nature of God. Truths of reason can be rationally proved or are empirically evident. Craig comments, "[Aquinas] maintains that we Christians must use only arguments that prove their conclusions with absolute certainty; for if we use mere probability arguments, the insufficiency of those arguments will only serve to confirm the non-Christian in his unbelief."[23]

Aquinas says God provided the evidence of miracles and prophecy to confirm the truths of faith. These signs ("confirmations," "arguments," and "proofs") do not demonstrate these truths directly. They enable persons to see the truths of faith.

They provide an adequate basis for accepting the truth of Christianity.

Aquinas taught that God's existence can be proved by reason and revelation. Reason can prove God, but since sin has obscured our thinking most people must just believe that God exists.[24]

William Lane Craig states Aquinas' view,

> The proofs of miracle and prophecy are compelling, although they are indirect. Thus, for example, the doctrine of the Trinity is a truth of faith because it cannot be directly proved by any argument; nevertheless, it is indirectly proved insofar as the truths of faith taken together as a whole are shown to be credible by the divine signs.
>
> Thomas' procedure, then, may be summarized in three steps: (1) Fulfilled prophecies and miracles make it credible that the Scriptures taken together as a whole are a revelation from God. (2) As a revelation from God, Scripture is absolutely authoritative. (3) Therefore, those doctrines taught by Scripture that are neither demonstratively provable nor empirical-

---

[23] William Lane Craig, *Reasonable Faith: Christian Truth and Apologetics*, 3rd ed. (Wheaton, IL: Crossway, 2008) 33. See Thomas Aquinas, *Summa Theologica* 1a.32.1 and *Summa Contra Gentiles* 1.9.

[24] Aquinas, *Summa Contra Gentiles*, 1.4, 3–5.

ly evident may be accepted by faith on the authority of Scripture. Thus, Aquinas can say that an opponent may be convinced of the truths of faith on the basis of the authority of Scripture as confirmed by God with miracles.[25]

In Aquinas's system faith is a path to truth, a way of knowing. What is known by faith is not knowledge but a truth of faith. "Faith was essentially intellectual assent to doctrines not provable by reason—hence, Aquinas's view that a doctrine cannot be both known and believed; if you know it (by reason), then you cannot believe it (by faith). Thus, Aquinas lost the view of faith as trust or commitment."[26]

According to Aquinas, by pure honest reasoning one can demonstrate the existence of God, the supernatural origin of Christianity, and the immortality of the soul. Faith is acceptance of what is given on authority—church or Scriptures. God revealed many things that can be known only by faith. Truth given by revelation can't contradict truth reached by reason.

His *Summa Theologica* (started in 1265, unfinished at his death, 1274) stands as his most influential writing. God has revealed himself in nature and Scripture. Nature shows one God, some of his characteristics, and the moral law. The Bible is the *only* divinely inspired and authoritative writing.

He began *Summa Theologica* with his Five Ways to demonstrate God's existence. He identified two objections to belief in God—evil in the world and the world can be accounted for by human reason. He then argued:

✧ From motion to an Unmoved Mover
✧ From effects to a First Cause
✧ From contingent beings to a Necessary Being
✧ From degrees of perfection to the Most Perfect Being
✧ From design in nature to a Designer

---

[25] Craig, *Reasonable Faith*, 33.
[26] Ibid.

He concluded that God is the necessary Being that is the cause of all contingent beings in the world.[27]

Aquinas rejected Plato's rationalism and accepted Aristotle's empiricism. He believed we were born with an innate capacity to know but not with innate ideas. All knowledge originates in the senses except the mind itself. Certain self-evident and undeniable first principles—identity, noncontradiction, excluded-middle, and causality—enable us to know reality.[28] He rejected the ontological arguments of Augustine and Anselm and their underlying rationalism.[29]

Edgar and Oliphint assess his impact, "Thomas Aquinas was without question the most important and influential figure of the medieval period. His intellect and influence are almost unmatched in the history of the church."[30]

The Middle Ages (450–1517)	
Apologists and Their Principal Works	**Primary Threat**
Anselm (1033–1109), *Monologion* and *Proslogion*	Jewish and pagan unbelief
Aquinas (1225–1274), *Summa Contra Gentiles* and *Summa Theologica*	Arabic naturalistic interpretation of Aristotle

The Reformation (1517–1648)

In the sixteenth century most Europeans at least nominally affirmed Christianity. Professing Christians argued with each other; defending the truth of the Christian faith was not the issue. The questions of the day were—What kind of Christianity? Was the Bible or the Church the final authority? Had the Catholic Church corrupted Christianity?

[27] Thomas Aquinas, *Summa Theologica*, 1a, 2, 3.
[28] Thomas Aquinas, *Summa Theologica*, 1a, 2ae.17, 3, 7.
[29] Thomas Aquinas, *Summa Contra Gentiles*, I, xi; *Summa Theologica*, II, 1.
[30] Edgar and Oliphint, *Christian Apologetics*, 395.

During the Middle Ages the Roman Catholic Church had developed several teachings and practices that were foreign to the church described in the NT—the authority of the pope, elevation of Mary into coredeemer, the mass, allegorical interpretation, purgatory, and the sacrament of penance including selling indulgences to purchase forgiveness. Catholic doctrine held that the church created the NT, hence it held authority over Scripture. The reformers believed that the spoken Word of God created the church and the written Word of God was the final authority for the church.

Martin Luther (1483–1546) led in challenging the Roman Catholic Church's claim to authority over the Bible and its system of justification by works. He greatly feared the wrath of God and found no relief in his Catholic religion. He concluded it was false religion and idolatry with only law and no gospel. He was born again by believing the gospel of grace with the free and full salvation in Christ. He knew the Bible was the Word of God through the witness of the Holy Spirit. This experience in his heart influenced Luther's apologetic. He believed the Bible was the inerrant and authoritative Word of God and the only norm for faith and life.

J. Theodore Mueller states,

> To Luther, however the canonical Scriptures were not only the normative authority of faith and life, but also the causative authority, that is, the living, powerful divine Word which engenders faith and works, and in the regenerate true sanctification. In other words, Luther regarded the divine Word of Scripture as the efficacious means of grace, by which the Holy Spirit works faith in men and keeps them in the true faith to the end.[31]

Luther believed the living and powerful divine Word is the means used by the Holy Spirit in doing his saving work in men

---

[31] J. Theodore Mueller, "Luther and the Bible," *Inspiration and Interpretation*, ed. John F. Walvoord (Grand Rapids: Eerdmans, 1957) 107.

and women. Persons know the objective truth of Scripture as they subjectively experience faith worked in them by the Holy Spirit. He rejected the idea that the Holy Spirit worked directly on people's hearts apart from the Word. The Spirit works through the Word to produce faith in the sinner. Mueller states, "Luther maintained that the Holy Spirit operates savingly in men only through the divine Word."[32]

He emphasized the inability of reason to save a person or to establish the redemptive love of God. He did not accept reason as an authority in matters of faith. He believed that the natural world was the realm of reason and the spiritual sphere is the place for faith. Reason before faith becomes arrogant, the "devil's whore," according to Luther. But if reason submits to revelation it can be a servant of faith.

Luther's comments on faith and reason were made in the context of human inability to attain salvation by one's own strength. The gospel, not reason, brings salvation. He feared that using apologetics to lead people to faith would be naturalistic and dependent upon works, violating *sola fide* (faith alone), *sola gratia* (grace alone), *sola Scriptura* (the Bible alone). Luther said, "It is most deplorable that we should attempt with our reason to defend God's Word, whereas the Word of God is rather our defense against all our enemies, as St. Paul teaches us."[33] To those who deny what Christ and the apostles spoke and wrote in the Word of God, Luther said, "Just say this: I will give you ample evidence from Scripture. If you believe this, fine. If not, be on your way."[34]

William Lane Craig says, "I think Martin Luther correctly distinguished between the magisterial and ministerial use of

---

[32] Ibid., 109.

[33] Martin Luther, "The Papacy at Rome," *A Compend of Luther's Theology*, ed. Hugh T. Kerr (Philadelphia: Westminster Press, 1966) 4.

[34] Martin Luther, W2, 9:1238. Quoted by Robert D. Preus, "Luther and Biblical Infallibility," *Inerrancy and the Church*, ed. John D. Hannah (Chicago: Moody Press, 1984) 128.

reason. The *magisterial use* of reason occurs when reason stands over and above the gospel like a magistrate and judges it on the basis of argument and evidence. The *ministerial use* of reason occurs when reason submits to and serves the gospel."[35]

"Luther's principle of *sola scriptura* outlaws not only the authority of pope, church, and council as sources and norms of doctrine but also human reason and experience," according to Robert D. Preus.[36] Reason can attempt to understand and submit to the Word but cannot sit in judgment of Scripture. Montgomery defends Luther from the charge of being a subjective fideist, noting Luther's objection to enthusiasts who put feelings above objective Scripture.[37]

Luther wrote, "All men have the general knowledge, namely, that there is a God, that he created heaven and earth, that he is just, that he punisheth the wicked. But what God thinketh of us, what his will is towards us, what he will give or what he will do, to the end that we may be delivered from sin and death and be saved, (which is the true knowledge of God indeed), this they know not."[38] Because of man's bondage to sin he cannot gain this true knowledge of God. Luther affirmed, "I believe that I cannot by my own reason or strength believe in Jesus Christ, my Lord, or come to him; but the Holy Spirit has called me by the Gospel, enlightened me with his gifts and sanctified and preserved me in the true faith."[39]

Luther did not develop a system of apologetics. His coworker, Philipp Melanchthon, (1497–1560), adopted a classical approach to apologetics. The person who most shaped

---

[35] Craig, *Reasonable Faith*, 47.

[36] Preus, "Luther and Biblical Infallibility," 126, cf. 139, W2, 18:1322.

[37] John Warwick Montgomery, "Lessons from Luther on the Inerrancy of Holy Writ," *God's Inerrant Word*, ed. John Warwick Montgomery (Minneapolis: Bethany Fellowship, 1974) 87.

[38] Martin Luther, *Commentary on Galatians*, in *A Compend of Luther's Theology*, 24.

[39] Martin Luther, *Small Catechism*, in *A Compend of Luther's Theology*, 65.

the Reformation's approach to apologetics was John Calvin—the reformer in Geneva, Switzerland.

John Calvin (1509–1564) was born in northern France. He studied law at the insistence of his father. After his father died, he returned to his first love, the study of theology and humanism. Within the next year or so he had a sudden conversion to Protestantism. He was a logician and systematizer as well as scholar of the Bible, the church fathers, and the classics. While twenty-six years of age he published his *Institutes of the Christian Religion* (1536) which he revised at least four times in the next thirty-three years until it reached 1,000 pages in its final edition (1559). The *Institutes* stands as the premier theological statement of the Protestant Reformation. In addition to his writing and teaching Calvin attempted to reform the Swiss city of Geneva. In the early chapters of the *Institutes* he states his apologetic.

Both Luther and Calvin agreed that the Scholastic theologians had not explored the effect of original sin on human reason. Both agreed that Christian faith did not need the support of philosophy or human arguments to make it credible. They represented a radical break from the Roman Catholic theologians.

Augustine's theology greatly influenced Calvin. He stressed the sovereignty of God and human depravity. God made a general revelation available to all mankind. Humans have a sense of deity as nature continuously gives testimony to God which makes us want to know and worship Him. Even the pagan has an innate sense of the natural law judging the just from the unjust. The evidence of intelligence and order in the universe bears witness to God's wisdom and glory. No one can plead ignorance of God.

In his providential care in human history God reveals himself demonstrating his goodness and faithfulness.[40]

---

[40] John Calvin, *Institutes of the Christian Religion*, I, 3.1, I.2.22.

The radical influence of mankind's sinful depravity keeps them from gaining a true knowledge of God from the evidence in general revelation. People can't understand the creation until they first understand the Creator. Knowing God involves love, worship, and a life of godliness. General revelation does not lead people to true faith and a proper knowledge of God due to the corruption of human depravity.[41]

Because people have a religious nature they are incurably religious and create false gods and false religions which do not conform to God's will. Without the guidance of divine truth they wander into error. Because they have an innate "sense of deity" they are without excuse. Enlightened human reason cannot overcome depravity. Even when thinkers approximate the truth of God they still suffer corruption. True knowledge of God is found only in Scripture.[42]

Special revelation alone can overcome a person's depravity and yield a true knowledge of God and bring one to the Redeemer who saves. Revelation given to prophets was recorded in their writings to remedy man's depravity.[43] Scripture provides the glasses that enable people to correctly read general revelation.[44]

The objective revelation in Scripture needs the witness of the Spirit for a person to accept it as the truth of God. The Spirit enables one to see the Scripture as revelation and persuades the person to accept it as the true redemptive Word of God.[45]

Calvin rejected Roman Catholic claims that the Church is the sole guarantee of the supernatural origin of Scripture. Human depravity blinds men to the majesty of Scripture. But the inner witness of the Spirit overcomes depravity so one can see

[41] Ibid., 1.4; 1, I.5. 6–11; 1.11.2.
[42] Ibid., 1.5. 11–15; 1.10.3.
[43] Ibid., 1. 6. 1–3.
[44] Ibid., I.6. 1.
[45] Ibid., I.7.4.

the majesty of Scripture. Arguments or reasoning can't remove doubt. The Spirit alone can give certainty.

Calvin did not vilify reason as Luther did. He believed reason could deal with mundane things but it was unable to deal with things divine until informed by the Word of God. The Church and human reason are subordinate to the witness of the Spirit. Calvin stated, "But I answer that the testimony of the Spirit is superior to reason. For as God alone can properly bear witness to his own words, so these words will not obtain full credit in the hearts of men, until they are sealed by the inward testimony of the Spirit."[46]

He continued, "Let it therefore be held as fixed, that those who are inwardly taught by the Holy Spirit acquiesce implicitly in Scripture; that Scripture, carrying its own evidence along with it, deigns not to submit to proofs and arguments, but owes the full conviction with which we ought to receive it to the testimony of the Spirit."[47]

Christian evidences provide "wonderful confirmations" but cannot overcome depravity. Calvin stated, "Of themselves they are not strong enough to provide a firm faith" so they should not be used to convince unbelievers that the Scriptures are the Word of God. "Scripture will ultimately suffice for a saving knowledge of God only when its certainty is founded upon the inward persuasion of the Holy Spirit. . . . It is foolish to attempt to prove to infidels that the Scripture is the Word of God."[48]

Ronald S. Wallace states Calvin's view, "It must be emphasized that the faith thus formed is not a natural response to the Word of God but is an entirely miraculous act of the Holy Spirit within the heart of the hearer of God's Word."[49] Calvin said,

---

[46] Ibid.

[47] Ibid., I.7.5.

[48] Ibid., I.8.1-13.

[49] Ronald B. Wallace, *Calvin's Doctrine on the Word and Sacraments* (Grand Rapids: Eerdmans, 1957) 127.

"We may hear perfectly everything that is spoken to us, but the words might as well be spoken to a tree-trunk till God has taken away this insensibility which is in our corrupt nature."[50] The Word of God cannot produce faith in the hearer until the Spirit creates faith in the person's heart by opening their mind to receive the Word. He did say it is unreasonable to say the Spirit works without the Word.[51]

For Calvin, evidences have a place of confirming Scripture *after* the witness of the Spirit. The internal witness gives assurance of the truthfulness of Scripture, and external evidences as secondary and "useful aids" give more objective verification. He listed the following as "signs of credibility": the majestic style and subject matter of Scripture, the honesty of the writers, the publicly attested miracles, fulfilled predictive prophecy, the amazing preservation of the biblical text, and the witness of martyrs.[52] These do not give full conviction unless confirmed by the witness of the Spirit. Those having the witness of the Spirit need no rational evidences.

Bernard Ramm summarizes Calvin's approach:

> Therefore the certification of the Christian faith is not to be found in the utterances of a proposed infallible Church; nor in rationalistic Christian evidences; nor in the appeals of philosophers to reason; nor as ecstatic experience of the Holy Spirit. It is to be found in the knowledge of God as Creator and Redeemer; it is to be found in the union of Word and Spirit; it is to be found in special revelation centering on the person of Christ and affirmed by the inner witness of the Holy Spirit.[53]

---

[50] Quoted in Wallace, *Calvin's Doctrine*, Calvin, Sermon on Acts 1:6-8, C.R. 48:605.

[51] Wallace, *Calvin's Doctrine*, 129-130.

[52] Quoted in Wallace, *Calvin's Doctrine*, C. R. 1.8.1-13.

[53] Bernard Ramm, *Varieties of Christian Apologetics* (Grand Rapids: Baker, 1961) 178.

Calvin appealed to Scripture first, not to reasonable evidence. The Holy Spirit then creates faith in the elect when they hear the Scripture.

The Reformation (1517–1648)	
Apologists and Their Principal Works	**Primary Threat**
Martin Luther (1483–1546).Throughout his writings. No work on apologetics.	Catholic authority and doctrine
John Calvin (1509–1564), *The Institutes of the Christian Religion*	Catholic authority and doctrine

The Modern Period (1648–1805)

During the seventeenth and eighteenth centuries, Christian apologists had to deal with the views of skepticism (God is unknowable) and rationalism (all truth must be proved by reason alone) and naturalism (denial of miracles). In the nineteenth century, scientism (only what can be proved by natural science is true) was a dominant foe of Christianity. In the twentieth century various forms of religious relativism, subjectivism, and pluralism made religious truth a matter of personal choice rather than a matter of objective truth.

Blaise Pascal (1623–1662), one of France's great geniuses, distinguished himself as a scientist, mathematician, inventor, writer, Bible scholar, mystic, and apologist.

The skepticism of Montaigne, rationalism of Descartes, and atheism of Vanini fueled the secularism of seventeenth-century France. After being exposed to skepticism and participating in the worldly life of Paris, Pascal underwent a (second) conversion experience at age thirty-one. As he read *John 17* he sensed the presence of God replacing the emptiness of his life with "certitude, heartfelt joy, and peace." This aspiring intellectual concluded that reason could not understand all of reality. He could not find meaning in life within himself but only in

Christ.[54] Renouncing self-will he surrendered in wholehearted commitment and passionate devotion to God in response to God's grace.

Constant sickness and pain plagued Pascal. He died at thirty-nine before he could write his anticipated book on apologetics. However he had written his thoughts about apologetics on scraps of paper tied together in bundles found after his death. These were edited and published in 1670 after his death as *Pensees* (Thoughts). He wrote to communicate Christianity to the unbelieving and indifferent.

Pascal proposed to put unbelievers in a frame of mind ready to accept Christianity and to give evidence for Christianity. He attempted to show the plausibility of belief in a world where rational certainty can't be obtained. People misunderstood themselves because of their indifference toward life, life after death, and God. He wanted to wake them out of their apathy.

Pascal believed God remains hidden because of people's sin. They rejected religion because they followed Descartes in basing religion on reason. By reason Pascal meant mathematical reason improperly applied philosophically. Using geometric reason in philosophy of religion makes people think they have infallibly demonstrated religious truth. Pascal insisted we do not learn truth in this abstract way. Reason must not be made an idol. Choosing mathematical reason as one's guide is foolish because of the corruption caused by original sin.[55]

Pascal states, "The heart has its reasons, which reason does not know."[56] "It is the heart which experiences God, and not the reason. This, then, is faith: God felt by the heart, not

---

[54] Blaise Pascal, *Pensees*, trans. W.F. Trotter (Mineola, NY: Dover Publications, 2003, of 1958 ed.) #547. Note that not all editions of *Pensees* use the same numbering.

[55] Ibid., #445, #446.

[56] Ibid., #277.

by the reason."[57] By heart he means the center of the human being not mere feeling. The heart intuitively responds to the entire experience of evidence.

Fundamental principles of philosophy and religion rest on an intuitive basis.[58] Descartes' philosophy doesn't deal with life and faith. Pascal viewed rationalism as a form of self-love and rebellion against God. Reason alone can't enable one to overcome self-will. Reason may do some groundwork, but humbly coming to the cross of Christ and experiencing conversion of imagination brings one into the grace and love of God. Faith is more than intellectually showing unbelief to be unreasonable and belief to be reasonable. It involves a passionate commitment of one's entire being to God.

Pascal considered the attempt to prove God from nature a sign of weakness.[59] Believers see all existence as the work of God, but unbelievers see only darkness. They can escape their darkness only through Jesus Christ.[60] "Men will never believe with a saving and real faith, unless God inclines their heart; and they will believe as soon as He inclines it."[61] Following reason one cannot find God. Persons find God who seek him with all their heart.

Pascal rejected theistic proofs because "without the Scripture, which has Jesus Christ alone for its object, we know nothing, and see only darkness and confusion in the nature of God, and in our own nature."[62] "Therefore I shall not undertake here to prove by natural reasons either the existence of God, or the Trinity, or the immortality of the soul, or anything of that nature; not only because I should not feel myself sufficiently

---

[57] Ibid., #278.
[58] Ibid., #282.
[59] Ibid., #428.
[60] Ibid., #229, 242-244.
[61] Ibid., #284.
[62] Ibid., #547.

able to find in nature arguments to convince hardened atheists, but also because such knowledge without Jesus Christ is useless and barren."[63] Natural theology has a place for believers, but has no possibility to bring unbelievers to faith in God.[64]

Pascal was not an irrationalist or a fideist. He said that the number of propositions known intuitively is small; most knowledge comes through reason. Reason helps us distinguish between true religion and superstition.[65] He wanted to avoid two extremes: "to exclude reason, to admit reason only."[66] "If we submit everything to reason, our religion will have no mysterious and supernatural element. If we offend the principles of reason our religion will be absurd and ridiculous."[67] "Men despise religion; they hate it, and fear it is true. To remedy this, we must begin by showing that religion is not contrary to reason; that it is venerable, to inspire respect for it; then we must make it lovable, to make good men hope it is true; finally, we must prove it is true."[68]

We are unable to reach the good by our own efforts and the present never satisfies, according to Pascal. He continues his analysis,

> What is it then that this desire and this inability proclaim to us, but that there was once in man a true happiness of which there now remain in him only the mark and empty trace, which he in vain tries to fill from all his surroundings, seeking from things absent the help he does not obtain in things present? But these are all inadequate, because the infinite abyss can only be filled by an infinite and immutable object, that is to say, only by God Himself.[69]

---

[63] Ibid., #555.
[64] Ibid., #242.
[65] Ibid., #187.
[66] Ibid., #253.
[67] Ibid., #273.
[68] Ibid., #187.
[69] Ibid., #425.

Having lost the true good, people search for the good in things of this world only leaving them unhappy and unsatisfied.

He wanted to shock people about their indifference to life after death. He explains man's glory as well as his misery. Man seeks happiness but experiences misery forgetting his former greatness. He seeks pleasure to find relief from his indifference which serves only as a drug as he marches to his death.

He described the misery of those without God because they cannot live a good life or know truth. Christianity correctly diagnoses the human condition and gives the right solution. It accounts for the contradiction of man's wretchedness and his greatness.[70] It shows the supreme good—the love of God. It gives remedy for man's condition—fellowship with God.

Pascal says that the evidences of God are clear and obscure:

> The prophecies, the very miracles and proofs of our religion, are not of such a nature that they can be said to be absolutely convincing. But they are also of such a kind that it cannot be said that it is unreasonable to believe them. Thus there is both evidence and obscurity to enlighten some and confuse others. But the evidence is such that it surpasses, or at least equals, the evidence to the contrary; so that it is not reason which can determine men not to follow it, and thus it can only be lust or malice of heart. And by this means there is sufficient evidence to condemn, and insufficient to convince; so that it appears in those who follow it, that it is grace, and not reason which makes them follow it; and in those who shun it, that it is lust, not reason, which makes them shun it.[71]

People want to know, "Why God has not openly and visibly revealed himself?" Pascal responded, "God has set up in the Church visible signs to make Himself known to those who should seek Him sincerely, and that He has nevertheless so

---

[70] Ibid., #434, #435, #435.
[71] Ibid., #563.

disguised them that He will only be perceived by those who seek Him with all their heart."[72] Sincere souls see through evidences—miracles and fulfilled prophecy and the perfect holiness of Christ—to God.[73]

In Pascal's wager he counsels believing in God in spite of the lack of absolute certainty because here one finds the eternal good. "Let us weigh the gain and the loss in wagering that God is. . . . If you gain, you gain all; if you lose, you lose nothing. Wager, then, without hesitation that He is."[74] Pascal asked people why they gamble with their eternal life. With Christian faith we have everything to gain and nothing to lose.

Os Guinness says, "No one seeking to recover the purpose and power of apologetics should bypass Pascal. Not only is he refreshingly different from the ineffectual approaches that passed for apologetics in his day as in ours, but he is one of the most brilliant persuaders in human history."[75] Dulles observes, "Few if any apologetical works have brought so many unbelievers on the way to faith."[76]

In the late seventeenth and early eighteenth centuries deism rose as a formidable opponent of Christianity. Deism taught that God created the world but has not supernaturally intervened by revelation or miracle since. They based religion and morality on a natural theology guided by reason and nature. Many leaders in modern science opposed deism— Robert Boyle (1627–1691, chemistry), Isaac Newton (1642–1727, physics), and John Ray (1627–1705, biology). These men argued that the organization and design in nature gave evidence of God's power, wisdom, and goodness.

---

[72] Ibid., #194. See also #242.

[73] See #546, #589, #590, #705 for more comments on proofs of God.

[74] Ibid., #233.

[75] Os Guinness, "Introduction," in *Mind on Fire: A Faith for the Skeptical and Indifferent*, ed. James M. Houston (Minneapolis: Bethany House, 1989, 1997) 35.

[76] Dulles, *A History of Christian Apologetics*, 166.

John Locke (1632–1704), a British empiricist, in his *Essay Concerning Human Understanding* (1689) rejected Descartes' absolute rationalism and held that religious knowledge could be built on the experience of the world around him. He believed that religious belief must have rational justification. He accepted the cosmological argument for God's existence. The idea of God was "naturally deducible from all parts of our knowledge" with a certainty comparable to the most evident theorems of geometry.[77]

He categorized propositions as: according to reason, above reason, and contrary to reason. "Thus the existence of one God is according to reason; the existence of more than one God contrary to reason; the resurrection of the dead, above reason."[78]

Revelation from God was confirmed and verified by evidences, such as miracles. Revealed truths are at times beyond reason but never contradict valid reason. *The Reasonableness of Christianity as Delivered in the Scriptures* (1695) pointed to the messiahship of Jesus verified by miracles and fulfilled OT prophecies as the essential Christian belief.[79]

Locke set forth three criteria for discerning a genuine revelation: First, it must not be dishonoring to God or inconsistent with natural religion and the natural moral law. Second, it must not inform man of things indifferent, insignificant, or easily discovered by natural ability. Third, it must be confirmed by supernatural signs, such as miracles. Jesus' miracles demonstrated he was the Messiah and his revelation from God was true.[80]

All deists were naturalistic. The early deists were rationalists while the later ones were empiricists. The deists of the

---

[77] John Locke, *Essay Concerning Human Understanding*, I.4.16.

[78] Ibid., IV.17.23.

[79] John Locke, *The Reasonableness of Christianity*, ed. I.T. Ramsey (New York: Black, 1958) 82.

[80] John Locke, *Discourse on Miracles* (1903) *Works*, rev. ed. (London, 1823) 9:262. Craig, *Reasonable Faith*, 3rd ed., 35.

eighteenth century (e.g., Tindal and Toland) were militantly anti-Christian and anti-supernaturalistic. Christian apologists produced many replies to the deists. Joseph Butler wrote the most significant response.

Joseph Butler (1692–1752), an Englishman, served as bishop of Bristol, dean of St. Paul's and then as bishop of Durham. Attracted to philosophy he passionately pursued truth and lived a life of godly piety and ethical conviction.

In 1736, he published *The Analogy of Religion, Natural and Revealed, to the Constitution and Course of Nature,* an apologetic for the plausibility of Christianity defended on the basis of analogy between revealed and natural religion. He showed that the deist argument against the biblical God would also apply to the God of nature if reason were the authority. He wanted to demonstrate that belief in Christianity was not unreasonable. Both Christianity and nature point to a single Author. He claimed only probability for his argument, admitting he could not prove his case beyond all doubt.

Many consider his *Analogy* to be the most effective answer to deism. Hume considered it the best defense of Christianity that he had read. In response to the deist's definition of religion on the basis of reason and nature, Butler also appealed to reason and nature in his defense.

Since the same laws govern nature and religion, then the method of analogy enables one to make transfer of truth from one realm to the other. Bush summarizes Butler's argument:

> We find a definite order in nature, he suggests, that is parallel to the order we find in divine revelation. Difficulties that we may discover in divine revelation bear a close analogy to similar difficulties that one can discourse in nature. He held that further scientific study may clear up some of the present difficulties in understanding nature, and, similarly, further theological study may clear up present difficulties in divine revelation. Nevertheless, he believed that the common pat-

terns found in both nature and Holy Scripture should serve as evidence of a common Author. If someone believes that God created the world (which is exactly what deists did believe) and recognizes the difficulties in understanding all aspects of nature, then that person could not deny the validity of divine revelation in Holy Scripture simply on the basis of having features that may be difficult to understand. Especially is this true if the difficulties can be shown to be analogous.[81]

He argued that since mysteries exist in nature made by God, we should expect mysteries in a revelation from God. Natural religion has just as many difficulties as revealed religion. Reason must test claims to revelation. The persistence of identity makes immortality probable. From what we know in nature the supernatural is probable. God has intervened through miracles and prophecies. Revealed religion is not only possible but it has happened.

His work seemed to be a refutation of Matthew Tindal's *Christianity as Old as Creation; the Gospel, a Republication of the Religion of Nature* (1730), often called "the Deist's Bible." Butler follows the empiricist and inductive approach of Newton and Locke. He rejected speculative metaphysics and acknowledged that all knowledge is based on probability. Natural reason is limited by information provided by the senses.

We do not possess absolute proof for anything in this life but we must base our beliefs on probability. Since our knowledge of the whole scheme of reality is partial, statements concerning our knowledge must be probability statements not absolute statements. Empirical evidence provides only probability of truth, never absolutely certain conclusions. "Probability is the very guide of life."[82]

While not claiming absolute certainty for the truth of Christianity, the totality of the evidence increases its probabil-

---

[81] Bush, *Classical Readings in Christian Apologetics*, 328.
[82] Joseph Butler, *The Analogy of Religion*, Introduction by Author.

ity to a practical certainty. This does not destroy our confidence in religious beliefs because all knowledge, including scientific knowledge, is based on the same kind of evidence. If one accepts the validity of any kind of knowledge, one must equally accept the validity of the evidence for Christianity.

When the evidences satisfy the standards of reason, reasonable men will assent. Butler held that reason was the only thing we had to judge anything, including revelation. Christianity answers the problems better than deism. He made a case against the improbability of miracles and for their probability. Fulfilled prophecies and miracles make revealed religion credible. He feared a religion that relied only on feelings and experiences.

Bernard Ramm observes,

> Butler's attack on deism was then a sort of within-the-camp attack. Traditional apologists were bombing deism from some distant position but by accepting this Lockian epistemology and the deists' theory of analogy Butler enters within their camp and by hand spikes their guns. So capable, so thorough, so devastating was Butler's attack upon deism that no real formal answer was ever made.[83]

Butler's *Analogy* and Hume's philosophy effectively undermined deism. As an intellectual movement deism did not extend much into the nineteenth century. The *Analogy* appeared frequently in reprints in Britain and America. Butler's works were standard reading at Oxford and Cambridge until about 1870. Butler stands as a representative of the evidentialist school of apologists.

William Paley (1743–1805) was another influential evidentialist. As a youth he showed little promise for scholarship being late for everything and often sleeping until noon. At the beginning of his third year at Christ's College at Cambridge

---

[83] Ramm, *Varieties of Christian Apologetics*, 109.

University one of his friends woke him at five o'clock to tell him he was a fool. He had much ability but was wasting his opportunity. This helped him decide to get serious about his studies.

He taught nine years at Cambridge. In 1782 he became the archdeacon of Carlisle and while there he published his three greatest works—*The Principles of Moral and Political Philosophy* (1785), *A View of the Evidences of Christianity* (1794), and *Natural Theology, or Evidences of the Existence and Attributes of the Deity Collected from the Appearances of Nature* (1802).

He opposed Enlightenment skepticism (Hume) with his evidential apologetic. Bush states, "He had a gift of effectively stating plain arguments in a way that made them very convincing to people."[84] He emphasized historical evidence of miracles to establish that God has revealed himself in the Bible and in Christ.

In *A View of the Evidences of Christianity* he saw miracles as credentials of a supernatural revelation. He agreed with Hume that the credibility of miracles depends upon the trustworthiness of the witnesses but disagreed with Hume's contention that all testimony to miracles was suspect because it was contrary to universal experience. He defended the historical reliability of the NT on the basis that the apostles held true to their report even in the face of persecution and threat of death. Jesus' miracles confirmed that he brought a divine revelation. Paley did not give blanket approval to all miracle claims. A true miracle is in support of a revelation. He rejected as exaggerations mere wonders that promoted the claimant's self-interest.

Paley gave classic statement to the argument for the existence of God from design in nature (teleological argument) in his *Natural Theology*. Paley begins by observing that if one kicks a stone he or she does not think much about it. It may have existed forever. When we encounter a natural object such as a

---

[84] Bush, *Classical Readings in Christian Apologetics*, 350.

watch with its organized interconnected parts functioning for the purpose of telling time "the inference we think is inevitable, that the watch must have had a maker . . . who comprehended its construction and designed its use."[85] A watch demands a watchmaker because design demands a designer.

Since the universe shows more complexity of design than a watch, it must also have had a Maker. He illustrates his argument from the human body—organs, bones, and muscles—demonstrating intelligent design. He goes into detail showing that the human eye is intricately designed for sight. Paley's argument that a watch proves a Watchmaker is the most famous expression of the argument from design.

His works were required reading for entrance to Cambridge University during the nineteenth century. Geisler underscores the importance of his apologetics, "Paley is one of the great apologists of the late eighteenth and early nineteenth centuries. Indeed, his influence continues. . . . Paley's arguments for God and for Christianity still provide the backbone for much of contemporary apologetics. The only major difference is that we now have much more 'meat' to put on the skeleton."[86] A strong Intelligent Design Movement has stressed scientific evidence of the anthropic principle showing how the universe is fitted for life, the irreducible complexity of biological systems, and the incredible amount of information in the DNA molecule as evidence of a Designer.

---

[85] William Paley, *Natural Theology*, Chapter 1.
[86] Norman L. Geisler, "Paley, William," *Baker Encyclopedia of Christian Apologetics* (Grand Rapids: Baker Books, 1999) 575.

The Modern Period (1648–1805)	
Apologists and Their Principal Works	**Primary Threat**
Blaise Pascal (1623–1662), *Pensees*	Skepticism, rationalism, and atheism
Joseph Butler (1692–1752), *The Analogy of Religion to the Constitution and Course of Nature*	Rationalism, naturalism, and deism
William Paley (1743–1805), *The Evidences of Christianity* and *Natural Theology*	Rationalistic biblical criticism, scientific naturalism

We conclude this history of how Christians defended the faith through the centuries at 1805. Some of the apologists of the nineteenth and twentieth centuries will appear in chapter 15 in the study of apologetic method.

In surveying the various apologists in their historical context, it is instructive to notice how these three factors influenced their apologetic approach: their personal experience of how they came to faith, their basic personality, and the specific threat to Christian faith which they were answering. Effective apologists have used the thinking of their day in answering the threats of their day.

Francis Schaeffer said, "The Christian must resist the spirit of the world *in the form it takes in his own generation.*" He urged heeding the words of Luther:

> If I profess with the loudest voice and clearest exposition every portion of the truth of God except precisely that little point which the world and the devil are at that moment attacking, I am not confessing Christ, however boldly I may be professing Christ. Where the battle rages, there the loyalty of the soldier is proved, and to be steady on all the battlefield besides, is mere flight and disgrace if he flinches at that point.[87]

---

[87] Francis A. Schaeffer, *The God Who Is There*, 2nd ed. 30th Anniversary Edition (Downers Grove, IL: InterVarsity, 1968, 1982) 31.

Review Questions

1. What apologetic response did Christians make to the challenge of Islam?

2. What is medieval Scholasticism? Name two thinkers from this movement.

3. State Anselm's view on faith and understanding, on the atonement, and on a rational argument for the existence of God.

4. Describe the threat that Aquinas sought to answer.

5. List the Five Ways Aquinas used to demonstrate the existence of God.

6. What did Luther believe about the role of the Scripture and the Holy Spirit in a sinner coming to saving faith?

7. Compare and contrast Luther's and Calvin's views on man's sinful depravity and one's coming to a knowledge of God.

8. What did Calvin believe about the witness of the Holy Spirit?

9. According to Calvin, what role do evidences have in regard to believing?

10. Write a brief paragraph describing Pascal.

11. Summarize Pascal's negative and positive comments about reason.

12. What role do theistic proofs and evidences have in Pascal's apologetic?

13. How did Pascal analyze man's predicament?

14. Locke said propositions fell into three categories in relation to reason. List them.

15. What was the point of Butler's *Analogy of Religion*? How effective was it in answering deism?

16. What degree of certainty did Butler claim for his argument for Christianity?

17. What was Paley's famous argument for the existence of God?

18. Assess Paley's influence as an apologist.

Suggested Reading

See resources listed on pages 323-324.

"For what we proclaim is not ourselves, but Jesus Christ as Lord, with ourselves as your servants for Jesus' sake. For God, who said, 'Let light shine out of darkness,' has shone in our hearts to give the light of the knowledge of the glory of God in the face of Jesus Christ."

2 Corinthians 4:5-6

15

Apologetic Method

Apologetic Method

Profile: C.S. Lewis—Apologist

I. Apologetic Methods
  A. Reasons for Faith
    1. Classical apologists
    2. Evidential apologists
    3. Cumulative case apologists
  B. Faith before Reasons
    1. Presuppositional apologists
    2. Fideist apologists
    3. Reformed epistemology apologists
II. Issues in Apologetic Method

"In the world of apologetics, each system is interrelated to the others due to its ultimate goal: defending Christianity in the context of an unbelieving and skeptical world. Each system begins at a point where it believes it can make a connection, and uses a method that it believes most effectively offers a convincing and compelling argument. There is, however, no universally accepted way of cataloguing these systems and showing how these systems agree or disagree with one another. While each method

A. The role of philosophy in apologetics
B. The relationship between faith and reason
C. The influence of sin on human reason
D. The validity and value of theistic arguments
E. The degree of common ground between believer and unbeliever
F. The role of evidences
G. The nature of faith
H. The view of knowledge and the test(s) of truth
I. The degree of certainty concerning the truth of Christianity
J. The role of the Holy Spirit
K. The role of divine revelation
III. Essential Elements in an Apologetic Method
   A. Rational
   B. Historical
   C. Personal

has its proponents and critics, categorizing the types of apologetic methods is somewhat akin to categorizing methods of evangelism. The systems are formally related (in purpose) and yet informally divergent (in assumptions)."[1]

Ergun Caner

---

[1] Ergun Caner, "Apologetics, Types of," *The Popular Encyclopedia of Apologetics: Surveying the Evidence for the Truth of Christianity*, eds., Ed Hindson and Ergun Caner (Eugene, OR: Harvest House, 2008) 64.

Profile: C.S. Lewis—Apologist

He disclaimed being a philosopher, a theologian, or a spiritual guide, yet in fact he has been all of these for millions. Many consider C.S. Lewis (1898–1962) the most successful English-speaking apologist in the twentieth century. Colin Duriez states, "From his teeming mind and imagination sprang stories and powerful rhetoric aimed at persuading people of the truth of Christian faith."[2] He searched for truth and longed for Joy which he found in Christianity.

In his happy early childhood, Lewis loved nature, read fantasy, and created his own imaginary world with stories that he illustrated. He wrote a history of Animal-Land. He believed that children exposed to the world of fantasy were better able to understand and relate to the real world as adults.[3] He defended the fairy tale as giving a better picture of truth than the so-called realistic stories. Clyde Kilby summarizes Lewis, "The fairy tale, like the myth, on the one hand arouses longing for more ideal worlds and on the other gives the real world a new dimension of depth. The boy 'does not despise real woods because he has read of enchanted woods: the reading makes all real woods a little more enchanted.'"[4] Lewis used the world of imagination to acquaint his readers with the order and values in the real world.

His original purpose was not to teach Christianity to children when he began to invent the allegorical stories about Narnia. It all started with images in his mind that bubbled up into stories. Then he said,

[2] Colin Duriez, "Lewis, C.S.," *New Dictionary of Christian Apologetics*, eds. W.C. Campbell-Jack and Gavin McGrath (Downers Grove, IL: InterVarsity, 2006) 402.
[3] Clyde Kilby in class lecture at Wheaton College in the fall of 1965.
[4] Clyde S. Kilby, *The Christian World of C.S. Lewis* (Grand Rapids: Eerdmans, 1964) 116.

> I thought I saw how stories of this kind could steal past a certain inhibition which had paralysed much of my own religion in childhood. Why did one find it so hard to feel as one was told one ought to feel about God or about the sufferings of Christ? I thought the chief reason was that one was told one ought to. . . . But supposing that by casting all these things into an imaginary world, stripping them of their stained-glass and Sunday school associations, one would make them for the first time appear in their real potency? Could one not steal past those watchful dragons? I thought one could.[5]

Lewis said, "I was therefore writing 'for children' only in the sense that I excluded what I thought they would not like or understand; not in the sense of writing what I intended to be below adult attention. . . . I never wrote down to anyone."[6]

The tremendous variety of his literary output demonstrates Lewis's creative imagination. He sets forth Christian truth in children's literature (*The Chronicles of Narnia*), satire (*The Screwtape Letters*), novels (*Till We Have Faces*), science fiction (*The Space Trilogy—Out of the Silent Planet, Perelandra,* and *That Hideous Strength*), allegory (*The Great Divorce, The Pilgrim's Regress: An Allegorical Apology for Christianity, Reason and Romanticism*), apologetic works (*Mere Christianity,*[7] *Miracles, The Abolition of Man,* and *The Problem of Pain*), autobiography (*Surprised by Joy, A Grief Observed*), word studies (*The Four Loves*), and poetry, essays, and speeches (*God in the Dock* and *Christian*

---

[5] C.S. Lewis, "Sometimes Fairy Stories May Say Best What's to Be Said," *C.S. Lewis on Stories and Other Essays on Literature,* ed. Walter Hooper (New York: Harcourt Brace Jovanovich, 1982) 47.

[6] Ibid., 47-48.

[7] *Mere Christianity,* his best known apologetics book, is a collection of his BBC broadcasts given during World War II.

Reflections). Believing God wanted him to answer each letter he received, he spent at least an hour each day answering people's questions.[8] He debated in the Socratic Club and engaged in conversations with his literary friends, the Inklings, on Tuesdays and Thursdays. He was sought after as a speaker and for many years was the most popular lecturer at Oxford and Cambridge.

His friend, Austin Farrer said, "He provided a positive exhibition of the force of Christian ideas, morally, imaginatively, and rationally. The strength of his appeal (as we have said) lies in the many-sidedness of his work."[9]

Having access to his father's ample library as a lad Lewis immersed himself in books. His mother started him on French and Latin. One of his schoolmasters, W.T. Kirkpatrick, taught him to think logically and communicate clearly. He graduated from Oxford and taught philosophy and then literature there. He continued his academic career at Cambridge 1954–1963. As a scholar he was a rational thinker with a brilliant mind and prodigious learning. His phenomenal memory enabled him to recall all he read (which he could demonstrate if challenged).[10]

Many hardships left their mark on Lewis. The death of his mother before he was ten resulted in his being put in one boarding school after another. He dealt with estrangement from his father. One of his schoolmasters was borderline insane. Lewis faced many difficulties in these schools

[8] Walter Hooper compiled and edited 3,228 of Lewis's letters publishing them in three volumes, *Collected Letters of C. S. Lewis* (2000–2006). See also *Letters to an American Lady* and *Letters to Children*.

[9] Austin Farrer, "The Christian Apologist," *Light on C. S. Lewis*, ed. Jocelyn Gibb (New York: Harcourt Brace Jovanovich, 1965), 26.

[10] Art Lindsley, *C.S. Lewis's Case for Christ: Insights from Reason, Imagination and Faith* (Downers Grove, IL: InterVarsity, 2005) 18-20.

including loneliness and unhappiness, being bullied, becoming an atheist, and losing his virtue. He was wounded in World War I. After accepting Christ, he faced professional hostility. Colleagues criticized his role as amateur theologian and blocked his professional advancement. In 1960 his wife of three years died. He faced a titanic struggle watching her suffer and die. He had to deal with the emotional problem of suffering after having written on the intellectual problem of suffering. These experiences deepened him and enabled him to be an emphatic apologist. He could sympathize with skeptics and strugglers because he had wandered those byways and wrestled with the same questions and difficulties.

His childhood was without personal religious experiences, though the family was formally Christian. His faith was shaken when God did not answer his prayers and magically heal his mother. He retreated into atheism, maintaining that God did not exist yet at the same time angry with God for not existing. His unbelief gave him a sense of relief.

He got involved in atheism, rationalism, materialism, the occult, spiritualism, pantheism, religious relativism, and philosophical idealism. He was troubled with the problem of evil, problems with prayer, denial of miracles, uncritical acceptance of the spirit of the age, and tension between imagination and reason. He appreciated firsthand the strengths and weaknesses in these worldviews and problems and addressed them in his books and essays.

David C. Downing observes:

> [Lewis's] Christian books are compelling precisely *because* he spent so many years as an unbeliever. He understood atheism; he felt the force of its arguments in his bones

and sinews. He knew the lure of the occult; indeed he wrote that if the wrong person had come along in his teenage years he might have ended up a sorcerer or a lunatic. And he was philosophically trained in idealism, the assumption that some unknowable Absolute lies behind the veil of appearances. He weighed all these worldviews himself, and eventually found them wanting. So when this 'reluctant convert'—eventually faced up to the meaning of his Christian commitment, he entered into it with his whole heart and mind and soul.[11]

Reading the writings of George Macdonald and G.K. Chesterton awakened in him a hunger for holiness and goodness. Christian friends including Owen Barfield, H.V.D. Dyson and J.R.R. Tolkien influenced him. In 1929 Lewis, convinced by the logic of theism, admitted God was God. He described himself as "the most dejected and reluctant convert in all England." His conversion to Christianity came without fanfare on the morning of September 28, 1931, as he was driven to Whipsnade zoo. "When we set out I did not believe that Jesus Christ is the Son of God, and when we reached the zoo I did." He developed a spiritual depth that attracted those searching for God. A single-minded devotion to Christ and to making him known to others dominated his life. He viewed his writings as "evangelistic" as well as written to help uneducated brethren deal with intellectual attacks on their faith.[12]

He attempted to see truth clearly, follow it honestly and fearlessly, and state it clearly and simply. He humbly emphasized his message without calling undue attention to himself. In debate he could be relentless in finding the

---

[11] David C. Downing, *The Most Reluctant Convert: C.S. Lewis's Journey to Faith* (Downers Grove, IL: Inter Varsity, 2002) 15.

[12] C.S. Lewis, "Rejoinder to Dr Pittenger," *God in the Dock* (Grand Rapids: Eerdmans, 1970), 183.

weakness of his opponent's argument and refuting it with clear logical argument.

His books are more in demand today than they were during his lifetime, selling in the millions, and his influence continues strong. He has ministered to the souls of millions of men, women, and children. He reached readers who would not read more technical, jargon-filled books. He expressed "mere" Christianity in popular terms and answered common objections. Cunningham says, "Sprinkled through his writings are approaches to the problems of revelation, miracle, pain, the relationship of faith and reason, the existence of God, the authority of the Bible, hermeneutics, language, science, philosophy, history, prayer, providence, and ethics."[13]

C.S. Lewis, a literary scholar without formal theological training, became perhaps twentieth century's most influential apologist. What made C.S. Lewis more effective than others in transmitting Christian truth? One factor is the clarity of his communication. He said, "My task was therefore simply that of a *translator*—one turning Christian doctrine . . . into the vernacular, into language that unscholarly people would attend to and could understand."[14] He had the ability to listen carefully and understand objections to his position and criticisms of his arguments. He also had the ability to objectively read or hear an argument without distorting it by his own bias. He refuted objections and argued effectively that Christianity was more reasonable than all alternatives.

Cunningham observes that Lewis:

---

[13] Richard B. Cunningham, *C.S. Lewis: Defender of the Faith* (Eugene, OR: Wipf & Stock, 2008 reprint of 1967 ed.) 20.

[14] Ibid., 183.

... teaches us that intellectual objections are often intimately interwoven with other factors—psychological, social, political and economic; with a naïve acceptance of a naturalistic world view and its uncritical rejection of supernaturalism. . . . He does not rest content with confronting the intellect. Rather, he probes the motives and characters of his readers and exposes psychological and social factors that contribute to unbelief.[15]

Richard L. Purtill says Lewis had "an imaginative power that enabled him to illuminate and illustrate his rational insights and arguments. One way in which imagination can serve intellect is by producing metaphors to illuminate unfamiliar or difficult topics, making parallels between what needs to be understood and some familiar area of experience."[16]

Friend Austin Farrer described Lewis:

Lewis was an apologist from temper, from conviction, and from modesty. From temper, for he loved an argument. From conviction, being traditionally orthodox. From modesty, because he laid no claim either to the learning which would have made him a theologian or to the grace which would have made him a spiritual guide. His writings certainly express a solid confidence; but it is the confidence that he can detect the fallacy of current objections to belief, and appreciate the superiority of orthodox tenets over rival positions; that he has some ability, besides, to make others see what he so clearly sees himself.[17]

Lewis did not fit any pattern as an apologist. He neither wrote a systematic apologetic nor described his apologetic method.

[15] Ibid., 65.
[16] Richard L. Purtill, *C.S. Lewis's Case for the Christian Faith* (San Francisco: Harper and Row, 1981) 5.
[17] Farrer, "The Christian Apologist," 24.

> He defended the faith by addressing with brilliant insight the obstacles that for years kept him from Christian faith. People in the mainstream of life relate to his writings. He fulfilled his stated purpose—"to explain and defend the belief that has been common to nearly all Christians at all times."[18]

Christian apologists have employed various approaches in how they defend Christian faith. This chapter will explore how Christian apologists believe we ought to do apologetics. The general intellectual climate of the age, the type of attacks raised against Christianity, and philosophical and theological assumptions influence how one approaches the apologetic task.

We will first look at various apologetic strategies and approaches. The issues or questions that an apologetic method needs to answer will be listed and discussed. The chapter will close by identifying elements that should be included in whatever apologetic method an individual adopts.

Apologetic Methods

Apologetic methods differ in fundamental philosophical and theological assumptions and viewpoints. Apologetics can be divided into positive and negative apologetics. In positive/offensive/affirming apologetics evidences and reasons for Christian faith present the case for the truth of Christianity, for example, arguments for the existence of God, evidences for the resurrection and deity of Jesus, and reasons for believing in the inspiration of the Bible. Negative/defensive/answering apologetics seeks to refute non-Christian worldviews and answer objections raised against Christian faith, for example, the problem of evil and suffering and the challenge of naturalistic science.

---

[18] C.S. Lewis, *Mere Christianity* (New York: Macmillan, 1952) vi.

Scholars have classified types of apologetic systems or strategies in various ways. The following chart gives four classifications.

Apologetic Methods	
Gordon R. Lewis[19] **Apologetic Epistemologies**	**Bernard Ramm**[20] **Varieties of Apologetic Systems**
Pure empiricism Rational empiricism Rationalism Biblical authoritarianism Mysticism Verificationism	Systems stressing the uniqueness of the Christian experience of grace Systems that stress natural theology as the point at which apologetics begins Systems that stress revelation as the foundation upon which apologetics must be built
Stephen B. Cowan[21] **Apologetic Types by Apologetic Strategy**	**Kenneth D. Boa and Robert M. Bowman, Jr.**[22] **Families of Apologetic Approaches**
Classical method Evidential method Cumulative case method Presuppositional method Reformed epistemology method	Classical apologetics emphasizing reason Evidential apologetics emphasizing fact Reformed apologetics emphasizing revelation Fideist apologetics emphasizing faith

[19] Gordon R. Lewis, *Testing Christianity's Truth Claims* (Chicago: Moody Press, 1976).

[20] Bernard Ramm, *Varieties of Christian Apologetics* (Grand Rapids: Baker, 1961) 14-17.

[21] Steven B. Cowan, ed., *Five Views on Apologetics* (Grand Rapids: Zondervan, 2000) 15-20.

[22] Kenneth D. Boa and Robert M. Bowman, Jr., *Faith Has Its Reasons: An Integrative Approach to Defending Christianity*, 2nd ed. (Waynesboro, GA: Authentic Publishing/Paternoster, 2005).

This chapter will consider two general approaches to doing apologetics. One type of apologetics seeks to present reasons and evidences for faith. Another approach begins with faith then sees reasons and evidences for faith taking a nonevidentialist approach to apologetics.

C. Stephen Evans observes that:

> When we look at actual individuals instead of ideal types, the differences between these types may be significantly reduced. . . . Practically, there may not be nearly so much disagreement about the methodology of apologetics as might at first be thought. The ideal types that inspired the organization of Cowan's book do, however, make a useful starting point for sorting out questions concerning apologetics.[23]

Reasons for Faith

This approach presents reasons and evidence supporting the truth claims of Christianity to unbelievers. It assumes that subjects can gain knowledge of the real external world. These apologists present rational arguments for the existence of God, generally stressing cause, design, and morality. They view historical evidences, including fulfilled prophecies and miracles, especially the resurrection, as credentials validating the supernatural claims of Christ and the Bible.

Classical apologists first argue for the existence of God, and then advance historical evidences supporting the truth of Christianity. The first step is philosophical; the second is evidential. Some begin by establishing philosophical first principles, such as the laws of logic and self-existence, then establish the existence of God through theistic arguments. They believe God has provided evidence of himself in nature which supports the reasonableness of belief in God and the Christian worldview. They develop arguments for the existence of God

---

[23] C. Stephen Evans, "Approaches to Christian Apologetics," *New Dictionary of Christian Apologetics*, eds., W.C. Campbell-Jack and Gavin McGrath (Downers Grove, IL: InterVarsity, 2006) 15.

before and apart from special revelation. Because every human being, believer or unbeliever, is made in the image of God he or she can understand the logical force of arguments and can accept the rationality of belief in God.

R.C. Sproul, John Gerstner, Arthur Lindsley, and Norman Geisler insist that the reality of God must be first established before any historical event can be accepted as a miracle—a two-step method.[24] They contend a direct appeal to historical miracles cannot make a successful argument for God's existence. After one is convinced by a rational case for God, then he or she can logically accept the possibility of miracles. Having established rational theism they make a case for Christianity being the true religion based on confirmed historical evidences including the reliability of the Scriptures, fulfilled prophecies, miracles, the resurrection of Jesus verifying the deity of Jesus and an authoritative Word from God. Jesus affirmed the OT as the Word of God and promised the inspiration of the NT. William Lane Craig considers himself a classical apologist but does not insist on a necessary order of these two steps.

Geisler's Classical Apologetics

1. Truth about reality is knowable.
2. Opposites cannot both be true.
3. The theistic God exists.
4. Miracles are possible.
5. Miracles performed in connection with a truth claim are acts of God to confirm the truth of God through a messenger of God.

[24] R.C. Sproul, John Gerstner, and Arthur Lindsley, *Classical Apologetics: A Rational Defense of the Christian Faith and a Critique of Presuppositional Apologetics* (Grand Rapids: Zondervan, 1984) 146-147, 276; and Norman Geisler, "Apologetics, Types of," *Baker Encyclopedia of Christian Apologetics* (Grand Rapids: Eerdmans, 1999) 41-42.

6. The NT documents are reliable.
7. As witnessed in the NT, Jesus claimed to be God.
8. Jesus' claim to divinity was proven by a unique convergence of miracles.
9. Therefore, Jesus was God in human flesh.
10. Whatever Jesus (who is God) affirmed as true, is true.
11. Jesus affirmed that the Bible is the Word of God.
12. Therefore, it is true that the Bible is the Word of God and whatever is opposed to any biblical truth is false.[25]

Evidentialist apologists stress evidence in support of the truth claims of Christianity. They appeal to rational, historical, and experimental evidences with the primary focus on historical evidence. They employ the same arguments for God and for Christianity as the classical apologists and agree that unbelievers can think logically and see the force of arguments. The key difference is that evidentialists do not view theistic arguments as the logically necessary first step. Theism is not the necessary precondition to validate historical apologetics. The evidentialist approach makes an inductive case for the truth of Christianity without any set order to the arguments. They believe that if one is open to the possibility of a God, then the argument from historical evidence for miracles can still be effective. The claims and credentials of Christ and Christianity show Christianity to be reasonable and true over all competing religious and philosophical views.

Historical evidence for the truth claims of Christianity is available to believer and unbeliever alike. Evidentialists focus on the historical evidence for the resurrection of Jesus as verifying his claim to be God in the flesh and thus demonstrating the existence of God. From the authoritative teachings of Christ

[25] Norman Geisler, "Argument of Apologetics," *Baker Encyclopedia of Christian Apologetic*, 36. See also Norman L. Geisler and Frank Turek, *I Don't Have Enough Faith to Be an Atheist* (Wheaton, IL: Crossway, 2004).

they affirm the Bible is the Word of God and Christianity is the true religion. William Paley, John Warwick Montgomery, Josh McDowell, and Gary Habermas are evidential apologists.

Some apologists hold to reasons and evidence for faith but do not fit strictly into either the classical or evidential methods. This approach has been called "the cumulative case method," "combinationalism," and "verificationalism." Rather than following specific steps in a method it considers Christianity to be a hypothesis that best satisfies all the data. Paul D. Feinberg summarizes, "It is a broad-based argument with many subjective and objective elements. They require some explanation and in some cases can be seen as reinforcing one another to strengthen the case for Christian theism. The case is like a lawyer's brief. The claim is that Christian theism gives the most plausible explanation of all the evidence."[26] This strategy shares the same general approach as the classical and evidential approaches, hence is not a clear-cut or sharply defined different method.

The classical, evidential, and cumulative case methods all assume we should give some kind of evidence to unbelievers in making a case for the reasonableness of Christianity. They differ on what evidence must be established first and on the ways evidence supports Christianity, yet they all recognize that apologetic arguments and evidence can lead to Christian faith.

Faith before Reasons

Another general approach holds that the unbeliever must come to faith first before apologetic arguments or evidence can be effective. These apologists hold that we believe in God without rational or evidential argument. Presuppositionalists, fideists, and those utilizing Reformed epistemology fit in this group.

---

[26] Paul D. Feinberg, "Cumulative Case Apologetics," in Cowan, ed., *Five Views on Apologetics*, 166.

Presuppositionalists have roots back to Abraham Kuyper (1837–1920) who viewed traditional apologetics as impious and usurping the work of the Holy Spirit. They view traditional rational, historical apologetics as useless and false. Kuyper said, "The starting point of every motive in religion is God and not Man. . . . God alone is here the goal, the point of departure and the point of arrival."[27]

Cornelius Van Til (1895–1987), founder of presuppositionalism, said that one must begin with his or her presupposition. We begin presupposing either God or man. If you begin with man learning facts in this world as your starting point, then you will end with man without knowledge. You will never end with knowledge of God. There is no true knowledge prior to faith. The only way to knowledge is to presuppose the reality of God and the truth of the Bible. Rational knowledge comes only as a result of believing in God and the Bible as his revealed Word. God is the beginning of the argument not the conclusion.[28]

Van Til believed that, because of the damaging effects of sin on the human mind, no common ground exists between the believer and unbeliever for communication. Facts have no meaning apart from the Christian worldview. They reject the validity of theistic proofs and historical evidences with unbelievers. Because of sin and the resulting depravity, one cannot believe until he or she is given faith by the Holy Spirit. Faith is a supernatural gift of God and is not based on rational or historical evidence.

Terry Miethe points out some differences within presuppositionalism:

---

[27] Abraham Kuyper, *Lectures on Calvinism* (Grand Rapids: Eerdmans, 1931) 46.
[28] Cornelius Van Til, "My Credo," in *Jerusalem and Athens: Critical Discussions on the Theology and Apologetics of Cornelius Van Til*, ed. E. R. Geehan (Nutley, NJ: Presbyterian and Reformed, 1977) 3-21.

The starting point of a presuppositionalist system is either the axioms of logic, God and the Bible (as Gordon Clark argues) or the autonomous Scripture and the Triune God (as Cornelius Van Til maintains). The common ground between believers and non-believers is either the thought-forms of the mind (Clark) or nothing, no common ground epistemologically (Van Til). The test for truth is consistency (Clark) or self-authenticating claims of the Bible (Van Til).[29]

Cornelius Van Til represents revelational presuppositionalism and Gordon Clark rational presuppositionalism. John M. Frame has modified some of the views of these men but he still employs the presuppositional method.

Part of the presuppositional strategy is to demonstrate the inability of non-Christian worldviews to explain the world or life. Only by assuming God and the truth of Christianity can one make sense of the world and life. They assume the biblical revelation is essential to any coherent system of truth. Some presuppositionalists believe that for a statement to be true it must be stated in Scripture or be a logical inference from a Scriptural statement. In response to the charge that presupposing God is a circular argument, presuppositionalists plead guilty affirming that this divine circle is given by God himself.

Fideism sees the intuitive apprehension of faith as the ultimate ground for Christian belief and commitment. Fideists minimize or deny rational argument any role in believing. Søren Kierkegaard exalted the paradoxical and absurd aspect of faith. Rather than establishing a case for the incarnation of God in Christ by a rational apologetic, he saw it as a paradox to human reason believed only by passionate faith.

Some presuppositionalists represent a moderate form of fideism. Terry Miethe observes:

---

[29] Terry L. Miethe, *The Compact Dictionary of Doctrinal Words* (Minneapolis: Bethany House, 1988) 164-165.

In one sense, all perspectives are fideistic because they all must start with presuppositions. There is, however, a great difference between a "presupposition of method," the assumption that a real, factual world exists and that it is possible to investigate it, and "presuppositions of content," an assumed body of truth that must be accepted as true before truth can be known.[30]

Assuming certain fundamentals about the human knowing process is far different from assuming the conclusion you are trying to establish.

Apologists employing *Reformed epistemology* have challenged any kind of evidentialist epistemology. They contend that theistic arguments and evidences are convincing to the evidentialist and unconvincing to the unbeliever. Kelly Clark says, "Reason is not neutral. It does not stand dispassionately, without prejudice (prejudgment), overlooking the evidence; it is not bias-free (at least on matters of fundamental concern). . . . We can't attain *the view from nowhere* to check our beliefs against the facts (independent of our beliefs). . . . we cannot stand outside ourselves to compare our beliefs to the reality we suppose they tell us about."[31] According to this view, reason accepts the evidence it agrees with and discounts the evidence it does not value.

The Reformed epistemologists insist that one can rationally believe in God without any supporting arguments or evidence. They disagree with believers who insist evidence is necessary for belief in God. They also reject the evidentialist objection to belief in God—that theism is irrational because of no evidence or insufficient evidence. They believe that both the evidentialist believer and evidentialist unbeliever depend upon classical foundationalism[32] which they reject.

---

[30] Ibid., 92-93.

[31] Kelly James Clark, "A Reformed Epistemologist's Closing Remarks," in *Five Views on Apologetics*, 365.

[32] See page 158.

Alvin Plantinga says we have perceptual beliefs we consider justified without arguments, for example, seeing people in a room, and concluding people are in that room. We have thoughts about God—"I need God's help"—in response to circumstances. Just as our perceptual beliefs not based on arguments are justified, so, according to Plantinga, are our beliefs about God.

Plantinga contends, "that belief in God can be perfectly rational even if none of the theistic arguments works and even if there is no noncircular evidence for it; . . . it is perfectly rational to take belief in God as *basic*—to accept it, that is, without accepting it on the basis of argument or evidence from other propositions one believes."[33] He concludes belief in God is rational and warranted.

The Reformed epistemologists affirm Calvin's view that we are born with a sense of the divine, hence one can have a direct belief in God without evidence. This belief is properly basic; hence one can be justified in believing in God without believing on the basis of arguments. Their strategy is to awaken in unbelievers the latent sense of the divine and to insist that those who claim Christian belief does not amount to knowledge must first prove Christian belief is false.

Presuppositionalists believe reason has no part before faith but see the rationality of Christianity after faith. Fideists generally see faith as nonrational and subjective holding that faith and reason have no relationship with each other. The Reformed Epistemologists believe faith in God is rational because it is a basic belief even though it is not based on rational evidence.

---

[33] Alvin Plantinga, "A Christian Life Partly Lived," in *Philosophers Who Believe: The Spiritual Journeys of 11 Leading Thinkers*, ed. Kelly James Clark (Downers Grove, IL: Inter Varsity, 1993) 74. See his "Reason and Belief in God," in *Faith and Rationality*, eds., A. Plantinga and N. Wolterstorff (Notre Dame: University of Notre Dame, 1983).

Efforts have been made to combine or integrate the evidentialist approach and the nonevidentialist approach. Ronald B. Mayers,[34] H. Wayne House,[35] and Kenneth D. Boa and Robert M. Bowman, Jr.[36] attempt to unite insights from classical/evidential and presuppositional approaches. Further classification could include experiential apologetics, scientific apologetics, cultural apologetics, and others. Describing these would be beyond the scope of this book.

Issues in Apologetic Method

The following eleven issues are important to one's approach to doing apologetics.[37]

1. The Role of Philosophy in Apologetics

Tertullian saw philosophy as having nothing to do with Christian faith, yet Justin Martyr saw Christianity as the truest philosophy. Augustine saw some value in philosophy as a servant to theology. Thomas Aquinas looked to Aristotle's philosophy as an essential tool in his apologetics. Pascal felt that philosophy existed in a category separate from Christianity and should not be combined with Christian faith.

Classical/Evidential apologists use philosophical arguments in their apologetic witness. Those who posit faith before reason generally either see philosophical arguments useful after one is a believer or not at all.

---

[34] Ronald B. Mayers, *Balanced Apologetics: Using Evidences and Presuppositions in Defense of the Faith* (Grand Rapids: Kregel, 1984); Ronald B. Mayers, "Both/And: A Biblical Alternative to the Presuppositional/Evidential Debate," *Evidential Apologetics*, Michael Bauman, David W. Hall, and Robert C. Newman, eds. (Camp Hill, PA: Christian Publications, 1996) 35ff.

[35] H. Wayne House, "A Biblical Argument for Balanced Apologetics: How the Apostle Paul Practiced Apologetics in Acts," *Reasons for Faith: Making a Case for the Christian Faith*, Norman L. Geisler and Chad V. Meister, eds. (Wheaton, IL: Crossway, 2007) 53-64.

[36] Boa and Bowman, *Faith Has Its Reasons*.

[37] I am indebted to Ramm and Mayers who compiled similar lists. Bernard Ramm, *Varieties of Christian Apologetics*; and Ronald B. Mayers, *Both/And: A Balanced Apologetic* (Chicago: Moody Press, 1984) 13.

Whether the apologist recognizes it or not, some basic philosophic assumptions and viewpoints are present in any apologetic method. Serious apologists need to recognize and identify the philosophical assumptions they are making in regard to knowledge (epistemology), reality (metaphysics), and values (axiology).

Paul warns, *"See to it that no one takes you captive by philosophy and empty deceit, according to human tradition, according to the elemental spirits of the world, and not according to Christ"* (Col 2:8). We need some basic understanding of philosophy to avoid being led astray by philosophy. C.S. Lewis says, "Good philosophy must exist, if for no other reason, because bad philosophy needs to be answered."[38] No human philosophy perfectly expresses God's truth. As believers we must always be prepared to alter our philosophy when it conflicts with God's Word rather than to change God's Word according to our philosophy.

2. The Relationship between Faith and Reason

The relationship between faith and reason stands at the heart of apologetic method. When faith is viewed as mystical and totally subjective, then reason will be rejected or downplayed. If we view faith as objective and logically necessary, then reason will be strongly emphasized. Both the worship of reason in rationalism and the irrationalism of anti-intellectualism should be rejected by the Christian apologist.

The classical and evidential apologists see the validity of a rational apologetic. Presuppositionalists reject a rational apologetic to non-Christians; however they often see the value of reason after faith. Others see rational argument as unnecessary to belief in God.

Much of society has divided truth into two separate realms—the realm of facts and reasons and the realm of morality, religion, and values. They deed separate territorial

---

[38] C.S. Lewis, "Learning in Wartime," in *The Weight of Glory and Other Addresses* (Grand Rapids: Eerdmans paperback ed,, 1965 of 1949 ed.) 50.

rights to reason and faith. Reason can function in the fact area and faith functions in the realm of values and religion. Reason and faith are each limited to one realm. See chapter 9 for more extensive discussion of the relationship of faith and reason.

3. The Influence of Sin on Human Reason (Noetic Effect of Sin)

How have sin and human depravity affected the ability of our human reason to function in recognizing truth and in believing? The noetic effect of sin refers to the damage sin has caused on the human mind. Some reject all rational or evidential apologetics because they believe sin has corrupted the mind of fallen persons so they cannot understand or believe God's revelation either in nature or in Scripture nor can they reason correctly. Because of this total depravity they cannot believe the gospel until God supernaturally gives them faith. Some believe that all knowing and interpretation by unbelievers is false.

Others admit that sin has defaced the image of God in human beings and in the general revelation but it has not erased it. The non-Christian can still reason correctly and know that two plus two equals four and recognize demonstrated facts. Passages such as *Romans 1:18-20* teach that the "plain" and "clearly perceived" evidence of God in nature renders the unbeliever "without excuse." R.C. Koons states,

> In order for sinful humans to be "without excuse", it is essential that God's existence and divine qualities still be made "plain" to them in what has been created, despite the damage their cognitive capacities may have suffered as a result of the fall. Paul lays the blame for unbelief squarely on our misuse of those capacities to "suppress the truth by wickedness", and not on any defects within the capacities themselves. We could not be held accountable for unbelief or idolatry had the fall effectively erased our knowledge of the one God to whom we owe our exclusive worship.[39]

---

[39] R.C. Koons, "Natural Theology," *New Dictionary of Christian Apologetics*, 476.

Advocates of the view that fallen man cannot be persuaded by evidence point to *1 Corinthians 2:14*: *"The natural person does not accept the things of the Spirit of God."* Norman Geisler observes that in this passage, "Paul does not say that natural persons cannot *perceive* truth about God, but that they do not *receive* (Gk. *dekomai*, "welcome") it."[40]

John Calvin believed that evidences in nature were sufficient to convince any rational mind but human minds did not function rationally in thinking about God. Fallen men suppressed their innate knowledge of God so they were darkened in their understanding. Without the Word of God and the action of the Holy Spirit we would not be directed to God. He believed that certainty comes only by the internal witness of the Holy Spirit. God speaks through the self-authenticating Word of God. Reason cannot demonstrate God's truth to unbelievers.

Reformed theologians such as B.B. Warfield and J. Gresham Machen believed that in spite of the effects of sin we can present reasons and evidences to unbelievers and the Holy Spirit would do his convicting work through the evidences.

The human heart seeking to justify one's sin can irrationally dismiss strong evidence, but those who sincerely seek God will know Him (*John 7:17*).

4. The Validity and Value of Theistic Arguments

Natural theology is the attempt to gain knowledge of God from nature apart from special revelation. Various arguments for God's existence include ontological (concept of a Necessary Being to that Being's existence), cosmological (cosmos to Creator), teleological (design to Designer), and moral (moral law to Moral Lawgiver) arguments.

Some apologists deny that theistic proofs have any apologetic validity with unbelievers, viewing them either as ineffective, illogical, or unbiblical irreligion pointing away from the true

---

[40] Geisler, *Baker Encyclopedia of Christian Apologetics*, 39.

God. Those who accept the apologetic validity of the theistic arguments range in their assessment of their value from strong proof and demonstration to the level of supporting evidence.

Several scriptures support natural theology. God revealed something of his nature in humans by making us in his image (*Gen 1:27*). *"The heavens declare the glory of God and the sky above proclaims his handiwork"* (*Ps 19:1*). Paul affirms that evidences of God in nature and in human beings show that an eternal power and divine being exists (*Rom 1:19-20*) and his moral law is in our heart (*Rom 2:14-15*). While general revelation may yield a knowledge of God, it does not lead to a saving faith.

What one believes about the role of reason, the value of evidences, and the noetic influence of sin all contribute to one's decision about the validity and value of theistic arguments. Theistic arguments can show that belief in God is not against reason. Showing the insufficiency of the finite opens people's minds to the possibility of the infinite Being.

Thomas Aquinas believed that we can know of God's existence, unity, and basic nature from natural revelation. He believed his Five Ways demonstrated the existence of God as the First Cause of motion and design and as the necessary Being who is the cause of all contingent beings.

Hume argued that one cannot reason to an infinite cause from finite effects. Swinburne counters that an infinite Creator provides a superior explanation to a finite creator. Kant held that God could not be known by the senses. Reason cannot prove God's existence because sense knowledge is our only valid knowledge. He did not deny God. He denied that God can be proved by pure reason.

Critics view natural theology as an illegitimate positing of a Creator to explain what isn't known. However, we can base an argument on what is known, for example the fine tuning of the universe and the incredible complexity of biological entities such as DNA. The study of origins is more akin to historical knowledge than to knowledge gained by repeatable, experimental science. Another criticism holds that theology and science are two separate realms of knowledge and reality. This objection stems from a philosophical assumption of scientific naturalism.

5. *The Degree of a Common Ground between Believer and Unbeliever*

Does a common ground exist between believer and unbeliever which functions as a basis for communication and argument? Do believers and unbelievers share a common ground of knowledge that can be a bridge that the believer can use to lead the unbeliever to Christian faith? Van Til argued that no such common ground exists. He believed the unbeliever is totally incapable of understanding rational and evidential arguments without special revelation. If one starts with anything (reason, evidence, human beings) other than God, he or she will end in ignorance.

Classical and evidential apologists hold that human beings have a rational capacity to make true judgments when false assumptions are rejected. A general revelation exists in the universe and in man's moral nature that can be a point of contact between believer and unbeliever. Even many Reformed theologians believe that common grace overcomes human depravity so that a person can recognize general revelation and then accept special revelation.

Francis Schaeffer contended that even though men and women are fallen sinners they can still accept the principles of correct thinking (logic) and recognize two plus two equals four. Some intellectual and moral common ground exists because all persons—believers and unbelievers alike—are made in the image of God, which sin has effaced but not destroyed.

6. *The Role of Evidences*

Evidences may include rational, historical, and experimental evidence. Popular evidences include evidence of design in the world, fulfillment of prophecy, miracles, especially the resurrection of Christ, transformation of lives, and the influence of Christianity. Classical apologists hold that the logical order is that the existence of God must first be established by rational evidences then, as a second step, historical and experimental evidences can be presented. Evidentialists do not believe that the existence of God has to be established before historical evidences can be presented. They believe that evidences are God's chosen means of authenticating the truth of Christianity. Any person can investigate the evidence and learn that Jesus rose from the dead. The resurrection establishes the deity of Jesus and this divine Jesus guarantees the truth of Christianity.

Reformed presuppositionalists hold that because of sin, persons are unable to recognize or believe in the truth of God. The Holy Spirit must create faith in the heart before one can accept evidences. Presuppositionalist John Whitcomb says, "Christian evidences can neither create, sustain, nor increase true faith in God."[41] He says the sign-miracles were not intended to change or convert unbelievers, they were intended to attract and hold the attention of unbelievers so they would listen to the gospel.[42] Some Calvinists, however, believe that the witness of the Holy Spirit uses evidences in bringing persons to faith. The Reformed epistemologists believe that evidence is unnecessary as a basis for Christian faith.

Postmodernists contend that presenting evidences and reasons for faith is ineffective in this postmodern age. Yet modern unbelievers want evidence. Carl Sagan "wanted to find evidence" and for people to ask the difficult questions even about religion. D. Wilkinson states, "This [Sagan's] sense of questioning and the importance of evidence even in a postmodern

[41]John C. Whitcomb Jr., "Contemporary Apologetics and the Christian Faith, Part IV: The Limitations and Values of Christian Evidences," *Bibliotheca Sacra* 135 (January 1978) 31.
[42]Ibid., 25-33.

context is important to note for apologetics."[43] Atheist Sam Harris accused Christians of being convinced "that our beliefs about the world can float entirely free of reason and evidence" having "no evidence whatsoever."[44]

The defense of the faith as practiced in Scripture gives a significant place to the use of evidences in commending and defending Christian faith. See chapters 11 and 12.

7. The Nature of Faith

Aquinas separated knowledge and faith, "We *know* all things which come into the orbit of our knowing faculties; we *believe* all those things that come into our orbit in virtue of divine revelation."[45] Others recognize faith as cognitive in the sense of believing credible testimony and consider faith a source of knowledge. Others reject this cognitive aspect of faith, limiting faith to a mystical religious experience, making faith subjective and knowledge objective. Some hold that faith is totally a gift of God without any action on the part of the person. Those holding to free will hold that God gave human beings freedom of choice so they can choose to believe in God or refuse to believe in God. I believe that faith is trust based on evidence. Believing includes both mental assent (believe that) and personal trust (belief in). See chapter 9.

8. The View of Knowledge and the Test(s) of Truth

One's approach to apologetics is largely shaped by one's epistemology—how one gains knowledge and what counts as knowledge and what test(s) of truth justify beliefs. Apologists stressing empirical evidence generally see validity in the cosmological, teleological, and moral arguments for God's exis-

[43] D. Wilkinson, "Sagan, Carl Edward," in *New Dictionary of Christian Apologetics*, 631.

[44] Sam Harris, *The End of Faith: Religion, Terror, and the Future of Reason* (New York: W.W. Norton, 2004) 17, 19.

[45] Ramm, *Varieties of Christian Apologetics*, 25.

tence. Those holding a rational epistemology are more open to recognizing value in the ontological argument.

Those stressing reasons for faith will accept reason, senses, and authority as proper sources of knowledge and usually employ the correspondence test of truth. They also see the importance of checking subjective views and experiences with objective reasons and evidence. Apologists who believe faith precedes reasons are usually more deductive in thinking and believe knowledge of God is innate.

Presuppositionalists look to the witness of the Spirit and divine revelation as test of truth. After faith has been given they see the coherence of the Christian faith. Fideists affirm an irrationalism or mystical subjectivism. Yet this leaves no way to distinguish truth from falsehood. See chapters 7 and 8 for discussion of knowledge and truth.

Peter Kreeft and Ronald K. Tacelli state, "We try to use commonsense standards of rationality and universally agreed principles of logic in all our arguing."[46] I believe that Christianity stands true in the sense that the affirmations of Christianity correspond with actual reality.

9. The Degree of Certainty Concerning the Truth of Christianity

Joseph Butler emphasized probability rather than absolute certainty. He held that we have the same certainty for the Christian faith that we have for everyday life. Ramm summarizes, "Life is not made up of absolutes and none of our lives is guided by absolutes. Our lives are guided by principles graced with a high degree of probability. Even if Christianity were absolute in its truth-status we as imperfect creatures would only *probably* know this."[47] Many apologists, while admitting that Christianity does not have mathematical certainty, believe

---

[46] Peter Kreeft and Ronald K. Tacelli, *Pocket Handbook of Christian Apologetics* (Downers Grove, IL: InterVarsity, 2003) 10.

[47] Ramm, *Varieties of Christian Apologetics*, 23.

the case for Christianity has such a high degree of probability that it is practically certain.

Presuppositionalists believe God gives them absolute certainty not probability. A common Catholic view holds Christianity's truth claims as demonstrably certain.

The function of apologetics is to present considerations that enable a person to come to the threshold of commitment. A person must make a personal decision in his or her mind and will to believe or not believe. Reason does not force faith. Those who believe in reasons before faith do not see faith as a leap in the dark but a leap of trust based on solid, convincing, converging lines of evidence. Reason and evidence can only lead one to the threshold. One can always evade the appropriate response if he or she chooses to do so.

10. The Role of the Holy Spirit

John Calvin's influence is strong among evangelical apologists. He said, "The testimony of the Spirit is more excellent than all reason. For as God alone is a fit witness of himself in his Word, so also the Word will not find acceptance in men's hearts before it is sealed by the inward testimony of the Spirit."[48] "Let this point therefore stand: that those whom the Holy Spirit has inwardly taught truly rest upon Scripture, and that Scripture indeed is self-authenticated; hence, it is not right to subject it to proof and reasoning. And the certainty it deserves with us, it attains by the testimony of the Spirit."[49] The only source for authenticating the truth of the Word of God is by the direct action of the Holy Spirit on the heart of the person. Calvin wrote a chapter on the objective evidences for the supernatural nature of the Bible, but he says such evidence is inadequate. "Without the illumination of the Holy Spirit, the Word can do nothing."[50]

---

[48] John Calvin, *Institutes of the Christian Religion*, trans. Ford Lewis Battle, ed. John T. McNeill (Philadelphia: Westminster, 1960) 1.7.4.

[49] Ibid., 1.7.5.

[50] Ibid., 1.8; 3.2.33.

This view holds that the Holy Spirit's witness gives immediate assurance of the truth of Christianity and is self-authenticating.

Classical apologist William Lane Craig says:

> The way we know Christianity to be true is by the self-authenticating witness of God's Holy Spirit. . . . I mean that the experience of the Holy Spirit is veridical and unmistakable (though not necessarily irresistible or indubitable) for him who has it; that such a person does not need supplementary arguments or evidence in order to know and to know with confidence that he is in fact experiencing the Spirit of God; that such experience does not function in this case as a premise in any argument from religious experience to God, but rather is the immediate experiencing of God himself; . . . such an experience provides one not only with a subjective assurance of Christianity's truth, but with objective knowledge of that truth; and that arguments and evidence incompatible with that truth are overwhelmed by the experience of the Holy Spirit from him who attends fully to it.[51]

"So then for the unbeliever as well as for the believer, it is the testimony of God's Spirit that ultimately assures him of the truth of Christianity."[52] Craig also believes the Spirit works through evidences. "It is the role of the Holy Spirit to open the heart of the unbeliever and to use the arguments as a means of drawing people to himself."[53]

John Warwick Montgomery poses some questions for Calvin's view. What is the point of Peter's command to give a defense (1 Peter 3:15)?

> Why did Jesus, at the beginning of His earthly ministry, heal a paralytic so as to demonstrate objectively that He has divine miraculous power, thereby convincing His hearers that

---

[51] William Lane Craig, *Reasonable Faith: Christian Truth and Apologetics*, 3rd ed. (Wheaton, IL: Crossway, 2008) 43.

[52] Ibid., 47.

[53] William Lane Craig, "Classical Apologetics," *Five Views on Apologetics*, 54.

He can also forgive sin (Mark 2)? What is the significance of the detailed, physical descriptions of the resurrected Christ, if not to convince doubters? The Apostle's entire apologetic strategy on the Areopagus at Athens (Acts 17:16-33) would have been meaningless if evidence presented to unbelievers had no power to convince.[54]

Montgomery continues:

The fundamental issue remains: Can evidence per se put the non-Christian in a position where he ought reasonably to accept the saving facts of the gospel and the truth, authority, inspiration, and canonicity of Scripture—or does he need the Spirit's illumination as a prerequisite for doing so?

Moreover, the question is not whether the Holy Spirit is the sole Master in spiritual things. Of course He is. What has to be determined is whether He works mediately—through the Scripture (whose veracity can be independently established)—to change people's hearts, or whether His work in the human heart is a precondition for the recognition of the Bible's veracity. It is doubtful that Calvin was correct in declaring that "without the illumination of the Holy Spirit, the Word can do nothing."[55]

Montgomery states that the Holy Spirit "applies what is preached and defended to produce salvation." If the witness of the Spirit creates faith, "there is no objective way of testing the Spirit's inner presence. The 'inward witness' remains as subjectively unverifiable as the Mormon claim to a 'burning in the bosom.'"[56] "Christians should place before unbelievers the 'many infallible proofs' of God's revelation of Himself in Christ and in the Scriptures, and the Holy Spirit, working through the objective gospel and the inherently persuasive evidence for it, will assuredly apply it; for God's Word never returns void."[57]

---

[54] John Warwick Montgomery, "The Holy Spirit and the Defense of the Faith," *Bibliotheca Sacra* 154 (October–December 1997) 389.

[55] Ibid., 390.

[56] Ibid., 392-393.

[57] Ibid., 395.

Nineteenth century preacher Benjamin Franklin wrote:

> The question is not whether God makes believers. We all admit that God makes believers. The question is not whether He makes believers by the Holy Spirit. Nor is it whether He does it by His Power. We all admit that God makes believers by the Holy Spirit and by His power. But does He put forth His power through Christ, through the apostles, through the Spirit in the apostles, through the Gospel preached by the apostles? Or does He put forth His power or influence to make the sinner, not through Christ, nor through the apostles, nor the word? This is the question to be settled by Scripture.[58]

These are the two main positions concerning the witness of the Spirit: (1) He works directly in a person creating assurance of the truth of Christianity, and (2) He works through the Word of God and evidences.

11. *The Role of Divine Revelation*

The Catholic position is that from the general revelation in nature apart from special revelation we can prove that God is. Then by God's grace one can receive special revelation—the Scriptures and church dogma. Luther and Calvin admitted that a general revelation of God did exist in nature but sin kept people from recognizing it. Therefore knowledge of God from nature does not exist because the unbeliever fails to see it. Only in special revelation is the truth of God known.

I am convinced that from general revelation in nature and human beings we can gain a true but limited knowledge of God. Only special revelation in Christ and Scripture provides the basis for a saving knowledge of God. God's Word is normative and authoritative for all Christians.

---

[58] Benjamin Franklin, "How Are Persons Made Believers?" in *New Testament Christianity*, ed. by Zach Sweeney (Columbus, IN: New Testament Christianity Book Fund, 1930) 3:302.

Essential Elements in an Apologetic Method

Rational

We cannot force faith or demand that people believe, but we can give reasons for faith. Austin Farrer said,

> It is commonly said that if rational argument is so seldom the cause of conviction, philosophical apologetics must largely be wasting their shot. The premise is true, but the conclusion does not follow. For though argument does not create conviction, the lack of it destroys belief. What seems to be proved may not be embraced; but what no one shows the ability to defend is quickly abandoned. Rational argument does not create belief, but it maintains a climate in which belief may flourish.[59]

Reason alone is limited. Human beings could not by reason alone deduce the content of Christian faith. At the same time we do not believe what our reason holds to be false or unreal. We do not believe something unless we consider it plausible. Reason can help remove barriers and obstacles that keep one from seeing Christian faith as possible and plausible. Faith involves one's will and imagination as well as intellect.

Human beings are capable of logical reasoning. Thinking anything is right or wrong assumes the function of reason. Those who attempt to prove irrationalism use reason to try to deny reason. God appeals to reasonable evidence such as fulfilled prophecy (*Isa 41:21*) and miracles (*John 5:36*) as supernatural credentials.

Trueblood said, "Revelation must be tested by reason for the simple reason that there are false claims to revelation."[60] God himself called upon men to test religious truth claims. That does not make reason above God, but humans are asked to recognize divine credentials. However, human reason is

---

[59] Farrer, "The Christian Apologist," 26.
[60] Elton Trueblood, *Philosophy of Religion* (New York: Harper and Row, 1957) 32.

incapable of originating revealed truth. If reason is invalid in making a case for a divine revelation in Scripture, then reason would also be invalid in accepting our experience as valid.

In reaching out to those without faith or with a weak faith we seek to recognize and remove any intellectual or moral barriers to their acceptance of the evidence. We show the irrationality and unlivability of non-Christian worldviews. This removal of obstacles may be necessary before they will be able to listen to the positive case for the truth of Christianity and the rationality of the Christian worldview.

Philosophical barriers must be addressed when they keep a person from accepting the evidence for faith. We must destroy unbelieving systems of thought (*2 Cor 10:5*). The NT preachers did not make an abstract, philosophical case for Christianity. However, neither were they ignorant of the thought patterns influencing those to whom they witnessed. Paul addressed the pagan presuppositions in his address on Mars Hill in Athens (*Acts 17:22-31*).

Machen says:

> Certainly a Christianity that avoids argument is not the Christianity of the New Testament. The New Testament is full of argument—no one can doubt that. But even the words of Jesus are full of argument in defense of the truth of what Jesus was saying. "If ye then, being evil, know how to give good gifts unto your children, how much more shall your Father which is in heaven give good things to them that ask him?" Is not that a well-known form of reasoning, which the logicians would put in its proper category? Many of the parables of Jesus were argumentative in character. Even our lord, who spoke in the plenitude of divine authority, did condescend to reason with men. Everywhere the New Testament meets objections fairly, and presents the gospel as a thoroughly reasonable thing.[61]

[61] J. Gresham Machen, "Christian Scholarship and Evangelism," in *Selected Shorter Writings*, ed. D.G. Hart (Phillipsburg, NJ: P & R Publishing, 2004) 144.

Tim Keller comments, "Christians are saying that the rational isn't part of evangelism. The fact is people are rational. They do have questions. You have to answer those questions. Don't get the impression that I think that the rational aspect takes you all the way there. But there's too much emphasis on just the personal now."[62] We must not abandon the rational but rather combine it with the relational as we commend and defend the gospel.

Historical

True Christianity does not exist if Jesus of Nazareth did not live in a specific time and place in history. Myths float free from historical investigation. Jesus' life, ministry, death, and resurrection stand rooted in historical reality. Christian faith at its essence centers in what God has done in human history. The gospel is not philosophical ideas or ethical ideals. It is good news about something that happened in time and space.

Philosophers and theorists may argue all day about what can or cannot happen. In the final court of appeal the issue of miracles will be decided by credible evidence that miracles have in fact occurred. "What has happened?" rather than "What can or cannot happen?" Assumptions and theories must be corrected by reality.

Historical evidence cannot furnish absolute certainty. In fact no worldview can honestly claim absolute certainty because they all assume what cannot be humanly proven. Any view claiming to be universal truth must agree with known facts. Clark Pinnock says, "To segregate Christian conviction from all empirical verification is to make nonsense of it and to go against the precise claims of the gospel to be historical."[63]

Establish the historical reliability of the Bible, especially the Gospels. From the evidence of prophecy and miracles,

---

[62] Susan Wunderink, "Tim Keller Reasons with America," *Christianity Today* (June 2008) 39.

[63] Clark H. Pinnock, *Biblical Revelation: The Foundation of Christian Theology* (Chicago: Moody Press, 1971) 46.

especially the resurrection, establish the deity of Jesus. Defend the inspiration and inerrancy of the Bible on the basis of Jesus' authority.

Personal

Our apologetic must include rational thinking and historical evidence, but these must be combined with the personal and relational aspects in order to have maximum persuasiveness.

Some of the most influential evidence that a Christian can present are to give testimony from your personal life of the great things God has done in your life. A life manifesting the fruit of the Spirit (love, joy, peace, etc., *Gal 5:22-23*) is a powerful confirming evidence of the rational and historical evidence for the truth of Christianity. Personal testimony is central in the role of a witness. We were not eyewitness to Jesus when he lived in a flesh-body on earth. We can tell what the eyewitnesses said they saw and heard. We can tell why we personally believe and share the peace, joy, and hope that comes from faith in Christ.

Machen states:

> We are pleading, in other words, for a truly comprehensive apologetic—an apologetic which does not neglect the theistic proofs or the historical evidence of the New Testament account of Jesus, but which also does not neglect the facts of the inner life of man. The force of such an apologetic is, we think, cumulative; such an apologetic is strong in its details; but it is even stronger because the details are embraced in a harmonious whole.[64]

We may reach an individual by one approach rather than another, but as that believer is brought to maturity of faith all three elements—rational, historical, and personal—will be involved.

---

[64] J. Gresham Machen, "Relation of Religion to Science and Philosophy," *Princeton Theological Review*, XXIV (1926) 64-65.

The goal of apologetics is to make believers, not to win arguments. Apologetics is not an academic exercise merely to refute opponents. We press for a personal decision regarding the truth claims of Christianity. In the NT believers in their defense of the faith commended the Christ so that the hearers might come to personal, saving faith in Jesus Christ.

Review Questions

1. What do you think made C.S. Lewis an effective apologist?

2. What is meant by negative and positive apologetics?

3. Of the four classifications of apologetic methods in the chart on page 371 which one appeals to you and why?

4. This chapter classifies apologetics approaches into what two general categories?

5. Compare and contrast the classical and evidentialist methods of doing apologetics.

6. List three contemporary examples of classical and evidentialist apologists.

7. What are the distinctive features of the presuppositional approach?

8. What do those who hold to the Reformed epistemology believe about the necessity of evidence as a basis for faith?

9. List the eleven issues in apologetic method listed in the chapter.

10. How does one's belief about the influence of sin on human reason (the *noetic* effect of sin) affect one's apologetic method?

11. Compare and contrast the view of common ground between the believer and unbeliever in classical/evidentialist approach and the presuppositionalist approach.

12. Explain the importance of one's epistemology in regard to apologetic method.

13. State differing views on the role of the Holy Spirit in the process of one's becoming a believer. What is your view?

14. List three essential elements in an apologetic method.

15. Summarize Austin Farrer's comment on the role of rational argument in regard to belief.

16. Why can't Christianity be true if the facts of the gospel are historically false?

17. Explain the importance of the personal element in our witness and defense.

Suggested Reading

Boa, Kenneth D., and Robert M. Bowman, Jr. *Faith Has Its Reasons: An Integrative Approach to Defending Christianity*, 2nd ed. Waynesboro, GA: Authentic Publishing/Paternoster, 2005. Summarizes and states strengths and weaknesses of approaches that emphasize reason, that emphasize evidence, that emphasize revelation, that emphasize faith, and those favoring an integration approach.

Cowan, Stephen B., ed. *Five Views on Apologetics*. Grand Rapids: Zondervan, 2000. Examines how apologists "do" apologetics. Identifies five approaches—classical, evidential, presuppositional, Reformed epistemology, and cumulative case—with interaction among the proponents.

Evans, C. Stephen. "Approaches to Christian Apologetics." *New Dictionary of Christian Apologetics*. Eds. W.C. Campbell-Jack and Gavin McGrath. Downers Grove. IL: InterVarsity, 2006. Discusses apologetic approaches but sees them under two general headings "evidential" and "nonevidential." He discusses Richard Swinburne as an example of the first and Alvin Plantinga representing the second.

Geisler, Norman. *Christian Apologetics*. Grand Rapids: Baker, 1976. Part One discusses the tests of truth. Part Two applies these tests to various worldviews. Part Three defends a theistic worldview and states the evidence for deity of Christ and the authority of the Scripture.

Geisler, Norman. "Types of Apologetics." *Baker Encyclopedia of Christian Apologetics*, pp. 41-44. Grand Rapids: Baker, 1999. He discusses classical, evidential, experiential, historical, and presuppositional types of apologetics.

Lewis, Gordon R. *Testing Christianity's Truth Claims*. Chicago: Moody Press, 1976. Classifies apologetics methods by the epistemology they employ.

Ramm, Bernard. *Varieties of Christian Apologetics*, rev. ed. Grand Rapids: Baker, 1961. Discusses the apologetics of nine apologists under three general systems—stressing subjective immediacy, stressing natural theology, and stressing revelation.

Sproul, R.C., John Gerstner, and Arthur Lindsley. *Classical Apologetics: A Rational Defense of the Christian Faith and a Critique of Presuppositional Apologetics* (Grand Rapids: Zondervan, 1984). Defense of natural theology and refutation of presuppositionalism.

*"For an overseer, as God's steward . . . must hold firm
to the trustworthy word as taught, so that he may be
able to give instruction in sound doctrine and also to
rebuke those who contradict it."*

Titus 1:7,9

*"We are ambassadors for Christ,
God making his appeal through us."*

2 Corinthians 5:20

16

Practical Uses
of Apologetics

Practical Uses of Apologetics
 	
 Profile: Roy Weece—
     Apologetics in Ministry
     and Life
  I. Apologetics in the Family
     A. Parents
     B. Grandparents
 II. Apologetics in the Church
     A. Preaching
     B. Teaching
     C. Worship
	"I have little doubt that the single greatest obstacle to the impact of the gospel has not been its inability to provide answers, but the failure on our part to live it out."[1]
	
	 Ravi Zacharias

[1] Ravi Zacharias, "The Pastor as an Apologist," in *Is Your Church Ready?* eds., Ravi Zacharias and Norman Geisler (Grand Rapids: Zondervan, 2003) 22.

D. Ministry to needy
III. Apologetics with
    Students
   A. School
   B. Colleges and universities
   C. Christian colleges
    and seminaries
IV. Apologetics in
    Everyday Life
   A. Personal evangelism
   B. Writing
    letters/emails
V. Raising up Effective
   Apologists
	"We should be praying that God will raise up a new generation of Christian communicators who are determined to bridge the chasm; who struggle to relate God's unchanging Word to our ever-changing world; who refuse to sacrifice truth to relevance or relevance to truth; but who resolve instead in equal measure to be faithful to Scripture and pertinent to today."[2]
	
	                   John R.W. Stott

Profile: Roy Weece— Apologetics in Ministry and Life[3]

Roy Weece appreciated his studies at Ozark Bible College which deepened his confidence in Christian truths. He determined to plan practical ways to present and defend the faith. These are methods he used in his local church ministry.

Apologetics Sermon Series. Weece devoted every January to preaching faith-building sermons. He dealt with topics such as existence of God, deity of Jesus, inspiration of the Bible, the Bible and science, archaeology, fulfilled prophecy, the resurrection of Christ, and subjective evidences.

[2] John R.W. Stott, *Between Two Worlds: The Art of Preaching in the Twentieth Century* (Grand Rapids: Eerdmans, 1982) 144.

[3] Roy Weece, "Practical Ways to Defend the Faith," in *The Mind of Christ: A Tribute to Seth Wilson,* ed. Lynn Gardner (Joplin, MO: College Press, 1987) 49-57.

He wanted to begin the year by strengthening the faith of Christians and equipping them to answer questions about their faith. These messages had a refreshing and revitalizing effect on the faith of both the preacher and church members.

Home Appointment Lessons. He developed eight lessons, later reduced to five, to teach non-Christians in their homes. Three of the lessons dealt with apologetics. Lesson one gave reasons for faith in God, the Bible, and Christ. Lesson two surveyed Bible history with illustrations of its reliability from archaeology. In lesson five he surveyed the life of Christ giving reasons for believing him to be the Son of God. Weece reported, "In the first year of using the series, ninety-five were baptized based on faith in Jesus and only one failed to yield."

Reclaiming Dropouts. Church leaders wanted to reclaim delinquent church members. They bathed the process in prayer. From the membership list they developed a "dead list" of thirty-nine persons. The elders and minister met with each person. The leaders asked these questions about what and why they believed. "Do you still believe in God? Why or why not? Do you still believe in the Bible? Why or why not? Do you still believe Jesus is God's Son and your Leader-Savior? Why or why not?" They found "one of the reasons for straying from Christ is the absence of good reasons for faith." Giving reasons for faith helped them gain or regain a living faith. Thirty-seven returned to following Christ.

Personal Evangelism. Weece often used apologetics in his conversations with others. He asked an attorney, "What do you do with the evidences of Christianity since you deal with evidence?" He asked the inventor of one of the Skylab computers, "Suppose your thirteen inventions were displayed in Washington, D.C., on a special honors day and some suggested your 'works' were an accident and had no mind behind them. Would you feel insulted and unappreciated?"

"Yes, I most certainly would!"

Weece responded, "Do you suppose the Designer of the universe, whose order and symmetry you depend on for your inventions, ever feels insulted and unappreciated when man suggests it's all an accident and the result of mindless evolution?"

The inventor answered, "I'd never thought of it that way."

Teaching Youth. Youth have questions and need solid answers. Weece taught evidences to young people. He encouraged them to write term papers, give speeches, and make book reports in matters relating to Christian evidences. He also used apologetics with tiny tots. While supervising three-to-five-year-olds he took a doll and asked, "Did someone make it? How do you know?" He suggested that it just happened, but they argued that someone made it. Then he held up a globe to represent the world and asked, "Did it just happen or did someone make it?" Again they insisted that someone made the world.

Campus Ministry. Weece served in campus ministry at the University of Missouri for over thirty years. He could not recall any non-Christian student with whom he had talked who did not have doubts. He constantly used apologetics in answering the students' questions.

Public Speaking. Weece identifies some opportunities he had in public speaking.

In both high schools in Columbia, Missouri, I have given reasons about creation, accuracy of the Bible, and the deity of Christ. At the State Convention of the Missouri Jaycees, I explained my reasons for God's existence. At the Convention of the Missouri Dieticians Association and the Missouri Hospital Association, I defended my belief in the creation of man. At the Missouri Professional and Business Women's Organization, I shared reasons for faith.

Family. He used every opportunity to defend the faith to his own children, all of whom are in Christian service today. He urged his children to ask questions when the school teacher taught evolution. "Is that the only explanation for how everything got here? Can we hear the other explanation?" After they suggested their father, teachers invited him several times to present the case for creation.

An important purpose of the study of apologetics is to prepare every Christian to be a more effective defender of the faith. We must not relegate apologetics to an isolated academic dustbin. It touches how we think, speak, and act. Our approach to apologetics shapes how we share our Christian convictions with others. This chapter will discuss many practical uses of apologetics.

Apologetics in the Family

Parents. How parents respond to the thousands of questions their children ask has a tremendous influence in shaping the thought life of their children. Many young adults abandon the faith of their childhood because they did not get satisfying answers to their questions. Perhaps they felt their questions were treated as unimportant. I am grateful to my wife for her knowledge of the Bible and apologetics because she fielded the majority of our children's questions. Parents should never underestimate their role in shaping the thinking of their children.

Home life shapes our earliest attitude, positive or negative, toward God and Christianity. Many have a negative image of God because they had a bad relationship with their father. Many famous atheists and unbelievers had an absent father or a bad relationship with their father. Paul Vitz in his *Faith of the Fatherless* documents this phenomenon.[4]

Parents have the responsibility to help their children develop into being good thinkers. When a child asks if such and such is right or wrong, instead of giving a quick answer we can ask what *they* think and why. Allow them to have opinions but insist they have good reasons for them. Help them learn to think about God, relationships, science, and the world. Force feeding them with pat answers and conclusions does not develop their maturity. They will make better decisions in their young adult years if they know *why* such things as lying, cheating, sexual immorality, and profanity are wrong.

Mark DeVries points out that in an image-centered culture with limited conversation with thinking adults young people are ill prepared to think logically and understand moral principles. He quotes a college history professor, "Students are ready to tell you how they feel about an issue but they have never learned how to construct a rational argument to defend their opinions." DeVries adds, "Without the habit of critical thinking, our teenagers become easy prey to anyone who has something to sell."[5] Young people who develop relationships with mature adults will be better prepared for adult life.

Use opportunities from evidences of design in nature and everyday life to point them to God. Conscientious parents don't rely on the church youth program to do all the Bible teaching to their children. From the earliest years reading Bible stories will acquaint them with the Word of God. Moses' instruction to parents about teaching God's Word still rings true, *"You shall*

---

[4] Paul Vitz, *Faith of the Fatherless: The Psychology of Atheism* (Dallas: Spence, 1999).

[5] Mark DeVries, *Family-Based Youth Ministry*, rev. ed. (Downers Grove, IL: InterVarsity, 2004) 51.

teach them diligently to your children, and shall talk of them when you sit in your house, and when you walk by the way, and when you lie down, and when you rise" (Deut 6:7).

As children mature, it is important that they accept Christianity because it is true not just because it is family tradition. A merely family-faith will not sustain one through the trials of life. Each person must make the faith his or her own—intellectually and personally.

William Wilberforce saw the value of teaching apologetics to children. He challenged parents to carefully instruct their children in the principles of the faith and in the arguments for the defense of the faith.[6] J.P. Moreland observes:

> Having witnessed hundreds of evangelical children hit the college campus, I can attest to the fact that we need to follow Wilberforce's advice and start early in teaching them the reasons for their faith. Make no mistake about it. Young children can ask profound intellectual questions about God and religion. And if we do not take seriously and work to provide them with good answers, it will impact the vibrancy of their Christian commitment sooner or later.[7]

Mothers and fathers should be the first apologetics teachers for their children. This does not mean forcing religion on their children. But as we help our children become independent of us, we have to help them be good thinkers and make mature judgments about life. Parents who daily live a life of faith, joy, love, and hope demonstrate to their children the reality and relevance of Christianity.

Nancy Pearcey expresses alarm that we are losing our children and suggests a solution:

---

[6] William Wilberforce, *Real Christianity* (Portland, OR: Multnomah Press, 1982, based on 1829 edition) 1-2.

[7] J.P. Moreland, *Love Your God with All Your Mind* (Colorado Springs: NavPress, 1997) 135.

It's a familiar but tragic story that devout young people, raised in Christian homes, head off to college and abandon their faith. Why is this pattern so common? Largely because young believers have not been taught how to develop a biblical worldview. Instead, Christianity has been restricted to a specialized area of religious belief and personal devotion.

As Christian parents, pastors, teachers, and youth group leaders, we constantly see young people pulled down by the undertow of powerful cultural trends. If all we give them is a "heart" religion, it will not be strong enough to counter the lure of attractive but dangerous ideas. Young believers also need a "brain" religion—training in worldview and apologetics—to equip them to analyze and critique the competing worldviews they will encounter when they leave home. If forewarned and forearmed, young people at least have a fighting chance when they find themselves a minority of one among their classmates or work colleagues. Training young people to develop a Christian mind is no longer an option; it is part of their necessary survival equipment.[8]

Christians in high school and college face intellectual assault with anti-Christian worldviews and attitudes. Apologist William Craig says:

As I speak in churches around the country, I continually meet parents whose children have left the faith because there was no one in the church to answer their questions. For the sake of our youth, we desperately need informed parents who are equipped to wrestle with the issues at an intellectual level.[9]

If parents are not intellectually engaged with their faith and do not have sound arguments for Christian theism and good answers to their children's questions, then we are in real danger of losing our youth. It's no longer enough to teach our children Bible stories; they need doctrine and apologetics.

---

[8] Nancy Pearcey, *Total Truth: Liberating Christianity from Its Cultural Captivity* (Wheaton, IL: Crossway, 2004) 19.
[9] William Lane Craig, *Reasonable Faith: Christian Truth and Apologetics*, rev. ed. (Wheaton, IL: Crossway, 1994) xv.

Frankly, I find it hard to understand how people today can risk parenthood without having studied apologetics.[10]

In the light of the hostile environment of college and university campuses Richard Howe gives this advice, "Parents should try to make sure that their children are grounded in apologetics before sending them off. This does not mean that the students would have to have all the answers before they go. But it does mean that, if the need arises for an answer, they will know where to go and with whom to consult when the intellectual battle starts to rage. And it most certainly will rage."[11]

Grandparents. Grandparents have a great opportunity to influence their grandchildren. They can reinforce the values taught by parents or can introduce Christian values when the parents are not believers. My wife and I have had a Bible club with our grandchildren. Many of our lessons include apologetic issues—science, archaeology, how we got the Bible, etc. How grandparents face limitations and hardships speak volumes to grandchildren concerning the practical relevance of Christian faith. Seeing their loved ones face sickness and death with grace and faith can inspire grandchildren to faithfulness. Godly, praying grandparents can instill and nourish faith in their grandchildren.

Apologetics in the Church

Emphasis on entertaining programming has left many Christians intellectually shallow and unprepared to face the challenges of culture. Much of the contemporary evangelical church has adopted the culture of the world rather than seeking transformation by the Word of God. The church has a

---

[10] Ibid., 19.
[11] Richard Howe, "Colleges Think Left, Students Think That's Right," *American Family Association Journal*, (August 2006), **http://www.afajournal.org/2006/august/0806colleges.html**.

responsibility to teach the fundamentals of the faith—teaching what we believe as well as why we believe.

Preaching. "But how are they to call on him in whom they have not believed? And how are they to believe in him of whom they have never heard? And how are they to hear without someone preaching? . . . So faith comes from hearing, and hearing through the word of Christ" (Rom 10:14,17).

John Milton lamented the weakness of the preaching in his day when he wrote, "The hungry sheep look up, and are not fed."[12] D. Martyn Lloyd-Jones stated "the decadent periods and eras in the history of the Church have always been those periods when preaching had declined."[13] E.C. Dargan agrees, "Decline of spiritual life and activity in the churches is commonly accompanied by a lifeless, formal, unfruitful preaching, and this partly as cause, partly as effect. On the other hand, the great revivals of Christian history can most usually be traced to the work of the pulpit."[14]

Preaching will not build and nourish faith in the hearers unless the preacher has a strong confidence in the reality of a personal living God who has spoken and speaks truth in Scripture. Preaching that clearly and forcefully declares the truth in the biblical text and applies it to living today builds faith in the hearers.

The preacher has the awesome responsibility to be a mouthpiece declaring the Word of the magnificent God of the universe. The preacher stands in the presence of God and speaks to bring his listeners into the presence of God. His messages feed our spirits. Challenged by God's character and truth we leave better able to live in his will.

---

[12] John Milton, *Lycides*, Line 123.

[13] D. Martyn Lloyd-Jones, *Preaching and Preachers* (London: Hodder and Stoughton, 1971) 24.

[14] E.C. Dargan, *History of Preaching*, 1:13, quoted in John Stott, *Between Two Worlds: The Art of Preaching in the Twentieth Century* (Grand Rapids: Eerdmans, 1982) 114-115.

Preaching and teaching the Word must be a priority. Pop psychology and feel-good sermons do not nourish the mind or the soul. Unless the congregation hears the Word of God preached, they leave as empty and confused as when they came regardless of being entertained or told to feel good about themselves.[15]

Preachers need to wrestle with the text until the truth of the text is clear in their minds and grips their hearts. Forceful, biblical preaching challenges minds, feeds souls, directs wills. Effective preaching relates and applies the truth of Scripture to the questions, problems, and needs that people are facing as they live in today's world. This kind of preaching builds and nourishes faith equipping the hearers to commend and defend Christ to others.

Ravi Zacharias states, "It is the sacred duty of a pastor to remind his people periodically of the very nature of truth, because if truth dies, even at the altar of cultural sensitivities, then so does the gospel in the listener's ears. The first and foremost task of the apologist, then, is to stand for the truth and to clarify the claims of the gospel."[16] God designed the church to be a pillar of truth (*1 Tim 3:15*).

Those ministering in the local church need to provide answers to those with questions or help individuals get in touch with someone who can provide answers and resources. Zacharias warns, "If we are unprepared to defend what we believe so that the defense is meaningful, we may as well give up on this generation."[17] Preaching must minister to both the mind and the heart.

---

[15] David F. Wells, *The Courage to Be Protestant: Truth-lovers, Marketers, and Emergents in the Postmodern World* (Grand Rapids: Eerdmans, 2008) 229-233.
[16] Ravi Zacharias, "The Church's Role in Apologetics and the Development of the Mind," in *Beyond Opinion*, ed. Ravi Zacharias (Nashville: Thomas Nelson, 2007) 314.
[17] Ibid., 315.

Teaching. The teaching program must include a faith-building component. Church leaders must give attention to the curriculum being taught in classes, in the youth program, and in small groups. Is it true to the Bible? Does it build and strengthen faith? Does it equip for ministry? The church becomes spiritually shallow when entertaining programming replaces teaching the word of God. Leaders in local churches can use popular-level resources to teach basic evidences and apologetics. The accompanying sidebar lists books, video curricula, and websites providing apologetics resources.

Resources for Teaching Basic Apologetics

Popular-level books:

Paul Little, *Know Why You Believe*, 3rd. ed. (Downers Grove, IL: InterVarsity, 1988).

Josh McDowell and Sean McDowell, *More Than a Carpenter*, rev. ed. (Wheaton, IL: Tyndale House, 2009).

Lynn Gardner, *Christianity Stands True* (Joplin, MO: College Press, 1994).

Lee Strobel, *The Case for Christ* (Grand Rapids: Zondervan, 1998).

Timothy Keller, *The Reason for God* (New York: Dutton, 2008).

Lee Strobel, *The Case for Faith* (Grand Rapids: Zondervan, 2000).

Norman Geisler and Frank Turek, *I Don't Have Enough Faith to Be an Atheist* (Wheaton, IL: Crossway, 1999).

William Lane Craig, *On Guard: Defending Your Faith with Reason and Precision* (Colorado Springs: David C. Cook, 2010).

Video Curriculum:

Rewired: A Teen Worldview Curriculum (Prison Fellowship). DVD presentation helping teens develop a Christian worldview and exposing false ideas promoted in culture. **www.breakpoint.org/resources/rewired-curriculum.**

The Truth Project (Focus on the Family). A DVD-based small group curriculum comprised of twelve video lessons taught by Dr. Del Tackett. Seeks to relate Christianity to all of life. **www.thetruthproject.org**.

Truth U (Focus on the Family). A DVD-based apologetic training series primarily geared to help prepare high school students for the challenges and attacks that will confront them on the university campus. **www.trueU.org**.

I Don't Have Enough Faith to Be an Atheist (Impact Apologetics). DVD series by Norman Geisler and Frank Turek based on their book with the same title. **www.impactapologetics.com**.

Curriculum from Summit Ministries:

Lightbearers. One or two semester video-based curriculum for 8th grade teaching the Christian worldview.

Understanding the Times. One- or two-semester video-based curriculum for 12th grade teaching the Christian world-view and answering leading worldviews of the day.

Worldview in Focus. Series of lessons addressing and comparing the Christian worldview with competing worldviews of the day. High school, college, and adult options. **www. summit.org/curriculum**.

Websites:

www.arcapologetics.org, Apologetics Resource Center (Craig Branch and Steven Cowan)

www.garyhabermas.com (Gary Habermas)

www.josh.org and **www.truefoundations.com** (Josh McDowell).

www.LeeStrobel.com (Lee Strobel)

www.normangeisler.net (Norman Geisler)

www.reasonablefaith.org, Reasonable Faith (William Lane Craig)

www.rzim.org, Ravi Zacharias International Ministries (Ravi Zacharias)

www.str.org, Stand to Reason (Greg Koukl)

www.equip.org, Christian Research Institute (Hank Hannegraaff)

www.ankerberg.com, Ankerberg Theological Research Institute (John Ankerberg)

www.seanmcdowell.org (Sean McDowell)

www.meeknessandtruth.org, Meekness and Truth Ministries (David Geisler)

www.bethinking.org, UCCF: The Christian Unions

www.thinkchristianly.org (Jonathan Morrow)

www.lynngardner.info (Lynn Gardner)

www.icr.org, Institute for Creation Research

www.answersingenesis.org, Answers in Genesis

www.creationresearch.org, Creation Research Society

www.discovery.org/csc/, The Center for Science and Culture, at the Discovery Institute

www.designinference.com (William Dembski)

When people drop out of church it often indicates a problem with their faith. Try the method Roy Weece used. Instead of asking why did you quit church, ask "Do you believe in God, Christ, and the Bible? Why? or Why not?" Asking these basic questions will reveal whether or not they have a solid faith. If weak faith is the problem, address it with good teaching.

In homes and in informal settings people are more willing to ask their real questions. Teaching the basis for faith should be a part of home teaching sessions and small group studies. *The Truth Project* developed by Focus on the Family is a resource helping to meet this need. People find small groups valuable as a place they can ask their questions, grow spiritually, and experience loving fellowship and community. Small group leaders can use these opportunities to build faith in those present.

Dan Kimball states:

In my dialogue and relationships with non-Christian and Christian young people for more than 18 years, I am not finding less interest in apologetics, but actually *more* interest. The

more we are living in an increasingly post-Christian and pluralistic culture, the more we need apologetics because people
are asking more and more questions. We desperately need to
be ready to answer the tough questions of today's emerging
generations.[18]

Sean McDowell expresses a similar experience:

For the past decade or longer, the Christian marketplace has
been flooded with books about how to do ministry in a postmodern world. Their authors rightly have pointed out many
cultural changes due to postmodernism but often have failed to
realize how much has actually remained the same. I am per-
plexed when I read contemporary writers, particularly some in
the emerging church movement, who question the need for
apologetics in ministry to postmodern youth. My experience
has been that young people today, even in our postmodern culture, are deeply interested in apologetic questions.[19]

Children ask serious questions from an early age. We can
introduce young children to the concepts of God as creator and
Christ's miracles. Classes on basic faith, evidences, Bible, doctrine, and science addressing current issues can be a big help
for youth. Researcher with the Barna Group, David Kinnaman,
writes, "We are learning that one of the primary reasons that
ministry to teenagers fails to produce a lasting faith is because
they are not being taught to think."[20]

A research survey questioned 1,000 young adults, ages
20–29, who formerly regularly attended evangelical churches
but had dropped out of church. The findings indicated that

---

[18] Dan Kimball, "A Different Kind of Apologist," *Apologetics for a New Generation: A Biblical and Culturally Relevant Approach to Talking about God*, Sean
McDowell, ed. (Eugene, OR: Harvest House, 2009) 29.

[19] Sean McDowell, "Apologetics for an Emerging Generation," in *Passionate
Conviction: Contemporary Discourses on Christian Apologetics*, eds. Paul Copan
and William Lane Craig (Nashville: B & H Academic, 2007) 259-260.

[20] David Kinnaman and Gabe Lyons, *UnChristian: What a New Generation
Really Thinks about Christianity and Why it Matters* (Grand Rapids: Baker
Books, 2007) 81.

forty percent began doubting the truthfulness of the Bible while in middle school and forty-four percent began doubting in high school.[21] This research raises serious questions about the effectiveness of the current Sunday School and youth programming in evangelical churches.

Sociologist Christian Smith conducted an extensive research of contemporary youth culture. His research suggests that today's youth need an intellectual reinforcement of their beliefs. He documents the dominance of "open and inclusive religious pluralism" and "individualistic subjectivism and relativism" among contemporary American teenagers. His findings revealed that the main reason kids with a religious background shed their religious beliefs in their teen years is because they didn't believe those beliefs were true.[22] We are failing our youth if we do not give them reasons to believe. Many experts in youth apologetics give ideas for presenting apologetics to today's youth in *Apologetics for a New Generation: A Biblically and Culturally Relevant Approach to Talking about God*, edited by Sean McDowell (Harvest House, 2009).

Greg Stier drawing on his experience with this generation of young people says the claims about the death of apologetics are greatly exaggerated. He lists the following topics relevant and important to today's youth:

✧ What are the evidences for the existence of a higher power?
✧ Why is there evil in the world?
✧ Can all religions be right?
✧ Who is Jesus?

---

[21] Ken Ham and Britt Beemer with Todd Hillard. *Already Gone: Why Your Kids Will Quit Church and What You Can Do to Stop It* (Green Forest, AR: Master Books, 2009) 32.

[22] Christian Smith and Melinda Denton, *Soul Searching: The Religious and Spiritual Lives of American Teenagers* (New York: Oxford University Press, 2005) 75, 145, 89.

✧ Is the Bible reliable?

✧ What is truth, and can I know it with certainty?

He affirms, "I *love* this generation of young people. They are more open to engage in spiritual truth than any generation I can remember in my four decades on this planet. In my experience, postmoderns have been misdiagnosed as being purely relational—they are rational as well and hungry to explore spiritual truth. Therefore we must equip Christian students to engage others effectively in spiritual conversations."[23]

Leaders need to train students to recognize and evaluate worldviews. Zacharias says, "*The most effective defense of the faith and offense against falsehood must be based on an examination of worldviews.*"[24] Apologetics is an important part of ministering to youth.

Josh McDowell is devoting his recent efforts to demonstrating "to our kids not only what is *objectively true* about the Christian faith but also how that is *relationally meaningful* to their lives."[25] He emphasizes we must combine truth and relationship in our apologetics.[26]

Worship. Former archbishop of England, William Temple defined worship:

> Worship is the submission of all of our nature to God. It is the quickening of the conscience by his holiness; the nourishment of mind with his truth; the purifying of imagination by his beauty; the opening of the heart to his love; the surrender

---

[23] "An Interview with Greg Stier," in *Apologetics for a New Generation*, 119.

[24] Zacharias, "The Church's Role in Apologetics," 319. Italics in original.

[25] Josh McDowell, "A Relevant Apologetic," *Reasons for Faith: Making a Case for the Christian Faith*, Norman L. Geisler and Chad V. Meister, eds. (Wheaton, IL: Crossway, 2007) 39. For information about his campaign True Foundations see **www.truefoundations.com**.

[26] Josh McDowell, "A Fresh Apologetic: Relationships that Transform," *Apologetics for a New Generation: A Biblical and Culturally Relevant Approach to Talking about God*, Sean McDowell, ed. (Eugene, OR: Harvest House, 2009) 57-69.

of will to his purpose—all this gathered up in adoration, the most selfless emotion of which our nature is capable.[27]

A congregation of believers vibrantly worshiping God gives a powerful witness to outsiders of the reality of the living God. When visitors experience a meaningful worship service, they often sense a spiritual presence of God which defies rational and natural explanations. This contact may awaken in them the hunger for God that he put within every human being.

John Guest observes, "It is to a congregation that believers invite friends whom they want to see come to faith. And it is in the experience of worship that the relational and rational aspects of the Christian meet. There the unbelieving inquirers see what faith looks like up close and lived out."[28]

Directing our hearts to God in worship draws us closer to one another. We do not gather as lone rangers doing our religious duty. We gather as brothers and sisters in one caring family seeking to express our trust, love, and devotion to God. Our teaching the truth and defending the faith becomes more plausible and powerful when outsiders sense a dynamic reality of a joyful and dynamic Christian community.

A church makes an apologetic witness to outsiders when faith is demonstrated, when truth is lived, when mercy is evident. Seeing faith and love in practice adds credibility and power to our witness to the reality of God and the truth of Christianity.

Influences in Western culture "have eroded confidence in rational and reasonable truth. But along with the cognitively grasped reasons for faith, the quality of life in and through the Christian fellowship becomes another powerful, persuasive

---

[27] William Temple, *Readings in St. John's Gospel* (London: Macmillan, 1940) 68. Quoted in Zacharias, "The Church's Role in Apologetics," 326.

[28] John Guest, "The Church as the Heart and Soul of Apologetics," in *Is Your Church Ready?* 41.

weapon in the Christian's armory."[29] Christian fellowship can provide the sense of community which contemporary people desperately seek. "A congregation can winsomely and gently disarm the common distrust of the rational process. It does so in the context of lived, relational reality."[30]

John Stott emphasizes that the reading and preaching of the Word are essential to worship:

> Our worship is poor because our knowledge of God is poor, and our knowledge of God is poor because our preaching is poor. But when the Word of God is expounded in its fullness, and the congregation begins to glimpse the glory of the living God, they bow down in solemn awe and joyful wonder before his throne. It is preaching which accomplishes this, the proclamation of the Word of God in the power of the Spirit of God. That is why preaching is unique and irreplaceable.[31]

Ways a Local Church Can Teach Apologetics

1. Faith-building sermon series and regular biblical preaching that forcefully relate the truth of God's Word to life in today's world.
2. Solid teaching of the Bible and doctrine at every level of church life.
3. Classes in apologetics topics with textbooks, tests, and grades. Elective Sunday classes, weekend courses, home study series, a night class for six or seven weeks.
4. Special speakers and videos/DVDs on apologetics topics.
5. Good apologetics resources for both youth and adults in the church library promoted in church lobby and in email and print materials.
6. Specific apologetics training in middle school and with high school seniors preparing them for high school and college.

[29] Ibid., 42.
[30] Ibid.
[31] Stott, *Between Two Worlds*, 82-83.

Ministry. Persons with an apologetic lifestyle will have a spirit of seeking to serve rather be served (*Mark 10:45*). The watching world will know we are Christ followers by our demonstrated love (*John 13:35*). The church should be a refuge for hurting people. Those damaged by the hard knocks of life often have a hard time trusting God because they blame him. Rather than kick these persons down, reach out to them in love. Many who ask "Why does God let me suffer?" have an emotional problem with God more than an intellectual problem. They can't trust God because they feel he let them down.[32]

Those broadsided by tough times, even if they have a Christian understanding of suffering, still experience emotions of helplessness and often a sense of abandonment. They need ministry of loving concern and fellowship before they are ready to deal with the intellectual questions about God.

A singles pastor in a west coast church which had 1,100 never-married and single-again people weekly reported this startling statistic. He said, "Sixty percent of those coming to our singles group feel God ripped them off. Many were angry with God because of divorce or death. 'He left me.' 'She left me.' 'He died.' 'She died.'"[33]

Being sensitive to people's hurts and ministering to their needs confirms in practice the reality of the God we proclaim. Many today perceive Christians as hypocritical, insensitive, arrogant, and judgmental.[34] We will be ineffective in commending Christian faith until people see the demonstration of love in our attitude and actions. When they see love in action, they are more open to the plausibility of belief in our loving God. Our ministry to people in times of tragedy, hardship, ill-

[32] Lynn Gardner, *Where Is God When We Suffer?* (Joplin, MO: College Press, 2007) 261-275.

[33] Reported to me October 31, 2009, by Willard Black, speaker and writer on singles, who interviewed this singles pastor.

[34] See Dan Kimball, *They Like Jesus but Not the Church* (Grand Rapids: Zondervan, 2007); and Kinnaman and Lyons, *UnChristian.*

Learn more about the Lakota (Sioux) culture at <u>stjo.org/culture</u>.

ness, and death of a loved one often is the bridge that will open people to listen to our witness to Christ. Genuinely loving people and caring for the needy is an essential element in our apologetic.

Apologetics with Students

School. Many practice Christian faith before they are exposed to logical reasons and evidence. Josh McDowell observes, "I know many people who came to Christ as children or teenagers, but it wasn't until they got to high school or university that their faith really started to be challenged; they didn't question it until then. That was when they needed apologetics."[35]

Young people can be encouraged to study apologetics topics and give speeches, write themes, and do book reports on related issues in school. Classes can challenge young people to study a topic and present it to the group. Youth workers can encourage the youth to come to them with questions that their school and social life raises. Together they can search for good answers.

Churches can provide a series of lessons ending with a training seminar for graduates of the 8th grade preparing them for high school. They need to be prepared for the social and intellectual challenges and temptations ahead of them in high school. We can teach them logical thinking and worldview thinking, and how to find help and available resources when they have questions.

Conduct a more extensive summer institute on apologetics for high school graduates preparing them for college and career. Additional teaching concerning evaluating worldviews should help them prepare to evaluate what they will encounter in college. They need to be warned about the pressures to par-

---

[35] Christy Tennant, "Josh McDowell on Defending the Faith," *Bible Study Magazine* (Now & Dec 2008) 12.

ticipate in premarital sex, drinking alcohol, and taking drugs; to adopt a humanistic viewpoint and lifestyle; and to abandon church. Current university students and an area campus minister could be resource people. We need to be more creative and intentional in equipping our young people for college.

Alex McFarland lists five core truths students should be taught before heading off to college:

1. Truth: Does absolute, universal truth exist?
2. God: Can we know that He exists?
3. Scriptures: How can we be sure that the Bible is trustworthy?
4. Jesus: Is He really the one and only Savior?
5. The problem of pain: Why does a supposedly loving God allow suffering in the world?[36]

In *College and University*. Charles Malik states:

All the preaching in the world, and all the loving care of even the best parents when there are no problems whatever, will amount to little, if not to nothing, so long as what the children are exposed to day in and day out for fifteen to twenty years in the school and university virtually cancels out, morally and spiritually, what they hear and see and learn at home and in the church. Therefore the problem of the school and university is the most critical problem afflicting Western civilization.[37]

David Embree, university professor of religion and campus minister, describes the university mindset, "On university campuses Christianity is often spoken of as a thing of the past, overwhelmingly discredited by the hard sciences. Anyone who possesses a life of faith is naïve at best and stupid at worst, neither of which fits the image students want to project."[38]

---

[36] Alex McFarland, "Making Apologetics Come Alive in Youth Ministry," in *Apologetics for a New Generation*, 153.

[37] Charles Malik, "The Two Tasks," in *The Two Tasks of the Christian Scholar: Redeeming the Soul, Redeeming the Mind* (Wheaton, IL: Crossway, 2007) 60.

[38] Personal communication to the author.

Christian students often find their faith openly ridiculed or facing a patronizing attitude. Roy Weece said, "Students often have their faith smiled away." Estimates suggest that up to 51 percent of those who enter college as Christians will renounce their faith before they graduate. They have not been trained to defend the biblical worldview.[39]

Alison Thomas describes the challenges and temptations she faced at university:

> From the moment I entered my university campus, my faith was attacked from every direction. My professors scoffed at the idea that I considered the Bible to be historically trustworthy. My classmates declared Christianity to be the cause of all the problems in the world, including violence, racism, and sexism. Members of my community reveled in the public disgrace of prominent evangelicals. There were lifestyle challenges that presented themselves to me daily: parties, sex, alcohol, drugs. Combine this with sleep deprivation, poor nutrition, lack of exercise, fickle relationships, and the absence of mentors and accountability partners, and it is a perfect recipe for disaster. The combination of all of these factors makes spiritual growth in college a unique challenge.[40]

When she was a teen her youth ministers brushed aside her intellectual questions and her campus minister gave her patronizing responses. She states, "I wish I had been prepared for the attack on my faith that took place in college, for I am absolutely convinced that I would have been spared from much doubt, sin, and heartache. This is why I work with teens just before they go to college."[41]

Alison Thomas writes:

> The good news is that, with proper training, Christian students can find their college years to be a time of God's blessing instead of a time of spiritual bankruptcy. It is in school

---

[39] Alison Thomas, "Challenges from Youth," in *Beyond Opinion*, 19.
[40] Ibid., 40-41.
[41] Ibid., 47.

that many students rededicate their lives to Christ or genuine-ly encounter him for the first time. In my collegiate years, I was tempted to ignore the difficult questions that plagued my mind and heart, but it was by facing them head-on and wrestling with them one by one that my faith was strength-ened and my life was transformed.[42]

Campus ministers can have a tremendous witness for Christ to students and faculty, but they need training in Bible and apologetics. Ministry on college and university campuses should include teaching apologetics and worldview analysis and answering questions and objections. This vital outreach of the church helps students navigate the challenges higher edu-cation presents. Winning internationals to faith in Christ and sending them home as Christian evangelists is an effective method of missions.

Resources for Preparing for and Surviving Spiritually at College

J. Budziszewski, *How to Stay Christian in College: An Interactive Guide to Keeping the Faith* (Think, 2004). A former athe-ist and radical, now professor at the University of Texas, gives straight advice on different worldviews and myths that students encounter at college.

Alex McFarland, *Stand Strong in College* (Tyndale House, 2007). Apologetics youth expert helps the student prepare for the academic, social, emotional, and spir-itual challenges he or she will face. Geared to high school students.

Jonathan Morrow, *Welcome to College: A Christ-Follower's Guide for the Journey* (Kregel, 2008). This guidebook provides wisdom from biblical truth and practical experience. It discusses intellectual challenges, finan-

---

[42] Ibid., 45.

cial problems, sexual snares, getting enough sleep and more.

Abby Nye, *Fish Out of Water* (Green Forest, AR: New Leaf Press, 2005). The author tells of her story of facing the anti-Christian atmosphere and pressures she experienced at Butler University and how she survived with her faith intact.

James W. Sire, *Chris Chrisman Goes to Colleges: And Faces the Challenges of Relativism, Individualism and Pluralism* (Downers Grove, IL: InterVarsity, 1993). Fictional account of three young men at college and how they confronted the dominant ideologies of the secular university.

David Wheaton, *University of Destruction: Your Game Plan for Spiritual Victory on Campus* (Bethany House, 2005). Professional tennis player and speaker relates his experience at Stanford University. He identifies perils faced in sex, alcohol/drugs, and humanism and gives a game plan for surviving spiritually.

Christian Colleges and Seminaries. Students in Christian colleges and seminaries need apologetic studies because most students enter as freshmen with little or no apologetic training and resources. Many Christian schools provide little instruction in apologetics. Vocational as well as volunteer Christian leaders and workers need to be well prepared to commend and defend Christian faith. Institutions preparing Christian leaders should offer at least a course giving grounding in Christian evidences for freshmen and sophomores and an advanced course in apologetics for upperclassmen.

Christian colleges and universities should be faith-building institutions. Regrettably in some cases liberal and postmodern views, negative biblical criticism, and moral relativism have invaded these schools. Budziszewski states, "But the worst stories about anti-Christian ideological assault I have heard so far come from nominally Christian colleges that have not remained true to their mission."[43] Douglas Groothuis says, "Christian colleges, seminaries, and churches should incorporate apologetics into their institutional/educational life, mission, and vision. Specifically, every Christian high school, college, university, and seminary should require at least one class in apologetics for every degree in their curriculum."[44]

Apologetics in Everyday Life

In our everyday conversation we can relate evidence concerning these basic facts: God is real. The Bible is true. Christ is alive. Sharing and building faith in Christ is the heart of evangelism not just recruiting people to join the church.

When the conversation is negative about everything, the economy, the weather, politics, sickness, etc. you can state your faith and hope in the future because Jesus lives and in your confidence that God keeps his Word. We can use everyday conversation as an opportunity to speak up for Christ.

People need to hear apologetics today, but often Christians assume they are not interested. Non-Christians today often start with a distrust of Christians, the church, and the Bible. We have to earn their trust so they will be interested in the answers we can provide. Often non-Christians are willing to discuss their religious questions with those they trust and consider a friend.

Personal Evangelism. We become more effective communicators and defenders of the faith by actually talking to people. Mark Mittelberg challenges, "If you want to become a well-rounded and effective Christian apologist, then don't just read

---

[43] J. Budziszewski, "Off to College: Can We Keep Them?" in *Is Your Church Ready?* 104.

[44] Douglas Groothuis, "Manifesto for Christian Apologetics: Nineteen Theses to Shake the World with the Truth," in *Reasons for Faith*, 405.

books and spend all of your time hanging out with like-minded believers. Get out there and actually *talk with real human beings* who have questions and objections."[45]

Dan Kimball realized he was hanging out all the time with Christians who enjoyed discussing apologetics. He said, "I wasn't spending time with the non-Christians who were asking these tough questions. . . . The more skilled in apologetics we get, the fewer people we know who actually need it. . . . But if we are focusing our energy and time listening mainly to Christians, how do we know what the questions non-Christian youth or young adults have?"[46] Kimball challenges us to ask ourselves: "How many discussions with non-Christians we have had in the last six months? Who are we praying regularly for who is a not a Christian?"[47]

Lifestyle apologetics means we live what we believe. If we do not pray, we can't expect people to believe us when we say we believe in a prayer-hearing and answering God. It is trite but true—what we *do* speaks louder than what we *say*. Seeing faith in living color in the lives of Christians makes Christianity plausible. Seeing the evidence of its truthfulness in real life makes it persuasive. People take notice when a Christian diagnosed with a terminal illness faces it with faith and hope in God.

Mark Mittelberg says, "I don't think evidence or reason alone leads people into God's family. . . . But I do believe, based on both Scripture and experience, that good arguments, logic, and evidence are used by God's Spirit to help clear the path of intellectual roadblocks" so people "can take the message seriously and eventually decide to follow the one who died to pay for our sins and rose to give us new life. . . . Apologetics is the handmaiden to evangelism."[48] Apologetics training gives

---

[45] Mittelberg, "An Apologetic for Apologetics," in *Reasons for Faith*, 22.

[46] Dan Kimball, "A Different Kind of Apologist," 31, 33, 34.

[47] Ibid., 33.

[48] Mittelberg, "An Apologetic for Apologetics," 18.

believers more confidence in sharing their faith. Study apologetics with a heart compassionate for the lost rather than developing arguments and skill in proving people wrong. Apologetics should be an integral element in giving our evangelistic witness to those outside of Christ.[49]

Writing Letters/Emails. Written communication can be an effective means of sharing evidences. *Letters to a Skeptic* is a collection of letters between a believing son and his unbelieving father that led to the father's conversion.[50] Arnold Lunn and C.E.M. Joad debated the question, "Is Christianity true?" by correspondence. Arnold said Joad, an agnostic who had published books of philosophy, did not know the case for Christianity. Lunn testified,

> And yet Joad died a practicing Christian, largely, so he told me, because of our correspondence. If Joad could be convinced once he was compelled to meet the rational case for Christianity, are we Christians perhaps not to blame for the fact that we have failed to induce the majority of our contemporaries even to examine the case?[51]

Lunn said,

> Of my own contributions to apologetics I believe the most useful to have been *Science and the Supernatural*, an exchange of letters with the late Professor J.B.S. Haldane. . . . That Haldane certainly failed to demolish the case for the supernatural could only be attributed to the strength of that case, for Haldane was obviously my intellectual superior.[52]

---

[49] Norman Geisler and David Geisler, *Conversational Evangelism: How to Listen and Speak So You Can Be Heard* (Eugene, OR: Harvest House, 2009). Seeks to combine apologetics and evangelism in practical ways.

[50] Gregory A. Boyd and Edward K. Boyd, *Letters from a Skeptic: A Son Wrestles with His Father's Questions about Christianity* (Wheaton, IL: SP Publications, 1994).

[51] Arnold Lunn, "An Apology for Apologetics," in *Christian Counter-Attack*, eds. Arnold Lunn and Garth Lean (New Rochelle, NY: Arlington House, 1969) 120.

[52] Ibid., 125-126.

Haldane admitted "that there was no scientific argument against the possibility that God might exist or that, if He did exist, He might permit the miraculous interference with the natural order."[53] Lord Longford stated, "Arnold Lunn's controversy with Haldane removed my sneaking suspicion that in a real showdown there would be materialist questions which the man of religion would not face."[54]

Ignatius, a bishop of the church in Antioch around the turn of the first century was persecuted for his faith and martyred for Christ. But on the way to his execution he wrote letters that emphasized that Jesus "really and truly" was crucified for our sins, that he rose again on the third day, and that this proved conclusively that he was the Son of God as he claimed. He used this means to commend and defend his Christian faith.

Sharing apologetic CDs and DVDs as well as books and websites can be a means of giving witness to nonbelievers.

Raising Up Effective Apologists

The forces of unbelief have forceful communicators in prominent and influential positions in the media, in education, and in the public square. The church of the Lord Jesus Christ must respond with well-prepared defenders of the faith who can make a persuasive presentation of the gospel and give intelligent answers to the critics.

Our times call out for persons to respond to these urgent appeals for effective apologists. Trueblood issued this plea:

> What we need desperately, at this particular juncture in the enduring human crisis, is the emergence of Christian intellectuals. If Basic Christianity is to survive, it must be served by a highly dedicated and highly trained group of persons who are unabashed and unapologetic in the face of opposition and ridicule. They must be able to outthink as well as outlive all

---

[53] Ibid., 126.
[54] Ibid., 128.

attacks on the central faith which we so sorely need as an alternative to confusion.[55]

A new day is dawning for Christian intellectuals who will prepare themselves for the arduous and much-needed task of helping their fellows to cut through the fog and confusion that mark the climate of current opinion. . . . An effective attack is possible, however, precisely because the enemies of the faith are themselves so obviously vulnerable. C.S. Lewis was highly successful as a Christian intellectual who followed such a course, but the shame is that he was so nearly alone and that he has so few contemporary successors.[56]

What we desperately need is the literature of witness in which men who have reached a firm place to stand are able to tell us the road by which they have come and why it was taken. We need a whole new group of thinkers who are willing and able to obey the injunction of I Peter 3:15, being prepared to make a defense of the "hope that is in them," but doing it "with gentleness and reverence."[57]

John Stott challenges:

I pray earnestly that God will raise up today a new generation of Christian apologists or Christian communicators, who will combine an absolute loyalty to the biblical gospel and an unwavering confidence in the power of the Spirit with a deep and sensitive understanding of the contemporary alternatives to the gospel; who will relate the one to the other with freshness, pungency, authority and relevance; and who will use *their* minds to reach *other* minds for Christ.[58]

I myself have a growing burden that God will call out more men for their teaching ministry today; that he will call men with alert minds, biblical convictions and an aptitude for teaching; that he will set them in the great capital cities and university cities of the world; that there, like Paul in

---

[55] Elton Trueblood, *A Place to Stand* (New York: Harper and Row, 1969) 20.
[56] Ibid., 29.
[57] Ibid., 30.
[58] John R.W. Stott, *Your Mind Matters* (Downers Grove, IL: InterVarsity, 1972) 52.

Tyrannus's hall in Ephesus, they will exercise a thoughtful, systematic teaching ministry, expounding the ancient Scriptures and relating them to the modern world; and that such a faithful ministry under the good hand of God will not only lead their own congregation up to Christian maturity but will also through the visitors who come briefly under its influence spread its blessing far and wide.[59]

Apologetics in action contributes to evangelism—leading men and women to saving faith in Christ and to discipleship—strengthening believers and encouraging their growth in Christ.

Review Questions

1. List the eight areas where Roy Weece used apologetics. Which one was most interesting to you and why?

2. Why is it important that parents have some knowledge of apologetics?

3. How can parents prepare their children for the assault on their faith which they will probably face at college?

4. How does preaching relate to the apologetic preparation of the congregation?

5. Suggest ways the teaching program of the local church can have a faith-building component.

6. Christian Smith's research suggests what is the main reason many young people with a religious background shed their religious beliefs during their teen years?

7. Why does Christian truth become more plausible when one experiences genuine Christian worship and fellowship?

8. Suggest ways a local church can teach apologetics.

[59] Ibid., 55.

9. At what age should children receive apologetics training?

10. Summarize the challenges and temptations Alison Thomas faced at college.

11. List resources dealing with the challenges college campuses present to a student's faith.

12. What does Mark Mittelberg say is necessary beyond reading books to prepare one to be an effective apologist?

13. Give examples where writing letters contributed to leading nonbelievers to faith in Christ.

14. Summarize Trueblood and Stott's call to raise up effective apologists.

Suggested Reading

McDowell, Sean, ed. *Apologetics for a New Generation: A Biblical and Culturally Relevant Approach to Talking about God.* Eugene, OR: Harvest House, 2009. Writers who work with teenagers and college-age persons address how to teach them to formulate a biblical worldview, articulate their questions in a safe environment, and develop their confidence in their faith and witness.

Smith, Wilbur M. *Therefore Stand.* Grand Rapids: Baker Book House, 1969. Smith gives suggestions for an immediate vigorous offensive in the defense of the Christian faith (478-522).

Trueblood, David Elton. *A Place to Stand.* New York: Harper and Row, 1969. Insists on a rational defense of Christianity and criticizes subjectivism's copout on apologetics (13-36).

Weece, Roy "Practical Ways to Defend the Faith," in *The Mind of Christ*, ed. by Lynn Gardner. Joplin, MO: College Press, 1987. Uses of apologetics in ministry, in church, and in life.

Zacharias, Ravi, ed. *Beyond Opinion: Living the Faith We Defend*. Wheaton, IL: Crossway, 2007. Addresses the challenges facing Christians today. Note especially the following chapters: "Challenges from Youth," Allison Thomas, and "The Church's Role in Apologetics and the Development of the Mind," Ravi Zacharias.

Zacharias, Ravi, and Norman Geisler, eds. *Is Your Church Ready? Motivating Leaders to Live an Apologetic Life*. Grand Rapids: Zondervan, 2003. Calls for a well-balanced apologetic in all of church life—pastors, church leaders, parents, college students, and internationals.

"A new commandment I give to you, that you love one another: just as I have loved you, you also are to love one another. By this all people will know that you are my disciples, if you have love for one another."

John 13:34-35

"Rather, speaking the truth in love, we are to grow up in every way into him who is the head, into Christ."

Ephesians 4:15

17
Guidelines for Apologetics

Guidelines for Apologetics	"So the positive side of apologetics is the communication of the gospel to the present generation in terms that they can understand."[1]
Profile: Bob Passantino— The Character of an Apologist	
Preparation for Commending and Defending Christian Faith	Francis A. Schaeffer
1. Know and love God	"I have found that nothing is more dangerous to one's own faith than the work of an apologist. No doctrine of that Faith seems to me so spectral, so unreal as one that I have just successfully defended in
2. Know the Bible	
3. Know why you believe	
4. Live a consistent Christian life	

[1] Francis A. Schaeffer, *The God Who Is There*, 30th Anniversary Edition, 2nd ed (Wheaton, IL: Crossway, 1982) 173.

5. Listen to the other person until you understand their point of view 6. Ask perceptive questions 7. Focus on Christ and his resurrection 8. Be honest 9. Be loving 10. Pray and depend upon God 11. The final apologetic	a public debate. For a moment, you see, it has seemed to rest on oneself: as a result, when you go away from that debate, it seems no stronger than that weak pillar. That is why we apologists take our lives in our hands and can be saved only by falling back continually from the web of our own arguments, as from our intellectual counters, into the Reality—from Christian apologetics into Christ Himself. That also is why we need one another's continual help—*oremus pro invicem* [Let us pray for each other]."[2] <div align="right">C.S. Lewis</div>

Profile: Bob Passantino—
The Character of an Apologist[3]

Bob Passantino died at age fifty-four. His passing left a void in Christian apologetics. He left an example for others to follow. Though he had little formal education he excelled as an apologist. In this profile we get acquainted with him through comments made by his friends.

Intellect. "I was always amazed . . . [at] the rapidity with which he absorbed information, picked apart arguments, and subjected everything to the critiques of

---

[2] C.S. Lewis, "Christian Apologetics," *God in the Dock* (Grand Rapids: Eerdmans, 1970) 103.

[3] The quotes in this profile come from E. Calvin Biesner, "The Character of the Good Apologist: An Appreciation for the Life and Labors of Bob Passantino," in *Reasons for Faith: Making a Case for the Christian Faith*, eds. Norman L. Geisler and Chad V. Meister (Wheaton, IL: Crossway, 2007) 77-92.

Scripture and logic." "He gave me, and countless others, the desire not only to know the truth, but to know how to study and think better."

Courage. "I never heard Bob talk down to anyone, and I never heard him back down either." They described him as "positively fearless" and "a bulldog, but in a friendly, disarming, almost naïve way."

Humility. His "breadth and depth of knowledge was truly staggering, surpassed only by the humility and graciousness by which he approached both people and ideas." He had "a mind like a steel trap, yet he never made those around him feel inferior." "Bob mirrored Christ the best in exhibiting humility with brains."

Passion. He exhibited "unrelenting enthusiasm for the gospel and the Christian life. . . . His only goal in life was to bring each person he had contact with to a realization of the logical truth of Christ."

Humor. People remembered "his smile, his wit." There was a "playfulness, and curiosity, about Bob's mind that was downright contagious." He was "so funny, so kind, so humble."

Patience. "One never felt rushed, like you had anything else to do than 'be there' for whatever need was before you." "Not only did he give brilliant answers, he asked brilliant questions and listened brilliantly." "He wanted to know what I thought. This stimulated me to think and learn."

Generosity. "He gave the most precious things to others that he had—his time, himself, and his beloved Lord Jesus." "He always made time for me, even if it was inconvenient."

Energy. He "contained boundless energy, a zest for life, and a genuine love for people that I have never seen duplicated." He would discuss with people until the wee hours of the morning. He quipped, "If I can't convince you I'm right, I can at least wear you out!"

Teamwork. Bob and his wife, Gretchen, worked as a team. "You and Gretchen have healed the damaged faith of thousands. You have allowed us to believe with both our minds and our hearts. You have taught us to rejoice in truth and not simply in good feelings. You have made a home with an open door and open hearth."

Friendship. "Bob always had a way of making you feel like you'd been friends forever." "He always treated me as though I was the most important person in the room."

Love. "Love was the key to [Bob's] life." "He was always there giving people help, advice, humor, etc. But the most I admire about him is his love for people and the Lord." "He loved and cared for me." "He cared about people who didn't know his Lord and used all his power to persuade them of the truth of the gospel."

"He had an elite Oxford mind in a blue-collar body. His heart was soft as a lamb's, but his skin was tough as steel wool. No matter the topic, over time I have never heard him be offended by the question. Truth and love lived in Bob comfortably. How refreshing was his laughter!"

Bob was "full of love, passion, and truth. In his search for wisdom, truth, or knowledge he was unrelenting. In his desire to speak to anyone interested in the exploration of the truth he was an instant friend and mentor. He exhibited a love, an openness and respect for others that fundamentally changed my life."

As Christians we are ambassadors for Christ to those in the world who do not know Christ. Through the Great Commission Christ calls us to share our witness with others. It is important that we prepare ourselves to be able to witness to the truth of our Christian faith. It is also important that as we do so we represent Christ, not misrepresent him. The following suggestions are given to better prepare you to commend and defend the faith.

Preparation for Defending the Faith

1. Know and Love God

Knowing and loving God our Father, Jesus Christ our Lord and Savior, and the Holy Spirit should be the greatest priority in our lives. Jesus said the great commandment is *"You shall love the Lord your God with all your heart and with all your soul and with all your mind"* (**Matt 22:37**). J.I. Packer said some might think that the priority for the Christian is

> . . . social witness, or dialogue with other Christians and other faiths, or refuting this or that '-ism,' or developing a Christian philosophy and culture, or what have you. But our line of study makes the present day concentration on these things look like a gigantic conspiracy of misdirection. Of course, it is not that; the issues themselves are real and must be dealt with in their place. But it is tragic that, in paying attention to them, so many in our day seem to have been distracted from what was, is, and always will be the priority for every human being—that is, learning to know God in Christ.[4]

In preparing our hearts to witness to lost men and women we need to pray with Paul, that the Father would grant us to be *"strengthened with power through his Spirit in your inner being, so that Christ may dwell in your hearts through faith . . . and to know the love of Christ that surpasses knowledge, that you may be filled with all the fullness of God"* (**Eph 3:16-19**).

William Lane Craig, after making his case for presenting rational arguments and evidence for the truth of Christianity, highlights the importance for those who commend and defend

---

[4] J.I. Packer, *Knowing God* (Downers Grove, IL: InterVarsity, 1973) 254.

the faith of having a loving relationship with God and a loving relationship with our fellow man. He believes that this is "the most effective and practical apologetic for the Christian faith that I know of. This apologetic will help you win more persons to Christ than all the other arguments in your apologetic arsenal put together."[5]

Arguing the truth of propositions is not the ultimate goal of evangelistic apologetics. The heart issue is introducing people to the person of God, helping them know and love the Lord Jesus Christ. If you do not have this personal relationship with the Lord yourself, you will be ineffective as an ambassador for Christ.

2. Know the Bible

As C.S. Lewis said, "A man can't be always defending the truth; there must be a time to feed on it."[6] Learning the Word of God is a faith-building exercise to those who seek truth. *"So faith comes from hearing, and hearing through the word of Christ"* (*Rom 10:17*). Misrepresentations and distortions of God and the Bible will be evident to the person who knows the Bible.

A liberal Episcopalian told me that he did not like the cruel God in the OT, but he liked the God of love shown by Jesus in forgiving the woman taken in adultery. Not long before this conversation I had an assignment in Bible college where we were to itemize the statements showing God's wrath and God's love in both the OT and the NT. Those data clearly show that in both the Old and New Testaments God is a God of wrath as well as of love. Knowing what the Bible actually says makes it easier to recognize and respond to misrepresentations.

A comprehensive knowledge of the Bible is not essential before one can defend the faith. However, the better under-

---

[5] William Lane Craig, *Reasonable Faith: Christian Truth and Apologetics*, 3rd ed. (Wheaton, IL: Crossway, 2008) 405.

[6] C.S. Lewis, *Reflections on the Psalms* (New York: Harcourt, Brace and World, 1958) 7.

standing we have of the Bible, the better prepared we are to respond to objections. Merely accumulating biblical information in one's brain does not assure faith or competence in apologetics. Many unbelieving scholars know what the Bible says, but they choose not to believe it. The honest seeker will find that knowing the Bible will be a faith-building enterprise. Faith in God's Word will issue in obedience to the will of God. Knowing and obeying God's Word builds one in the faith and helps one be a more effective witness and defender of the truth of God.

3. Know Why You Believe

Study the evidences for Christianity first. A guide in the Mint in Washington, D.C., described the training of workers preparing them to recognize counterfeit money. He said first they spend several days looking at and learning the characteristics of good money. Then the trainees are taught to recognize the counterfeit. It is important to study the truth about Christianity before studying the objections that are raised against it.

Twentieth-century defender of the faith, J. Gresham Machen, warned against studying what is said against the Christian religion without ever obtaining any really orderly acquaintance with what can be said for it. Study the fundamentals of Christianity first, he advocated, then investigating the objections against Christianity will only make you a better defender of the faith.

This does not mean that ministerial students should be shielded from the attacks on Christianity. Machen stated:

> I am telling him that the logical order is to learn what a thing is before one attends exclusively to what can be said against it; and I am telling him further, that the way to learn what a thing is is not to listen first to its opponents, but to grant a full hearing to those who believe in it with all their minds and hearts. After that has been done, after our students, by pursuing the complete course of study, have obtained something

like an orderly acquaintance with the marvelous system of truth that the Bible contains, then the more they listen to what can be said against it, the better defenders of it they will probably be.[7]

In evangelizing the lost and in teaching new Christians, introduce them to key information about God and Christ so that they know basic Christianity. Teaching evidences provides a foundation for their Christian faith and should be taught before studying the cults, alternative religions, or world religions. No longer can we assume people's acquaintance with the evidences of Christianity. Christian homes, local churches, Bible colleges, and Christian colleges need to teach the evidences for believing in God, Christ, and the Bible.

4. Live a Consistent Christian Life

The lives of changed, consistent committed Christians constitutes one of the strongest arguments for Christianity. It is also true that one of the greatest stumbling blocks for non-Christians is the example of inconsistent Christians. Neither proves Christianity to be true or false. Both get people's attention and either encourage or discourage faith. Ravi Zacharias says, "I have little doubt that the single greatest obstacle to the impact of the gospel has not been its inability to provide answers, but the failure on our part to live it out."[8]

Zacharias tells of a Hindu who denied anything supernatural in Christian conversion. He said it was nothing more than a decision to live a more ethical life. He asked, "If this conversion is truly supernatural, why is it not more evident in the lives of so many Christians I know?"[9]

---

[7] J. Gresham Machen, *What Is Christianity?* (Grand Rapids: Eerdmans, 1951) 136.

[8] Ravi Zacharias, "An Apologetic for Apologetics," *Beyond Opinion: Living the Faith We Defend,* ed. Ravi Zacharias (Nashville: Thomas Nelson, 2007) xiii.

[9] Ravi Zacharias, "The Pastor as an Apologist," in *Is Your Church Ready?* eds. Ravi Zacharias and Norman L. Geisler (Grand Rapids: Zondervan, 2003) 23.

A nineteenth-century apologist, Theodore Christlieb stated:

Where we wish to defend the Word of Life, our own life cannot be separated from the Word. *The strongest argument for the truth of Christianity is the true Christian,* the man filled with the Spirit of Christ. The best means of bringing back the world to a belief in miracles is to exhibit the miracle of regeneration and its power in our own life. The best proof of Christ's resurrection is a living Church, which itself is walking in a new life.[10]

Our faith grows stronger as we exercise our faith by living in genuine dependence upon God. Persons manifesting a growing spiritual maturity present a case for the plausibility and power of Christian faith. A changed life is not an absolute proof, but lives changed by Christ furnish a practical demonstration of the truth of Christianity.

Maintaining Christian vitality as a loner is difficult. Paul emphasized that the church is a body, a community of believers. We need to be nourished in a body of believers where we are edified and encouraged. A young man, who almost lost his faith at a Christian liberal arts college while majoring in anthropology, testified that the ministry of the local congregation was crucial in keeping his faith. Christians who are joyfully serving in a local congregation are growing Christians.

Athenagoras contrasted unbelievers with Christians. He asked, ". . . who of them have so purged their souls, instead of hating their enemies, to love them; and, instead of speaking ill of those who have reviled them, . . . to bless them; and to pray for those who plot against their lives?" He continued:

But among us you will find uneducated persons, and artisans, and old women, who, if they are unable in words to prove the benefit of our doctrine, yet by their deeds exhibit the benefit arising from their persuasion of its truth: they do not rehearse speeches, but exhibit good works; when struck, they do not

---

[10] Quoted by Wilbur M. Smith, *Therefore Stand* (Natick, MA: W.A. Wilde, 1954) 512. Emphasis in the original.

strike again; when robbed, they do not go to law; they give to those that ask of them, and love their neighbours as themselves.[11]

To a large extent the impact of our witness to skeptics will depend upon the kind of life we are living. William Lane Craig reminds us, "More often than not, it is what you *are* rather than what you *say* that will bring an unbeliever to Christ." The ultimate apologetic is "your life."[12]

The perception of Bible-believing Christians being intolerant and hypocritical can be a barrier to non-Christians giving a fair hearing to the truth of the gospel. We need genuine humility and a spirit seeking to grow in grace, regularly confessing sins (*1 John 1:9*), and turning away from wickedness (*2 Tim 2:19*). When we are hypocritical, we lose spiritual power and genuineness in witness. Jean-Paul Sartre, an atheist, said to a Christian witnessing to him, "I understand what you are saying, but you know, there are so many so-called Christians. . . . When I see the actions of certain persons like that, I am not able to believe."[13]

David Kinnaman, researcher with the Barna Group, documents some of the negative opinions outsiders have of Christians—hypocritical, too focused on getting converts, antihomosexual, sheltered, too political, and judgmental.[14] Even though responses can be made to these perceptions, honestly and openly considering the criticisms of non-Christians can help us see our flaws and better prepare to communicate the

---

[11] Athenagoras, "A Plea for the Christians," in L. Russ Bush, ed., *Classical Readings in Christian Apologetics: A. D. 100–1800* (Grand Rapids: Zondervan, 1983) 44.

[12] Craig, *Reasonable Faith*, 302. Emphasis in the original.

[13] Quoted by Timothy George and John Woodbridge, *The Mark of Jesus: Loving in a Way the World Can See* (Chicago: Moody, 2005) 107.

[14] David Kinnaman and Gabe Lyons, *unchristian: What a New Generation Really Thinks about Christianity . . . And Why It Matters* (Grand Rapids: Baker Books, 2007) 31-32.

gospel effectively. Kinnaman's *unchristian: What a New Generation Really Thinks about Christianity . . . And Why It Matters* and Dan Kimball's *They Like Jesus but Not the Church: Insights from Emerging Generations* are two resources documenting how believers are perceived by those outside the church.[15]

Many will not trust Jesus as their living Lord until they see Christ living in a believer's life. In order to commend and defend Christian faith we must consistently live and practice the faith we profess.

5. Listen to the Other Person until You Understand Their Point of View

Trainers teach sales persons first to restate the potential buyer's objection to buying the product before they give an answer to that objection. Machen said, "Mere denunciation does not constitute an argument; and before a man can refute successfully an argument of an opponent, he must understand the argument that he is endeavoring to refute."[16] As we seek to persuade unbelievers of the truth of Christianity, we need to be good listeners and learn what they are actually saying. Ask what they think and listen to their answers. Sometimes you have to listen for quite a while to establish rapport before they begin to ask you why you believe what you do.

Jim Petersen says, "When a non-Christian begins to study the Bible with you, one of his biggest unspoken questions will be, 'To what degree will I be able to express what I really think with him? What will be the reaction if I express my true doubts and questions?' The person will first send out some rather 'safe' trial questions. How we react to these questions will affect the level of communication between us from then on." He points out that we can respond with dogmatism or defen-

---

[15] Ibid. and Dan Kimball, *They Like Jesus but Not the Church* (Grand Rapids: Zondervan, 2007).

[16] Machen, *What Is Christianity?* 134.

siveness which will hinder the person's openness. Or we can encourage honest questions and doubts, which will increase the effectiveness of open communication and dialogue.[17]

After graduating from Princeton Theological Seminary, Machen studied in Europe. He was a bachelor and his mother feared that he would lose his faith because he was studying under liberal theologians. In a letter to his mother he defended the need to study the other side, "As long as he feels that he has not fully learned to appreciate the arguments on both sides and (particularly the side to which he is inclined to be opposed)—just so long must he continue to be a doubter."[18]

One could reason that it would be safer not to study the unbelievers' attacks. However not to confront the attacks is to yield the ground to the opponents of the faith. It is better to study such attacks in an atmosphere of faith than to be shielded from them and later be broadsided by the attacks because we are unprepared.

We should follow the "golden rule of apologetics" formulated by Bob and Gretchen Passantino. *"We should do unto other's arguments and texts as we would have them do unto ours."*[19]

6. Ask Perceptive Questions

Gregory P. Koukl said the reputation of some apologists is that "Defenders don't dialogue. They fight." He suggests that "our engagements should look more like diplomacy than combat."[20]

Koukl recommends the "Columbo tactic." The TV detective often asks, "Do you mind if I ask you a question?"

---

[17] Quoted in Peter J. Grant, "The Priority of Apologetics in the Church," in *Is Your Church Ready?* 58.

[18] Quoted in Ned B. Stonehouse. *J. Gresham Machen: A Biographical Memoir* (Grand Rapids: Eerdmans, 1954) 140.

[19] Alan W. Gomes, "The Value of Historical Theology for Apologetics," in *Reasons for Faith*, 181.

[20] Gregory P. Koukl, "Tactics: Applying Apologetics to Everyday Life," in *Is Your Church Ready?* 47-48. See also Koukl's *Tactics: A Game Plan for Discussing Your Christian Convictions* (Grand Rapids: Zondervan, 2008).

The key to Columbo is to go on the offensive by advancing the conversation—and eventually dismantling another person's viewpoint—with carefully selected questions which move the discussion along in an interactive way. . . . Simply put, instead of making assertions, ask questions. . . . The Columbo tactic allows you to make good headway without actually stating your case. More importantly, a carefully placed question shifts the burden of proof to the other person where it often belongs.[21]

Jesus frequently used questions, for example, *"Was the baptism of John from heaven or from man?"* (**Luke 20:4**).

When someone says, "All religions are true in their own way," one might ask "What do you mean by *true?*" "Do you mean that even when two religions contradict each other that they are still true?" To the statement "The Bible is full of errors," ask "What convinced you of this? Can you give me an example?" This forces the person to justify his or her beliefs.

Koukl says:

It's not enough for followers of Christ to have accurately informed minds. They also need an artful method. They need to combine their knowledge with wisdom and diplomacy. . . . Asking simple, leading questions is an almost effortless way to accomplish balance. You can advance the dialogue . . . without seeming abrupt, rude or pushy. Questions are engaging and interactive, probing yet amicable. . . . Most critics are not well-equipped to defend their own faith. They have rarely thought through what they believe and have relied more on generalizations and slogans than on careful reflection. To expose their error, take your cue from Columbo. Scratch your head, rub your chin, pause for a moment, then say, "Do you mind if I ask you a question?"[22]

Asking probing questions can help people think seriously about what they believe and why they believe it.

---

[21] Koukl, "Tactics," 48-49.
[22] Ibid., 55.

Josh McDowell states that when he is in a dialogue with one who says Abraham is a myth, and not a real person, he tries to find out what led them to that conclusion. He asks, "What are you assuming to be true? What would convince you that Abraham was a real person? Or what has convinced you that he wasn't a real person?"[23]

In developing a relationship asking questions and listening to their answers will establish trust which can become a bridge making possible future conversations about the truth of Christianity.

7. Focus on Christ and His Resurrection

Don't be sidetracked by minor issues. Questions like whether we should celebrate Christmas, the length of the days of creation, or theories of the millennium are worthy of discussion, but these matters are not the priority issues when seeking to lead one to faith in Christ. In the book of *Acts* the person of the risen Christ was central in their witness. John Stott says, "Our struggle today is how to be faithful to this apostolic gospel, while at the same time presenting it in a way which resonates with modern men and women. What is immediately clear is that, like the apostles, we must focus on Jesus Christ. . . . It is impossible to preach the gospel without proclaiming Christ."[24] Even when Paul presented general evidence for God to the men of Athens, he led up to the resurrection of Christ.

The central issue is "Who is Jesus?" In commending and defending the faith focus on helping men and women come to know and believe in God and in Christ. Here is the heart of the matter. W. Edgar states:

the most central issue of all, one which has always been primary, and which is more crucial than ever, is the call to know

---

[23] Quoted in Christy Tennant, "Josh McDowell on Defending the Bible," *Bible Study Magazine* (Nov & Dec 2008) 13.

[24] John R.W. Stott, *The Message of Acts* (Downers Grove, IL: InterVarsity, 1990) 79-80.

God and to worship him. The centre of apologetics would quite naturally be the centre of the Christian message. Though we have fallen from God's presence, Jesus Christ has come into the world to save sinners. Because of Christ's finished work at Calvary, and because of his resurrection from the dead, we now have access to the grace of God through faith in his Son. The first task of apologetics is to persuade men and women that salvation is freely offered to all, and that their only hope in life or in death is Jesus Christ, God's Son, the Saviour of the world.[25]

Avery Dulles agrees:

The best apologetics in my opinion has always directed attention to the figure of Jesus Christ, with his challenging message, his powerful deeds, his loving self-sacrifice, and his glorious vindication by the Father. He is the great witness of God, and the Church bears witness to him. Where the story of Jesus Christ becomes clouded over with secondary questions, apologetics loses itself in fruitless and inconclusive debates.[26]

8. Be Honest

Francis Schaeffer emphasized that the Christian's task is "to be able to give an honest answer to an honest question, and then to give it."[27] J. Gresham Machen emphasized that as defenders of the faith we must be frank, perfectly open and aboveboard.[28] Do not ridicule or laugh at honest questions. Life and its deep questions are for real. Do not just give superficial treatment in a slighting manner when people state their honest

---

[25] W. Edgar, "Christian Apologetics for a New Century," in *New Dictionary of Christian Apologetics*, eds. W.C. Campbell-Jack and Gavin McGrath (Downers Grove, IL: InterVarsity, 2006) 14.

[26] "The History and Purpose of Apologetics—An Interview with Avery Cardinal Dulles, S.J.," by Carl E. Olson, **http://ignatiusinsight.com/features2005/print 2005/carddullesint_july05.html**.

[27] Francis A. Schaeffer, *The Mark of the Christian* (Downers Grove, IL: InterVarsity, 1970) 17.

[28] Machen, *What Is Christianity?* 133.

doubts and questions. If you do not know the answer or how to respond, admit you do not know. Help the person find the answer or someone who can help them find the answer. If you have made a mistake, admit it. If you have been unloving to an individual, say you are sorry. Cover-ups and pretense in the end undermine one's testimony. Our reputation as brilliant apologists is not the issue. The issue is helping this person come to faith.

Integrity in character, accuracy in research, and excellence in presentation will contribute to the power and effectiveness of our witness.

9. Be Loving

Jesus states, *"A new commandment I give to you, that you love one another; just as I have loved you, you also are to love one another. By this all people will know that you are my disciples, if you have love for one another"* (*John 13:34-35*). Schaeffer says that Jesus "gives the world the right to judge whether you and I are born-again Christians on the basis of our observable love toward all Christians."[29] In Jesus' response to the question about the greatest commandment, he said the second was *like* or the *same* as the first. Loving others shares importance with loving God (*Matt 22:38-39*).

Peter reminds us,

> *In your hearts regard Christ the Lord as holy, always being prepared to make a defense to anyone who asks you for a reason for the hope that is in you; yet **do it with gentleness and respect**, having a good conscience, so that when you are slandered, those who revile your good behavior in Christ may be put to shame.* (*1 Pet 3:15-16*, emphasis added)

Jude encourages us to *"have mercy on those who doubt"* (*Jude 22*). Paul instructs Timothy, *"The Lord's servant must not be quarrelsome but kind to everyone, able to teach, patiently enduring evil, cor-*

---

[29] Francis A. Schaeffer, *The Mark of the Christian*, 13.

recting his opponents with gentleness." Always with the hope that they may come *"to a knowledge of the truth"* (*2 Tim 2:24-25*).

Our attitude and manner of defense are important. Seth Wilson emphasizes, "They won't care how much you know until they know how much you care."[30] John Guest says, "Love is the ultimate apologetic; it reaches the whole person."[31] Our love for others must be observable in our actions, not merely in our words.

God loves all human beings. Our responsibility is to love all persons because they are made in the image of God and because Christ died for them just as he died for us. In Christian witness there is no excuse for cold, brutal harshness. Dogmatic, arrogant defenders of the faith turn people away from Christ. We are to commend the faith. Arrogance and tactlessness betray rather than portray Christ. Don't club people over the head with truth. Lead them to the one who invited all to come unto him and learn from him (*Matt 11:28*).

Craig J. Hazen states, "Apologists are sometimes out to win arguments and not souls, impatient with illogic from their counterparts, and arrogant in their demeanor. . . . The most effective apologist is not one who has the greatest academic prowess alone, but the one who has excellent preparation *and* reflects Christ's love in every way."[32]

Genuine love knows "There but by the grace of God go I." If we self-righteously express shock or condemnation at people's doubts and questions, we forfeit the opportunity to help them. I remember attending a state university in the 60s, an era of rebellion on college campuses. I found the dress and

---

[30] H. Lynn Gardner, *"Brother Wilson": The Life and Work of Seth Wilson* (Joplin, MO: College Press, 2007) 134.

[31] John Guest, "The Church as the Heart and Soul of Apologetics," in *Is Your Church Ready?* 43.

[32] Craig J. Hazen, "Defending the Defense of the Faith," in *To Everyone an Answer: A Case for the Christian Worldview*, eds. Francis J. Beckwith, William Lane Craig, and J.P. Moreland (Downers Grove, IL: InterVarsity, 2004) 45.

actions of some of the students offensive. I had to keep reminding myself, "They are persons for whom Christ died." Love cares even for the unlovely. Believers are only sinners saved by grace. We don't have all the answers and aren't perfect, but we have the opportunity of introducing people to the one who does have the answers and is perfect.

Dan Kimball in *The Emerging Church* states,

> I am finding that emerging generations really aren't opposed to truth and biblical morals. When people sense that you aren't just dogmatically opinionated due to blind faith and that you aren't just attacking other people's beliefs out of fear, they are remarkably open to intelligent and loving discussion about choice and truth."[33]

Sean McDowell says, "I have found that although they clearly are turned off by people who arrogantly think they have all the answers, *young people respond positively to someone who can lovingly lead them to truth.*"[34]

Unloving attitudes and bitterness between Christians undermines our Christian witness. Francis Schaeffer says in *John 17* Jesus is stating, "We cannot expect the world to believe that the Father sent the Son, that Jesus' claims are true, and that Christianity is true, unless the world sees some reality of the oneness of true Christians."[35] Jesus makes it clear that practical, visible unity among believers is important to persuading those of the world to believe. Our Lord prays that believers *"may all be one, just as you, Father, are in me, and I in you, that they also may be in us, so that the world may believe that you have sent me" (John 17:21).*

If the world does not see observable love and unity among Christians, Schaeffer reminds:

[33] Dan Kimball, *The Emerging Church* (Grand Rapids: Zondervan, 2003) 86.
[34] Sean McDowell, "Apologetics for an Emerging Generation," in *Passionate Conviction*, eds. Paul Copan and Willliam Lane Craig (Nashville: B & H Publishing, 2007) 268.
[35] Schaeffer, *The Mark of the Christian*, 15.

. . . it will not believe that Christ was sent by the Father. People will not believe only on the basis of the proper answers. The two should not be placed in antithesis. The world must have the proper answers to their honest questions, but at the same time, there must be a oneness in love between all true Christians. This is what is needed if men are to know that Jesus was sent by the Father and that Christianity is true.[36]

10. Pray and Depend upon God

The struggle for the soul of a person is a spiritual battle not just an intellectual matter. Theodore Christlieb, German apologist, said, "Instead of at once fulminating *against* unbelievers, let us first wrestle *for* them with the power of intercessory prayer that they may be enlightened by the Lord. . . . Let no combatant enter the arena without putting on the spiritual as well as the intellectual panoply."[37] William Tyler, a professor at Amherst, tells of a "concert of prayer for the colleges" born in 1823. They prayed for the colleges every Sunday morning. Revivals resulted in many colleges.

As we witness for Christ, intellectual and personal preparation is important. We do not go in our own strength or we will fail. We must rely on God and pray for his help. Zacharias says, "Over the years I have discovered that praying with people can sometimes do more for them than preaching to them."[38]

Paul says,

Finally, be strong in the Lord and in the strength of his might. Put on the whole armor of God, that you may be able to stand against the schemes of the devil. For we do not wrestle against flesh and blood, but against the rulers, against the authorities, against the cosmic powers over this present darkness, against the spiritual forces of evil in the heavenly places. (*Eph 6:10-12*)

---

[36] Ibid., 18.

[37] Quoted in Smith, *Therefore Stand*, 511.

[38] Ravi Zacharias, "Arrows and Swords in the Church," in *Is Your Church Ready?* 87.

He tells us to put on the whole armor of God including truth, righteousness, readiness to preach the gospel, faith, salvation, and the Word of God. He continues,

> *praying at all times in the Spirit, with all prayer and supplication. To that end keep alert with all perseverance, making supplication for all the saints, and also for me, that words may be given to me in opening my mouth boldly to proclaim the mystery of the gospel, for which I am an ambassador in chains, that I may declare it boldly, as I ought to speak.* (**Eph. 6:18-20**)

If the apostle Paul needed prayer for boldness to witness for Christ, how much more is it a necessity for us?

Os Guinness warns us:

> Christian apologetics is in crisis today. Cut loose from its missionary and evangelistic setting, it has become caught between the opposing tendencies of a broad conservative movement ("Don't persuade, proclaim!") and a broad liberal movement ("Don't debate, dialogue!"). In the process, apologetics has been either misunderstood (as an abject apology) or narrowly defined (in a purely defensive role) and critically constricted (to certain types of argument and certain levels of educational development). Its concern and capacity to persuade real people has almost been lost.[39]

As prayerful apologists we must never lose sight of the evangelistic goal of leading men and women to a saving faith in Jesus Christ.

11. The Final Apologetic

The Christian before the watching world is the final apologetic. Francis Schaeffer says:

> The world has a right to look upon us and make a judgment. We are told by Jesus that as we love one another the world will judge, not only whether we are His disciples, but whether

---

[39] Os Guinness, "Introduction," in *Mind on Fire: A Faith for the Skeptical and Indifferent*, ed. James M. Houston (Minneapolis: Bethany House, 1989, 1997) 34-35.

the Father sent the Son. The final apologetic, along with the rational, logical defense and presentation, *is what the world sees* in the individual Christian and in our corporate relationships together. The command that we should love one another surely means something much richer than merely organizational relationship.[40]

Douglas Groothuis issues this challenge:

The essential issue is whether or not one has a passion for God's transforming truth—reasonably pursued and courageously communicated—and a passion for the lost because of the love of God resident and active in one's life (Rom. 9:1-3; 10:1). Like the apostle Paul at Athens, we should be "greatly distressed" because of the rampant unbelief in our day. We, like that great apologist, should also be intellectually equipped and spiritually prepared to enter the marketplace of ideas for the cause of Christ (Acts 17:16-34).[41]

[40] Schaeffer, *The God Who Is There*, 185. Emphasis is in the original.
[41] Douglas Groothuis, "A Manifesto for Christian Apologetics: Nineteen Theses to Shake the World with the Truth," in *Reasons for Faith*, 402.

Review Questions

1. What impresses you most about Bob Passantino as an apologist?

2. What does William Lane Craig believe to be the most effective and practical apologetic for Christian faith?

3. How can a comprehensive knowledge of the Bible help one be a better apologist?

4. Which should be studied first—evidence for Christianity or objections to Christianity? Why?

5. Why should ministerial students not be shielded from the arguments against Christianity?

6. How does our life relate to our credibility as defenders of the faith?

7. What does Craig say is your ultimate apologetic?

8. Why is listening to a non-Christian's objections essential to effective apologetics?

9. Describe the apologetic use of the "Colombo" tactic.

10. In commending Christian faith what is the central issue?

11. Quote Schaeffer's comment about honest questions.

12. State how love is important to effective apologetics.

13. What does Jesus say about the unity of believers in relationship to apologetics?

14. What spiritual practice is essential to preparing to give a defense of the faith?

Suggested Reading

George, Timothy, and John Woodbridge. *The Mark of Jesus: Loving in a Way the World Can See.* Chicago: Moody,

2005. Emphasizes the importance of the character of the apologist.

Koukl, Gregory P. *Tactics: A Game Plan for Discussing your Christian Convictions.* Grand Rapids: Zondervan, 2008. Shows how to initiate conversations, use diplomatic questions, present truth persuasively, graciously expose faulty thinking, maintain a disarming style as you present truth about Christianity. For a brief account see Koukl, Gregory P. "Tactics: Applying Apologetics to Everyday Life," in *Is Your Church Ready?* eds. Ravi Zacharias and Norman L. Geisler. Grand Rapids: Zondervan, 2003.

Lindsley, Art. *Love, the Ultimate Apologetic: The Heart of Christian Witness.* Downers Grove, IL: InterVarsity, 2008. Explores the persuasive power of Christlike love expressed in commitment, conscience, character, community, and courage as a witness to the truth in Christ.

Schaeffer, Francis. *The God Who Is There.* Downers Grove, IL: InterVarsity, 1968. Most comprehensive statement of Schaeffer's cultural apologetics. A challenge to listen to the philosophical ideas expressed in culture and fearlessly challenge non-Christian views speaking the truth in love.

Schaeffer, Francis A. *The Mark of the Christian.* Downers Grove, IL: InterVarsity, 1970. A short essay advocating observable love as the final apologetic.

Zacharias, Ravi, and Norman Geisler, eds. *Is Your Church Ready?* Grand Rapids: Zondervan, 2003. Builds a case for apologetics in the local church, home, school, and in everyday life.

Terms Used in Apologetics

Absolute. As an adjective it means perfection, universality, and nonrelative. As a noun it designates a necessary being depending on nothing else and upon whom all else depends or a concept that is invariable or not open to revision and not relative to circumstances.

Agnostic. One who believes it is not possible to know if God exists. One who is undecided on the question of God's existence.

Agnosticism. A view which professes inability to determine whether or not God exists. Literally means "no knowledge." Some agnostics claim the evidence is insufficient for them to be able to decide the question of God's existence while others claim that no one can decide this question so the only reasonable view is to suspend judgment.

Anti-intellectualism. Minimizing or rejecting the role of reason in favor of emotion, tradition, experience, or authority. An overreaction to deifying the mind (intellectualism).

Antithesis. An idea in opposition to or in contradiction to a particular proposition or thesis.

Apologetics. A reasoned defense of the truth of Christianity. Presents arguments for the existence of God, the deity of Christ, the inspiration of the Bible and Christian experience. Seeks to remove barriers to faith by responding to critical challenges.

Apostle. As a general term refers to a person sent on a mission. Christ's chosen apostles were his authorized representatives guided by the Holy Spirit to establish his church. The Twelve and Paul were apostles in this sense.

Argument. Discourse in which a conclusion is inferred from reasons or evidence (premises).

Arminianism. A system of Christian doctrine advocated by Dutch theologian, Jacobus Arminius (1560–1609), He taught that

God's election to salvation was conditional based on God's foreknowledge of human freedom of choice.

Assumption. An unproved first principle.

Atheism. The lack of belief in a divine being and/or the denial of the existence of a divine being or beings.

Atheist. One who does not believe God exists.

Authenticity. Concerns the historical trustworthiness and accuracy of a document.

Authority. The right to command belief and obedience. While Protestants have looked to the Bible as the final and ultimate authority, the Roman Catholic Church and the Orthodox Church have given more weight to the church officials and historical tradition.

Autonomy. The individual self is the only source of moral obligation. Human beings are independent, free from all external restraints and authorities.

Axiology. The branch of philosophy that deals with values (including morality, arts, religion, economics, politics, laws, and social customs).

Basic belief. A belief held independent of other beliefs. It is not based on any other belief.

Belief. A mental state that is affirmed in a proposition.

Biblical theology. Study of the biblical teaching as it unfolds in each portion of the biblical text rather than organizing it under topics, for example, theology of the prophets or Pauline theology.

Bibliolatry. The worship of the Bible, making the book an idol.

Bibliology. A comprehensive study of the doctrine of Scripture.

Buddhism. Eastern religion based on the teaching of Gautama Buddha (5th century BC) The solution to suffering is liberation coming through mental and moral purification.

Calvinism. A theological system taught by John Calvin (1509–1564) and his followers emphasizing the knowledge of

God and the sovereignty of God. Calvin taught that before the foundation of the world God by his sovereign will determined who would be saved and who would be lost. He extended his saving grace to the elect.

Calvinism, Five Points of. Formulated at the Synod of Dort (1618–1619) in response to Arminians. Often identified as TULIP.

✦ Total depravity. Fallen human beings are incapable of believing the gospel.

✦ Unconditional election. God chooses what persons will be saved without any conditional response on the individuals' part.

✦ Limited atonement. The saving work of Christ is limited only for the elect.

✦ Irresistible grace. God's gift of his grace for those pre-chosen can't be rejected by those persons.

✦ Perseverance of the saints. God guarantees that once a person receives his grace and is saved, they will never lose their salvation.

Not all Calvinists accept all five points.

Canon. A list of books accepted as holy and authoritative Scripture.

Causality. The relationship between cause and effect. The principle that all events or phenomena have sufficient causes.

Cause and effect. Subsequent events are made to happen by previous events or conditions. Also referred to as causality.

Christian evidences. Historical, rational, and personal evidences supporting the truth of Christianity.

Christology. The study of the person and work of Jesus Christ.

Circular argument. An invalid argument that begins by assuming the conclusion to be proved.

Classical apologetic. A method of defending Christianity that first rationally establishes the existence of God by natural theology, then presents evidences for the truth of Christianity.

Classical foundationalism. As held by Descartes attempts to establish certain starting points not justified by any other knowledge on which all knowledge could rest that would lead to indubitable truth. He began with indubitable first principles gained introspectively and then drew inferences from them. All beliefs are justified by being derived from these self-evident starting points or foundational beliefs.

Coherence test of truth. Logical consistency is the test of truth. A proposition is true if and only if it agrees with other beliefs the person accepts.

Correspondence definition of truth. Truth means correspondence with reality.

Correspondence test of truth. Agreement with reality is the test of truth. A proposition is true if and only if it corresponds to the way things actually are.

Cosmological argument. The existence of the universe demands a theistic cause. An argument for the existence of God from the effect (the universe) to the cause (God). A universe made up of limited, changing beings points to an infinite, uncaused noncontingent First Cause. There cannot be an infinite regress of causes, therefore an uncaused Cause exists.

Cosmology. The study of the origin and nature of the universe.

Creation. The view that God created the physical universe out of nothing by an act of his will. He created the physical world and life forms. God created human beings after his own image.

Cultural relativism. The view that moral values are merely the customs of a culture and are not objective or universally binding. What is right varies with each culture.

Darwinism. The theory of naturalistic evolutionary development of biological life advocated by Charles Darwin

(1809–1882) which holds that the mechanism for the survival of the fittest is made up of chance variations and natural selection. Social Darwinism applied the concept of naturalistic evolution to society, including family, religion, ethics, and social structures.

Deconstruction. According to Derrida, deconstruction is the process of exposing the conflicting elements within any view or expression. Meaning of language is indeterminate and is not objective and has no extralinguistic reference. A text is to be read looking for contradictions between what the author intends to say and what the text actually says. The meaning in a statement is not what the speaker or writer intends but what the hearer or reader finds the statement says to him or her.

Deduction. A form of logical reasoning in which the conclusion is necessarily true if the premises are true and the rules of inference are not violated. In a valid deductive argument the conclusion inferred from the premises necessarily follows and is absolutely certain. Flows from the general to the specific.

Deist. One who believes that God created the world but has been uninvolved since.

Deism. The belief in a God that created the universe but left it to run by fixed natural laws. God does not supernaturally intervene in the world either by miracle or divine revelation. Deists exalt reason over faith, revelation, and ethics. The early deists were rationalists (Herbert of Cherbury, 1583–1643) and the later deists were empiricists (Matthew Tindal, 1653–1733). As a movement, deism flourished in the seventeenth and eighteenth centuries.

Deity of Jesus. Jesus possessed all the qualities of deity. He was God in the flesh.

Depravity, Total. A view describing the state of mankind after the Fall. The corruption of human sinfulness affects all the faculties of human nature. Calvinism teaches that fallen human beings in their natural state are unable to understand, believe, or obey the gospel and every person inherits this corruption from Adam. Arminianism denies *total* depravity with the belief in the inheritance of the guilt of original sin and the loss of free will. They believe we have a tendency to sin but not a sinful nature.

Determinism. All events, including human choices, are made necessary by previous conditions and cannot happen any other way. Denies genuine free will since all actions are determined by previous causes.

Dialectic. Used differently by various philosophers. In general is a type of thinking that involves contradictions and their resolution in an ongoing process.

Doubt. Uncertainty as to what to believe about a proposition, a person, or a worldview.

Dualism, Epistemological. The view that accepts the distinction between knower and known.

Dualism, Metaphysical. The view that the universe is made up of two fundamental principles, the physical or material and the spiritual or immaterial. Some views see good and evil as two eternal, opposite realities involved in a never-ending conflict.

Emergent Church Movement. A group of churches holding divergent ideas that came together in the 1990s. They distanced themselves from classical evangelicalism as having adopted the rationalism of modernity and the seeker church movement as driven by marketing and consumerism. Strongly influenced by postmodernism, the authority and truthfulness of Scripture and doctrine are minimized. They prefer mystery to certainty, experience to reason. They oppose any foundationalism.

Empiricism. A theory of knowledge which holds that all knowledge comes through sense experience or gives priority to sense experience in the knowing process.

Enlightenment. A seventeenth- and eighteenth-century philosophical and cultural movement emphasizing the autonomy of human reason and skepticism of traditional authorities. Often hostile to Christianity. Led to modern scientific naturalism and rationalism.

Epistemology. The study of how we know what we know. Examines the sources, nature, and validity of knowledge. Theory of knowledge, its limits, and validity (justification of beliefs).

Ethical relativism. Moral values are a matter of personal preference and are not absolute, objective, or universally true.

Ethics. The study of the principles of moral conduct. Concerns how we determine right from wrong.

Evidences of Christianity. The study of the facts supporting the truth of Christianity. Stresses historical and biblical evidences, including fulfilled prophecy and miracles.

Evidentialism. An apologetic approach which holds that the truth claims of Christianity can be verified by appealing to historical and rational evidences available to believer and unbeliever alike. The term also designates an epistemological view holding that it is irrational to accept a belief that is not supported by sufficient evidence.

Evil, Problem of. The problem of reconciling the existence of evil (both moral and natural) in the world with the existence of an all-powerful and loving God. The intellectual problem of evil includes the logical or deductive problem of evil which holds that the existence of evil refutes the existence of God and the evidential or probabilistic problem of evil which holds that evil makes the existence of God unlikely. The emotional problem of evil holds feelings of abandonment by God because of suffering and tragic experiences.

Evolution. Can mean a process of change. Usually means the biological theory that all life developed by natural processes gradually from simpler life forms. Macroevolution or the general theory of evolution is the "amoeba-to-man" development. The origin of the universe, life, and human beings are usually viewed as accomplished by natural processes. Microevolution refers to development within species.

Evolution, Theistic. A belief that God used the process of evolution by natural causes in creating the world and life.

Ex Nihilo. Literally "out of nothing." Refers to the concept that God created the physical universe without preexisting material. Before the creation matter did not exist.

Existentialism. A philosophy, popular in mid-twentieth century, holding that truth is subjective, personal, and individualistic, and not universal or absolute. Metaphysics and science cannot explain reality. Stresses absurdity of human existence and the human response of anxiety. Existence precedes essence. Human beings have no fixed human nature but are totally free to define life's meaning and make themselves whatever they choose. An existential may be a theist or an atheist.

Fact. An event which has occurred in time and space.

Faith. Trust based on adequate evidence. It may refer to mental assent to the truth of a statement or to a personal commitment of trusting submission to a person. Also can refer to the content of beliefs held by a person or to the religion believed.

Fall, The. The sin of Adam and Eve in the Garden of Eden that resulted in a world of sin and death for the human race.

Fideism. The view that truth in religion ultimately is based on faith rather than reason or evidence. Reason has nothing to do with faith. Some forms of presuppositionalism are close to fideism.

Finite. That which is limited.

Foundationalism. The view that some truths or unprovable first principles or basic beliefs form the basis for learning other truths. See **Classical foundationalism** and **Modest foundationalism.**

Free will. Ability of moral agents to make genuine choices between alternatives without being predetermined by external causes.

Fundamentalism. A conservative movement in the late nineteenth and early twentieth centuries opposing liberalism with its rationalistic and naturalistic reinterpretation of biblical religion. Stressed the inerrancy of the Bible, the virgin birth, substitutionary atonement, resurrection, and deity of Christ. In recent days used to refer to a traditional and conservative form of a religion or worldview holding that that particular viewpoint is so exclusively true that other options are eliminated. Often used in a derogatory sense.

General revelation. The knowledge of God available to all persons apart from the Bible in the natural universe and man. Also called natural theology. Distinguished from special revelation.

Genuineness. Concerns the authorship of a book. Seeks to determine if the book was written by the claimed author.

Hermeneutics. The study of the principles of interpretation of literature including Scripture.

Higher criticism. A study which seeks to determine the author, date of writing, composition including sources, literary nature, and historical trustworthiness of a document. Sometimes it designates the negative and naturalistic literary analysis of the Bible documents.

Hinduism. A family of divergent beliefs which together make up the main religion of India based on religious writings called Vedas and the Upanishads. Teaches reincarnation—the transmigration of souls; karma—one's actions determine his destiny in the next existence; and nirvana—the absorption of the person into the whole of reality.

467

Holocaust. The slaughter of six million Jews by the Nazis during World War II.

Humanism. Can be used to mean respect for the value of human beings. Generally refers to the view that human beings are the highest value in the universe. See **Secular humanism** and **Religious humanism**.

Idealism. As a theory of reality, holds that reality is more akin to ideas than to things. Mind or ideas constitute the ultimate reality. Denies the reality of the physical world or assigns to it a lesser reality.

Image of God. Human beings are created in the image of God (*Gen 1:27*). The unique aspect possessed by human beings mirroring God—one's inner person including mind, will, emotions, and conscience. Often referred to as Imago Dei—Latin for image of God. Theologians argue about whether the image of God was lost or merely defaced in the Fall.

Immanence. God is actively involved in the universe and in human history.

Incarnation. God became man in the person of Jesus of Nazareth.

Induction. A form of logical reasoning in which a conclusion is based on some evidence. A general conclusion is reached on the basis of particular instances. At its best the conclusion can only be said to be probably true, not absolutely certain.

Inerrancy. Characterized by being without error and completely truthful in all it teaches. Often used interchangeably with infallibility.

Infallibility. Incapable of error. Often used interchangeably with inerrancy. Some use infallible to mean the Bible is able to accomplish its purpose. Some say the Bible is infallible in matters of faith and morals but has errors in history and science.

Inference. A mental leap from reasons or evidence to conclusion.

Inspiration. Guidance by Holy Spirit ensured that the writers of Scripture wrote the truth that God wanted written—without error or omission of necessary truth. The word used in *2 Timothy 3:16* is literally "God-breathed." What the inspired writers wrote is God's Word written.

Intelligent Design. Scientific evidence that the natural universe manifests a degree of complexity that requires an intelligent Designer. Naturalistic explanations cannot account for the natural world.

Intuition. Immediate insight or apprehension or cognition without being an obvious rational inference.

Irreducible complexity. The observation that certain biological systems are only beneficial as they are and that lessening any part of that system would render the whole nonbeneficial to the organism.

Islam. A monotheistic religion founded by an Arab leader named Mohammed (570–632 AD). Islam means submission to Allah. Based on the Koran (Qur'an), a record of Mohammad's claimed revelation. Islam's five pillars are: a declaration of faith, prayer, fasting, almsgiving, and the pilgrimage. Adherents are known as Muslims.

Kerygma. Greek word meaning the message preached or proclaimed. In Christian use refers to the gospel of Jesus Christ preached by the early disciples.

Knowledge. Propositional knowledge is justified true belief. Used in a general sense as recognition or understanding of something.

Laws of Logic. Three fundamental principles of logic—the law of identity, the law of noncontradiction, and the law of excluded middle.

Law of identity. Every proposition is identical with itself.

Law of noncontradiction. No proposition can be both true and false in the same sense and at the same time.

Law of the excluded middle. A factual statement and its denial cannot both be true. A proposition is either true or false.

Liberalism, Theological. A movement which began in 19th-century Europe that reinterpreted Christianity in the light of rationalism, naturalism, and humanism. Also called Modernism.

Liberation Theology. A group of movements arising from theologically liberal Christianity that stress deliverance from some type of social or economic bondage. Often advocating Marxist socialism.

Logic. A study of the principles of clear and correct thinking. Identifies fallacies which are mistakes in thinking and reasoning.

Logical positivism. A twentieth-century movement insisting that any proposition that is not verified by sense experience is nonsense. Affirmed that all metaphysical or theological propositions are meaningless and ethical propositions only express emotional preference. The verification principle held that all cognitive propositions (either true or false) are either analytic (true or false by definition of terms) or are verified by sense experience. Lost influence because its own verification principle was unverifiable by sense experience.

Lower Criticism. The study which seeks to recover the exact wording of the original text of a document by examining manuscripts, translations, and quotations of the book. (In documentary studies also referred to as textual criticism and integrity of the text.)

Materialism. In philosophy refers to the view that the physical material world is all that exists. No nonmaterial reality exists.

Metanarrative. A comprehensive explanation of all that exists.

Metaphysics. The study of the nature of reality.

Methodological naturalism. A view of the scientific method which believes that science gives a naturalistic explanation of all phenomena. Any supernatural explanation is unscientific.

Miracle. An event in the physical world, worked by the direct power of God, intended as a sign. Miracles are called powers, wonders, and signs in the New Testament. Supersedes the observed uniform pattern of the natural world. Not accountable by natural secondary causes.

Modernism. The viewpoint arising from modernity characterized by rationalism, naturalism, humanism, metaphysical skepticism, and rejection of traditional authorities. Theological liberalism, also called modernism, attempted to update Christianity by reinterpreting it to harmonize with rationalism, naturalism, and humanism. Postmodernists consider one modern who recognizes the validity of reason and science.

Modernity. The culture brought about by the scientific, industrial, intellectual, and political revolutions of the past three or four hundred years resulting in industrialization, technology, communications, economy, and globalization of our time.

Modest foundationalism. The view that some of our core beliefs serve as first principles, not being derived from other beliefs or cultures or persons, e.g., the laws of logic. Some properly basic beliefs are defensible, yet are subject to forthcoming evidence. All beliefs are not necessary truths or empirically demonstrable. (Also called weak foundationalism or a fallibilist version of foundationalism.)

Monism. The view that only one kind of reality exists, e.g., all spirit or all matter.

Monotheism. The belief that only one God exists.

Moral Argument. An argument for the existence of God holding that man's moral nature and the existence of an objective moral law point to the existence of a Moral Creator.

Moral Imperative. Kant's teaching that persons should be treated as ends and not as means.

Mystery. As used in the New Testament that which surpasses human reason and comprehension but can be revealed to us by God.

Mysticism. The view that knowledge is gained through direct apprehension and inner personal experience transcending reason and sense experience. Also called subjectivism.

Naturalism. A philosophical view that nature is all that exists. Denies any supernatural being exists. The view that the physical universe is the whole of reality. Man is only a biochemical machine. Rejects the existence of a supernatural God or any transcendent spiritual reality.

Natural Law. A statement describing observed uniformity in nature. In ethics refers to universal moral standards common to mankind.

Natural Theology. Attempt to gain knowledge of God from the natural world and human nature apart from special revelation. See **General Revelation.**

Neoorthodoxy. Twentieth-century theology led by Karl Barth in reaction to liberalism. Accepted biblical criticism, God's transcendence, human sinfulness. Influenced by existentialism, held to a subjective view of truth. The Bible is not the propositional word of God but can become the word of God through personal encounter.

New Age Movement. A late twentieth-century social movement advocating a form of spirituality incorporating Eastern mysticism and pantheism, the human potential movement, and occultism. Adherents are unified on the concept that the age of Western monotheistic religion is over.

Nihilism. A radical philosophical skepticism in respect to objective truth and moral values. Believes that existence is senseless often leading to destructive behavior in individuals and society.

Noetic effects of sin. The damage sin has caused to the human mind. Some hold that special divine grace is necessary for a person to understand and obey biblical truth. Some feel that the effect of sin on fallen humans influenced the ability to respond to God's truth but did not destroy it.

Objective truth. A statement or statements correctly describing reality that is not dependent on any creature's circumstances, emotions, or desires. It is true regardless of whether or not a person or persons believe it. Belief in objective truth does not deny the subjectivity of the person in coming to know and accept objective truth.

Omnipotence. The attribute of God as being all-powerful or having infinite power. He can do anything logically possible or consistent with his nature that he wills to do.

Omniscience. The attribute of God as having perfect knowledge of all things—past, present, and future.

Ontological Argument. An argument for the existence of God based on the concept of the greatest of all conceivable beings points to the existence of God. The idea of God implies his existence.

Ontology. A study of the nature of being or existence. Generally synonymous with metaphysics.

Open theism. A recent view that God does not have foreknowledge of future human actions.

Original sin. The classical view advocated by Augustine, Luther, and Calvin teaches that every person is born inheriting the guilt of Adam's sin, and his or her spiritual nature is corrupted and without free will so that the person is unable to believe or obey the gospel unless the Holy Spirit intervenes and grants them grace and faith. The Arminian view holds that humans inherit the consequences of Adam's sin but not the guilt, and they believe human free will was not destroyed by the fall.

Panentheism. A view that God is *in* the universe and evolves with it. Differs from pantheism which says God *is* the universe. As the soul is in the body but is not equated with the body, so God is in the world but not equated with the world. Advocated by process theology.

Paradox. An apparent contradiction.

Pantheism. God and nature are the same. The whole of reality is identical with the Absolute. Particular items are only appearances. Since all is god, humans are gods also. Denies a transcendent personal God.

Phenomenology. Originated by Edmund Husserl (1859–1938). Attempts to describe the process of human thinking and experience as it is experienced. We can only know for certain our own experience or possible experience. Physical objects are just collections of sense objects.

Philosophy. Serious thinking and reflection on the most important and fundamental questions of life: How do we know truth? What is real? What is of value in human conduct? Branches of philosophy include the study of knowledge (epistemology), reality (metaphysics), and values (axiology).

Philosophy of Religion. Usually refers to a branch of philosophy that critically evaluates the beliefs, practices, and fundamental issues in religions. Investigates the nature and grounds of religious truth claims concerning the existence of God, the nature of religion, and life after death. Sometimes used as a synonym of apologetics.

Pluralism. Holds that all viewpoints are equally true and have equal validity. It may express a simple recognition that in certain cultures there are multiple choices of worldviews commonly accepted and practiced.

Polytheism. A belief in many gods.

Positivism. A philosophical view that holds what cannot be observed does not exist. The only valid knowledge is that verified by empirical science.

Postconservatism. Designates former evangelicals who want to reshape traditional theology. They see the essence of

Christianity not in doctrine but in the experience of God's community. Avoid affirming the inerrancy of the Bible and are uncomfortable with saying Jesus is the only way to salvation.

Postmodern. Refers to the period of time beginning in late twentieth century in which some thinkers have rejected modernism's optimistic rationalism in favor of the philosophy of postmodernism.

Postmodernism. Term used to designate a cluster of philosophies unified by their rejection of the Enlightenment's optimistic rationalism and scientism. Postmodernists hold that there are no absolutes and that truth, meaning, and individual identity do not exist. They are distrustful of any statement or system claiming universal validity and truth. Truth is socially and linguistically constructed. All social relationships, all institutions, all moral values are expressions of the basic will to power. Some forms hold to religious pluralism and moral relativism.

Pragmatic test of truth. Utility is the test of truth. Useful results validate truth. Truth is made not discovered. Rejects the correspondence theory of truth.

Pragmatism. An American philosophical movement that began late in the 19th century defining truth as what works. Truth is determined by practical results. Influenced by Darwinism.

Predictive Prophecy. A declaration of events before they actually happen.

Presupposition. An assumption or first principle of thinking.

Presuppositionalism. An apologetic method which holds that the biblical revelation is the presupposition upon which all truth is based. All true statements are either stated in the Bible or are logically inferred from statements in the Bible. As an apologetic method holds that an unbeliever cannot be convinced by reasons or evidences until the Holy Spirit creates faith in him or her.

Process philosophy. The philosophical view developed by Alfred North Whitehead (1861–1947) holding that all of reality, including God, is evolving.

Process theology. A 20ᵗʰ-century theology holding that all reality including God as well as the universe is evolving. Based on process philosophy. Accepts panentheism.

Prophet. One who speaks under supernatural inspiration of the Holy Spirit declaring God's message, including teaching, admonition, warning, and prediction.

Proposition. A statement in which the predicate affirms something of the subject.

Propositional knowledge. Statements affirming certain facts are true or states of affair obtain.

Rationalism. A system of thought holding that all truth is established by reason. Human reason is the highest test of truth. Affirms that all or most knowledge is derived from reason rather than from the senses.

Realism. The belief that actual entities exist apart from human knowers. We can have knowledge of the real world which is external to our minds.

Realism, Scottish Common Sense. A philosophical viewpoint developed by Thomas Reid (1720–1796) holding that a person can know external reality. Knowledge is possible because we accept fundamental first principles, such as self-existence and existence of the external world.

Reason. The mental ability to think logically and draw inferences from evidence and to evaluate arguments. Ability to make judgments.

Reincarnation. The belief that after death a person's soul or spark of life is reborn in the next life in another form— god, person, animal, or plant. This reincarnation continues successively according to karma (one reaps what one sows) until final purification is achieved and the wheel of reincarnation is escaped.

Relativism. A denial of any objective or absolute standard for truth or for morality. Truth and goodness depend on and are determined by the individual (subjectivism) or the culture (cultural relativism). Truth varies with the particular situation.

Religious Humanism. A nontheistic religion based on a naturalistic view of the universe and human beings. Stresses human improvement by education and social programs.

Revelation. The knowledge God has disclosed about himself and his will. Special revelation discloses knowledge of God and his will through supernaturally guided messengers. General revelation is the disclosure of God through nature. See **General revelation** and **Special revelation.**

Romanticism. A philosophical and literary movement in the early nineteenth century stressing subjectivity, personal experience, freedom, and spontaneous feeling. It was a reaction against rationalism. Adopted an optimistic view of human nature.

Scholasticism. An approach to philosophy and theology that flourished in Europe primarily in the eleventh through the fourteenth centuries that attempted to synthesize Christian thought with Greek philosophy. For example, Thomas Aquinas (1225–1274) based much of his thought on Aristotle's philosophy.

Science. A systematic search for knowledge based on empirical research, including investigation, experimentation, verification, and organization. Usually divided into natural sciences (physics, chemistry, geology, and biology) and social sciences (economics, sociology, anthropology, psychology, and political science).

Scientific Revolution. An intellectual movement in which the scientific research and discoveries of men like Copernicus (1473–1543) and Galileo (1564–1642) overturned the Aristotelian conception of the world. The application of the scientific method led to modern technology and the economic and social changes that resulted.

Scientism. The view that scientific knowledge, especially that of the natural sciences, is the highest, if not the only, valid knowledge.

Scientific Naturalism. The view that the physical world is the only reality and scientific knowledge is the only valid knowledge.

Scripture. Traditionally Christians have viewed both the Old and New Testaments of the Bible as God's Word written.

Secular Humanism. A worldview holding that human beings have the highest value in the universe. Denies the existence of any supernatural Being. Human values are not God-given but are based on human beings themselves and are relative and subject to change. Stresses reason, science, education, and art.

Secularism. A viewpoint, attitude, or lifestyle that ignores or denies God and bases cultural values and standards on naturalism.

Skepticism. A view that denies that human beings can have genuine knowledge of the external world or of other minds.

Socialism. An economic theory advocating group ownership of the means of production.

Soundness. In logical analysis a deductive argument is sound if it is valid in form and has true premises.

Special revelation. The communication of knowledge of God and his will through supernaturally informed messengers (prophets and apostles) recorded in Scripture and through Christ.

Subjectivism. The view that truth is limited to one's personal experience. Truth and values are mere personal feelings and have no independent reality or relationship to objective or absolute standards. Values and truth claims are merely based on desire, hope, opinion, or preference.

Supernaturalism. The belief in an ultimate spiritual being beyond the physical universe who can intervene in the natural world.

Systematic theology. A study of biblical teaching organized topically. Draws upon philosophical theology, biblical theology, and historical theology to give a comprehensive study of God and his relations with his creatures.

Teleological argument. An argument for the existence of God based on order and design in the universe. The purposeful design and fine tuning of the universe necessary to support intelligent life and the intricate and irreducible complexity of biological systems point to an intelligent Designer and can't be accounted for by an accident or chance. Design demands a Designer.

Teleology. The study of the evidences of design in nature.

Textual Criticism. See **Lower criticism**.

Theism. A belief in a personal God, who is creator and ruler of the world yet involved in the world. An infinite, all-powerful, all-knowing, personal God exists and has created and sustains the universe. The term may also refer to the study of the existence and nature of God.

Theistic arguments. Arguments for the existence of God, including the ontological argument, cosmological argument, the teleological argument, and the moral argument.

Theodicy. An answer given attempting to explain the presence of evil in a world created and sustained by an all-powerful, all-wise, and all-loving God.

Theology. The study of God and his truth. See **Biblical theology** and **Systematic theology.**

Tolerance. Traditionally the term has referred to a character trait that allows others to hold views with which one may disagree or even disapprove. Recently it has been used to mean a relativistic pluralism claiming to accept all views as equally true.

Totalitarianism. Complete centralized control by a dictator or hierarchy. The rights of individuals are all subjugated to the strict control of the state in regard to all aspects of life, government, and culture.

Transcendence. An aspect of God as being different from every other being. God is infinite, uncaused, omnipotent, and omniscient.

Truth. A statement that corresponds to and agrees with reality.

Unbelief. A deliberate refusal to believe in a personal God or a lack of belief or trust in any ultimate being. From a Christian perspective, unbelief is a rejection or lack of belief in the living, personal God who is revealed in Scripture and in Jesus Christ.

Unitarianism. A religious worldview that denies the trinity, holding that God is a unity. Jesus is viewed as a good human being who is a model for us to follow but not God in flesh. Embraces nearly all spiritual paths as equally valid.

Universal. Applying to all people, at all times, and in all places.

Universalism. The view that eventually all will be saved. Rejects the teaching that some people will be eternally lost in hell.

Validity. In logic an argument is valid if its conclusion follows from the premises according to the laws of logic. See **Soundness.**

Verification. A confirmation or establishment of the truth or accuracy of a statement.

Worldview. A set of basic beliefs about the nature and meaning of the world and life. Includes beliefs about the basic questions about the world and life—including: What is real? What is knowledge and how can it be gained? What is truth? What do I believe about God? What is a human being? Is there life after death? How do we decide what is right and what is wrong? What is the meaning of human history?

Scripture Index

482

Index of Subjects and Persons